VARIETIES OF RIGHT-WINᴜ EXTREMISM IN EUROPE

Beginning with an analysis of the complex relationship between fascism and the post-war extreme right, the book discusses both contemporary parties and the cultural and intellectual influences of the European New Right as well as patterns of socialization and mobilization. It then analyses the effects of a range of factors on the ideological development of right-wing extremism including anti-Semitism, Islamophobia, religious extremism and the approach towards Europe (and the European Union). The final parts investigate a number of activist manifestations of the extreme right from youth participation and the White Power music scene to transnational rallies, the Internet and football hooliganism. In the process, the book questions the notion that the contemporary extreme right is either extremely novel or only populist in character.

Drawing together a wide range of contributors, this is essential reading for all those with an interest in contemporary extremism and fascism. The book is a companion volume to *Mapping the Extreme Right* (Routledge, 2012) which has the same editors.

Andrea Mammone is a Lecturer in Modern European History at Royal Holloway, University of London, UK.

Emmanuel Godin is Principal Lecturer in the School of Languages and Area Studies at the University of Portsmouth, UK.

Brian Jenkins was formerly a Senior Research Fellow in the Department of French at the University of Leeds, UK. He co-edits the *Journal of Contemporary European Studies*.

Routledge Studies in Extremism and Democracy

Series editors: Roger Eatwell, *University of Bath* **and**
Matthew Goodwin, *University of Nottingham*
Founding series editors: Roger Eatwell, *University of Bath* **and**
Cas Mudde, *University of Antwerp-UFSIA*

This new series encompasses academic studies within the broad fields of 'extremism' and 'democracy'. These topics have traditionally been considered largely in isolation by academics. A key focus of the series, therefore, is the (inter-)*relation* between extremism and democracy. Works will seek to answer questions such as to what extent 'extremist' groups pose a major threat to democratic parties, or how democracy can respond to extremism without undermining its own democratic credentials.

The books encompass two strands:

Routledge Studies in Extremism and Democracy includes books with an introductory and broad focus which are aimed at students and teachers. These books will be available in hardback and paperback. Titles include:

Understanding Terrorism in America
From the Klan to al Qaeda
Christopher Hewitt

Fascism and the Extreme Right
Roger Eatwell

Racist Extremism in Central and Eastern Europe
Edited by Cas Mudde

Political Parties and Terrorist Groups (Second Edition)
Leonard Weinberg, Ami Pedahzur and Arie Perliger

The New Extremism in 21st Century Britain
Edited by Roger Eatwell and Matthew Goodwin

New British Fascism
Rise of the British National Party
Matthew Goodwin

The End of Terrorism?
Leonard Weinberg

Mapping the Extreme Right in Contemporary Europe
From local to transnational
Edited by Andrea Mammone, Emmanuel Godin and Brian Jenkins

Varieties of Right-Wing Extremism in Europe
Edited by Andrea Mammone, Emmanuel Godin and Brian Jenkins

Routledge Research in Extremism and Democracy offers a forum for innovative new research intended for a more specialist readership. These books will be in hardback only. Titles include:

VARIETIES OF RIGHT-WING EXTREMISM IN EUROPE

Edited by Andrea Mammone,
Emmanuel Godin and Brian Jenkins

Routledge
Taylor & Francis Group

LONDON AND NEW YORK

First published 2013
by Routledge
2 Park Square, Milton Park, Abingdon, Oxon OX14 4RN

Simultaneously published in the USA and Canada
by Routledge
711 Third Avenue, New York, NY 10017

Routledge is an imprint of the Taylor & Francis Group, an informa business

British Library Cataloguing in Publication Data
A catalogue record for this book is available from the British Library

Library of Congress Cataloging in Publication Data
Varieties of right-wing extremism in Europe/edited by Andrea Mammone,
Emmanuel Godin & Brian Jenkins.
  p. cm. – (Routledge studies in extremism and democracy)
  Includes bibliographical references and index.
  1. Right-wing extremists – Europe.   2. Radicalism – Europe.
  3. Fascism – Europe.   4. Europe – Politics and government – 1989–.
  I. Mammone, Andrea.   II. Godin, Emmanuel.   III. Jenkins, Brian,
  1944–.
  HN380.Z9R394 2013
  303.48'4 – dc23
  2012035139

ISBN: 978-0-415-62719-1 (hbk)
ISBN: 978-0-415-62717-7 (pbk)
ISBN: 978-0-203-08046-7 (ebk)

Typeset in Bembo
by Florence Production, Stoodleigh, Devon, UK

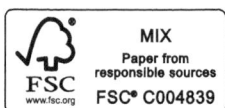

CONTENTS

CONTRIBUTORS

Joan Antón-Mellón is a Professor of Political Science at the University of Barcelona (Spain).

Gary Armstrong is a Reader in Sociology of Sport at Brunel University (UK).

Tamir Bar-On is a Professor of International Relations and Humanities at the Tecnológico de Monterrey, Querétaro (Mexico).

Manuela Caiani is an Assistant Professor in Comparative European Politics at the Institute for Advanced Studies (HIS), Wien (Austria).

Jean-Yves Camus is a Senior Researcher at the Institut de Relations Internationales et Stratégiques (IRIS), Paris (France).

Stéphanie Dechezelles is an Assistant Professor in Political Science at the Institut d'Études Politiques, Aix-en-Provence (France).

Emmanuel Godin is a Principal Lecturer in French and European Studies at the University of Portsmouth (UK).

Gabriel Goodliffe is an Assistant Professor of International Relations and International Political Economy at the Instituto Tecnológico Autónomo de México, Mexico City (Mexico).

Leila Hadj-Abdou is a Ph.D. Researcher in Political and Social Sciences at the European University Institute, Florence (Italy).

Jérôme Jamin is a Professor in Political Science at the University of Liège (Belgium).

Brian Jenkins is a Senior Research Fellow in French Studies at the University of Leeds (UK). He co-edits the *Journal of Contemporary European Studies*.

Martin Langebach is a Ph.D. candidate in Sociology at the University of Düsseldorf (Germany).

Andrea Mammone is a Lecturer in Modern European History at Royal Holloway, University of London (UK).

Birgitta Orfali is an Associate Professor of Sociology at Paris Descartes University and an Associate Researcher at Sciences Po-CEVIPOF (France).

Linda Parenti is a Ph.D. Researcher in Political Science at the University of Florence (Italy).

Jan Raabe is Head of a community centre and Adviser for Argumente und Kultur gegen Rechts, Bielefeld (Germany).

Sieglinde Rosenberger is a Professor of Political Science at the University of Vienna (Austria).

Alberto Testa is a Lecturer in Sociology of Sport at Brunel University (UK).

Emily Turner-Graham is an independent scholar.

Fabian Virchow is a Professor of Social Theory and Theories of Political Action at the University of Applied Sciences, Düsseldorf (Germany).

Bénédicte Williams is a Ph.D. Researcher in Political Science at the Central European University, and a journalist at the *Budapest Times* and *Budapester Zeitung*, Budapest (Hungary).

Jim Wolfreys is a Senior Lecturer in French Politics and European Studies at King's College London (UK).

ABBREVIATIONS

FN	Front National
FPÖ	Freiheitliche Partei Österreichs
GEPECS	Groupe d'Étude pour l'Europe de la Culture et de la Solidarité
GRECE	*Groupement de Recherche et d'Études pour la Civilisation Européenne*
GUD	Groupe Union Défense
HVIM	Hatvannégy Vármegye Ifjúsági Mozgalom
IRCA	Islamic Religious Community in Austria
JN	Junge Nationaldemokraten
Jobbik	Jobboldali Ifjúsági Közösség (Movement for a Better Hungary)
LEPS	Laboratoire Européen de Psychologie Sociale
LiF	Liberales Forum
LPF	League of Polish Families
MDI	Mouvement des Damnés de l'Impérialisme
MG	Magyar Gárda (Hungarian Guard)
MGP	Movimento Giovani Padani
MHP	Milliyetçi Hareket Partisi
MIÉP	Magyar Igazság és Élet Pártja (Hungarian Party of Justice and Life)
MNA	Magyar Nemzeti Arcvonal (Hungarian National Front)
MNR	Mouvement National Républicain
MSI	Movimento Sociale Italiano
ND	Nouvelle Droite
NF	National Front
NHW	Nordisches Hilfswerk (Northern Relief Organization)
NP	Nyilaskeresztes Párt (Arrow Cross Party)
NPD	Nationaldemokratische Partei Deutschland
NR	New Right
NSBM	National Socialist Black Metal
NSDAP	Nationalsozialistische Deutsche Arbeiterpartei (German National Socialist Party)
NSF	Nationalsocialistisk Front
NSHC	National Socialist Hardcore
NVU	Nederlandse Volks Unie
OAS	Organisation Armée Secrète
ONC	Occupazioni Non Conformi
ÖVP	Österreichische Volkspartei
PCF	Parti Communiste Français
PCN	Parti Communautaire National-Européen
PiS	Prawo i Sprawiedliwosc
PNF	Partito Nazionale Fascista
PPF	Parti Populaire Français
PxC	Plataforma per Catalunya
RAC	Rock against Communism

RFJ	Ring Freiheitlicher Jugend
RS	revolutionary syndicalists
RSI	Italian Social Republic
RSS	Rashtriya Swayamsevak Sangh
SFIO	Section Française de l'International Ouvrière
SGP	Staatkundig Gereformeerde Partij
SMR	Svenska Motståndsrörelsen (Swedish Resistance Movement)
SPÖ	Sozialdemokratische Partei Österreichs
SVP	Swiss People's Party
UISP	Unione Italiana Sport
VHP	Vishva Hindu Parishad
YNF	Young National Front
ZOG	Zionist Occupation Government

INTRODUCTION

Andrea Mammone, Emmanuel Godin and Brian Jenkins

I

The year 2009 ended with the extremist leader Nick Griffin – following the British National Party (BNP)'s 'achievements' at the European Union elections – being invited onto *Question Time*: a 'blackshirt' in one of the temples of the British media, complained the many protesters. It was predictable that the BBC's invitation to an alleged heir of Nazi-fascism would cause a sensation. Fascism and Nazism have always aroused great interest among scholars, mass media and public opinion. Likewise, over the past two decades across Western Europe, the rise of right-wing extremist parties and movements has generated an abundance of comments, debates, analyses and disputes making right-wing extremism one of the most controversial phenomena of the contemporary period.

Among these controversies, the debate about the precise political nature of such parties and movements has been the dominant topic for academics, journalists and politicians. When observing developments on the right of the right, are we witnessing the emergence of a new political phenomenon, whose nature, because it is rooted in a post-industrial society, is markedly different, in terms of ideological orientation, political objectives and organization, from its historical (Nazi-fascist and neo-fascist) ancestors? Rather than seeking to give a categorical answer to this crucial question, one of the aims of this volume is to demonstrate the complexity of the nature of the extreme right and to raise some doubts about the contention that what we are witnessing is a new phenomenon, or simply the by-product of a post-industrial society. Contributions in this volume will remind the reader that, if the notion of new radical-right populism has acquired a degree of currency in academia, it must nevertheless be approached with some caution. In this volume, we offer a different perspective. First, some of our contributors have chosen to revisit theoretical debates about the nature of what is happening on the right of the right. Taken together, their conclusions, drawing from different disciplines (and, in some cases, based on long-term analyses), tend to point to a more complex, but also more significant, series of linkages with fascism – or to what is usually considered an 'old' extreme right now almost disappeared or marginal – than is usually accepted. In the three subsequent parts, contributors aim to examine critically and empirically some of the theoretical claims made in the first part of this volume. The second part assesses, with some surprising results, the way old 'mobilizing passions', to use historian Robert Paxton's famous expression, such as anti-Semitism, the fight against the decline of nations and Western civilization have evolved over the years and to what extent new passions, such as Islamophobia, are fundamentally novel and distinct from older ones. On the whole, this part highlights both major readjustments and enduring obsessions: pragmatic concessions to electoral politics are combined with the capacity to repackage old hatreds into new crusades. Part III addresses what is happening within these parties: by focusing on members and activists rather than voters, by analysing their recruitment, socialization and mobilization, by examining organizational issues rather than public discourses, this part provides readers with an original but intricate map of these parties, insisting not only on their diverse culture, but also on internal fractures and factions. Viewed from this specific angle, it becomes more difficult to assert that these parties are markedly different from past fascist organizations: at the very least this debate deserves to be revisited. Part IV recognizes that right-wing extremism cannot be reduced to its strict party dimension: the Internet, ecology, music and sport provide alternative and admittedly less regulated vectors of right-wing extremist expression. They are also powerful vehicles for party organizations to convey their message to a (younger) public, less interested by conventional forms of political participation but more likely to be confident in using new technologies and to find in ecology, music and sport engaging and exciting forms of sociability.

This is therefore a trans-disciplinary volume on one of the most debated phenomena in contemporary Europe: a phenomenon able to provoke passions, controversies, and, above all to attract a substantial share of the vote, sometimes in a proportion that gives access to decision-making at local, but also national levels. Case studies in this volume will show how, why and under which conditions right-wing extremism is a potential threat to liberal democracy and multi-ethnic society. It is our editors' contention that there is much that is 'old' within the latest manifestations of right-wing extremism. Our objective is to encourage readers to assess critically the nature of contemporary phenomena in the light of the theoretical perspectives and empirical evidence presented in this volume. Of course, we are aware of the huge diversity of parties located on the right of the right as well as the specific local and national context in which they have emerged, and in which they operate today. We also acknowledge that these parties have changed, or have attempted to modernize themselves (or simply to present a different external image), over the past twenty years or so. We accept that most parties are ridden with internal factions ('modernizers', 'old guards', etc.), whose relative influence may fluctuate.

But we believe that the nature and intensity of such change need to be reassessed. We wish to argue that not all the European right-wing extremist parties have undergone a process of genuine democratization, *even if* they have moved 'from the margins to the mainstream', to borrow from the title of a significant previous edited volume (Hainsworth 2000). Our hypothesis is that such a realignment is not necessarily synonymous with democratization: the arguments used by such parties, their use of 'new' mobilizing themes, their organizational cultures, their use of new media, tend to point to a *neo-fascist* form of modernization or adaptation to a multi-ethnic society that is dominated by patterns of popular insecurity and, at times, 'fear'.[1] At the same time, more sophisticated electoral strategies, emphasizing respectability and using firm but 'reasonable' language, attract a growing portion of voters. Whether such electoral strategies have a profound, rather than superficial, effect on the overall culture of these parties is a matter of debate. In this sense, Wolfreys's opening chapter lays the ground well. It places the extreme right in a comparative context and suggests that it represents the different (*Paxtonian*) phases or stages of a somewhat 'classic extreme right'.[2] Wolfreys, in particular, interestingly locates the contemporary extreme right 'at different points in Paxton's second stage of fascist development, attempting to forge alliances as part of their integration into the political system'.

II

As suggested above, the very first part of the book (but this is also evident in other sections) attempts to raise doubts on the now 'accepted' post-neo-fascist nature of the contemporary extreme right and thus reveals that some forms and strands of fascism and neo-fascism may have survived in Europe within the cosmology of contemporary parties and intellectual think tanks. This includes the specific case of the powerful European Nouvelle Droite (New Right, ND). The ND first developed in post-1968 France under the leadership of Alain de Benoist. It called for a synthesis or new paradigm between the left and the right, or, more precisely, between some New Left ideas and the German Konservative Revolution. It became an intellectual enterprise quite influential in England, France, Italy and Germany and across the Atlantic – but also in the right-wing music scene through an esoteric neo-Paganism that influenced several bands (François 2007). However, it is debatable whether ND has really 'made a political "conversion" from the revolutionary Right (or conservative revolutionary) milieu to "democracy" and [created] . . . a "post-fascist" political synthesis' (Bar-On 2009: 243), or whether it has superficially but convincingly learned how to mime the political requirements of a democracy? In this volume, both Antón-Mellón and Bar-On seem to share the idea that some lines of continuity can be drawn between some inter-war extreme-right ideas and post-war followers of de Benoist.[3] Such lines of continuity are also central to Goodliffe's argument, as he explains how in a context of globalization and the crisis of the so-called Fordist model of regulation, the French Front National has been able to achieve electorally an enduring sociological synthesis between the working class and the petty bourgeoisie that previous French extreme-right parties less successfully sought to bring about.

We have therefore tried to link past and present times, historical movements or ideas with contemporary practices, and possibly to lay the ground for some further research on the historical, and 'philosophical', evolution of ultra-rightist forces and cultures. To an extent, this approach is at odds with attempts to conceptualize what is happening on the right of the right uniquely as a form of populism. *Varieties of Right-Wing Extremism* is both sceptical and critical about the notion of populism. In some ways, we argue that the indistinct usage of the term 'populism' often acts as a form of academic, media or public legitimization of right-wing extremism. Populism, if it describes a political style based on easy, catchy, emotional slogans rather than a certain value ascribed to rational debate, is of course not the exclusive preserve of right-wing extremism.[4] If it is meant to describe the reaction of a 'virtuous' people against a corrupt elite, then populism becomes a convenient concept allowing us to brush under the carpet important questions about the nature of this 'virtuous' people (which 'people'?) and its political objectives (what sort of democracy?). Right-wing extremist parties rather like to be described as populist: it is like offering them a free ticket to the pantheon of democracy without asking too many questions and without discussing their ideologies, taking their stated conversion to parliamentary rule at face value. As Mammone suggests elsewhere, characterizing such parties as populist 'might in fact lead (1) to the bypassing of the (uncomfortable) burden of the (fascist) past as well as (2) to different perceptions of such parties which thereby seem less dangerous in people's eyes' (Mammone 2009: 174).

In this volume, *Varieties of Right-Wing Extremism*, Jamin discusses in his chapter the meaning and differences between populism and right-wing extremism and the confusion between the two concepts in the current literature. He suggests that right-wing extremist ideology is much more defined and structured. This latter is shaped around three focal points: (a) the idea of inequality and hierarchy in the human world, (b) an ethnic form of nationalism that guarantees an holistic and multi-ethnic free community against all *enemies* and, finally, (c) a possible radicalism/extremism to carry out ultra-right goals and establish or defend an imagined society.[5] These features are certainly not a novelty in European history, and, with different degrees, are shared by the majority, if not all, right-wing extremist movements and groupings analysed in both our volumes.

III

In *The Anatomy of Fascism*, Paxton argues that 'fascism is more plausibly linked to a set of "mobilizing passions" that shape fascist action than to a consistent and fully articulated philosophy' (Paxton 2005: 41). The US historian characterizes these passions by their structure rather than a formal, prescriptive content: for instance, fascism is defined by 'a Manichean view of history, as a battle between good and evil camps [. . .] in which one's own community or nation has been the victim', and 'the need for closer integration of a purer community, by consent if possible, or by exclusionary violence if necessary', and so on (Paxton 2005: 41–2).

In our volume, we have already suggested that several core 'mobilizing passions' are examined and situated in a longer time frame in order to assess their resilience and mutation. For example, in 'The European extreme right and religious extremism' chapter, Camus charts the evolution of religious extremism since the end of the Second World War, explaining how a weakening of Catholic fundamentalism has been displaced by a renewed interest in Paganism, a religious position which, he argues, has far more in common with fascism than ultra-Catholicism's antiquated vagaries. Pursuing his argument within the framework of a specific case study (the following Chapter 7), Camus then explains how over the past sixty years, changing permutations between anti-Semitism and anti-Zionism remain a defining and enduring feature of the extreme right in France 'even if it takes different forms and is expressed with varying degrees of intensity'.

At the same time, a surge in Islamophobia replicates similar reflexes and a comparable logic to those that underpin anti-Semitism. That Islamphobic discourses yield better electoral returns than anti-Semitism today is one thing: but to take a relative – a very relative – decline in the use of anti-Semitism in public discourses as a sure sign of moderation would be a rather dubious conclusion. If in the name of anti-Semitism and Western spiritual decadence, a number of Islamist groups in Europe have sought alliances with right-wing extremist parties, this shows just how complex, and sometimes convoluted, linkages between politics and religion can be. Yet, as Camus reminds us, such linkages are not necessarily new, and certainly not the direct product of a post-9/11 context: their roots are deep in the past. Camus does demonstrate how over the past decades relations between religion and right-wing extremism have changed, sometimes dramatically: but such changes, he argues, are not enough to indicate increased moderation or to be taken as a sign of normalization. Further, as Rosenberger and Hadj-Abdou's chapter suggests, some 'religious', or for that matter anti-religious, extreme-right stances are often linked to particular political opportunity structures and to strategic patterns of national party competition.

However, Rosenberger and Hadj-Abdou's conclusions about anti-Islamic mobilization in Austria point to another potent mobilizing passion: the defence of the nation against what are perceived as internal and external threats (though this 'defensive' approach towards the 'enemies' of the nation is an extreme-right mantra). On the other hand, in the book we have also chosen to explore this passion through the complex articulation between the nation and Europe. Historically, right-wing extremism has not always embraced a narrow nation-based stance rejecting the external world. The most common example is Sir Oswald Mosley's concept of 'Europe. A Nation', which was an attempt to define the terms of a single (blackshirt and corporative) European super-state where all neo-fascists had to develop a self-awareness of being genuine 'Europeans'. As we have already indicated in our companion volume (Mammone *et al.* 2012), this enthusiasm for a certain kind of Europe remains an enduring feature of the post-war extreme right: the neo-fascist summits of Rome (1950) and Malmoe (1951) which promoted the creation of the European Social Movement are testimony to this (Mammone 2011). Bar-On also explores some of this ground for the important French ND.

Naturally, the EU hardly represents the sort of Europe that extreme-right parties would aspire to and, on the whole, such parties remain critical towards Brussels, even if such criticisms, as Williams reminds us, have evolved with time and need to be qualified depending on whether they are directed towards the principles upon which the EU is based, the way it operates or the direction it intends to take. Clearly, as opposed to an idealized Europe, à la Mosley or otherwise, much debated within intellectual circles and fringe political gatherings, extreme-right parties that take the electoral game seriously offer an assessment of the EU project that varies greatly in relation to the specific competitive environment in which they operate. Analysing the Austrian FPÖ and French FN manifestos over the past twenty-five years, Williams convincingly demonstrates how extreme-right parties are able to take a more pragmatic approach on the EU than usually expected, contrive programmes more in tune with voters' aspirations, and thus often maximize their electoral competitive advantage. Depending on what is deemed to be yielding maximum results, extreme-right parties can deploy a variety of ideological resources. Whereas the Nouvelle Droite remains obsessed with Europe's cultural identity, extreme-right parties insist far more on the EU's political ineffectiveness and economic costs and direct their strongest criticism against an ever-voracious, but ineffective Brussels. This stance also reflects a well-established, classical extreme-right vision of Europe, quite different from Mosley's: a 'Europe of Fatherlands', whose strength resides in the vitality of its member-states and whose object is to defend a continent assailed by harmful external forces. For instance, as Rosenberger and Hadj-Abdou demonstrate, in Austria the extreme right has used Islamophobia to attract voters whose Austrian and European identity Islam supposedly threatens, and it castigates the EU, not so much for its failure to offer protection against Islam but for sapping national vitality without which resistance to such global threats becomes futile.

However, there is much more than this. By taking a longer historical perspective, Bar-On seeks to evaluate whether there is a degree of continuity between past fascist representations of a European space and culture and the way such space and culture are presented today within extreme-right milieus. Bar-On shows that since the Second World War, the extreme right has embraced 'Europe' as a space to orchestrate *revenges* (also against 'war' enemies such as Soviet communism and the USA). This political and cultural Europe remains the preserve of the white race and is almost monocultural. Interestingly, Rosenberger and Hadj-Abdou seem to suggest (correctly) that Islamophobia is now used as a sort of (white) European flag: it creates an opportunity for like-minded parties to cooperate across state boundaries, and to 'discuss' the existence of some core European values within a common European space.[6] Likewise, the Internet, music and sport help consolidate this common, European space by promoting a collective right-wing extremist worldview across national borders.

Europe, Western Europe for our purposes here, decidedly remains a *battlefield* for the extreme right. In other words, 'Europe' is perceived as a contested space (against the EU bureaucracy and its impositions) as well as an imagined space (to unify forces and to escape from the ghetto of isolation). As we have partially mentioned, this is, once more, not a new theme or extreme-right dimension. This idea to unify forces and create a sort of European (right-wing) nationalism and space was used from the early 1950s by some rightist thinkers and movements – it was also considered as a 'response' to the mainstream European integration that had just started (Mammone 2011). If we do not consider this historical legacy (and all its contradictions), our 'approach' may appear problematic. In this volume, Virchow underlines the inherent ambiguities of such a position with references to neo-Nazi rallies. The willingness to mobilize and, crucially, to socialize members across national borders is often limited by irreconcilable national and local interests and a political culture that valorizes polarization (vividly illustrated by the continuing historical clash between Italian and German right-wing extremists about South Tyrol).

IV

Without entering into the troubling waters of definitions and debates on terminology, this volume, nonetheless, intends to encourage readers to reassess critically the attempt to define what is happening on the right of the right as a 'new populism'. 'Populism' has now become a popular term not only in academia (for example, Mény and Surel 2000; Mudde 2007; Taggart 2000), but also in countries where there is some reluctance to confront the fascist past (such as in Italy or Austria, but also in France where the Front National is often described as 'national populist').[7]

Whether the label 'populism' actually contributes to the legitimization of right-wing extremism is open to debate. What seems less contested, however, is the role played by the media in explaining the relative success of right-wing extremist parties (Carter 2005; Ellinas 2009).[8] In this volume, Orfali also examines the role of the media in triggering recruitment to right-wing extremist parties. She argues that 'reaction to a specific event', often staged today on television, appears to be an important reason for extreme-right membership in France:

> [M]any activists related their decision to join the party [. . .] to a specific event like the TV broadcast '*l'Heure de vérité*', where Jean-Marie Le Pen was invited, or the 1984 European elections where the Front National 'suddenly' emerged on the French political scene.

It seems to us that the identity of right-wing extremism and the passions that it conveys cannot be understood without assessing the relations between mass communication (including the new media that is so influential today) and the 'extremist galaxy'.

This also leads us to the discussion in our volume of the use of new media by the extreme right. The interaction between the Internet and right-wing extremism has hitherto been largely under-studied. Both Caiani and Parenti and Turner-Graham show how the Internet is used to spread ideas and attract voters and, crucially, to build an imagined society and collective identity – or a 'cyber-landscape' to use Turner-Graham's own words. What is most striking is the nature and content of ideas, images, slogans and references, which are often badly controlled – if at all – by party machines. While the Internet is indeed a modern form of communication, socialization and mobilization, the ideas promoted through it are often recycled from the past: references to the fascist and Nazi imaginary, along with overtly racist statements, illustrate that what is modern can serve a traditional agenda. Away from the glossy pages of manifestos and the respectable public images presented to voters, one is struck by the permanence of old-fashioned and contentious arguments.

The use of new technologies has contributed to the success of the contemporary extreme right: it has become an effective entrepreneur in terms of recruitment and mobilization. However, why has it become so attractive? Orfali's chapter takes a socio-psychological perspective and argues that ideological motivations are not enough to understand why people decide to join an extremist party or movement: the personal expectations of new members also needs to be taken into account. Indeed, as she puts it:

> [T]hese expectations can be realized through party activism and this is certainly the specificity of extreme-right parties: they suggest a minority action and consider all the other parties, indeed society in general, as the 'enemies' against which they have to fight. Members then find what they are looking for, the possibility to overcome a feeling of powerlessness which they felt before.[9]

Parties on the extreme of the political spectrum often act as a 'counter-society' or provide members with a family-like environment where they are able to share the values, socialize with like-minded comrades, and develop feelings of solidarity, loyalty and discipline. Above all, this community forms a protective environment where members can share their emotions and express their feelings without fear of stigmatization (Klandermans and Mayer 2006). This leads to the creation of a collective identity which, in Dechezelles's chapter, is fundamentally based 'on a double strategy of homogenization and differentiation: the creation of an inclusive and positive *Us* that can be opposed to the irremediably different and negative *Them*'. The French scholar focuses her analysis on youth participation in right-wing extremist organizations and studies their political socialization of youth activists who are meant to become the party's future cadres. Dechezelles claims that it is important to open and analyse the 'cultural box' through which this socialization is structured. As (implicitly or explicitly) suggested by other contributors to this volume, Dechezelles argues that this 'box' is composed of three key elements: an ideal model of society, a legendary narrative and a symbolic territory. All these elements are grounded in and inspired by some old ideological references.

Particularly interesting here is, in fact, the controversial case of the National Alliance (Alleanza Nazionale, AN). The party has been one of the key components of Silvio Berlusconi's political coalitions. It is now fully merged into Berlusconi's latest enterprise, the Popolo della Libertà, which is the largest Italian party. Gianfranco Fini, the former AN leader, left the party and founded a somewhat centrist movement, but AN politicians strongly influence contemporary Italian politics. On the other hand, AN was/is often perceived to be 'post-fascist' (see for example Ruzza and Fella 2007). Yet, as Cheles suggests it would be wrong to treat this (now basically disappeared or non-autonomous) party 'as a monolithic block. Its leading figures' adherence to the values of fascism vary' (Cheles 2010: 277). Cheles also interestingly argues that AN propaganda incorporated two levels of meaning: one is for the public and is quite moderate; the other is more hidden and is for activists celebrating fascism and showing that the party has not betrayed its (fascist/neo-fascist) roots. In similar vein, Wolfreys points out that 'the AN leadership is attempting to bridge the gap between its role at the heart of the Berlusconi regime and the political culture of its membership, steeped in notions of the "purity of origins"'. Dechezelles specifically shows the salience of the fascist heritage in the cultural box framing the political socialization of many young AN sympathizers.[10] Youth activists are indeed clearly influenced by references to (a family or public) fascist or neo-fascist event and the myth of this 'purity of origins', which commands a certain degree of pride. Thus, 'the historical and family "proximity" with certain past events/figures therefore allows the young activists to place themselves in a direct line of historical continuity with a private (family) and public (political) genealogy'.

Virchow also insists on the importance attached to the development of a 'collection of emotions' in the socialization of activists, especially when such emotions are generated outside the strict confines of party politics and are woven into activities such as marches, music and sport. During such events, party activists attract sympathizers and make contacts. Ethnographic observations of extreme right-wing marches have led Virchow to suggest that these contacts

> become friendships, visits are followed by return visits, thereby contributing to the emergence or strengthening of an informal network [. . .]. Marches function as acts of initiation where a first-timer to the extreme right can admit his/her affiliation openly . . . the repetition of this act can become an important ingredient of a political socialization process.
>
> (Virchow 2007: 154)

Marches and rallies provide a fertile ground for recruitment and socialization of members, and Virchow also highlights in this volume how they serve to promote cooperation between actors, and facilitate ideological cross-fertilization and the development of common political actions.

Sporting events often play a similar role too. In our book, Testa and Armstrong's analysis is based on the Italian context – specifically the case of Rome's two very important football teams (Rome and Lazio) – that is to say in a country where *calcio* is generally perceived as a sort of secular religion. Through the football terraces, supporters (especially the so-called 'Ultras') spread a doctrine based on fascist and neo-fascist myths, racial prejudice and ultra-nationalism. Testa and Armstrong argue that this significant mobilizing passion has wider European ramifications: politicized football supporters respect their fellows from all over Europe, 'a shared transnational enthusiasm for football and neo-fascist ideology has given rise to Ultras [. . .] twinning-friendships based on a sense of [. . .] mutual respect'. For example, Rome and Lazio maintain strong links with like-minded neo-fascist supporters of Benfica Lisbon, Hammarby of Sweden, Espanyol Barcelona, Real Madrid, Werder Bremen, Lokomotiv Leipzig, Panathinaikos and Paris St Germain.[11] Indeed, exactly as in the case of the rallies described by Virchow, the origin of such transnational networks across countries is often due to personal contacts:

> Representatives of the Ultra Sur [Real Madrid] attend games as guests of the Irriducibili [Lazio] *Direttivo* (management board) who display the team scarves of the twinning clubs in their Head Office. The twinning is first and foremost a declaration of friendship based on a shared enthusiasm for neo-fascism.

For Langebach and Raabe, music is another interesting new vector facilitating not only the diffusion of extreme-right doctrine (including through YouTube clips or downloadable music on extremist websites, as described by Turner-Graham) but also the recruitment of activists. *RechtsRock* (also called White Power, neo-Nazi music or White Noise) is a truly international phenomenon with a world-wide distribution and market. In countries such as Germany, it is the most important means used to activate young people around neo-Nazi and extreme-right groups. Lyrics are naturally based on 'nationalism, racism, anti-Semitism or on the glorification of National Socialism/fascism'. Indeed, if the Internet can be immediately considered as a place of 'encounters', sport stadiums, concerts and gigs (in particular rock and hard rock), commemoration sites and demonstrations are increasingly cross-national spaces where political identities are manufactured. In that respect, the music scene plays a fundamental socializing role across the European continent:

> Music is something entirely social, maintaining complex relationships with the social world. It holds a position that has become central amongst the elements that form our perception of the world, the sense of hearing rivalling more than ever what we see and what we read [. . .]. Music can also be a method of engagement, at the same time individual (those who listen) and/or collective (those who play) – a medium for resistance to cultural or political domination.
>
> (François 2007: 35)

Thus, similar lifestyles and involvement in apparently non-political events such as a football match or a concert or the direct engagement in more politicized movements certainly help to establish and propagate a collective political identity, increasingly so across borders.

To summarize, this volume also offers an overview of extreme-right forms of recruitment, socialization and mobilization across spaces – whether geographical, contested or virtual. The use of traditional methods of socialization and, at the same time, the reliance on new technologies guarantee the continuity and proper transmigration of genuine extreme-right cultures across time and space. Moreover, it is suggested and demonstrated that the extreme right still displays in its message a certain fascination with the past. Themes, or mobilizing passions, are often borrowed from a 'blackshirt' history, and the Internet, rallies, stadiums, concerts, often help to spread racism, xenophobia and the sort of ideals and myths that are common currency in the pantheon of the most extreme fringes of the right: references to the ideas and slogans promoted in their time by Mussolini, Hitler, Julius Evola or the Iron Guards are never far away, even today.

V

The expression 'long journey' is frequently deployed in the prefaces and introductions of academic books, to describe personal and academic trajectories often extending over years. Our book has a very similar story. It was 2007 when we launched our original Call for Papers on the 'Far Right in Europe' and this volume represents the last step in a project that has produced two special editions of the *Journal of Contemporary European Studies* (*JCES*) and another Routledge Extremism and Democracy volume entitled *Mapping the Extreme Right in Contemporary Europe: From Local to Transnational*. We are therefore deeply indebted to Jeremy Leaman and the other editors of *JCES* for helping us in launching this venture, as well as all Routledge editors (Extremism and Democracy series, etc.). We would also like to thank the anonymous reader(s) for their perceptive and helpful observations on earlier versions of the text.

While our companion volume (*Mapping the Extreme Right*) above all explored the *spatial* dimensions of the extreme right (local, regional, national, comparative, transnational) and was therefore deliberately continental in its scope, the focus in this successor publication is on the ideological character of the extreme right, its mobilization themes, its vectors for the transmission of ideas and the socialization of militants. The emphasis is thus on the cultural thickness/richness of the phenomenon rather than on its territorial ubiquity/diversity. This thematic differentiation between the two volumes has had one quite unanticipated and certainly unintended consequence, namely that the second volume has a predominantly 'Western European' focus, but, as we briefly already suggested, we attach no particular significance to this outcome.

Through an exploration of the nature and political culture of the extreme right, its use of media and its diverse techniques of mobilization, this volume (re)introduces the image of a Janus-faced party family able to adapt itself to the modern world without renouncing its fundamental ideas. Hence, it is argued that alleged new rightist themes are often instrumental, pandering opportunistically to the electorate's own cost–benefit assessment of a given subject, or linked with the usual neo-fascist and fascist vision of society (for instance a racialized, holistic and homogeneous community).

Finally, we also contend that the extreme right is only superficially moderating its ideology. It has never produced any sort of *Godesberger Programm*, democratizing its beliefs and abandoning neo-fascism.[12] By revealing patterns of sociological and ideological continuity within the history and imaginary of parties and rightist cultures, our book aims to show that it is difficult to demonstrate convincingly that the European extreme right has undertaken a process of genuine demo-cratization. Much may have changed in the form, but what is striking are elements of continuity with a fascist past, thus raising questions about the threat that such parties and movements pose to contemporary democracies and multi-ethnic society. Given the extreme right's transnational dimension and the attractiveness of its methods of recruitment and socialization (music, the Internet, sport) among the younger generations, these questions are surely worth asking.

Notes

1 For example, according to Mammone (2009: 187):

> by not dismissing their backward looking and extremist philosophies, these new movements may thereby come to represent a sort of adaptation of some traditional 'old' political streams as well as a modernization of some classic fascist ideas. This could be conceptualized as a contemporarization of neofascism within a post-materialist and global society.

In reference to the BNP, Copsey (2007: 79) similarly suggests that the party 'despite clearly dissociating itself from inter-war fascism, [it] remains intuitively fascist. To locate the BNP on the national–populist right is ill-advised', thus this is 'fascism recalibrated – a form of neo-fascism – to suit contemporary sensibilities' (Copsey 2007: 66). In line with this, and in reference to the new 'nativist job ideology' (national jobs for national citizens), Richardson and Wodak – through a deconstruction of terms and slogans widely used by the contemporary extreme right – argue that this allegedly new rhetoric 'stems from antisemitic, nationalistic, and fascist ideologies from the nineteenth and twentieth cen-turies, although implemented in significantly different ways' owing to national differences (such as colonialism, fascism or Nazism). In this sense, their contemporary world-vision is made up of references to the past and to refined and narrow ideas of belonging: 'their "British worker" is white, and only white, with "racial foreigners" only here on suffer-ance, to be repatriated at the earliest convenience. Similarly, the "real Austrian" is conceived as being Christian and white' (Richardson and Wodak 2009: 264).

2 In a recent contribution to neo-fascism, Cento Bull has convincingly adopted a 'diachronic approach' for the study of the phenomenon in question (Cento Bull 2009: 598). She basically borrows – as Wolfreys has similarly done in our book – Robert Paxton's idea of different contexts and stages of fascism, and uses it to analyse post-1945 right-wing extremism up to recent times. In doing so, she traces the evolution of an extreme-right journey that is prevalently still fascist in its ideological core and legacy (Cento Bull 2009: 603).

3 Bar-On made this point even clearer by assuming that

> the '*nouvelle droite*'s political 'conversion' process was only *exoteric* in nature by
> mimicking the ideas of the New Left and that its *esoteric* orientation was of 'true
> believers' who never left a political pantheon of conservative revolutionary ideas
> with roots largely in the 1920s and 1930s.
>
> (Bar-On 2009: 243)

4 Indeed, the term 'populism' was historically coined around the turn/end of the 1800s,
and referred to various agrarian movements in North America, Russia, and parts of
Western Europe along with some urban movements in Latin America. It was thus a feature
of past movements as well – including leftist ones. In terms of imaginary, populists are
perceived to be close to the underprivileged and under-represented common citizens,
close to their needs and desires, against elites, traditional political class and intellectuals.

5 We also share Jamin's view that it is only the concept of the 'enemy' – as when it represents
the hated elites – that unifies populists and rightist extremists.

6 In our first volume, we specifically suggested that it is this 'rhetoric of exclusion' that
immediately characterizes the extreme right in the eyes of many Europeans – it is an
evident common feature across state borders (Mammone *et al.* 2012: 5–6). This discourse
can be in fact extended to a number of countries and movements. Mammone, for example,
argues that a sort of 'Euroracism' (also grounded in the Front National's 'national
preference' worldview) which particularly, and transnationally, unifies the extreme right
in contemporary France and Italy (Mammone, forthcoming).

7 David Art (2006), for example suggests that the differences in dealing with the Nazi past
led to diverse outcomes in terms of local political cultures and partisan politics in Austria
and Germany. While in Germany the idea of guilt led to an environment in some way
less fertile to the resurgence of Hitler's heirs, Austrian's imaginary of 'first victims of
National Socialism' contributed to the rise and successes of (powerful) extreme-right
movements. For a specific critique of the use of *national populisme* in the French context
see Collovald 2004 and 2003, and Mammone 2009.

8 In particular, Ellinas (in a special edition of the *Journal of Contemporary European Studies*
which we have edited) questions the idea that electoral achievements are *all* about party
organization. This view is indeed too static and it is useful only to understand why some
parties *survive* after the first successes while others disappear. 'The media can help parties
overcome their early organisational deficiencies, but can also undermine future
organisational growth' (Ellinas 2009: 209).

9 Interestingly enough, and linked with our idea of an 'old' contemporary extreme right,
Orfali continues,

> the fact that 'new' extreme-right movements have to be understood through a
> reference to 'old' ones shows how the cognitive process works: in any country,
> today's extreme right is necessarily related to some identical party or ideology from
> the past. In France for example, the Front National will bring a reference to Pétain
> and the Nazi collaborationists [. . .]; in Italy, the Fascists will be quoted when Alleanza
> Nazionale, Forza Nuova, Fiamma Tricolore or Azione Sociale are discussed.

This is something that also comes up in Wolfreys' and other chapters. It is however worth
noting that the insistence on a past 'exclusively national ancestry' has also been used (e.g.
the French 'immunity thesis' towards fascism as described in Jenkins 2007) to deny
transnational historical resemblances (e.g. with fascism, or with other foreign neo-fascist
movements as also discussed in Mammone, forthcoming).

10 Similar attitudes can be found, for example, in Britain – but also in many other places
– where the British National Party proved to be rather ambivalent around issues of racism,
immigration and national identity. Indeed the party

> conceals this core racist ideology, acknowledging its aim for a white Britain only
> in documents rarely read by non-members. In its more widely disseminated

election materials, the party emphasises 'Britain', cultural identity and a range of political commonplaces that most democratically minded Britons would be hard-pressed to object to.

(Richardson and Wodak 2009: 252)

11 As in the case of the rallies described by Virchow,

the origin of such relationships is often down to personal contacts – representatives of the *Ultra Sur* [Real Madrid] attend games as guests of the Irriducibili [Lazio] *Direttivo* (management board) who display the team scarves of the twinning clubs in their Head Office. The twinning is first and foremost a declaration of friendship based on a shared enthusiasm for neo-fascism.

12 At the 1959 Congress of Bad Godesberg, the German Social Democrats officially foreswore ideas based on Marxism that had hitherto influenced the party's discourse and official aims.

References

Art, D. (2006), *The Politics of the Nazi Past in Germany and Austria* (Cambridge: Cambridge University Press).

Bar-On, T. (2009), 'Understanding political conversion and mimetic rivalry', *Totalitarian Movements and Political Religions*, 10(3–4), 241–64.

Carter, E. (2005), *The Extreme Right in Western Europe* (Manchester: Manchester University Press).

Cento Bull, A. (2009), 'Neofascism', in R.J.B. Bosworth (ed.), *The Oxford Handbook of Fascism* (Oxford: Oxford University Press).

Cheles, L. (2010), 'Back to the future: The visual propaganda of Alleanza Nazionale (1994–2009)', *Journal of Modern Italian Studies*, 15(2), 232–311.

Collovald, A. (2003), 'Le "national-populisme" ou le fascisme disparu: Les historiens du "temps présent" et la question du déloyalisme politique contemporain', in M. Dobry (ed.) *Le mythe de l'allergie française au fascisme* (Paris: Albin Michel), pp. 279–321.

Collovald, A. (2004), *Le 'Populisme du FN': Un dangéreux contresens* (Broissieux: Éditions du Croquant).

Copsey, N. (2007), 'Changing course or changing clothes? Reflections on the ideological evolution of the British National Party. 1999–2006', *Patterns of Prejudice*, 41(1), 61–82.

Ellinas, A. (2009), 'Chaotic but popular? Extreme-right organisation and performance in the age of media communication', *Journal of Contemporary European Studies*, 17(2), 209–21.

François, S. (2007), 'The Euro-Pagan scene: Between Paganism and radical right', *Journal for the Study of Radicalism*, 1(2), 35–54.

Hainsworth, P. (2000), *The Politics of the Extreme Right: From the margins to the mainstream* (London and New York: Pinter).

Jenkins, B. (ed.) (2007), *France in the Era of Fascism: Essays on the French authoritarian right* (New York: Berghahn Books).

Klandermans, B. and Mayer, N. (eds) (2006), *Extreme-right Activists in Europe: Through the magnifying glass* (London and New York: Routledge).

Mammone, A. (2009), 'The eternal return? Faux populism and contemporarization of neo-fascism across Britain, France and Italy', *Journal of Contemporary European Studies*, 17(2), 171–92.

Mammone, A. (2011), 'Revitalizing and de-territorializing fascism in the 1950s: The extreme right in France and Italy, and the pan-national ("European") imaginary', *Patterns of Prejudice*, 45(4), 279–302.

Mammone, A. (forthcoming), *Transnational Neofascism in France and Italy* (New York and Cambridge: Cambridge University Press).

Mammone, A., Godin, E. and Jenkins, B. (2012), 'Mapping the "right of the mainstream right" in contemporary Europe', in A. Mammone, E. Godin and B. Jenkins (eds), *Mapping the Extreme Right in Contemporary Europe: From local to transnational* (London and New York: Routledge), pp. 1–14.

Mény, Y. and Surel, Y. (2000), *Par le peuple, Pour le peuple. Le populisme et les démocraties* (Paris: Fayard).

Mudde, C. (2007), *Populist Radical Right Parties in Europe* (Cambridge: Cambridge University Press).

Paxton, R. (2005), *The Anatomy of Fascism* (London: Vintage).

Richardon, J.E. and Wodak, R. (2009), 'Recontextualising fascist ideologies of the past: Right-wing discourses on employment and nativism in Austria and the United Kingdom', *Critical Discourse Studies*, 6(4), 251–67.

Ruzza, C. and Fella, S. (2007), *Re-inventing the Italian Right: Territorial politics, populism and 'post-fascism'* (London and New York: Routledge).

Taggart, P. (2000), *Populism* (Buckingham and Philadelphia: Open University Press).

Virchow, F. (2007), 'Performance, emotion, and ideology: On the creation of "collectives of emotion" and worldview in the contemporary German far right', *Journal of Contemporary Ethnography*, 36(2), 147–64.

PART I

Fascism and post-war right-wing extremism

1

THE EUROPEAN EXTREME RIGHT IN COMPARATIVE PERSPECTIVE

Jim Wolfreys

Is the extreme right 'coming in from the cold'? (Eatwell 2000: 424). The revival across Europe over the past twenty-five years of various organizations founded by fascist activists in the post-war period, and the entry of some of these parties into national and local government, has given rise to a bewildering array of terms in search of the formula that best defines this phenomenon, from far right, extreme right and radical right to populist, national-populist, authoritarian and neo-fascist. Some studies have been preoccupied with isolating templates or models while others have underestimated the role of strategy in a different way, by giving too much credence to the pronouncements of party leaders. As Annie Collovald has shown, 'populism' has become the dominant prism through which the extreme right is viewed in France, yet the term is used with no sociological foundation, as studies seek 'an explanation for political phenomena or behavior in proclaimed "political ideas" or "values" and not in social or political practice' (Collovald 2004: 25).[1] Definitions, as Robert Paxton argues, are static. 'They succumb all too often to the intellectual's temptation to take programmatic statements as constitutive.' In the case of fascism, they identify it 'more with what it said than what it did' (Paxton 2004: 14).[2]

The problem facing anyone attempting to understand the contemporary extreme right is not simply that the study of fascism has been dominated by idealism, giving priority to doctrine over party organization and strategy, but that the re-emergence of the phenomenon has coincided with, and contributed to, a reconfiguration across Europe of the party system itself. Integral to the development of the myth of the nation-state in the nineteenth century was the extension of representative democracy and the replacement of elite parties by mass organizations that performed a key role throughout the first half of the nineteenth century in linking citizens to the state or, in the case of fascist parties, mobilizing them against established institutions. In the post-war period parties gradually lost their mobilizing capacity and became more entwined with the state until, from the 1970s, this relationship began to change, so much so that some have argued that, 'the political party as a primary link between the society and the state disappeared and a vacuum was created' (Pedahzur and Weinberg 2001: 54).

The question that preoccupies those studying organizations such as Alleanza Nazionale (AN) – how and when does an organization formed by fascists become something other than fascist? – could therefore also apply to other political formations. The abandonment of its defence of the Mussolini regime and the adoption of the 'post-fascist' label have been widely taken as grounds for accepting that the AN is no longer an extremist, still less a fascist party. Should, then, the acceptance of the free market and the abandonment of redistributive state interventionist policies by European socialist parties be taken as evidence that they are no longer social democratic organizations? Does the embrace of socially liberal policies by right-wing formations imply that they are no longer conservative? A further complication arises when we take into account the fact that an avoidance of open identification with fascism and an acceptance of democratic institutions were acknowledged by the fascists themselves as a prerequisite of being able to function in the post-war period. A dislocation between word and deed therefore became intrinsic to the development of these parties.

This chapter draws on Robert Paxton's *The Anatomy of Fascism* to provide an assessment of the threat to democracy posed by the contemporary extreme right in Europe. It will offer a comparative analysis of three contrasting case studies: the French Front National, the British National Party and the Alleanza Nazionale (heir of the neo-fascist Movimento Sociale Italiano). At one extreme, Gianfranco Fini's 'post-fascist' Alleanza Nazionale appears to have become part of the mainstream of Italian politics, while at the other, Nick Griffin's BNP, despite local and European election advances, has achieved limited success in ridding itself of the image of a racist neo-fascist organization. In France, the Front National has cultivated both legitimacy and outsider status, taking local office while seeming to retain an implicit identification with the fascist and anti-Semitic traditions of France's counter-revolutionary right.

This chapter will ask what has governed the different trajectories of these parties over the past fifty years, given their common roots in pro-fascist organizations of the immediate post-war period. Do their contrasting experiences derive from aims that now diverge from common origins, or do they reflect different stages of development in pursuit of similar ends?

Theorizing fascism

If analyses of the extreme right tend to focus on what is said rather than what is done, two recent studies have bucked this trend. Michael Mann's monumental survey of European fascism is blunt in its dismissal of the recent vogue, led by Roger Griffin, for studies preoccupied with fascism's 'mythic core':

A myth cannot be an agent driving or integrating anything, since ideas are not free-floating. Without power organisations, ideas cannot actually do anything . . . Fascism was not just a collection of individuals with certain beliefs. Fascism had a great impact on the world only because of its collective actions and its organisational forms.

(Mann 2004: 12–13)

Although Mann incorporates a version of Griffin's notion of national rebirth as the core ideological feature of fascism, his focus on the paramilitary organizational forms of the movement means that his analysis goes beyond an abstract preoccupation with ideology. But the rigidity of Mann's definition of the phenomenon ('transcendental and cleansing nation-statism through paramilitarism'), means that he is unable to conceive of it existing outside the inter-war period: 'European fascism is defeated, dead and buried' (Mann 2004: 370).

Robert Paxton offers a more subtle approach and an explanation of what makes analyses confined to fascist ideology counterproductive. Fascism developed as a reaction against modern democratic society, liberal individualism, constitutionalism and the left. It arrived later on the scene than its older, more established rivals – socialism, conservatism, liberalism – at the point when mass democracy was experiencing its first difficulties and when socialists were beginning to participate in, and be compromised by, government. Fascism grew from these circumstances, rather than a pre-existing set of ideas. As Mussolini put it, 'The democrats of *Il Mondo* want to know our programme? It is to break the bones of the democrats of *Il Mondo*. And the sooner the better' (cited in Paxton 2004: 17). A preoccupation with doctrine therefore misses the key feature of fascism between the wars: its appeal was based more on action than dogma and had a strong performative, aesthetic and affective aspect. Based on a rejection of universal values, it was more disparate than other political movements, making it impossible to classify as a manifestation of 'the same fixed essence'. Fascism is less defined by its themes, argues Paxton, than by their function. Analyses of fascism therefore only make sense if they are attuned to historical contexts, which are prone to shift.

While ideology and doctrine played a role in the development of the movement, it was the irrational appeal of fascism, the set-piece rallies with their symbols and rituals, the emotional charge of the cult of the leader, the excitement of the culture of violence and voluntarism, that drew people into its ranks, compelled by the dramatic, sensual intensity of the promise of empowerment and subordination rather than persuaded by careful argument. Paxton identifies five stages in the development of fascism: the creation of a movement; its rooting in the political system; the seizure of power; the exercise of power; its fate in the long term.

Fascist parties are not static phenomena. The various processes that shape their development – establishing a following, forging alliances with those outside their ranks, laying claim to power, governing – impose different imperatives. 'The conceptual tools that illuminate one stage may not necessarily work equally well for others' (Paxton 2004: 23). Crucially, fascism is forced to adapt to the possibilities presented to it, reshaping itself as it grows into whatever space becomes available, seeking out the most appropriate themes in the national culture within which it develops in order to mobilize support. 'The themes that appeal to fascists in one cultural tradition may seem simply silly to another' (Paxton 2004: 39). Mussolini, for example, eschewed the socialist rhetoric of his early career once it became clear that the Italian left had occupied that terrain. Similarly, those who became allies of fascism did so less out of ideological affiliation than because, as options narrowed, polarization pulled them towards the fascist camp. Here Paxton's method echoes that developed by Michel Dobry, whose 'relational' analyses of fascism stress the role played by political allies and rivals in shaping a phenomenon that *develops*, rather than simply *exists* (Dobry 2003).[3]

'Settings and allies' therefore need to be considered with as much care as the fascists themselves (Paxton 2004: 207). The emphasis on political space means that the art of understanding fascism does not have to rely on checklists, ticking off features of modern movements against a 'fascist minimum', or finding 'exact replicas of the rhetoric, programmes or aesthetic preferences of the first fascist movements of the 1920s' (Paxton 2004: 174). Rather than a fixed essence, fascism in action 'looks much more like a network of relationships' (Paxton 2004: 207). These relationships embed tensions within the movement, between radical or revolutionary activists and more conservative elements, and, once in power, between existing state institutions and the 'party state'. As a movement, fascism builds its own parallel structures in order to demonstrate its ability to carry out the functions normally considered the preserve of the state. These structures are, for Paxton, a defining feature of fascism. Once in power, fascism either radicalizes or atrophies. Here Paxton echoes a perspective developed in the inter-war period by, among others, Trotsky. The tension between the movement's mass base and the existing state would be resolved either through radicalization, with the 'party state' taking precedence, or accommodation to the status quo, fascism mutating into Bonapartism.

The Front National

The origins of the Front National (FN), like those of the Movimento Sociale Italiano (MSI) and the British National Party (BNP), were fascist. The organization was the direct consequence of a reassessment of the role of fascism in the post-war period and the possibilities that were open to it in new circumstances. This discussion took place in a variety of books and periodicals, from Maurice Bardèche's *Défense de l'Occident* to François Gaucher's *Le Fascisme est-il actuel?* and Dominique Venner's *Europe-Action*.[4] A synthesis of these debates was presented to the self-styled 'revolutionary nationalist' organization Ordre Nouveau in the summer of 1972 by two of its leading members, François Duprat and François Brigneau. The document, *Pour un ordre nouveau*, drew the same conclusions as those reached by the MSI in the immediate post-war period: if fascists were to escape from their 'ghetto' they would have to adopt a strategy of 'insertion'.[5] The practical consequence of this analysis was the Front National, formed the following October with Jean-Marie Le Pen at its head and Duprat and Brigneau on its political bureau.[6] For the founders of the FN this conclusion was imposed in the French context by the following factors:

1   The experience of inter-war fascism and the legacy of its defeat meant that fascist organizations would have no hope of success if they proclaimed themselves so. Biological determinism, fascist regalia, armed struggle and violence against the left could play no part in post-war fascism if it was to reach a wider audience.

2   The rebuilding and consolidation of state institutions meant that parliamentary democracy had greater credibility in the post-war period. In France, the establishment of a large state bureaucracy, combined with sustained economic growth, meant that the frenzied petty bourgeoisie of the inter-war period had been largely supplanted by a white-collar middle class.

3   Greater economic and social stability made society less polarized, limiting the threat from the left.

Revolutionary nationalism could not win through the armed struggle of a comparatively small number of activists. These activists needed to reach a wider audience through an electoral strategy. This strategy was only viable if they acquired a respectable image. Aided by the work of the right-wing think tanks collectively known as the Nouvelle Droite (ND), which found ways of expressing racism in terms of cultural difference rather than biological supremacy, the Front National fashioned a structure for itself inspired by Jacques Doriot's Parti Populaire Français, a structure that combined official bodies and satellite organizations on the fascist model.[7] Among the inadequacies of analyses of the FN as a 'national–populist' organization is a lack of explanation as to how, when or why the former Waffen SS officers, Vichy militiamen and self-styled 'revolutionary nationalists' that peopled the leadership of the FN throughout the 1970s, most remaining with the organization following its electoral breakthrough, became populists. Having founded the FN with a deliberate strategy of courting respectability in order to build a fascist organization, did they consciously choose an alternative path? Or were they 'domesticated' by the party system, re-appropriated by the establishment?[8]

There is a rich vein of historical analysis of phenomena such as Boulangism, the populist authoritarian movement that rose to prominence in the late 1880s, that is sensitive to the different currents and divisions that shaped its rise and fall, identifying both internal tensions between traditional counter-revolutionary monarchists and the more radical elements that would later form anti-Semitic leagues during the Dreyfus Affair, and external tensions imposed by political competition, itself influenced by broader social and economic developments. These studies, by

American historians, portray Boulangism as a living movement, whose trajectory was not preordained or determined by an ideological 'essence'.[9] No studies of comparable depth or acuity have been produced by the many observers to have identified the Front National as a 'national–populist' organization. This label derives from analyses of FN discourse which locate the party's xenophobia and cultural pessimism in a lineage stretching from Boulangism to the present day via Pétainism and Poujadism.[10] Such studies tend to obscure the complex interaction that exists between the different levels of discourse that operate within the FN, mediating relations between different elements within the organization's sphere of influence. Le Pen's apparent 'gaffes', for instance, his remarks on the Holocaust as a detail of the Second World War, his pun on the gas ovens in reference to the centre-right minister in the Socialist Michel Rocard's government, Michel Durafour, and his claims about racial inequality, all served to confirm media perceptions of him as a buffoonish populist, prone to damaging slips. This superficial reading of his outbursts not only missed the point, but distracted from their function.

The 'detail' remark appeased hard core members whose political education had included regular and prolific negationist tracts provided by FN founder François Duprat, and presented a challenge to those who had either voted for the FN, joined it, or been elected under its colours. Some left the organization. Those who were prepared to accept his views had, however passively, been radicalized. The 'Durafour-crématoire' controversy was more than crass wordplay, the remarks having been trailed in the FN press for several weeks by articles claiming that the Rocard government's policy of opening up posts to the centre-right was part of a Jewish conspiracy masterminded by an international grouping of Jews and freemasons, of which Rocard was a part. Le Pen's public acknowledgement of such views provided the core membership with the means to engage with wider layers of support on such issues. The same was true of his 1996 references to racial inequality, dressed up in 'populist' inanities about the absence of black athletes from the finals of Olympic swimming events and their disproportionate representation on the track in the sprints. Parallel to his pontifications, the FN press was running articles about the American Civil War, linking the North's fight against slavery to the establishment of capitalist (and Jewish) domination of the economy.[11]

For an organization founded on the premise that its 'true' aims would have to be euphemized in order to pursue a strategy based on winning electoral legitimacy it is entirely logical that the relationship between propaganda and ideology should be a complex one. Academia and the media were obliging enough to obscure this relationship behind a one-dimensional 'populist' label, which the FN was happy to embrace. The above examples are small illustrations that the organization is pursuing a political strategy, not a populist agenda. Other examples range from Le Pen's decision to have an effigy of the head of a Socialist mayor served up to him on a plate at an election rally in 1997, his physical assault on another female Socialist candidate during the same campaign and his reluctance to engage in the

Islamophobia embraced by more traditionalist rivals such as Philippe de Villiers in the wake of the 9/11 attacks. Since the FN's emergence as a major political player, Le Pen's concern, in line with the founding aims of his party, has generally been to avoid sacrificing his organization's outsider status for the sake of electoral gain. In the late 1990s he was prepared to split the Front rather than see its cadre develop the kind of independence from his leadership that would risk the FN's integration into the political establishment through alliances with a still resilient mainstream party system.

In January 2011 the party chose Marine Le Pen to take over as leader following the retirement of her 82-year-old father. Media attention focused on her 'modern' image – her 'tailored jeans . . . high-heeled boots, silk shirts and strict blazers' (*Daily Telegraph*, 16 January 2011), her defence of abortion and her espousal of 'Republican values'. The election of a woman, four decades younger than the previous incumbent, to lead the FN, prompted claims that the Front's integration into the mainstream political establishment would now be accelerated. The new leader's identification of Muslim prayers in the street with the Occupation and her claim that globalization was a form of totalitarianism, however, indicated that her approach would not differ significantly from the party's long-term aim of fashioning itself into 'an iron hand in a velvet glove' (Wolfreys 1993). This consideration – how to court legitimacy without becoming 'a party like the others'? – remains central to the Front's strategy, and to the development of the extreme right in Britain and Italy, as we shall see below.

The British National Party

The forerunner of the BNP, the National Front, was never able to achieve what its French counterparts had managed by the 1980s, its neo-Nazi image proving a constant target for anti-fascist activity. The BNP itself, founded by former NF leader John Tyndall in 1982, achieved its first electoral breakthrough in 1993 when Derek Beackon won a council seat in Millwall, east London. The following year Beackon lost his seat and the party experienced a crisis. Tyndall's solution, a 'return to the streets', was rejected by the membership. A number of its leading cadres resigned from the party. As one of them put it, 'Activities like marches gave an impression to the public that the (media) accusations might be true . . . our tactics amounted to "attract-a-mob-to-attack-us" . . . such an approach to politics is not exactly calculated to encourage people to join' (*Patriot*, Summer 1999). In rebuilding the organization along more 'respectable' lines, the BNP looked to the Front National.[12]

A section of the BNP leadership attributed the Millwall victory to the adoption of a 'minimalist' agenda. This meant 'adopting the line of least resistance that is still consistent with the core ideology. It means that all excess baggage is discarded' (*Patriot*, Autumn 1999). This was the line advocated by Nick Griffin, who replaced Tyndall as leader in 1999:

> Why do nationalists, and nationalists alone, insist on spelling out in words of one syllable where they come from and where they want to go? . . . This is a life and death struggle for white survival, not a fancy dress party . . . As long as our own cadres understand the full implications of our struggle, then there is no need for us to do anything to give the public cause for concern. Rather, since we need their support in order to be able to turn impotent theory into practical reality, we must at all times present them with an image of moderate reasonableness.
>
> (*Patriot*, Spring 1999)

Under Griffin the party toned down some of its propaganda, dropping calls for the compulsory repatriation of immigrants, and adopted an official policy of avoiding confrontation with the left. BNP propaganda focused on four central themes: freedom (opposition to the European Union and state bureaucracy); democracy (plebiscitary calls for the return of the death penalty and tougher immigration policies); security (crime and unemployment); and identity. Explaining the function of these themes, Griffin stressed that members should try to 'create links between the BNP and those four idealistic, unobjectionable, motherhood and apple pie concepts' (*Patriot*, Spring 1999).

Among Griffin's political influences were the Italian fascist Julius Evola and the French Nouvelle Droite. His desire for respectability does not detract from his understanding of the role of an extra-parliamentary movement. In 1997 he gave an interview to journalists posing as representatives of the Front National. Referring to Beackon's 1993 success he told them:

> The electors of Millwall did not back a Post-Modernist Rightist Party, but what they perceived to be a strong, disciplined organisation with the ability to back up its slogan 'Defend Rights for Whites' with well directed boots and fists. When the crunch comes, power is the product of force and will, not of rational debate.
>
> (*Searchlight*, June 1997)

Griffin set up a front organization, the European Martial Arts Association, to train 'young men capable of defending our operations'. But he saw the BNP's priority as attracting the support of the 'frustrated and disorientated traditional middle class' (*Searchlight*, October 1999), since the kind of people who had voted for Beackon in east London were 'too stupid to do anything about it'. The BNP might win their votes, but 'you can't build a movement on those people' (*Searchlight*, June 1997). When Griffin met Le Pen during the 2003 local election campaign he apparently sought his advice 'on how to emulate the success of the French National Front in attracting educated, well-paid members' (*Sunday Times*, 4 May 2003). For the BNP leader, the development of marginal extreme-right groupings into viable alternatives to the establishment on the FN model is not the result of 'large numbers of people spontaneously turning to overt nationalism':

Rather, in every country where nationalists have begun to make serious breakthroughs it is because they have first made a real effort to turn towards the people. This means finding ways to describe the nationalist position in terms which ordinary people feel comfortable . . .

(*Identity*, January/February 2000)

Leading BNP figures see the FN as a model, proof of the possibility of metamorphosis 'from a far right party with embarrassing figures and strident language into a slick, sophisticated, more electorally appealing party . . . while the Front maintained its hardcore support, it could also reach a much wider audience'.[13]

Griffin overhauled the BNP's publications, introducing a glossy bi-monthly magazine whose title, *Identity*, is taken from the 'theoretical' publication produced by the FN. The party runs a Red-White-And-Blue Festival on the FN model, part of a concerted although as yet unfulfilled attempt to sink significant social roots. BNP satellite organizations also bear similarities to FN-affiliated organizations, from the 'Land and People' campaign to the Association of British Ex-Servicemen, the BNP Youth Group, the 'Renaissance' family circle, the Pensioners' Awareness Group and the British Students Association.

During the campaign against Tyndall, Griffin made much of the extremist image attached to his rival, often pictured in anti-fascist literature wearing the neo-Nazi uniform of the Greater Britain Movement. Griffin's views, however, are not significantly different from Tyndall's. In April 1998 he enlisted the support of the Holocaust revisionist Robert Faurisson to defend himself against charges of incitement to racial hatred following an anti-Semitic article in a BNP publication. 'Proud' of his subsequent conviction (*Patriot*, Summer 1999), Griffin expressed his negationism in forthright terms:

> I am well aware that the orthodox opinion is that 6 million Jews were gassed and cremated or turned into lampshades. Orthodox opinion also once held that the earth is flat . . . I have reached the conclusion that the 'extermination' tale is a mixture of Allied wartime propaganda, extremely profitable lie, and latter witch-hysteria.
>
> (Cited in *Searchlight*, May 2000)

Like Jean-Marie Le Pen, Griffin has a firm grasp on the importance for fascist organizations of contesting the existence of the Holocaust:

> The reason people like me aren't polite and reasonable sometimes about the Holocaust is . . . to do with frustration with how it is used to prevent any genuine debate on questions to do with immigration, ethnicity and the cultural survival of western nations.
>
> (*The Observer*, 1 September 2002)

For the benefit of BNP members, the message is spelt out even more clearly:

> For the last fifty years the vision underlying all the vile sickness of this age of ruins has been the so-called 'Holocaust' . . . The New World struggling to be born cannot do so until this lie is publicly exposed, ridiculed and destroyed . . . If nationalists don't bury this deadly lie, nobody will. In the case of Britain, that means that members of the British National Party have a duty to be involved as active participants in the revisionist struggle.
>
> (*Searchlight*, September 2002)

While the FN has spent many years educating its members in how to approach issues such as race and anti-Semitism by using language designed to deflect accusations of racism, the BNP's veneer of 'respectability' is much thinner. 'We must preserve the white race,' Griffin told *Wales on Sunday* in 1996, 'because it has been responsible for all the good things in civilisation'.[14] *Identity* carries articles that insist on 'the survival and ultimately the advancement of the White Race' as the party's 'ultimate objective'; 'once our race is mongrelised and mulattoised, how could we ever get it back?' Griffin's attitude to the presentation of the issue of race has long been shaped by the work of the Nouvelle Droite. As early as 1987, Griffin and his 'Political Soldiers' faction were using their editorial influence over NF publications to steer the British far right along lines developed in France by the GRECE and the Club de l'Horloge in the 1970s:

> The negative racism which infected sections of the Front until recently was largely a product of British imperialism, which sought to justify the domination of other peoples' countries by portraying them as members of 'inferior' races who needed to be 'civilized' and turned into coloured Britons . . . In complete contrast, the *racialist* position now adopted by the National Front is based on the Nationalist principle that self-rule and the preservation of racial and cultural identity is the inalienable right of all the peoples of the world, regardless of creed or colour.
>
> (*National Front News*, August 1987)[15]

BNP publications constantly stress the need to express racist ideas in terms of culture:

> The BNP is not a 'race supremacist' party. The BNP does not claim that any race is superior to any other, simply that they are different . . . Neither has the BNP any connection with 'race hate'. Indeed it is the multi-racialists who are the haters since it is they who are determined to destroy all cultures and all races to achieve a multi-racial mishmash.
>
> (*Identity*, January/February 2000)

This outlook informs the party's 'Rights for Whites' propaganda, a more trenchant version of the FN's notion of *la préférence nationale*, threatening discrimination against blacks in the job market, the deportation of black people (including those born in Britain) who commit crimes, and the outlawing of mixed-race relationships. That the BNP can affirm its opposition to 'race-mixing' while acknowledging that the racist label attached to the party remains 'the biggest political obstacle that we have to overcome', underlines the contradictions that underpin BNP 'respectability', and the value of compliant news editors to the organization's pursuit of it (*The Voice of Freedom*, February 2003).

Electoral success has prompted the BNP leadership to focus on bringing its fascist hard core into line. Party publications constantly stress the need for restraint:

> flight jackets, Prussian-style polished heads, black polo-neck sweaters and similar attire are just not good politics for a movement which is trying to win over ordinary Britons . . . It only takes one or two scruffy ones, one juvenile 'extreme' badge or magazine, an offensive and highly visible tattoo, or one over the top piece of invective to convince the sensible but cautious that there is substance to the media smears . . .
>
> (*Identity*, March/April 2000)

The party's efforts to court legitimacy were boosted by the New Labour government and its campaigns against asylum seekers, warnings against the 'swamping' of British schools by their children, and condemnation of 'black racism towards white people'.[16] Such attitudes were greeted with glee by Griffin:

> The asylum issue has been great for us. We have had phenomenal growth in membership. It has been quite fun to watch government ministers and the Tories play the race card in far cruder terms than we would ever use, but pretend not to. The issue legitimises us.[17]

Recession created a new situation that the party was keen to exploit, seeking to agitate among those identifying with the xenophobic slogan of 'British jobs for British workers'. In the wake of his election to the European parliament, moreover, Griffin quickly demonstrated his understanding of the tactics adopted by Le Pen when he called on the European Union to sink boats carrying illegal immigrants. The organization's awareness of the need to combine electoralism with more radical propaganda and street mobilizations was illustrated during the months that followed as BNP supporters took part in anti-Muslim demonstrations in several British cities organized by the English Defence League, a racist street league with close links to the party whose influence was to grow significantly as the BNP's electoral strategy stalled in 2010.

On one level the electoral strategy has been successful. The party won over 800,000 votes in the 2004 European elections and close to 300,000 in the 2007 local elections. Following several local electoral breakthroughs, notably in north-west England, in 2008 the BNP won a seat on the Greater London Assembly and could boast around fifty local councillors nationally. In 2009 it won two seats in the European parliament with close to a million votes (up 1.3 per cent on 2004). These advances, however, were interrupted in 2010 when the party failed to win a parliamentary seat (its overall vote rising only 1.8 per cent to 514,819 despite a year of unprecedented media exposure) and lost all its representatives in the chamber of its flagship council in Barking and Dagenham.

The party's ability to translate electoral success into organizational reserves has been limited. In 2008 a leaked party membership list of 12,800 names revealed only around a quarter of them to be active members. BNP membership has grown but efforts to organize large gatherings have yet to draw together more than a few hundred people at any one time. The disparity between 'populist' electoral propaganda and the demands of building a fascist party organization is an important feature of the modern European far right. Although the BNP nationally is in a stronger position than in 1993, the tension between its fascist hard core and its electoral ambitions remains. This has provoked tensions in the organization, notably in 2007, when two leading members were expelled taking a few dozen activists with them, and in the aftermath of the party's comparatively poor showing in the 2010 elections, when several activists were expelled, including various local councillors and the party's representative on the Greater London Assembly, Richard Barnbrook, amid rumours that the party was experiencing serious financial difficulties.

The Alleanza Nazionale (AN)

While a number of founding members of the FN in France had served under the Vichy regime, or the Waffen SS, their counterparts in Italy, the MSI, had not only a much higher proportion of fascist veterans, but they were open in their identification with the Mussolini regime. Although only ever on the fringes of the mainstream, the party sustained an electorate of around 5 per cent until the 1990s when, recast as the AN, its vote more than doubled.

The MSI/AN therefore represents a curious counterpoint to the French and British examples discussed above. Unrepentant for five decades after the fall of Mussolini about the legacy of inter-war fascism, in a way that the British NF or the French FN never permitted themselves to be, the AN has over the past decade achieved a level of integration into the political system that far out-strips its European counterparts. Many of these differences derive from contrasting aspects of particular national contexts. The reality of fascism in Italy made it impossible to claim that the nation had consistently united against it – the notion that underpinned the British myth of the Blitz (Calder 1991) – or that it was imported from elsewhere – the basis of the resistance myth and the Vichy syndrome in France (Rousso 1991). Moreover, the boundaries between insider and outsider status with regard to the political mainstream all but dissolved in the wake of the *Tangentopoli* scandal in the mid 1990s. Once the party system had collapsed, insider and outsider roles were reversed. The latter became almost a prerequisite for legitimacy and allowed the MSI, the xenophobic and federalist Northern League and the right-wing adventurer Silvio Berlusconi's Forza Italia to unite and win power in 1994.

What are we to make of the AN's integration into mainstream politics? AN acceptance of the role of anti-fascism came only after the collapse and fragmentation of anti-fascist political representation. Studies of the 1995 conference which heralded the formation of the AN have emphasized the deep-seated affiliation to fascism that characterized the political culture of AN cadre at this point, with the overwhelming majority identifying with Mussolini, his regime and his philosophical acolytes. Whether such attitudes were genuinely counterbalanced by a 'silent' embrace of liberal views, as Piero Ignazi has argued, is unlikely. A quarter of party cadres believed strikers should be sacked and that homosexuals should not be employed in bars or restaurants, over 40 per cent wanted the 'elimination' of conscientious objection. Even higher proportions expressed antagonistic attitudes towards immigrants, a belief in racial superiority and an identification with anti-Semitism. The most that can be said is that the AN leadership, like its counterparts in Britain and France, was ahead of its membership in grasping the need for moderation (Ignazi 2004: 146–56).

The official policy on immigration that emerged after the Fiuggi congress was similar to the Nouvelle Droite influenced approach adopted by the FN in France. Anti-Semitism, racism and racist violence were condemned. Instead the party stressed the need to protect 'authentic' cultures by preserving ethnic autonomy in the face of globalization and the 'egalitarian myth'. In Italy this meant that Italians came first. The party went further than the FN's proposals for a repatriation scheme, advocating cooperative programmes with developing countries aimed at stemming the flow of immigrants to Italy, but it also expressed its identification with ethnic nationalism in more direct terms, asserting that the state 'should be an expression of ethnic community' and that those who did not belong to it were 'excluded from the nation' (Ter Wal 2000: 39–47).

For the Italian extreme right, the stakes were higher than elsewhere. The prize for those able to profit from the collapse of the Christian Democratic Party that had dominated the right for fifty years was a role in government. Notwithstanding the fact that Fini may have experienced genuine remorse at having spent his entire political career up to that point defending – prominently, publicly and with gusto – Mussolini's crimes,[18] it is worth highlighting that it was now, with this prize at stake, that he chose to reveal that he considered fascist forces to have been 'on the wrong side' at the end of the Second World War. Did he believe it? He was leading a party that by 1998 was still recruiting new members who generally held positive views of the fascist regime. Does this allow us to conclude, as many have done, that 'the AN is progressively and unambiguously leaving the territory of right-wing extremism'? Are 'official declarations and platforms', along with the AN's 'estrangement from extremist groups in the domestic and international arena' and 'the party's behavior in representative assemblies', sufficient criteria to warrant the qualification of the AN as 'a post-fascist, proto-conservative party'? (Ignazi 2004: 152). If the leadership of the party has reached a 'moderate-conservative political space' while the 'middle-level elite seems still trapped in fascist nostalgia' it is surely worth asking why the party leadership manifests such a 'feeble willingness' to complete the political education of its local cadre. A plausible line of enquiry would be to ponder the hiatus between public and internal party consumption.

The key question here is the relationship between 'self-representation' and 'latent ideology' (Tarchi 2003: 137). The 'Theses of the Fiuggi Congress' (25–29 January 1995), for example, refer to 'democracy and liberty as inalienable values' but also assert, in words echoing Maurice Barrès, that 'nothing can be separated, nothing is destroyed in the formation of a cultural and historical memory' (Tarchi 2003: 141–2). The adoption of a neoliberal economic outlook and the embrace of democracy have an external function, then, in signalling the party's willingness to play by the rules of the game. But neoliberalism also allows enough scope to satisfy the deep-seated internal attitudes towards liberty and authority. What mainstream figures, from Tony Blair to Nicolas Sarkozy, refer to as the 'rights and responsibilities' of citizenship are integrated into the MSI/AN worldview as a historical relationship between individual liberty and the authority of the national community: 'real liberties do not end with the rights and freedom of the isolated individual, but extend to the dimension of the community denied since the French Revolution' (Tarchi 2003: 143).

Marco Tarchi's analysis of the theses produced by the AN at successive congresses since the 1990s concludes by dividing the organization's attempts to remodel its programme into three periods: a 'populist' phase between 1995 and 1997 during which the party positioned itself as a representative of 'civil society' against the establishment yet within the existing democratic framework; a 'national–liberal' period between 1998 and 2000 characterized by a conversion to neoliberalism and a stand against political corruption; and a third period, from 2000, when aspects of the MSI outlook were reintegrated, in a modified form, into the party's outlook – a restatement of the state's role in directing economic affairs and enforcing law and order and a renewed emphasis on the national community. Internal power relations are judged to be less significant in determining political choices by the AN than the 'affinities and frictions' with coalition partners in government (Tarchi 2003: 178).

A notable aspect of the reconfiguring of the AN was that revision of the programme was not accompanied by an influx of new leaders from the conservative right. Moreover, a restructuring of the party, which reinforced the authority of the leader over local branches (where nostalgia for the party's neo-fascist tradition ran deepest), was, as one study put it, 'a change of name rather than logic' and 'failed to overcome the previous internal setting' (Ignazi 2005: 337). While the redrafting of the AN programme and the restructuring of the organization are widely considered to have been ambiguous in outcome, there is widespread agreement that Fini's declarations, in particular his acknowledgment that fascism was an 'absolute evil', have been 'path-breaking' acts (Ignazi 2005: 339). Yet studies of the AN in the late 1990s insisted that the party's 'conversion' was ambiguous, that its support for democracy was a prerequisite for establishing an anti-communist alliance of the right in the wake of the collapse of the party system and that the lack of a serious debate on the meaning and role of fascism meant that its legacy had been remodelled for new times but kept intact (Sznajder 1997–8). The party had taken advantage of the availability of a mainstream political ally – in the albeit unconventional form of Silvio Berlusconi – and the historical revisionism of Renzo de Felice, which allowed the MSI/AN to abandon 'defensive and desperate positions' (Gallego 1999: 18), and occupy the political space that had opened up at the heart of the political establishment. This allowed the AN to present itself as part of a reaction against the 'parasitic bourgeoisie' that it claimed had dominated post-war Italian politics – the old parties, the banks and the unions – and to recast the role of fascism as a departure from the historical tradition of the Italian right, made necessary by the imperative of defeating communism in the inter-war period (Sznajder 1997–8: 4–8).

The capacity of the far right to bring its cultural and political heritage into the mainstream became clear following Berlusconi's election victory in April 2008, at the head of the People of Freedom coalition. The AN, which formally dissolved itself to join the coalition, returned significant numbers of deputies, as did Umberto Bossi's Northern League. The coalition's partners also included Azione Sociale, the fascist current led by Mussolini's granddaughter, Alessandra. Berlusconi acknowledged this heritage on winning office, claiming, 'We are the new Falange'. His victory was followed by that of Gianni Alemanno as mayor of Rome. A former AN minister who received his political education in the MSI, Alemanno's election was greeted by supporters giving Roman salutes and shouting 'Duce! Duce!' The first targets of the new government were Italy's Roma population. Measures were announced that would require the fingerprinting of all Roma adults and the threat to remove custody from parents who allowed their children to beg on the streets. In Naples Roma camps were evacuated in May 2008 after angry crowds set fire to their homes. In July the Court of Cassation made public a decision to overturn the conviction for racial discrimination handed out to the Northern League mayor of Verona who had claimed in 2001 that wherever there are gypsies 'there are robberies' (*The Guardian*, 1 July 2008). If such scapegoating reflected a determination to set a new political agenda, Bossi, with typical bravado, indicated that there was scope for its parameters to shift yet further, marking the first session of the new parliament with a warning to his opponents: 'I don't know what the left wants [but] we are ready. If they want conflicts, I have 300,000 men always on hand' (*The Guardian*, 30 April 2008). His Northern League colleague in Berlusconi's cabinet, Roberto Calderoli, now rivals Alessandra Mussolini as a leading anti-Muslim figure, desecrating land set aside for building mosques by taking pigs to walk on it (Mammone and Peace 2012: 8). The relationship between the ex-AN, the Northern League and Mussolini's Azione Sociale underlines Anna Cento Bull's claim that taxonomies are of limited use in forming an assessment of the contemporary far-right's development, which must take into account ideology, 'dynamic trajectory' and the distinction between leadership and rank and file (Cento Bull 2009: 602). The trajectory of the Italian far right is neither static nor linear but, as Dechezelles has shown in this volume, shot through with tension. On the one hand, the AN leadership has attempted to bridge the gap between its role at the heart of the Berlusconi regime and the political culture of its membership, steeped in notions of the 'purity of origins'; the Northern League, meanwhile, has found that radicalization has paid electoral dividends; in their shadow are more overtly fascist groups such as Azione Sociale whose positions are legitimized by the success of their bigger rivals (see also Dechezelles's chapter). Fini's break from Berlusconi in the summer of 2010 and the establishment of a new formation, Future and Freedom, with former MSI members at its core and Fini at its head, further underlines the fluidity of these tensions.

Conclusion

The above examples show the extreme right at different points in Paxton's second stage of fascist development, attempting to forge alliances as part of their integration into the political system. In Britain the BNP leadership has achieved limited, local success and been offered a propaganda platform by a media establishment that broadly considers it a legitimate political player. In France the Front National has deliberately limited the extent of its political integration, and shed a significant number of party cadres, by preserving its outsider status at the expense of sealing electoral pacts with potential allies. A likely factor in Le Pen's – *père et fille* – assessment of this situation is a consideration of the party's ability to withstand the blandishments of the establishment and maintain its outsider status. In Italy a place on the fringes of the mainstream as a permanent outsider had been won over a period of several decades by the MSI/AN. Fini's turn towards a more moderate line is most convincingly explained in strategic terms, rather than as a genuine conversion to the values of democratic anti-fascism. The AN simply took advantage of the political space that opened up in the mid 1990s, and occupied it. This does not preclude the party's mutation into a different form of authoritarianism, located on the continuum that links fascism to conservatism.[19]

Inter-war fascism took aspects of the context in which it found itself – notably militarism and imperialism – and made them its own. Those who have attempted to preserve fascist political traditions in the post-war period have sought to mould it to a new context, taking into account public revulsion at the fascist heritage and the consequences of a more sophisticated state and party system. Contexts shift and the responses of the Italian, French and, to a lesser extent, British extreme right, have achieved varying degrees of durability. The economic crisis that will shape the period ahead will test these formations and their opponents and place greater pressure on mainstream political traditions already in difficulty. Each of the parties discussed above, steeped in a political culture characterized by anti-egalitarianism, an identification with a hierarchy of leaders and the subordination of individuals to an ethnocentric community of destiny from which outsiders are excluded, possesses a capacity for mutation, either towards incorporation into the mainstream – a form of atrophy – or its opposite: radicalization.

Notes

1 On the tendency for electoral studies of the FN to take correlations for explanations see Collovald 2004, pp. 119–62, 'Vote FN: vote populaire'.
2 For a discussion of Paxton and Mann see Wolfreys 2006.
3 See also Dobry 2005.
4 See, for example, Bardèche 1961 and Gaucher 1961.
5 On the great influence of the MSI on the creation of the FN see Mammone 2008.
6 On the formation of the Front National see Algazy 1989; Lorien *et al.* 1985; Fysh and Wolfreys 2003.
7 These structures were put in place by Victor Barthélemy, former general secretary of the PPF in the 1930s and later an advisor to Mussolini. See Barthélemy 1978.
8 One of the few books to address this question is Camus 1996.
9 See Nord 1986; Seager 1969; Rutkoff 1981.
10 See, for example: Winock 1993; Taguieff 1989; or, more recently, Lecoeur 2003.
11 See Fysh and Wolfreys 2003, Chapter Five.
12 For a more detailed version of this analysis, see Wolfreys 2003.
13 Tony Lecomber, review of J. Marcus, *The Front National in French Politics*, Basingstoke, Macmillan, 1995, in *Patriot*, Spring 1999.
14 *Searchlight*, 'The Politics of the BNP a summary' (www.s-light.demon.co.uk/presspack).
15 Cited in Eatwell 1996, p. 109.
16 These remarks were made by Phil Woolas, MP for Oldham, in 2002 (*The Sunday Times*, 2 February 2002). Made a government minister in 2005, he argued in 2008 that birth defects in Muslim children could be attributed to 'inbreeding'.
17 *Searchlight*, 'The Politics of the BNP: a summary' (www.s-light.demon.co.uk/presspack).
18 In 1991 the MSI was described by its secretary as a party of 'fascists, heirs of fascism, postfascists or fascists of the twenty-first century'. Cited in Tarchi 2003, p. 140.
19 See Soucy 2005 for an elaboration of this notion.

Bibliography

Algazy, J., *L'Extrême Droite en France de 1965 à 1984*, Paris: L'Harmattan, 1989.

Bardèche, M., *Qu'est-ce que le Fascisme?*, Paris: Les Sept Couleurs, 1961.

Barthélemy, V., *Du Communisme au Fascisme, Histoire d'un Engagement Politique*, Paris: Albin Michel, 1978.

Calder, A., *The Myth of the Blitz*, London: Cape, 1991.

Camus, J.-Y., *Le Front national, histoire et analyse*, Paris: Olivier Laurens, 1996.

Carter, E., *The Extreme Right in Western Europe*, Manchester and New York: Manchester University Press, 2005.

Cento Bull, A., 'Neofascism', in *The Oxford Handbook of Fascism*, ed. R. Bosworth, Oxford: Oxford University Press, 2009.

Collovald, A., *Le 'Populisme du FN' un dangereux contresens*, Paris: Éditions du Croquant, 2004.

Dobry, M., *Le mythe de l'allergie française au fascisme*, Paris: Albin Michel, 2003.

Dobry, M., 'February 1934 and the discovery of French society's allergy to the "fascist revolution"', in *France in the Era of Fascism: Essays on the French authoritarian right*, ed. B. Jenkins, Oxford and New York: Berghahn, 2005, pp. 185–213.

Eatwell, R., 'The esoteric ideology of the National Front in the 1980s', in *The Failure of British Fascism: The far right and the fight for political recognition*, ed. M. Cronin, Basingstoke: Macmillan, 1996, pp. 99–117.

Eatwell, R., 'The rebirth of the "extreme right" in Western Europe?' *Parliamentary Affairs*, 53(3) (2000), 407–25.

Eatwell, R. and C. Muddle eds, *Western Democracies and the New Extreme Right Challenge*, Oxford: Routledge, 2004.

Fenner, A. and E.D. Weitz eds, *Fascism and Neofascism: Critical writings on the radical right in Europe*, Basingstoke: Palgrave Macmillan, 2004.

Fysh, P. and J. Wolfreys, *The Politics of Racism in France*, Basingstoke: Palgrave Macmillan, 2003.

Gallego, F., 'The extreme right in Italy from the Italian Social Movement to Post-Fascism', *ICPS Working Paper*, no. 169, Universitat Autònoma de Barcelona (1999).

Gaucher, F., *Le Fascisme est-il Actuel?*, Paris: Librairie française, 1961.

Ignazi, P., *Extreme Right Parties in Western Europe*, Oxford: Oxford University Press, 2003.

Ignazi, P., 'Changing the guard on the Italian extreme right', *Representation*, 40(2) (2004), 146–56.

Ignazi, P., 'Legitimation and evolution on the Italian right wing: Social and ideological repositioning of Alleanza Nazionale and the Lega Nord', *South European Society and Politics*, 10(2) (2005), 333–49.

Klandermans, B. and N. Mayer eds, *Extreme Right Activists in Europe: Through the magnifying glass*, London: Routledge, 2006.

Lecoeur, E., *Un néo-populisme à la française. Trente ans de Front national*, Paris: La Découverte, 2003.

Lorien, J., K. Criton and S. Dumont, *Le Système Le Pen*, Brussels: Éditions EPO, 1985.

Mammone, A., 'The transnational reaction to 1968: Neo-fascist national fronts and political cultures in France and Italy', *Contemporary European History*, 17(2) (2008), 213–36.

Mammone, A. and T. Peace, 'Cross-national ideology in local elections: the case of Azione Sociale and the British National Party', in A. Mammone, E. Godin, and B. Jenkins (eds), *Mapping the Extreme Right in Contemporary Europe: From local to transnational*, London: Routledge, 2012.

Mann, M., *Fascists*, Cambridge: Cambridge University Press, 2004.

Nord, P., *Paris Shopkeepers and the Politics of Resentment*, Princeton, NJ: Princeton University Press, 1986.

Norris, P., *Radical Right*, Cambridge: Cambridge University Press, 2005.

Paxton, R., *The Anatomy of Fascism*, London: Penguin, 2004.

Pedahzur, A. and L. Weinberg, 'Modern European democracy and its enemies: The threat of the extreme right', *Totalitarian Movements and Political Religions*, 2(1) (2001), 52–72.

Rousso, H., *The Vichy Syndrome: History and memory in France since 1944*, Cambridge, MA: Harvard University Press, 1991.

Rutkoff, P.M., *Revanche and Revision: The ligue des patriotes and the origins of the radical right in France, 1882–1900*, Athens, OH: Ohio University Press, 1981.

Seager, F.H., *The Boulanger Affair: Political crossroad of France, 1886–1889*, Ithaca, NY: Cornell University Press, 1969.

Soucy, R. 'Fascism in France: Problematising the immunity thesis', in *France in the Era of Fascism: Essays on the French authoritarian right*, ed. Brian Jenkins, Oxford and New York: Berghahn, 2005, pp. 65–104.

Sznajder, M. 'Continuity or change in the ideology of the Alleanza Nazionale', *Anti-Semitism Worldwide 1997/8*, The Stephen Roth Institute, Tel Aviv: Tel Aviv University, 1998, www.tau.ac.il/Anti-Semitism/asw97–8/sznajder.html.

Taguieff, P.-A., 'Un programme révolutionnaire?' in *Le Front National a Découvert*, eds N. Mayer and P. Perrineau, Paris: Presses de la FNSP, 1989, pp. 195–227.

Tarchi, M., 'The political culture of the Alleanza Nazionale: An analysis of the party's programmatic documents (1995–2002)', *Journal of Modern Italian Studies*, 8(2) (2003), 135–81.

Ter Wal, J., 'The discourse of the extreme right and its ideological implications: The case of the Alleanza Nazionale on immigration', *Patterns of Prejudice*, 34(4) (2000), 37–51.

Winock, M., *Histoire de l'Extrême Droite en France*, Paris: Seuil, 1993.

Wolfreys, J., 'An iron hand in a velvet glove: The programme of the French Front National', *Parliamentary Affairs*, 46(3) (1993), 415–29.

Wolfreys, J., 'Sur les pas du FN: le British National Party', *Contretemps*, no. 8 (2003), 123–33.

Wolfreys, J., 'What is Fascism?', *International Socialism*, 2(112) (2006), 189–95.

2

TWO DIFFERENT REALITIES

Notes on populism and the extreme right

Jérôme Jamin

Populism and the extreme right: two problematic concepts

The concepts of populism and the extreme right play a full part in structuring the political debate in Europe and the United States. While in some respects they refer to specific realities that are easily identifiable, they can also lead to confusion. The frequent, often incorrect use of these concepts in the media, journalism, politics and political science contributes to the conceptual vagueness that characterizes the literature on this issue. This chapter is grounded in the idea that populism is not the extreme right and does not embody the same kind of threat to liberal values and democracy. To demonstrate such an assertion, we will study and compare here the precise significance of these two categories.

There are several reasons why confusion reigns in this field. First, the particularly evolving, complex and multiple nature of the phenomena to which the concepts of populism and extreme right refer makes using these concepts difficult. The diversity of situations and contexts, the sometimes very different national circumstances, the changes within parties and political groups and the brisk pace of elections prevent any exhaustive analysis.

Second, although research in political science is not the same thing as daily, 'urgent' journalistic analysis of political phenomena, it cannot completely ignore the sources on the subject if it is to evaluate their impact on political players and voters, stay informed, or clarify and if appropriate criticize them. Journalistic urgency, which itself responds to a certain extent to the pace of political events, therefore makes it difficult to attain the objectivity required for analysis from a 'political science' perspective.

The third reason is that scientific literature and research need to be based on several levels of analysis in order to correctly grasp and describe these phenomena as a whole. Thus the question of whether it is the discourse, the programme, the structure, the people or the acts (in opposition or in power), or some of these elements, or all of them at once that make up populism and the extreme right is a decisive one. This question makes the task of description and analysis arduous.

Fourth, as a result of the above there are fierce disagreements and contradictory proofs in the literature in respect of these concepts and the realities they describe. The explanations are 'resources that fuel the balance of power between scholars, journalists and politicians' (Le Bohec 2005: 55), and in terms of analysing populism in France for example, Collovald accuses Taguieff in his writing of seeking only to protect his expertise (Collovald 2004). There are numerous articles on populism and the extreme right, and many of their introductions highlight the confusion that reigns in the field.

The fifth and final reason is that the complexity of these concepts and the difficulty of defining what they cover is also explained by their prescriptive nature, by their use to demonize and discredit. These concepts are used just as much to pass judgement on a reality as to describe it. This applies to populism, which has the disadvantage of having become an anathema that categorizes the person using it just as much as those being criticized (Hermet 2001: 18). Far from simply describing, the concept of populism discredits (Zawadzki 2004: 61).

This also applies to the extreme right. Labelling a party as belonging to the extreme right means indirectly situating it as part of the extension of fascism and its crimes, morally disqualifying it and excluding it from the democratic political arena (Mayer 2002: 26, 27).

Although confusion and differing analyses dominate the literature, several authors have managed to 'clear' the ground in order to establish lists of descriptive terms that stand up to the multiple definitions and especially the variety of phenomena referred to by the concepts of populism and the extreme right. According to these authors (Backes 2001; Eatwell and O'Sullivan 1989; Laclau 2008; Mudde 1996; Rioux 2007), it can be said that populism refers to a political discourse placing the glory of the people in opposition to the corrupted elite, and that the former must take back control of the democracy that was confiscated by the latter. In the same way, it can be said that the extreme right is an ideological movement based on an extreme nationalism that is anxious to defend a given people in a given territory. A nationalism that justifies xenophobia, anti-Semitism and the development of a strong police state to protect the future of that people from a racial, territorial and cultural point of view.

While it is possible to select the terms most commonly used to describe the meaning of these two concepts and to use them to sketch out definitions supported by a degree of consensus, such definitions cannot mask the numerous disagreements and differences in the literature in this field that maintain the confusion about these two concepts, not only within themselves, but also between them. Indeed it is possible to raise a series of questions that are embarrassing for researchers in political and social science. In support of this, we have to ask ourselves if it is, for example, the stigmatization of the elite that exclusively characterizes populism, and in response say that this characteristic also describes 'extreme-right discourse' such as the Flemish Vlaams Blok[1] programme, or Geert Wilders' ambiguous and ambivalent discourse in Holland (Jamin 2011: 43–5). We also need to ask ourselves whether extreme nationalism is specific to the extreme right, and in response say that there are several phenomena considered to be populist that were based on exacerbated 'local' nationalism, such as the Lega Nord in Italy or the Union Démocratique du Centre in Switzerland.

Populism and the extreme right are of interest insofar as their political programmes, albeit in different ways, defy certain principles and values of contemporary Western democracies. It is therefore naturally the ideology and the political programme that will take precedence in our analysis of the concepts and in strictly defining their content. It is the idea of democracy in populist and/or extreme-right discourse, and their relationship to its most fundamental principles and values that count here.

Defining populism

While, as Canovan states, populism refers to a political style, demagogy, or an electoral strategy rather than to a specific political ideology or doctrine (Canovan 1981), we can add, as Hermet does, that unlike the other political families, from monarchist traditionalism to liberalism, socialism, fascism, anarchism and Marxism, populism does not have any theorists of great stature or any elaborate doctrines (Hermet 2001: 70). Ideology is a relatively coherent set of normative, empirical beliefs and thoughts relating to the problems of human nature, the development of history and social and political dynamics (Eatwell and Wright 1999: 17). If populism is first and foremost a discourse or style rather than a doctrine or ideology, we should not ignore the representation of society and politics running through populist movements. It appeals to the people and the elite, and attributes very specific characteristics to them that are of relevance (Jamin 2009: 91–115).

The people

In order to study populism, the concept of the 'people' is an inevitable starting point. 'Populist' leaders, parties, discourses and political programmes develop all their arguments based on a certain idea of the people and their role in history. The people in the populist discourse simultaneously evoke the ideas of majority, homogeneity (the idea of a homogeneous identity) and hard work (the idea of hard working people who do difficult physical work). These three traits implicitly appear in the literature on populism and indirectly in populist discourse.

Although the people evoked in populist discourse are often people portrayed as being excluded from the system, outside the places where decisions are made and far from the centre or heart of society, they nonetheless represent the greatest number and therefore personify the majority of the 'man in the street', 'ordinary people' (Taggart 1995: 37; Taguieff 2002: 127), 'Joe public' (Federici 1991: 26; Ignazi 2001: 370). The 'people' of populism are systematically presented as the majority, and merge with the idea of the greatest number, the masses, and the 'world of the little people' (Wieviorka 1993: 82) that together form the vast majority of the population. The 'people' of populism are the masses that embody democratic sovereignty.

By referring to the majority and to the greatest number, the concept of the 'people' has two important but contradictory meanings. On the one hand, with its majority dimension, the 'people' can represent a vast number of segments (social classes, etc.) of the population and therefore the concept is fundamentally vague. On the other hand, however, given its 'unifying', 'gathering' and 'simplifying' use in populist rhetoric, it also refers to a radically homogeneous social group (Mazzoleni 2003: 117). The idea that a majority group of individuals in society shares common traits, objectives and aspirations is important in populist discourse, whether those things are real or not.

Finally, the homogeneous majority also has a third specific and easily identifiable characteristic: its hard working nature. Indeed, there are few populist discourses that do not refer to the hard work of the population. The rejected, the little people and the 'man in the street' are above all honest people who work hard – or would like to work hard – to earn their living. They are people who respect honest success through work, explains Taguieff, in a description of the people to whom Thatcher's discourse was addressed (Taguieff 2002: 116).

In a comparison of the populist discourses of Pat Robertson and Jesse Jackson in the United States,[2] Hertzke goes along the same lines when he highlights criticism in this type of discourse of the exploitation of the poor by the rich, of the 'people by the elite', of workers by multinationals, bankers and other financiers (Hertzke 1993: 4). All the time the theme of the exploitation of the majority by a few recurs, developing the image of a society that pits the productive, tax-paying majority against a minority of politicians, bureaucrats and their clients, who consume the fruits of the labours of the latter (Betz 1998: 5).

The majority status, homogeneity and hard-working nature of the people enables populist leaders to attribute a number of qualities to them. Indeed, the idea of the popular majority (the first characteristic) gives rise to the idea of legitimacy. Legitimacy implies the idea of majority, which justifies and gives substance to the populist argument. Next, the legitimate majority also possesses truth. The sum of the opinions of the greatest number (the majority and legitimate opinion) is similar to the idea of truth, the idea of just discourse on what should be done, thought or decided.

The elite

The characteristics of the elite in populist discourse are exactly opposite to the characteristics of the people. The elite are in the minority, heterogeneous and lazy.

The elite never represents more than a handful of individuals, and while the number can vary considerably, it is always significantly smaller than the majority group. When referring to one of the major features of populism, Singh highlights the antipathy that the American Federal Government inspires in populist leaders as diverse as David Duke, Pat Buchanan and Louis Farrakhan. Each time, he says, it is 'us against them' (Singh 1997: 183, 184), the people against the Washington elite, the majority of Americans against the Federal Government controlled by a handful of individuals. Whoever the individuals in 'power' referred to are, they are systematically described as a secret minority, 'professional liars' (Taguieff 1991: 43).

The meaning of the concept of the elite can change radically from one discourse to another, depending on who is the originator and who it is addressed to. In his comparison of Jesse Jackson and Pat Robertson, who he considers to be American gospel populists, Hertzke demonstrates the difference between the 'economic elites', who according to Jackson exploit the poor, and the 'cultural elites' who according to Robertson undermine moral values. The former attacks multinationals, financiers, bankers and those owning the major capital, while the latter condemns educators, secular teachers, the owners of the media, 'pretentious artists', 'liberal academics', government bureaucrats, feminists, ACLU[3] lawyers, etc. (Hertzke 1993: 4). In both cases, the objective of their discourse was to stigmatize a handful of individuals who were always numerically inferior.

The majority, homogeneous, hard-working people are placed in opposition to the minority, heterogeneous, lazy elite. Thus the people who work in the fields are succeeded by the elite of the town who live off the work of others and who therefore have no merit. 'It is impossible to honestly earn the fortune of a plutocrat', the People's Party was already saying in the late nineteenth century.[4]

The elite embody evil and dishonesty. Populist leaders deduce these characteristics from the minority, disparate, lazy and cosmopolitan aspect of the elite. What does the populist ideology in fact suggest?

> [That] the solution to the problems that exist could not be easier, and has even already been found, as only the malice of a group of hypocritical politicians and servile penpushers has so far prevented it from being applied in all its clarity.
>
> (Hermet 2001: 78)

Populist rhetoric simplifies to the extreme the challenges that drive history and politics, but also and above all the number of players that could have an influence over these things. Thus social struggles, inequalities, economic crises, insecurity, unemployment and many other major political themes are referred to through a simplifying prism that places two sole players in opposition to each other in an extremely tense relationship, who are supposedly impervious to one another. This prism gives a dual vision of the social and political struggle in which two specific forces alone suffice to explain history and politics (Rioux 2007). The 'simplifying dualism' of this narrative excludes all the other players involved from the analysis and in general excludes all the other causes that are usually evoked in this field.

'By constructing a political battle focused around a bitter struggle between "us" and "them"', explains Singh (Singh 1997: 184), populists exploit the fear and resentment of the people and direct them towards groups and institutions that they deem responsible. Thus, in populist style, 'the majority of contemporary extreme right-wing parties reject intermediary institutions in favour of a direct relationship between the people and its leaders' (Betz 2002: 199), and to some extent, they reject politics (Laclau 2008).

Defining the extreme right

The most frequent characteristics used to define the extreme right include extreme nationalism, racism, ethnocentrism, anti-communism, law and order thinking, anti-pluralism and hostility to democracy (on the link between the extreme right and fascist ideologies, see Wolfreys and Antón-Mellón in this volume). Alongside these things there are also other elements, sometimes 'logically associated' with these characteristics (Dohet 2010): social Darwinism, xenophobia/heterophobia, authoritarianism, Führer worship, militarism, unwillingness to compromise, fanaticism, dogmatism, conspiracy thinking, a tendency to violence, etc.

While extremists and extremism can legitimately be set in opposition to democrats, and as Pipes maintains, extremism can simply and logically be defined as taking an idea to excess and applying it or wishing to apply it with excessive means (Pipes 1997: 29), the concept of extremism poses a problem raised by Billig in a contribution on the anti-Semitism of the extreme right. He explains that one of 'the difficulties with the "extreme right" label is that it gives the impression of saying that these movements are like the non-extreme right, but just a little more to the right' (Billig 1989: 146).

In order to deal with the problem of the numerous characteristics involved in defining it, Backes proposes analysing the extreme right as a sub-phenomenon of political extremism, and he therefore thinks that a definition of right-wing extremism should have two components: the first should show in what way the phenomenon is extremist, the second should show in what way the phenomenon is right wing. First, he explains that political extremism can refer to all political movements that are aggressively deployed against the most important values, institutions and rules of operation of constitutional democracy (Backes 2001: 24). Referring to the work of Norberto Bobbio (1996) on the difference between the right and the left, Backes goes on to describe the difference between the extreme right and the extreme left, based on the different relationship they have with the principle of equality. Right-wing extremism, he explains, refutes this principle, while left-wing extremism accepts it, but interprets in an etymologically speaking total way – with the consequence that the principle of total equality destroys the freedoms guaranteed by the rules and institutions of the rule of law' (Backes 2001: 23, 24). Along the same lines, de Stexhe explains that the reason the extreme right arouses a more ethically marked resistance than the extreme left when both of these movements are dangerous to democracy is because 'the extreme left claims, in its aims, universalism, which is the ethical source of democracy, while the extreme right challenges it more or less explicitly' (de Stexhe 2000: 119).

Aside from the definitions, three elements run through all the texts analysing the extreme right: an acknowledgement of inequality between people as a basic premise and axiom, nationalism as the proposal in support of the acknowledgement of inequality, and extremism, which is understood to mean absolute, violent and extreme positions on certain ideas, policies, parties, groups or people, but also as a means, a mode of action to achieve its objectives.

Inegalitarianism

The existence of races and the inequality between them are traits that appear unremarkably in works dedicated to the extreme right. They are present when discussing openly racist and violent groups in the United States (neo-Nazis, KKK, skinheads, etc.), and also characterize extreme-right political parties in Europe that take part in the electoral process (this is also highlighted in some of the later chapters in this volume). Ignazi talks about the major characteristics of the extreme-right paradigm and in particular mentions the subversive anti-egalitarian movement that characterizes it (Ignazi 2001: 371). In the same vein, Bihr attempts to erect a permanent structure of extreme-right thinking and shows that it is based on 'raising up inequality as a fundamental ontological and axiological category' (Bihr 1998a: 16). A little later on, Bihr shows how extreme-right thinking is profoundly inegalitarian, and that it sees inequality as a value to be promoted and defended, and that it is therefore right and fair that there should be people who are superior and those who are inferior, because that is quite simply 'the natural order' (Bihr 1998a: 26, 27).

Inequality between the races appears in an article on the Flemish Vlaams Blok and the French Front National by Swyngedouw and Ivaldi, in which they show that for these parties, egalitarianism is intrinsically false and goes against the law of nature (Swyngedouw and Ivaldi 2001: 6). Among those that illustrate the importance of racial inequality, Vlaams Blok is a prime example. The ideology of this party prioritizes the concept of a nationalist state structure, which perceives the people as an 'ethnic community with hereditary links'. The concept of nationality is thus based on 'biological consanguinity' and as the state structure must follow the 'natural ethnic structure', the party opts for a Flanders that is structured in an organic and hierarchical way. According to de Witte and Scheepers, placing the emphasis on a state structure based on ethnic nationalism also implies that it must be monocultural and monoracial (de Witte and Scheepers 1998: 100, 101). Ethnicity is perceived by Vlaams Belang as a blend of cultural, racial, linguistic and identity traits that point to both biological inequality between ethnic groups and nationalism as a method of protecting the superior ethnic group.

Nationalism

Nationalism responds to the acknowledgement of inequality, not this time as a basic premise but as a proposal, as an ultimate political structure to put in place in support of the basic axiom relating to inequality. Nationalism is the second concept that combines a series of characteristics of the ideological world of the extreme right. What is a nation? According to Anderson, it is

> an imaginary political community, imagined as intrinsically limited and sovereign. It is imagined because even the members of the smallest of nations will never know most of their fellow citizens: they will never encounter them or hear of them, even though the image of their communion lives in the mind of each person.
>
> (Anderson 2002: 19–20)

In a text discussing Vlaams Blok and its voters in Flanders, de Witte and Scheepers establish a difference between ethnic nationalism and state nationalism, and present the Flemish extreme-right party's programme on two levels (de Witte and Scheepers 1998).

The first level relates to the Flemish people, which is an ethnic community with hereditary links and biological consanguinity. The Flemish people conform to a natural ethnic structure that obliges each member of the community to form a large family, to promote monogamous marriage and to categorically reject other types of relationship (de Witte and Scheepers 1998: 103). In Vlaams Blok discourse, national interests are more important than individual interests, and each person must submit to the 'organic whole'. The second level concerns the structure of the state, which supports the natural and ethnic structure. The state is nationalist to protect the Flemish ethnic group; it advocates the independence of Flanders, rejects immigrants, who threaten the integrity and homogeneity of the biological social body and condemns the 'political mafia' and the traditional parties that encourage immigration and corruption.

The differing interpretation of the concept of 'nationalism' is at times one of the elements that hinder collaboration between the various extreme-right parties in Europe (on the collaboration and the organization of extreme-right parties at an international and cross-national level see Virchow's chapter in this volume). For example, the fact that Vlaams Blok is an ethnic-nationalist party sometimes hinders it from collaborating with 'state-nationalist' parties such as the French Front National and the former Italian MSI (Italian Social Movement). These parties are opposed to any division of their national territory, unlike Vlaams Blok, which, for ethnic reasons, is prepared to 'get rid' of Wallonia, but above all, in the long term wants 'French Flanders' to be annexed to Flanders, because the inhabitants of this region of Northern France are in their eyes part of the Flemish people (de Witte and Scheepers 1998: 103; on the 'organic ultra-regionalism' of the New Right see also Bar-On's chapter in this volume).

The extreme right promotes an exacerbated nationalism based on the ethno-national community, a community that is sometimes mobilized under the term 'people' ('the French people'), considered in terms of its ethnic, 'racial', cultural, linguistic and historic unity. The nation and the people are threatened by enemies and forces acting within and outside them.

The internal threat is mainly at the level of the well-being, health, survival and the 'biological' future of the social community. The people are in danger. The threat lies in falling birth rates in the majority of European countries at a time when the population is growing ever older. For the extreme right, a falling birth rate is the first sign of the disappearance of the ethnic group, people or 'white race' in general. The threat also lies in the legal and medical methods developed in Western countries to interrupt (abortion) or prevent (contraception) birth on demand, which are causing the birth rate to fall even further and therefore increasing the risks threatening the future of the community. Finally, the threat lies in the new forms of living together that no longer place procreation at the centre of their interests, thereby aggravating the problems mentioned above: relationships outside marriage, homosexuality, feminism, singleness, etc.

The external threat to the social community, meanwhile, comes from international migratory flows and the presence of a growing population that is foreign or of foreign origin in the 'national territories' defended by the extreme right. The threat is perceived to be on three levels. The first danger follows a biological and physical metaphor: immigrants are 'foreign bodies' that penetrate a healthy and homogeneous social body, and in doing so threaten the health and balance of that body. The second danger lies in interbreeding and the meeting between 'nationals' and foreigners. Mixing of people, peoples, and ethnic groups is considered by the extreme right to be a factor in degradation, decline, disease and levelling. Finally, the third danger lies in the emergence of what are known as multicultural societies that, in the eyes of the extreme right, embody the triumph of disease and perversion within the ethnic community.

Extremism

The third and final idea to investigate in order to clarify the ideology of the extreme right is extremism. As an attitude that aims to act in a radical way, on the root (*radix*), on the deep cause of the effects or the phenomenon where change is desired, extremism represents a type of 'absolute' action, a 'total' way of acting to give shape to the nationalist project in support of the acknowledgement of inequality. As extreme behaviour aimed at the prime cause that drives a project or obstacle, the elementary root, the heart of a reality or fact, extremism represents a 'complete' procedure, extreme behaviour to give substance to nationalism.

When we delve into the literature on the extreme right and more particularly into the texts that aim to clarify its characteristics, in particular in terms of ideology and programmes, we discover numerous adjectives of the 'anti-X', 'anti-Y', etc.

type. The ideology of the extreme right is therefore described sometimes as anti-pluralist, anti-universal or anti-parliamentarian, sometimes as anti-American, anti-communist, anti-Zionist, anti-intellectual and, more recently since 9/11, anti-Muslim, such as the ambiguous speech of the anti-Islamic leader Geert Wilders in Holland (Jamin 2011). The examples are numerous and we have seen the criteria used by Backes (Backes 2001). In a pioneering work on the extreme right in the United States, Lipset and Raab systematized the functioning of these oppositions. Right-wing extremism, they explain, is the rejection of pluralism, politics and negotiations, the rejection of difference, divisions and ambivalence. In extreme right-wing ideology, difference means dissidence. In other words, they conclude, right-wing extremism is characterized by a sort of 'monism' and philosophical, political and ideological simplism (Lipset and Raab 1973: 6–8).

Anti-ism unambiguously marks out the enemy. It reinforces the 'us' in a process that was formulated by Anne Tristan in France when she described how Front National activists 'loved to hate together',[5] but also by White in the United States, who explains that right-wing extremism is defined by hatred and that extremists 'do not simply love, they love in conjunction with hate'. For example, they love Christians because they hate those who are not Christians. They love whites because they hate those who are not white (White 2001: 945).

Ignazi explains that while it is well known that the majority of the parties that are on the extreme right of the right–left scale do not openly describe themselves as anti-democratic, it is nevertheless true that they express anti-system attitudes and that the culture that emerges from internal publications and the leaders' discourse, propaganda and the worldview of the executives and activists can be considered to be anti-egalitarian, anti-pluralist and fundamentally opposed to the principles of the democratic system (Ignazi 2001: 371). Other authors follow the same lines, such as Betz, who bases his definition of the extreme right on the fundamental rejection of the rules of the democratic game, individual freedom, the principle of equality and equal rights for all members of the political community (Betz 1998: 3), Eatwell, who talks about hostility to democracy (Eatwell 2000: 411), and Mudde, who talks about anti-democratism (Mudde 1996: 229). Anti-democratism is also among the traits studied by Billig when he explains that the principles of nationalism blended with the extreme right are formulated in such a way that democratic rights and freedoms are threatened (Billig 1989: 147).

Conclusion

In support of the above, it can be said that populism and the extreme right refer to very different realities. Populism mobilizes a discourse glorifying the honest people against the corrupt elite, the extreme right postulates racial and cultural inequality between peoples and nations and advocates extreme nationalism as a form of political organization that can protect the people from their enemies. In the name of democracy, populism rejects the elite and the institutions they represent while the extreme right rejects the principles, values and foundations of democracy.

From populist rhetoric to extreme-right ideology, the discourse becomes more radical and racial, but otherwise the two tendencies evolve together because they are complementary. This process takes place mainly at the level of the enemy as it is identified in the two types of discourse. In populist discourse, the enemy is judged for what he does and for his bad intentions, the elites are identified with 'parasites' that are at the top of the social order. For example, in the Geert Wilders' radical discourse against the elite from Brussels and against Muslims in Holland, the leader does not oppose both as human beings but the elite as lazy and corrupted people and Muslims as dangerous radical believers. In extreme-right discourse, the enemy is not only judged for what he does but also for what he is. He is judged for the way that his racial, biological and cultural membership unsettles the homogeneous, stable nation. Moving from judgement of acts to judgement of acts accompanied by judgement of the ethno-racial or ethno-cultural identity represents a radicalization of the political discourse that fits the two meanings mentioned above: seeking the root of a problem and proposing extreme means of solving it.

We have seen that the right and the left could be differentiated by their relationship to the issue of equality or inequality between humans. By basing its whole ideology on the premise of racial and cultural inequality between humans and peoples, extreme-right ideology does not strictly have anything to do with extreme-left ideology (de Stexhe 2000: 119), even if in practice regimes inspired by these different ideologies can lead to similar consequences (Backes 2001: 23, 24).

As a discourse opposed to the elite, populism can, however, be just as much a right-wing as a left-wing phenomenon. In a contribution on populism and communism in France, Lazar describes left-wing populism as an idealized representation of a people who are exploited but united, hard-working and collectively productive, profoundly fair and good, virtuous and invincible (Lazar 2004: 84). When discussing populism in the United States, Berlet considers that populist movements may be right-wing, left-wing or in the centre. They can be egalitarian or authoritarian, and rely either on a decentralized network or on a charismatic leader. They may demand new social and political relations or romanticize the past (Berlet and Lyons 2000: 4, 5). Populist movements may promote certain forms of anti-elitism that aim either at genuine oppressive structures or at scapegoats that are allegedly members of a secret plot. They may define the 'people' in a way that is inclusive and questions traditional hierarchies, or in a way that reduces to silence and demonizes certain oppressed groups (Berlet and Lyons 2000: 4, 5).

If populism and the extreme right refer to such different discourses, it is legitimate to wonder why they contribute so much to the confusion mentioned in the introduction to this chapter. A first answer to this question lies in the evolution of the enemy in extreme-right discourse, in particular in Europe since the signing of the Maastricht Treaty in 1992. The traditional internal enemy in extreme-right discourse is personified by Jews, communists, feminists or freemasons. The external enemy, meanwhile, is personified by foreigners, immigrants, or 'false' refugees who try to enter the national territory. Since the late 1980s and the signing by the member states of the various treaties establishing the European Union, a new category of enemy has had to be added to extreme-right discourse, which is both within and outside the nation: 'the stateless, vagrant bureaucrats who control Brussels and Washington and are seeking to make the world into a vast market with no people and no soul, without a nation and without a culture' (Jamin 2009: 234–42).

As we have seen, the populism is not the extreme right, it does not embody the same threat to democracy and liberal values. Both need to be correctly defined to avoid the confusion linked to the shared rejection of Europe, but also to avoid the use of 'populism' to describe the extreme right and the kind of 'democratic legitimization' such a use might provoke (Mammone 2009).

In twenty years, 'the Brussels elite' has gradually begun to appear in extreme-right discourse (on the rejection of technocratic Europe by the New Right, see Bar-On's chapter in this volume; but see also Williams' chapter for a discussion on the extreme right and its policy towards Europe and European Integration). It is portrayed in discourse as being both everywhere and nowhere, it has no cultural or national connections and is seeking to establish a multicultural and interbred global society that is at the mercy of the markets and finance (The New World Order). In certain respects, and given their influence, the 'stateless cosmopolitan bureaucrats' are now a greater threat than foreigners in numerous contemporary extreme-right discourses.

The shared rejection of Europe maintains confusion between the populist discourses that are traditionally opposed to the elite and the extreme-right discourses that have been opposed to Brussels since Maastricht. With the erosion of national sovereignty, opposition to the European programme has become central. The elite of the populist discourse merges today with the elite of Brussels who now personify the new enemy in extreme-right discourse, a faceless enemy that is both internal and external, an enemy that is added to immigrants, refugees, Muslims, Jews, Freemasons, homosexuals, feminists and communists.

If populism and the extreme right refer to such different discourses, it is legitimate to wonder why they contribute so much to the confusion mentioned in the introduction to this chapter. A second answer to this question lies in the evolution of radical speech against foreigners. In many European countries, both populist and extreme-right parties have changed their line of arguments, leaving behind open racist rhetoric to embrace an ambiguous progressive and secular speech against 'totalitarian Islam'. Taking advantage of the numerous debates in Europe about Islam, feminist values and equality between men and women, populist and extreme-right leaders have embraced today a new struggle against Muslims in the name of democracy. This change, which is more recent than the common opposition to the elite of the European Union we wrote about before, make it more difficult to dispel the confusion between nevertheless two very different kinds of speech.

Notes

1 We shall retain the name 'Vlaams Blok' in our text as we are going to refer to a series of facts concerning the party before it changed its statutes and its name (Vlaams Belang) in 2005.
2 A similar comparison has been made in France between Jean-Marie Le Pen and Bernard Tapie. See T. Saussez (1992), *Tapie-Le Pen. Les jumeaux du populisme*, Paris: Édition No. 1.
3 The American Civil Liberties Union is one of the main American associations defending fundamental rights such as freedom of expression, equal opportunities, minority rights, etc.
4 Extract quoted by Canovan (Canovan, 1981: 52, 54).
5 According to Albert Cohen's formula quoted by Anne Tristan (1987), *Au Front*, Paris: Gallimard, p. 257.

Bibliography

Anderson, B. (2002) *L'imaginaire national. Réflexions sur l'origine et l'essor du nationalisme*, Paris: La Découverte.
Backes, U. (2001) 'L'extrême droite: les multiples facettes d'une catégorie d'analyse' in Perrineau, P. (ed.), *Les croisés de la société fermée: L'Europe des extrêmes droites*, Paris: Editions de l'aube, pp. 13–29.
Berlet, C. and Lyons, M. (2000) *Right-wing Populism in America*, New York: Guilford Press.
Betz, H.-G. (1998) *The New Politics of the Right*, New York: St Martin's Press.
Betz, H.-G. (2002) 'Conditions favouring the success and failure of radical right-wing populist parties in contemporary democracies' in Meny, Y. and Surel, Y. (eds), *Democracies and the Populist Challenge*, New York: Palgrave, pp. 197–213.
Betz, H.-G. (2004a) 'Une mobilisation politique de la droite radicale: le cas autrichien' in Taguieff, P.-A. (ed.), *Le retour du populisme. Un défi pour les démocraties européennes*, Paris: Encyclopaedia Universalis, pp. 35–46.
Betz, H.-G (2004b) *La droite populiste en Europe. Extrême et démocrate?*, Paris: CEVIPOF/ Autrement.
Bihr, A. (1998a) *L'actualité d'un archaïsme. La pensée d'extrême droite et la crise de la modernité*, Lausanne: Éditions Page deux.
Bihr, A. (1998b) *Le spectre de l'extrême droite, Les Français dans le miroir du Front national*, Paris: Les Éditions de l'Atelier.
Billig, M. (1978) *Fascists: A social psychological view of the National Front*, London: Harcourt Brace Jovanovich.
Billig, M. (1989) 'The extreme right: Continuities in anti-Semitic conspiracy theory in post-war Europe' in Eatwell, R. and O'Sullivan, N. (eds), *The Nature of the Right*, London: Pinter, pp. 146–66.
Bobbio, N. (1996) *Droite et Gauche*, Paris: Seuil.
Braun, A. and Scheinberg, S. (eds) (1997) *The Extreme Right: Freedom and security at risk*, Boulder, CO: Westview Press.
Canovan, M. (1981) *Populism*, London: Junction Books.
Canovan, M. (1999) 'Trust the people: Populism and the two faces of democracy', *Political Studies*, 47, 2–16.
Collovald, A. (2004) *Le 'Populisme du FN' un dangereux contresens*, Broissieux: Éditions du Croquant.
De Stexhe, G. (2000) 'Qu'est-ce qui est et n'est pas démocratique? La démocratie comme logique et comme projet' in Dumont, H., Mandoux, P., Strowel, A. and Tulkens, F.

(eds), *Pas de liberté pour les ennemis de la liberté. Groupements liberticides et droit*, Bruxelles: Bruylant, pp. 103–23.

De Witte, H. and Scheepers, P. (1998) 'En Flandr: le Vlaams Blok et les électeurs', *Pouvoirs*, 87, November, 95–114.

Dohet, J. (2010) *Le darwinisme volé*, Liège: Les territoires de la mémoire.

Eatwell, R. (2000) 'The rebirth of the "extreme right" in Western Europe?', *Parliamentary Affairs*, 53, 407–25.

Eatwell, R. and O'Sullivan, N. (1989) *The Nature of the Right*, London: Pinter.

Eatwell, R. and Wright, A. (1999) *Contemporary Political Ideologies*, London: Continuum.

Federici, M. (1991) *The Challenge of Populism*, London: Praeger.

Hainsworth, P. (1992) *The Extreme Right in Europe and the USA*, London: Pinter.

Hainsworth, P. (ed.) (2000) *The Politics of the Extreme Right (from the Margins to the Mainstream)*, London: Pinter.

Hermet, G. (2001) *Les populismes dans le monde. Une histoire sociologique XIXème–XXème siècle*, Paris: Fayard.

Hertzke, A. (1993) *Echoes of Discontent: Jesse Jackson, Pat Robertson, and the resurgence of populism*, Washington: Congressional Quarterly Press.

Ignazi, P. (2001) 'Les partis d'extrême droite: les fruits inachevés de la société postindustrielle' in Perrineau, P. (ed.), *Les croisés de la société fermée: L'Europe des extrêmes droites*, Paris: Éditions de l'Aube, pp. 369–84.

Ivaldi, G. (2004) *Droites populistes et extrêmes en Europe occidentale*, Paris: La documentation française.

Jamin, J. (2009) *L'imaginaire du complot. Discours d'extrême droite en France et aux Etats-Unis*, Amsterdam: Amsterdam University Press.

Jamin, J. (2011) 'Vieilles pratiques, nouveaux visages: Geert Wilders et l'extrême droite en Europe', *Vacarme*, Paris, spring, 11, 55, 43–5.

Kazin, M. (1998) *The Populist Persuasion: An American history*, London: Cornell University Press.

Laclau, E. (2008) *La raison populiste*, Paris: Seuil.

Lazar, M. (2004) 'Populisme et communisme: le cas français' in Taguieff, P.-A. (ed.), *Le retour du populisme. Un défi pour les démocraties européennes*, Paris: Encyclopaedia Universalis, pp. 83–94.

Lazar, M. (2006) *L'Italie à la dérive*, Paris: Editions Perrin.

Le Bohec, J. (2005) *Sociologie du phénomène Le Pen*, Paris: La Découverte.

Lipset, S. and Raab, E. (1973) *The Politics of Unreason: Right-wing extremism in America, 1790–1970*, New York: Harper Torchbook.

Mammone, A. (2009) 'The eternal return? Faux populism and contemporarization of neo-fascism across Britain, France and Italy', *Journal of Contemporary European Studies*, 17, 2, 171–92.

Mayer, N. (2002) *Ces Français qui votent Le Pen*, Paris: Flammarion.

Mazzoleni, O. (2003) *Nationalisme et populisme en Suisse. La radicalisation de la 'nouvelle' UDC*, Lausanne: Presses polytechniques et universitaires romandes.

Mudde, C. (1995) 'Right-wing extremism analysed: A comparative analysis of the ideologies of three alleged right-wing extremist parties (NPD, NDP, CP'86)', *European Journal of Political Research*, 27, 203–24.

Mudde, C. (1996) 'The war of words: Defining the extreme right party family', *West European Politics*, 19, 2, April, 225–48.

Mudde, C. (2007) *Populist Radical Right Parties in Europe*, Cambridge: Cambridge University Press.

Pipes, D. (1997) *Conspiracy: How the paranoid style flourishes and where it comes from*, New York: The Free Press.

Rioux, J.-P. (2007) *Les populismes*, Paris: Seuil.

Saussez, T. (1992) *Tapie-Le Pen. Les jumeaux du populisme*, Paris: Édition No. 1.

Singh, R. (1997) *The Farrakhan Phenomenon*, Washington DC: Georgetown University Press.

Surel, Y. (2002) 'Populism in the French party system' in Meny, Y. and Surel, Y. (eds), *Democracies and the Populist Challenge*, New York: Palgrave, pp. 139–54.

Swyngedouw, M. and Ivaldi, G. (2001) 'The extreme right utopia in Belgium and France: The ideology of the Flemish Vlaams Blok and the French Front National', *West European Politics*, 24, 3, July, 1–22.

Taggart, P. (1995) 'New populist parties in Western Europe', *West European Politics*, 18, 1, January, 34–51.

Taguieff, P.-A. (ed.) (1991) *Face au racisme* (2 volumes), Paris: La Découverte.

Taguieff, P.-A. (2002) *L'illusion populiste*, Paris: Berg International.

Tristan, A. (1987) *Au Front*, Paris: Gallimard.

White, J. (2001) 'Political eschatology: A theology of antigovernment extremism', *American Behavioral Scientist*, 44, 6, February, 937–56.

Wieviorka, M. (1993) *La démocratie à l'épreuve. Nationalisme, populisme, ethnicité*, Paris: La Découverte.

Zawadzki, P. (2004) 'Les populismes en Pologne' in Taguieff, P.-A. (ed.), *Le retour du populisme. Un défi pour les démocraties européennes*, Paris: Encyclopaedia Universalis, pp. 61–71.

3

THE *IDÉES-FORCE* OF THE EUROPEAN NEW RIGHT

A new paradigm?

Joan Antón-Mellón

Introduction

This chapter explores the axioms and core beliefs, or *idées-force*,[1] of the European New Right (NR)[2] and analyses their internal coherence. In doing so, the aim is to contribute to the ongoing academic debate regarding the movement's ideological affiliation.[3]

My main hypothesis is that this affiliation should be situated, unequivocally, in the area of the extreme right or the radical right; and that the NR's own analysis, which claims that the movement has established a new theoretical and political paradigm beyond the left and the right, should be dismissed on the grounds that it is tendentious and false. In order to test my hypothesis, I describe the analogies and divergences between the core concepts of the NR and those of classical fascism (1919–45), the most important variant of the European radical right of the first half of the twentieth century.

My analysis is based on a study of the writings of the NR,[4] paying special attention to four main questions. The first is how they define themselves – their self-definitions. The second is their diagnosis of the current historical situation. The third refers to their aims and means, their aspirations, their utopia, and also what they reject; and the last comprises their worldview and their conception of man, nature and history. The chapter ends with a comparison of the similarities and differences between the NR and classical fascism.

To test the internal coherence of the NR's ideas, Alain Bihr's theoretical model is particularly useful. In this model, the three decisive factors in the ideologies of the extreme right in the West are the defence of ultra ethno-nationalist ideas, elevating the collective identity to the category of a fetish, the insistence on inequality as a fundamental ontological and axiological category, and the defence of a bellicose conception of existence that glorifies combat as one of the supreme elements of existence.[5]

The sources consulted for this chapter include a selection from the abundant theoretical works of the orthodox French NR, in particular the writings of Alain de Benoist, and of the breakaway NR headed by Guillaume Faye; second, editorials and articles from GRECE's official magazine *Éléments pour la culture européenne* (first issue September/October 1973); articles from the publications of the Italian NR *Trasgressioni* (first issue May/August 1986) and the Spanish NR *Hespérides* (1993–2000); and finally works such as *Manifeste: La Nouvelle Droite de l'an 2000*, by de Benoist and the current editor of *Éléments*, Charles Champetier, and the Spanish NR's *Manifiesto del Proyecto Cultural Aurora; ¿Qué hacer? Elementos para un discurso de contestación*, published at the end of the 1990s, and *El Manifiesto contra la muerte del espíritu y de la tierra*, published in 2002.

The NR comprises a group of cultural associations that subscribe to a particular ideology. Since the 1960s, the movement has tried to reinvent the classical discourse of the European radical right of the early twentieth century in order to influence the various groups on the right: extreme, moderate, populist and neo-traditionalist. In the democratic post-1945 West, the NR faces massive opposition from the mainstream, which it defines as the product of Christianity and the political thought of the Enlightenment in a new modern guise. However, the decline of the radical left has created a political and cultural vacuum[6] that the NR aims to occupy by presenting ideological alternatives to what it sees as the stale technocracy of conservative liberalism and social democracy. The NR savages the dysfunctions of postmodernity (anomie, hyperindividualism, ultra-materialism, problems of identity) and offers its remedies for society's alienation and decadence, all of which involve, as a *sine qua non*, the recovery of the authentic 'European identity'.

The NR's flagship is the association *Groupement de Recherche et d'Études pour la Civilisation Européenne* (GRECE) founded in January 1968 in Nice and, at the same time, in Paris and Toulouse, by roughly forty people from the French extreme or radical right. Inside this group, dissidents such as Faye, Steuckers and Vial made their own proposals regarding strategy that diverged significantly from the party line.[7] The NR's influence is limited to the traditional areas of support of the European radical right, thrown into disarray by the defeat of classical fascism and the collaborationist governments of occupied Europe and the subsequent repudiation of the ideology of the radical right under the political and cultural pressure of anti-fascism in the second half of the twentieth century. The existence of GRECE has propitiated the creation of associations or groups in Italy, Belgium, Great Britain, Spain and Russia, whose efforts to establish themselves have met with varying degrees of success. GRECE's journal *Éléments*, for example, inspired similar publications in all these countries, even reproducing the name in four cases (the exceptions being *Hespérides* in Spain and *The Scorpion* in Britain).

The movement's cultural influence in France reached its apogee in the 1980s[8] although it has gradually lost ground since then. The rest of the European groups have not expanded outside the social base of the radical and extreme right, although some of them have managed to contribute to the ideologies, doctrines and proposals of populist parties of the radical right such as the Forza Nuova/ Mouvement National Républicain (FN/MNR) in France, the Freiheitliche Partei Österreichs (FPÖ) in Austria and the Plataforma per Catalunya (PxC) in Catalonia.

Because of its insistence on maintaining a metapolitical option (and its scorn for mainstream politics) GRECE has lost several of its leading figures at regular intervals, most of whom have left for populist parties on the radical right such as the FN or the MNR or even for liberal–conservative parties. The medieval historian Pierre Vial, for example, one of the founders of GRECE, joined the FN and later supported the splinter group, the MNR, led by Bruno Mégret (another founder member of GRECE) in 1996: Vial created a neo-Nazi cultural movement *Terre et Peuple* in the same year.[9]

Another leading dissident is Guillaume Faye, together with Benoist, GRECE's most important intellectual voice until his departure in 1986. A typical product of the right-wing version of May 1968, on his return to the intellectual arena in the late 1990s he analysed the reasons for GRECE's loss of influence, dismissed the metapolitical option as pointless and reaffirmed the NR's earlier positions rejecting the politically correct euphemisms so profusely used, in his view, by the orthodox NR. Echoing Nietzsche, Faye calls for the rejection of Enlightenment values and advocates the institution of a heterogeneous world formed by large ethnically homogeneous territorial units with radical inequalities in the social and productive structure to guarantee the ecological sustainability of the system and the progress of its peoples.[10]

The self-definitions of the European New Right

Throughout its history the European NR has seen itself as a radical, and special, variant of the right and as the contemporary representative of revolutionary conservatism. In 1994 Benoist defined the NR as a 'dissident' group at odds with 'the institutionalized Right'.[11] For his part, J.J. Esparza, one of the leaders of the Spanish NR, stated that the movement had gone through a series of stages that had signified as a continuous distancing from the conventional right.[12] Advocating metapolitical action, the European NR defines itself as a 'laboratory of ideas', a 'school of thought', a 'community of the spirit', a 'space of resistance against the system'.

This metapolitical option derives from Gramsci and his concept of hegemony (although Faye considers this reading of the Italian communist thinker superficial, and his breakaway NR rejects the metapolitical position). The orthodox view is that the conquest of political power must be preceded by victory – hegemony – in the ideological and cultural conflict. This stance is quite revealing. It shows that, as far as theory is concerned, the NR is pragmatic and eclectic: it uses anything that might be useful for the defence of its core concepts, whether the argument in question comes from the right or the left: Nietzsche, Heidegger, Evola, Gramsci,

Schmitt, Lorenz, Dumont, Koestler, Locchi, Dumezil, Rougier or the revolutionary conservatives of the early twentieth century are all called upon at different moments. In the NR's exhaustive search for intellectual endorsement (obviously from a political perspective rather than a scientific one) the inconsistencies and contradictions that inevitably arise from this approach are conveniently ignored.

The European NR aims to raise awareness of the deep-seated causes of the decline of European civilization, in three stages: first, via ideological and cultural engineering to influence public opinion; second, by providing intellectual leadership in the task of reversing this decline; third, via the construction of a harmonious, powerful European political community that acknowledges the authenticity of its identity going back into the past and builds its future in the present. This means that its struggle is cultural but also political. Faced with powerful opponents and enemies, it has had to start at the most elementary level: in its own words, to create 'a space of resistance against the system'.[13] Gradually this space will grow, and eventually the disastrous political and sociocultural consequences of the Enlightenment and modernity will be overcome.[14] But the main problem is a hangover from an earlier time: the triumph of Christianity.

Significantly, in the year 2000 the orthodox NR defined itself as 'based on community, based on citizenship, European, and pagan'.[15] The ideals of the Enlightenment are merely a lay version of Christianity; for its part, Christianity is a noxious foreign body totally alien to the Indo-European roots of our culture. Liberalism and socialism are merely negative epiphenomena of the Enlightenment and Christianity.

According to the NR's analyses, its 'laboratory of ideas' performs the vital role of achieving radical cultural change in the decadent world of the bourgeois West. The latter, led by the US, has imposed its Judeo-Christian ideals as the predominant doctrine of human rights (the lowest common denominator of egalitarianism). To use Nietzsche's term, this is the morality of the herd, destined to alienate the masses in the West, stultified by consumption and infantilized by the welfare state.[16] The NR sees itself as 'a promise of renewal in the depths of a cold, grey winter . . . an adventure of the spirit'[17] of 'active pessimists'[18] during the interregnum. The age of Kali-Yuga, in the Sanskrit terminology used by Evola and Eliade, is a period in which the truth lies buried by ignorance and awaits its redeemers.

And it is as redeemers that the NR's thinkers see themselves, visionaries who, following Nietzsche, believe that the future belongs to those with the longest memory. The NR's thinkers are revolutionaries in a context, Europe, which is plagued by the bourgeois materialist values of mercantilism, individualism, egalitarianism and universalism, primarily because of a misapprehension of the nature of man. In contrast, the NR advocates the hegemony of politics over economics, of the community over the individual, of hierarchy over equality and of heterogeneity over universalist homogeneity. Benoist quotes Carl Schmitt: 'the essential contents of democracy is a people not humanity. If democracy has to continue to be a political form, there are only democracies of peoples, and not democracies of humanity.'[19]

Diagnosis

The NR's diagnosis of the West could hardly be more pessimistic. With the triumph of individualism and the economy and the abandonment of spirituality, the West has reached the point of exhaustion. At the end of the 1990s the Spanish NR denounced the existence of 'a progressive and inexorable tendency towards death'; in June 2002, it proclaimed a new *Manifesto against the death of the spirit and the land* mentioned above. For its part, the French NR speaks of the 'threshold of sterility', and the 'senility' of European or Western civilization. A profound sense of loss has invaded contemporary society. In the NR's apocalyptic vision:

> As Konrad Lorenz noted, Western civilisation is dragging us along to a slow death. Its ways of life have psychological, neurotic and pathogenic effects: we become domesticated, fragile beings. Demographic decline, weakness of character, the genetic degradation of the Westerners, are facts confirmed by medical practitioners.[20]

Hypermaterialism, productivism, egalitarianism and hedonism smother all forms of transcendence, spirituality and beauty. The individualistic cult of well-being alienates and corrupts, incapacitating men for the task of developing their potential both as members of their community and as individuals. This cult was engendered by Christian dualism in defending the view that the true life was the future life in heaven. The liberal creates heaven on earth, in the belief that the sole aims of human life are to amass material goods and to achieve a more comfortable existence – the only individual satisfaction possible in a society understood as a depoliticized aggregate of isolated, unconnected units.

The corollary of this alienating reality is the role played by the state (seen as a *'technocratic organism at the service of the economy'*).[21] Its mission is to safeguard the individual rights that guarantee the maximum yield on the investments made. Meanwhile, egalitarian values triumph in the 'public capitalism of the welfare state' (repeatedly described as the 'dinosaur state'), dressed up in the garb of the universalist declaration of human rights. Even the nation-states today are being superseded by a worldwide techno-structure which is the entity that truly governs the world (albeit indirectly). This 'system' functions through the internalization of its objectives; it needs minimal political coordination, since everyone subscribes to the ideology that underpins it. Economics prevails over politics; the people equate personal happiness with the acquisition of material possessions, and are profoundly alienated from what should be their most prized value: their capacity to form part of a community through their individual will. The society in which they live is dominated by the economy and the market, in which goods produce yet more goods in a constant, circular process.

The government of men is replaced by the government of objects at the service of production, a world of producers, consumers and false needs, a process of homogenization and of the destruction of ethnic difference. The alchemy of this cancerous growth always comprises the same ingredients: supranational techno-economic structures, the universal and egalitarian ideology of human rights, and rampant mass consumerism. For the NR, the true political frontier is not between the right and the left, but between a 'plurivocal, polycentric, diverse, polytheist' perception of the world on the one hand, and the old 'Manichean' and 'monotheist' mentalities on the other.

In this bleak scenario, the NR raises the banner of a mythical European (not Western) civilization and ethnic biodiversity, the right to difference, and the subordination of the economy to political and social ends, in a society that teaches that sacrifice for the community is the highest honour that an individual can achieve.

Since the fall of communism as a political model, the NR's principal enemy has become liberalism, as an ideology and a system of values, and the US – deemed the new Carthage – as the leader of the West, a country born bourgeois, lacking an aristocracy or tradition.[22] For the NR, liberalism is a wholly misguided political philosophy and ideology, because it makes the abstract individual the lynchpin of the system. In the political arena, liberalism bears a certain resemblance to anarchy. It imposes as little authority as possible; at the social level it denies the holistic principle and the notion of collective interest, making the society the sum of all individual interests. To quote the NR:

> [L]iberalism is a machine that produces disenchantment . . . never has social apathy been as strong as it is at present . . . liberalism destroys collective identities and established cultures, and creates uniformity . . . to fight liberalism is to fight the root of the evil.[23]

In spite of the gravity of the current historical situation, however, there remains some room for hope. According to Guillaume Faye, the twenty-first century will bring a succession of catastrophes – economic, social, political, ecological, migratory, and so on – that will sweep away the current system and usher in a new civilization. In earlier years, Faye had already argued[24] that, beyond a certain limit, the regulation of a system in crisis is impossible. With the collapse of a civilization, the values and ideas that legitimize it come crashing down; Faye calls for revolutionary alternatives oriented towards organic visions of the world.

Aims and means

The main objective of the NR is, in its own terms, 'to take over from the dominant ideologies . . . after reconstructing a vision of the world' and, given their diagnosis of the situation outlined above, 'to bring ideas to a world which has none'.[25] For the NR, ideas constitute arms at the service of a project; its ambition is to propose ideas that will rouse people to action: 'But this ambition is combat. We fight because not to fight is to die, because the world that surrounds us is a world of passivity and slumber, where the energy of the people has faded away.'[26] The NR claims to have created a sophisticated new theoretical paradigm that leaves behind the traditional categories of right and left: an ideological and political Third Way. In their eyes, the real political division of the twentieth century was not between right and left but between universalists and identitarists. In opposition to the slogan of the left-wing social movement 'SOS Racisme' they devise their own: '*SOS Racines*' – 'SOS Roots'.[27]

The NR's vision is of a heterogeneous world comprised of ethnically homogeneous units – union without confusion, to quote Benoist. The movement defends the right to difference and the rights of peoples. Like de Maistre, the NR holds that mankind does not exist in the abstract, but comprises individuals forming different peoples, races and culture. So one must '*take the side of ethno-national doctrines, against pacifism and humanitarism*'.[28]

Faced with the decadence of modern times, the strategic and tactical objectives of the NR are palingenetic. The most important are: to promote the concept (at once ancient and modern) of freedom inside a community; to replace the hegemony of bourgeois values with aristocratic values; to revive Europe – or, in the case of Spain, to recover the nation's soul (in the opinion of the Spanish NR, the two aims are perfectly compatible); to revitalize the idea of community and to keep the legal concepts of nationality and citizenship separate; to place ethnonationalist criteria at the forefront of political activity and to make the peoples of Europe aware of their true historical identity; to fight egalitarianism[29] and universalism; to subordinate the economy to politics; to achieve harmony; to preserve biodiversity; to defend ecology;[30] and to promote a 'genuinely participative, radical and plural democracy' that turns the citizens of European communities into agents of their own history.

The achievement of these objectives will redeem society, restore the individual's true essence as a non-alienated being, and open the way for a glorious destiny in place of neutered, hypermercantilized banality. A future of this kind is possible: to achieve it, the ideas of the NR must become the basis of society and create broad national movements inspired by its ideas of 'regeneration':

> The future belongs to cultural, spiritual and national revolutions. In the future the international economic order will be destroyed and replaced by an idea that is already making its way forward today: the concentration of autonomous economic spaces around large cultural nuclei.[31]

The NR's worldview: the conception of man, nature and history

The NR's worldview revolves around a series of per se convictions or first principles that are worth outlining here. The first is the conviction that there are laws of nature that govern all living beings and can be extrapolated to individuals and human communities: selection, inequality and hierarchy are phenomena as natural as the land and the sea. The second is the paramount importance of the philogenetic information that human communities pass on from one generation to the next. The third is the idea that conflict is another of the laws of nature: to fight is to live[32] and weakness is a prelude to death;[33] and the fourth is the idea of the importance of the will to the living of an authentic, fulfilling existence. As Benoist claims in a famous article that was published widely in the European NR literature, the aim is not to find an objective truth, outside the world, but to create one voluntarily, on the basis of a new values system: a neo-Paganism that allows the development of a full, authentic mode of existence.[34]

The NR's vision is empiricist: only nature (including man) is observable, therefore either God does not exist or God is nature and therefore man is, or can be, God. The NR concludes that human life aspires towards transcendence, an aspiration that is alien to Enlightenment and post-Enlightenment rationalism. Out of fear, reason rejects everything that is not logos. Reason is constantly at war, but rejects war as a concept; it denies that law is force,[35] it proclaims equality, but never achieves it; it rejects any authority that is not based on utilitarian arguments.

The NR's worldview spurns rationality and offers an alternative to the 'pensée unique' of modernity. The disappearance of aristocratic values has been a catastrophe for Europe, only comparable to the replacement of Paganism in Indo-European communities by the dualist,[36] universalist and egalitarian Christianity. The NR points to what it sees as a glaring contradiction: on the one hand, Western society is based on a capitalist system that lauds the survival of the fittest, but on the other it insists on advocating human rights – an absurd product of the corrupt modern age, grounded on the conviction that all human beings are equal and free.

The NR rejects out of hand a vision of individual freedom, the belief that men hold a series of inherent, inalienable rights by virtue of their humanity and not granted by any higher authority. The NR's conception of freedom, stated explicitly by Julius Evola, holds that there is no general and abstract freedom, but a series of freedoms articulated in accordance with the nature itself of the beings involved. Freedom belongs to a practical and political plane, not to a philosophical or moral one. It must be conquered. No one is born free, but some, either individuals or groups, attain freedom through action.[37]

As an individual, then, one is free via membership of a community. And, as the whole is greater than the sum of the parts and possesses qualities that are characteristic of it (holism), the state should promote not the prosaic objective of the material well-being of its citizens, but that of guaranteeing their existence and of their power in history. So happiness is no longer an individual matter but a collective concept, since – and this is another core belief of the NR – the protagonists of history are peoples, communities, nations and/or cultures in a constant dialectic of confrontation. Rather than nature, man has culture and history which develop from certain constant biological characteristics. There will always be hunters and warriors, strong and weak, superior and inferior, say the ideologues of the NR,[38] however much the supporters of human rights reject these distinctions. The NR's vision of the world is organicist, pluralist and differentialist.

For this reason the NR's legal conception of individual rights is non-universalist. It proposes that each political, historical and cultural community should be entitled to establish the rights of its members; this is the basis of its criterion for distinguishing between citizenship and nationality. And, obviously, rights are granted by the community to the individual. Therefore, if men cannot be considered equal, have different needs and belong to different human communities, why do we establish the same universal and abstract rights for all on a 'one size fits all' basis?

The NR blames this on the triumph of bourgeois Christian values: individualist, economicist, egalitarian and universalist, the values of Christianity are based on a misconception of the world and man. It is the mission of the NR to alert the world to its errors and to spread an alternative worldview, one that is visionary with respect to the future and lucid with respect to the present and past.

So lucid and powerful is the NR's vision that it is able to harmonize opposites (just as classical fascism had sought to do):[39] instinct and culture; rationality and irrationality; hypermodernism/postmodernism and tradition; ecology and technological development; nation and supranational community (Europe); the maximum sovereignty of the state and individual economic freedom; right and left; individual sacrifice and freedom and/or collective happiness. Kant and Marx were wrong and Nietzsche, Heidegger and Evola were right. Blood is worth more than gold.[40]

The NR's worldview is the antithesis of bourgeois-liberal views and values. Exalting the sacred, the irrational and the spirit of adventure, it urges Europeans to shake off the alienating domestication that is the legacy of Christianity and liberalism. It calls for generosity of spirit instead of calculation, idealism and altruism instead of materialism and pragmatism, sacrifice instead of hedonism and collective adventure instead of selfish conformism. In the European NR, with its political and ideological unity,[41] this ideal way of 'being in the world' replaces the absurd, aimless way of life of modernity.

Therefore the worldview of the NR reflects the prototypical convictions of the radical right, advocating inequality, the idea of life as combat, the importance of tradition and an organic conception of ethnically homogeneous communities. The aristocrat confronts the bourgeois.[42] Benoist himself confirms this hypothesis in revealing to us in the preface to his *Le grain de sable* that the origin of his most frequent pseudonym, Robert de Herte, is a tribute to a maternal ancestor, Charles-Germain de Herte, an aristocrat and lieutenant in a regiment of musketeers who was guillotined during the French Revolution at the age of thirty-eight.

Conclusions

The defeat of fascism in 1945 meant the political and cultural rejection of its ideas in the liberal countries and the victory of democratic values. Fascism became a demonized ideology for all but a few minorities and was prosecuted by the authorities. Its fall from grace and from power obliged its adherents, both old and new, to seek refuge in the realm of ideas, in culture and in philosophy. After the collapse of the 'authoritarian compromise' of the 1930s[43] and the 'preventive counterrevolution',[44] the European NR aims to be the ideological leader of the radical right. In this setting, it has emerged as the most sophisticated modern version of fascist ideas (Griffin 2007; Spektorowski 2003).

The continuity between inter-war fascism and the NR is expressed in six main ways. The first is the homogeneity of the core of the ideological and philosophical foundations that the two schools share: their conception of man, nature and history. Their vision of man begins with the radical rejection of the Enlightenment view that all men are born free and equal. Their concept of freedom follows Nietzsche: only the select few become free, because their acts reflect their greater will to power, and it is they who must rule over the weak, impotent masses. Combat reveals superiority and puts each individual (or nation, or even firm) in its rightful place. The authentic, natural essence of human beings is aggressiveness, inequality, hierarchy and territoriality. Clearly, anti-Enlightenment and social Darwinism are features of the NR that follow on directly from classical fascism, as are its respect for capitalism and certain cultural reference points such as the radical conservatives of the early twentieth century.

Second, with regard to their conception of history, both schools of thought hold that the protagonists are ethnically homogeneous peoples: this is the root of their anti-universalist ultra-nationalism. This ultra-nationalism is cultural and political or biologically based racism in classical fascism, or differentialist (a new form of cultural racism) in the NR. One major novelty in the NR is the replacement of national myths by the myth of Europe as the imagined community[45] and the replacement of 'stale' nation-states by the Empire. As a larger sovereign political unit, a federalist 'Europe of the peoples' would be compatible with the (ethnically exclusive) identity of the continent's historical nationalities.

Third, their diagnoses and their prime objectives are the same: society is decadent, in crisis. Only palingenesis, promoted by the healthy part of the community, can create a broad-based movement able to achieve regeneration. The palingenetic and nativist character[46] of their political proposals highlights another of the key aspects of the two ideologies: the vital importance of the idea of community in ultra-nationalist thought.[47] Both classical fascism and the NR champion a homogeneous community with a collective destiny: racially or culturally pure in the case of classical fascism, and respecting ethnic differences and avoiding universalism and multiculturalist miscegenation in the case of the NR, a position that has been termed differentialist or culturalist racism.[48]

Fourth, recalling the positions of the 1930s, the NR proposes that this broad movement should unite and harmonize the community.[49] It must be above party politics, social divisions and ideologies. The NR defends a third way, neither right nor left wing: what they call *ninisme* (from '*ni . . . ni . . .*', 'neither . . . nor . . .'). In Eatwell's analysis: 'the Fascist "matrix" . . . At the heart of Fascist thinking was the creation of a new elite of men, who would forge a holistic nation and build a new third way state.'[50]

Fifth, the rejection, common to both ideologies, of liberalism as a political philosophy, together with the acceptance (from a social Darwinist perspective) of capitalism as an ideal productive system provided that it is subordinate to political guidance.

Sixth, fascism and the NR both propose political and cultural change, but not economic or social change; their axiology is organicist, metaphysical, transcendental and spiritualist.[51]

Taken together, these six factors highlight the great homogeneity between the *idées-force* of classical fascism and of the NR. Following Bihr's model (Bihr 1999), we can conceptualize these two models as extreme right/radical right, with their fetishistic concept of the collective identity, their defence of inequality[52] and their conception of life as eternal struggle.

Finally, fascism constituted a 'right-wing extremism' that offered a remedy for the miseries, contradictions and problems of modernity. It was a political and cultural alternative, not a social or economic one. In much the same way, the ideas of the NR are a political and cultural response to the ills of the postmodern world from the perspective of the post-war extreme right (Antón-Mellón 2007), but they leave social hierarchies and capitalist production systems in place. This disposition highlights the tactical differences between classical fascism and the NR (and indeed certain strategic differences, such as the acceptance or rejection of totalitarianism) and the movement's adaptation to the prevailing historical conditions in order to safeguard its *idées-force*.

The NR's leaders want to be the revolutionary conservatives of the twenty-first century. To quote the dissident NR theorist Guillaume Faye, their utopia is an 'archaeofuturist'[53] world, divided into ethnically homogeneous blocks, with vast socio-economic differences between the inhabitants of the technologically developed cities and the inhabitants of the primitive towns on the periphery, in order to ensure an ecologically sustainable society. The idea is obviously perverse: in fact Faye's theory (which he proposes in the interests of 'sustainability') is pure classical fascism.

Above all else, the NR believes that the protagonists of history are ethnically homogeneous communities,[54] and that freedom is only within the reach of a few select human beings. A harmonious human society is one in which men define themselves as aggressive, hierarchical and territorial – the very antithesis of the Enlightenment conception in which human beings are born free, equal and rational – and develop a political theory and political institutions in consonance with this definition. There is little here that distinguishes the NR from classical fascism. In fact, the NR's position is aptly summed up in the words of an old Buenos Aires tango:

The worst kind of nostalgia is missing things that never happened.

Notes

1 For Martin Seliguer, these are the fundamental nucleus of an ideology: see 'Fundamental and operative ideology: The two principal dimensions of political argumentation', *Policy Sciences*, 1 (1970). Seliguer distinguishes between an ideology's fundamental and operative nuclei. For another definition, see Michael Freeden, 'Political concepts and ideological morphology', *The Journal of Political Philosophy*, 2, 2 (1994).

2 Both its orthodox version (de Benoist, Champetier), and its heterodox version (Faye, Vial and Steuckers). Studying the core concepts of the NR will help us to understand the ideological framework of the extreme or radical right from its beginnings in the early twentieth century until the present day.

3 See Thomas Sheehan, 'Myth and violence: The fascism of Julius Evola and Alain de Benoist', *Social Research*, 48, 1 (Spring 1981); Pierre-André Taguieff, *Sur la Nouvelle droite*, Descartes, Paris, 1994; Roger Griffin, 'Plus ça change! El pedigrí fascista de la Nueva Derecha', in Miguel Angel Simón (ed.), *La Extrema Derecha en Europa desde 1945 a nuestros días*, Tecnos, Madrid, 2007; Joan Antón-Mellón, 'La cultura e ideología política del Neopopulismo en Europa Occidental: MNR/FN (Francia), FPÖ (Austria) y Lega Nord (Italia)', in Simón, *La Extrema Derecha en Europa desde 1945 a nuestros días*; Tamir Bar-On, *Where Have All the Fascists Gone?*, Ashgate, England/USA, 2007 and Diego Luís Sanromán, *La Nueva Derecha*, CIS, Madrid, 2008.

4 A small part of the empirical material used here was presented in an earlier study: Joan Antón-Mellón, 'Las ideas-fuerza de la Nueva Derecha Europea (ND) y su continuidad/discontinuidad con el Fascismo Clásico (1919–1945)', in *Afinidades. Revista de literatura y pensamiento*, 03 (2010).

5 Alain Bihr, *L'actualité d'un archaïsme*, Éditions Page deux, Lausanne, 1999. The applicability of this model is demonstrated in its assessment of the core concepts of classical fascism: see Joan Antón-Mellón, 'Las concepciones nucleares, axiomas e ideas-fuerza del Fascismo Clásico (1919–1945)', in *Revista de Estudios Políticos*, 146 (October–December 2009).

6 Marco Revelli, 'La nuova destra', *Iride*, 18 (May–August 1996).

7 See Taguieff, *Sur la Nouvelle droite*, and Ariane Chevel d'Appollonia, *L'Extrême droite en France*, Complexe, Brussels, 1996.

8 See M. Vaughan, 'Nouvelle droite: Cultural power and political influence', in D.S. Bell (ed.), *Contemporary French Politics*, Groom Helm, London/Canberra, 1982.

9 See Christopher Flood, 'The cultural struggle of the extreme right and the case of *Terre et Peuple*', *Contemporary French Civilization*, 24, 2 (2000), 241–66.

10 Guillaume Faye, *Archéofuturisme*, L'Aencre, Paris, 1998.

11 Alain de Benoist, *Le grain de sable. Jalons pour une fin de siècle*, Le Labyrinthe, Marsat, 1994, p. 15.

12 José Javier Esparza, 'La Nueva Derecha en su contexto', *Hespérides*, 16/17.

13 Manifesto of the Spanish NR: ¿*Qué hacer? Elementos para un discurso de la contestación.*

14 To quote Benoist: 'The promotion of the individual requires a long process of disaggregation from society which leads to anomie and atomization. With modernity, the social connection becomes pure contingency.' Alain de Benoist, *Más allá de la Derecha y la Izquierda/Antología a cargo de Javier Ruíz Portella*, Altera, Barcelona, 2010, p. 164.

15 'Entrevista a Charles Champetier', *Hespérides*, 16/17, 701.

16   What is it that all the hyperhumanitarian, hyperegalitarian, hyperdemocratic harangues from the supporters of the welfare state are hiding? . . . Isn't it their aim to construct a 'homo occidentalis', residing in an 'Americanosphere', in which the difference between socialism and liberalism only has any meaning during the charade of the electoral process?

Alain de Benoist and Guillaume Faye, *Las ideas de la Nueva Derecha. Una respuesta al colonialismo cultura*, Ediciones de Nuevo Arte Thor, Barcelona, 1986, p. 160.

17 Editorial de *Éléments*, 56 (1985).
18 A. de Benoist and G. Faye, *Las ideas de la Nueva Derecha*, p. 180.
19 Alain de Benoist, *Más allá de la Derecha y la Izquierda*, Altera, Barcelona, 2010, p. 149.
20 Guillaume Faye, 'Critique du système occidental', *Orientations*, 5 (1984), 7.
21 A. de Benoist and G. Faye, 'Contre l'État-providence', *Éléments*, 44 (1983) (emphasis added).
22 'America is among us: were this terrible formula to come true, it would make us the living dead.' G. Faye, *Actes du XV colloque national du GRECE*, Le Labyrinthe, Paris, 1982, p. 47.
23 Editorial, *Éléments*, 68 (1990).
24 Guillaume Faye, 'La modernité: Ambiguités d'une notion capitale', *Études et Recherches*, 1 (1983), 5.
25 De Benoist and Faye, *Las ideas de la Nueva Derecha*, pp. 157–8.
26 Guillaume Faye, 'Pour un Gramscisme de Droite', *Actes du XVI colloque national du GRECE*, Le Labyrinthe, Paris, 1982.
27 Proposed by Benoist at the Nineteenth National Meeting of GRECE (November 1985).
28 A. de Benoist and G. Faye, *Las ideas de la Nueva Derecha*, p. 472 (emphasis added).
29 This is because: 'Egalitarianism supposes the destruction of all that is elevated and differentiated inside all that is homogeneous, undifferentiated: it involves the inversion of the hierarchies.' Editorial, *Éléments*, 28/29 (1979).
30 Ecology is one of the points on which the French NR changed its position, from initial contempt to the acceptance of its radical criticism of capitalism. Compare the first and the last editorials of *Éléments* (above all no. 21/22 (1977) and no. 79 (1994).
31 Guillaume Faye 'Pour en finir avec la civilisation occidentale', *Éléments*, 34 (1980), 9.
32 '[Man possesses] an agonistic temperament which makes struggle – and in principle the struggle with himself – the very essence of life', A. de Benoist and G. Faye, *Las ideas de la Nueva Derecha*, p. 198.
33 'Modern ethology and biology have demonstrated (. . .) the importance of hunting and warlike behaviours in the philogenetic formation of humanity as key criteria in natural selection and in the orientation of evolution. We are the "children of Cain".' Ibid., p. 299.
34 Alain de Benoist, 'La religion de l'Europe', *Éléments*, 36 (1980), 20.
35 'The existence of men shows that in spite of their protests, they have always associated force and law . . . Bismarck . . . "force precedes law"', A. de Benoist, 'Ni fraiche ni joyeuse', *Éléments*, 24/25 (1982), p. 28. Alain de Benoist, 'La religion de l'Europe', *Éléments*, 36 (1980), 20.
36 The attempts to specify the values of paganism have listed features such as an eminently aristocratic conception of the human being, a system of ethics based on honour ('shame' rather than 'sin'), a heroic attitude in face of the challenges of existence, the exaltation and sanctification of the world, of beauty, or the body, of strength and health, the rejection of the 'other world', the inseparability of aesthetics and morals, and so on. We subscribe to all this, but in a way it seems secondary: the fundamental characteristic, in our view, is the rejection of dualism.
    (A. de Benoist and G. Faye, *Las ideas de la Nueva Derecha*, p. 191)

37 This conception of human freedom is closely linked to a certain conception of history: 'nature', the innate and the past condition the future of man, but do not determine it. It is inside this semantic space between 'condition' and 'determine' where freedom lies, man can only act with what he has; but with what he has he can be and do what he wants.
    (A. de Benoist, 'La religion de l'Europe', p. 12)

38 '[N]othing authorises the statement that reason is shared equally among all men', A. de Benoist and G. Faye, *Las ideas de la Nueva Derecha*, p. 397.

39 Joan Antón-Mellón, 'Las concepciones nucleares, axiomas e ideas-fuerza del Fascismo Clásico (1919–45)', ibid.
40 'From the huge stones raised at Stonehenge to the symbols of the bull at Knossos, the same idea has always been expressed: blood is worth more than gold', A. de Benoist and G. Faye, *Las ideas de la Nueva Derecha*, p. 474.
41 In fact, in the early 1970s several members of GRECE who rejected the NR's antiliberal stance broke away to found the *Club de L'Horloge*. In the 1980s, another group of GRECE members (J.C. Barder, P. Vial and J.Y. Le Gallou) actively supported J.M. Le Pen and the FN. In 1986, Faye decided to leave GRECE.
42 '[The] 'new bourgeois' . . . are only those who, in a world modelled entirely by the bourgeois mentality, are a caricature of the old aristocratic ways . . ., nobility, honour, giftedness, that is, everything that gives meaning to existence . . .' Editorial, *Éléments*, 72 (1991).
43 Philippe Burrin, 'Politique et société: les structures du pouvoir dans l'Italie fasciste et l'Allemagne nazi', *Annales*, 3 (1998).
44 Norberto Bobbio, 'Riforme e rivoluzioni', in P. Farneti (ed.), *Politica e Societá*, La Nuova Italia, Florence, 1972.
45 See Spektorowski (2003).
46 On the concept of nativism, see Cas Mudde, *Populist Radical Right Parties*, Cambridge University Press, New York, 2007, and Hans-Georg Betz, 'Contra el "totalitarismo verde": nativismo antiislámico en los populismos radicales de derecha en Europa occidental', in Simón, *La Extrema Derecha en Europa desde 1945 a nuestros días*, Tecnos, Ibid.
47 '[T]he minimum definition of the party family should be based on the key concept, the nation,' Mudde, ibid.
48 Xavier Torrens, 'Racismo y antisemitismo', in Joan Antón-Mellón (ed.), *Ideologías y Movimientos Políticos Contemporáneos*, Tecnos, Madrid, 2006.
49 The quest for a united society is probably the most important core idea of classical fascism. For the Spanish Fascist leader Primo de Rivera, 'Fascism is not a tactic – violence – but an idea – unity', *Textos*, (1959) 85.
50 Roger Eatwell, 'The nature of fascism: Or essentialism by another name?', *Ethik*, 2004. http://people.bath.ac.uk/mlsre/EWE1&2.htm.
51 See Sheehan (1981).
52 'GRECE retained an ideological core . . . This was the defence of identity (of whatever kind) and a refusal of egalitarianism . . . Ideological contradictions between NR factions did occasionally emerge, but the core ideology remained untouched', McCulloch, 2006, p. 161.
53 See Faye (1998).
54 This prerequisite of homogeneity echoes the most important core belief of Fascism [Esta es la Idea del fascismo: el unitarismo ultranacionalista palingenesico y violento]. Antón, 'Las concepciones nucleares, axiomas e ideas-fuerza del Fascismo Clásico', ibid., p. 61.

Bibliography

Antón-Mellón, Joan (2007), 'La cultura e ideología política del neopopulismo en Europa Occidental: MNR/FN (Francia), FPÖ (Austria), y Lega Nord (Italia)', in Simón, Miguel Angel (ed.), *La Extrema Derecha en Europa desde 1945 a nuestros días* (Madrid: Tecnos), pp. 281–311.
Antón-Mellón, Joan (2009), 'Las concepciones nucleares, axiomas e ideas-fuerza del Fascismo Clásico (1919–1945)', *Revista de Estudios Políticos*, 146, 49–79.
Antón-Mellón, Joan (2010), 'Las ideas-fuerza de la Nueva Derecha Europea (ND) y su continuidad/discontinuidad con el Fascismo Clásico (1919–1945)', in *Afinidades. Revista de literature y pensamiento*, 3, 97–106.

Bar-On, T. (2007), *Where Have All the Fascists Gone?* (Aldershot: Ashgate).

Benjamin, Walter (1973), *Discursos interrumpidos* (Madrid: Taurus).

Bihr, Alain (1999), *L'actualité d'un archaïsme* (Lausanne: Éditions Page Deux).

Bobbio, Norberto (1972), 'Riforme e rivoluzione', in Farceti, P. (ed.), *Politica e Società*, 2 vols (Florencia: La Nuova Italia).

Bobbio, N. and Matteucci, N. (eds) (1981), *Diccionario de Política*, 2 vols (Madrid: Siglo XXI).

Buchignani, Paolo (2006), *La Rivoluzione in Camicia Nera* (Milano: Mondadori).

Burrin, Philippe (1998), 'Politique et société: les structures du pouvoir dans l'Italie fasciste et l'Allemagne nazi', *Annales*, 3, 615–37.

Chevel d' Appollonia, Ariane (1996), *L' Extrême droite en france* (Brussels: Complexe).

de Benoist, Alain (1980), 'La religion de l' Europe', *Éléments*, 36.

de Benoist, Alain (1982), 'Ni fraiche ni joyeuse', *Éléments*, 24/25.

de Benoist, Alain (1994), *Le grain de sable. Jalons pour une fin de siècle* (Marsat: Le Labyrinthe).

de Benoist, Alain (2010), *Más allá de la derecha y la Izquierda/Antología* (edited by Javier Ruíz Portella) (Barcelona: Altera).

de Benoist, Alain and Faye, G. (1983), 'Contre l'Etat-providence', *Éléments*, 44.

de Benoist, Alain and Faye, G. (1986), *Las ideas de la Nueva Derecha* (Barcelona: Ediciones de Nuevo Arte, Thor).

del Rio Cisneros, Augustín (ed.) (1959), *Textos de Doctrina Política. Obras completas de José Antonio Primo de Rivera* (Madrid: Delegación Nacional de la Sección Femenina de F.E.T y de las J.O.N.S).

Eatwell, Roger (1992), 'Towards a new model of generic Fascism', *Journal of Theoretical Politics*, 4, 2, 161–94.

Eatwell, Roger (2004), 'The nature of fascism: Or essentialism by another name?', *Ethik*. http://people.bath.ac.uk/mlsre/EWE1&2.htm (accessed November 2008).

Eley, G. (1983), 'What produces fascism: Preindustrial traditions or a crisis of a capitalist state', *Politics and Society*, 12, 53–82.

Esparza, José Javier, 'La Nueva Derecha en su contexto', *Hespérides*, 16–17, 547–874.

Faye, G. (1980), 'Pour en finir avec la civilisation occidentale', *Éléments*, 34, 5–11.

Faye, G. (1982), 'Pour un gramscisme de Droite', *Actes du XVI Colloque National de GRECE* (Paris: Le Labyrinthe) pp. 71–80.

Faye, G. (1983), 'La modernité: Ambiguites d'une notion capitale', *Études et Recherches*, 1, 3–10.

Faye, G. (1984), 'Critique du systeme occidental', *Orientations*, 5, 4–12.

Faye, G. (1998), *L'Archéofuturisme* (Paris: L'Aencre).

Faye, G. (2001), *Porquoi nous combattons. Manifeste de la Résistance européenne* (Paris: L'Aencre).

Fennema, Meindert (2004), 'Populist parties of the Right', *ASSR Working Paper*, 04/01.

Flood, Christopher (2000), 'The cultural struggle of the extreme right and the case of terre et people', *Contemporary French Civilization*, 24, 2, 241–66.

Freeden, Michael (1994), 'Political concepts and ideological morphology', *The Journal of Political Philosophy*, 2, 2, 140–64.

Gallego, Ferran (2006), *Todos los hombres del Führer* (Barcelona: Debate).

Gentile, Emilio (2002), *La religión fascista* (Mesnil-sur-l'Estrée: Perrin).

Gentile, Emilio (2004), *Fascismo, historia e interpretación* (Madrid: Alianza Editorial).

Griffin, Roger (2000), 'Between metapolitics and apoliteia: The Nouvelle Droite's strategy for conserving the fascist vision in the "interregnum"', *Modern and Contemporary France*, 8, 1, 35–53.

Griffin, Roger (2002), 'Cruces gamadas y caminos bifurcados: las dinámicas fascistas del Tercer Reich', in Antón-Mellón, Joan (ed.), *Orden, Jerarquía y Comunidad. Fascismos, Dictaduras y Postfascismos en la Europa Contemporánea* (Tecnos: Madrid) pp. 103–49.

Griffin, Roger (ed.) (2005), *Fascism, Totalitarianism and Political Religion* (London/New York: Routledge).

Griffin, Roger (2007), 'Plus ça change! El pedigrí fascista de la Nueva Derecha', in Simón, Miguel Ángel (ed.), *La Extrema Derecha en Europa desde 1945 a nuestros días* (Madrid: Tecnos).

Herf, G. (1990), *El modernismo reaccionario* (México: Fondo Cultura Económica).

Laqueur, Walter (1996), *Fascism, Past, Present, Future* (New York: Oxford University Press).

McCulloch, Tom (2006), 'The Nouvelle Droite in the 1980s and 1990s: Ideology and entrism, the relationship with the Front National', *French Politics*, 4, 158–78.

Mammone, Andrea (2008), 'The transnational reaction to 1968: Neo-fascist national fronts and political cultures in France and Italy', *Contemporary European History*, 17, 2, 213–36.

Mann, Michael (2006), *Fascistas* (Valencia: Publicaciones de la Universidad de Valencia).

Mayer, Arno (1986), *La persistencia del Antiguo Régimen* (Madrid: Alianza Editorial).

Mudde, Cas (1996), 'The war of words: Defining the extreme right party family', *West European Politics*, 19, 2, 225–48.

Mudde, Cas (2007), *Populist Radical Right Parties* (New York: Cambridge University Press).

Paxton, Robert O. (2005), *Anatomía del Fascismo* (Barcelona: Península).

Prowe, Diethelm (1994), 'Classic fascism and the new radical right in Western Europe: Comparisons and contrasts', *Contemporary European History*, 3, 3, 289–313.

Revelli, Marco (1996), 'La nouva dresta', *Iride*, 18, May–August.

Seliguer, Martin (1970), 'Fundamental and operative ideology: The two principal dimensions of political argumentation', *Policy Sciences*, 1, 325–7.

Sheehan, Thomas (1981), 'Myth and violence: The fascism of Julius Evola and Alain de Benoist', *Social Research*, 48, 1 (Spring), 45–73.

Spektorowski, Alberto (2000), 'The French New Right differentialism and the idea of ethnophilian exclusionism', *Polity*, 33, 2 (Winter), 283–303.

Spektorowski, Alberto (2003), 'Ethnoregionalism: The intellectual New Right and the Lega Nord', *The Global Review of Ethnopolitics*, 2, 3, 55–70.

Taguieff, Pierre-André (1994), *Sur la Nouvelle droite* (Paris: Descartes).

Torigian, Michael (1999), 'The philosophical foundations of the French New Right', *Telos*, 117, 6–42.

Torrens, Xavier (2006), 'Racismo y antisemitismo', in Joan Antón-Mellón (ed.), *Ideologias y Movimientos Políticos Contemporáneos* (Madrid: Tecnos).

Trevor-Roper, Hugh (ed.) (2004), *Conversaciones privadas de Hitler* (Barcelona: Crítica).

Tugendhat, Ernst (2002), *Problemas* (Barcelona: Gedisa).

Vaughan, M. (1982), 'Nouvelle droite: Cultural power and political influence', in D.S. Bell (ed.), *Contemporary French Civilization* (London/Canberra: Groom Helm) pp. 52–68.

4

FASCISM TO THE NOUVELLE DROITE

The quest for pan-European empire

Tamir Bar-On

Introduction

Led by Alain de Benoist, the French Nouvelle Droite (ND) is a cultural movement distinguished from extreme-right political parties and extra-parliamentary formations of the revolutionary right (see also Virchow in this volume for the revolutionary right). Created in 1968, the ND has ultra-nationalistic, pro-colonialist roots. It is a response to the loss of French Algeria, the growing ascendancy of liberalism and the New Left (NL), and the weakness and divisiveness of the extreme-right and neo-fascist milieu in an 'anti-fascist' era (Bar-On 2007b). In line with the prevailing neo-fascist post-war trend led by French writer Maurice Bardèche (1907–98), the ND superseded narrow nationalism and embraced pan-Europeanism. Yet, there were earlier pan-European strains on the extreme right: the monarchical, counter-revolutionary tradition of Joseph de Maistre (1753–1821) and Donoso Cortés (1809–53) (Schmitt 2002: 100–15) to elements within the Italian Fascist Party (PNF) (Ledeen 1972: 104–32; Griffiths 2005: 72–88).

The goal of this chapter is to trace historical continuity in the ND's primordial attachment to a homogeneous notion of pan-European identity. Early post-war neo-fascism and significant fascist elements in the inter-war years were similarly obsessed with the decline of homogeneous pan-European or Western identities. It is my thesis that despite the ultra-nationalistic origins of historical fascism, early post-war neo-fascism and the ND in different historical periods, the thread tying them together is the notion of a unified, homogeneous, pan-European empire regenerated in defence against the dominant 'materialist' ideologies from liberalism to socialism. All three political outfits argued that superpowers such as the former Marxist–Leninist Soviet Union and liberal democratic United States (US) embody a common egalitarian, 'materialist' and 'decadent' ideological framework, which seeks to impose itself globally to the detriment of homogeneous, rooted European cultures. Fascism and neo-fascism's ultra-nationalism or the ND's origins in defence of French Algeria obscures the Europeanizing thrust of these political projects. Moreover, the ND's indebtedness to the inter-war Conservative Revolution (CR) (including Ernst Junger and Carl Schmitt) (Griffin 1995: 104–14) and post-war neo-fascists such as Bardèche, as well as influence on contemporary extreme-right political parties such as the French Front National (FN), undermines ND claims of forging a 'post-fascist' *Weltanschauung* (see Antón-Mellón and Wolfreys in this volume).

The point of rupture between historical fascism and early post-war neo-fascism and the ND is that the latter two schools of thought turned more *explicitly* pan-European owing to the defeat of Fascism in 1945 and the lack of significant popular support for post-war fascist movements until the early 1980s (see also Virchow's chapter for post-war pan-European Nazism). One major exception was Italy's neo-fascist Italian Social Movement (MSI). While there were important currents of pan-Europeanism such as the Italian PNF, the British fascist Oswald Mosley or Pierre Drieu La Rochelle in France, it is in the early post-war period that the pan-European orientation of fascist thought supersedes the traditional ultra-nationalistic framework. The ND continues this pan-European framework inherited from post-war French neo-fascism.

Right, left, Nouvelle Droite

For this paper, right and left are defined by Norberto Bobbio (1996: 60–79). The 'pole star' separating the left and right, argues Bobbio, is equality versus inequality. For the liberal-left, equality has three meanings: equality of opportunity, legal equality of citizens, or the socialist notion of equality of condition.

ND positions in the 1990s *appeared* to have more in common with the left. After the fall of the Berlin Wall in 1989, the ND appealed to disgruntled leftists in North America and the ecological movement (de Benoist 1993–4; 1999; 2007). After liberalism's 'victory', the ND entered into dialogue with *Telos*, a critical theory journal with anti-capitalist, NL roots (Piccone 1993–4: 3–23).

Like fascists, the ND attacks inequalities associated with global capitalism that tear asunder national or regional communities (de Benoist 1996; 1998), yet it also rejects administratively enforced equality (Piccone 1993–4: 19). De Benoist has argued that egalitarianism is *the* major ill of the modern world and he looks for inspiration to organic, hierarchical, Indo-European societies of the pagan period (de Benoist 1979a: 16, 25). For de Benoist, egalitarianism is rejected because it undermines *diversity*, arguably a code word for inequality, the fundamental principal of the right. Egalitarianism, de Benoist posits along Nietzschean lines, produced all subsequent 'decadent' and 'materialist' ideologies, including the Judeo-Christian tradition and its secular derivatives – liberalism, socialism, social democracy and communism (de Benoist 1979a: 16). The ND, then, is a right-wing movement that insists on the necessity of inequalities between people and is opposed to formal, juridical equality in the context of a liberal, multicultural society. Yet, while a right-wing movement, the ND mimetically borrows from competitors on the left and NL in order to survive and stay faithful to an inter-war CR tradition that inspired Nazism and fascism (Bar-On 2001: 331–51; 2007b). Despite extensive linkages with the anti-immigrant FN with the ND acting as one important party faction (McCulloch 2006: 158–78), around the new millennium de Benoist turned more pan-European, federalist, regionalist, environmentalist and 'leftist' by praising 1968 icons such as Che Guevara, Herbert Marcuse and Daniel Cohn-Bendit (GRECE 1998; Bar-On 2007b: 57–77).

The ND sought to spread its ideas in a metapolitical framework throughout the European continent. Since its formation in 1968 with the creation of *Groupement de Recherche et d'Études pour la Civilisation Européene* (GRECE – Research and Study Group for European Civilization), the ND moved beyond French neo-fascism and ultra-nationalism towards pan-European ultra-regionalism (Spektorowski 2000: 352–61; Bastow in Blamires 2006: 88). Its transnational links with Italian, Belgian, Spanish, Romanian and other European think tanks, journals and organizations cemented its pan-European identity (Griffin 1993: 21–5; Bar-On 2007b: 142–4; Bar-On 2011).

If the ND is pan-European, it is also a right that borrows from numerous French, German and European traditions that rejected liberal democracy. It attacks the egalitarian thrust of 1789 and simultaneously rejects reactionary conservatism (Bellamy in Eatwell and Wright 2003: 58–61). Today the ND harkens back to an anti-Jacobin, anti-capitalist and regionalist right-wing tradition. It is a right that, as one ND fellow traveller argues, is 'indebted' to diverse right-wing traditions: liberal, radical and ultra-nationalist rights (Sunic 1990: 6). Yet, it is also a right that has been shaped by the defining moments of the left and NL such as the events of May 1968. The ND worldview can be summarized in the synthesis of Conservative Revolution (CR) and NL ideals (Bar-On 2007b: 1–19). Or, in this equation: CR + NL = ND. As a historical comparison, fascism synthesized organic ultra-nationalism, anti-Marxist socialism (or class transcendence), extreme statism, and paramilitarism combined with ethnic cleansing goals (Mann 2004: 13). The ND continues the first three aspects of the fascist tradition, but makes cosmetic changes by substituting organic ultra-regionalism for ultra-nationalism; questioning extreme statism yet vindicating an immigrant-free Europe of homogeneous regions; and rejecting paramilitarism but valorizing martial themes of CR thinkers such as Ernst Jünger, revolutionary neo-fascists such as Julius Evola, and non-fascist elitists such as Friedrich Nietzsche (for further theorizing on the ND's relationship to fascism, see also Antón-Mellón's chapter).

ND appeals to both revolutionary right and NL is an attempt to create a political synthesis for the new millennium. By reconciling the ideas of right and left, the ND hopes to attract a constituency of supporters around issues that transcend the materialist left–right divide: the pace of immigration, the nature of European identity, the political direction of the European Union, the environmental catastrophe, regionalism or the corruption of established party and political systems along populist lines (Taggart 2000). These transversal issues are what the ND has in mind when it claims to transcend outmoded, 'imbecile' categories such as right and left (de Benoist 1995a: 89). If conflicts are no longer material in the post-communist age, then presumably they might be cultural or civilizational. De Benoist officially rejects the notion of a 'clash of civilizations' (de Benoist 2001; see also Huntington 1998), yet echoes the Huntingtonian thesis in the ND's official manifesto written in 1999 (de Benoist and Champetier 1999: 11–23). In seeking to forge an organic, ultra-nationalist Third Way beyond liberalism and socialism (Sternhell 1994; Eatwell 1996), the ND echoes a fascist tradition that longed for class transcendence to solve the social question and questioned the validity of parliamentary institutions. Like fascists who claimed to save both the nation and Europe from 'materialist decadence', the ND perpetuates a tradition of cultural and ideological pessimism vis-à-vis liberal democracy and simultaneous optimism at overcoming a hated system.

A common link: an elitist, sovereign Europe

Whereas today the ND is pro-European, regionalist and federalist, it rejects the technocratic, pro-capitalist, pro-globalization thrust of the EU. Like many contemporary extreme-right political parties, the ND criticizes the distant, pro-capitalist, bureaucratized 'EU of the politicians' that undermines the voices of the European 'heartland' in a spirit of direct democracy (de Benoist and Champetier 1999: 11–23) (see also Williams in this volume for the multifaceted electoral positions of extreme-right parties in respect of the EU). As Mudde (2004: 14) correctly points out, 'Most right-wing extremists are not against European cooperation *per se*, they are against the form of cooperation that the EU stands for.' In Habermasian terms, the ND favours technological modernity, yet rejects the effects of cultural modernity – liberalism, egalitarianism, multiculturalism and pluralism (Woods 2007: 132).

Similarly, post-war fascists such as Bardèche were adamant that Europe's historic role was as a united, sovereign political force, which obeyed the dictates of neither Washington nor Moscow (Bardèche 1970: 176–8). Yet, Bardèche was also clear that a reborn fascism would be a *third way*, which rejected liberalism or socialism, but harkened back to revolutionary 'movement fascism' or the Italian Social Republic (RSI) (Bardèche 1970: 17–19). Like the ND, Bardèche does not reject European unity and even prefers it, provided it is an elitist, authoritarian, pan-European unity.

We often forget that Mussolini's claim that fascism was not for export contradicted attempts of Italian fascists to Europeanize the movement as early as 1925 (Ledeen 1972; de Caprariis 2000: 151–83).

On the question of Europe, it was Julius Evola, author of the Fascist regime's manifesto of 'spiritual racism', who best embodied the notion of an elitist, hierarchical, sovereign Europe. Evola called for pro-Europeanism in public affairs, as well as a 'unity of fighters' against liberal and communist enemies within (Griffin 1993: 1). He supported a united Europe that 'must not be a stage towards the Westernization of the world, but a move against it, in fact a revolt against the modern world in favour of what is nobler, higher, more truly human' (Griffin 1993: 1). That is, a

Europe that Evola argued would be 'spiritually distinct' vis-à-vis other powers such as the US (Griffin 1993: 1). In short, a more revolutionary, fascist, spiritual, elitist European empire that longs for the 'golden age' before the Enlightenment and its *egalitarian* principles 'destroyed' Europe's collective cultural heritage. Although they work from different right-wing traditions, de Benoist's anti-Western, pan-European turn in the 1980s echoed Evola's anti-Western, pro-European unity orientation (de Benoist 1982; 1986).

Fascism's European identity: the fascist international

When we think of internationalism, our gaze normally turns towards the left: the two Internationals, the Paris Commune, Soviet Marxism–Leninism, the International Brigades of communists and anarchists in the Spanish Civil War, the anti-colonialist struggles, the NL, or the contemporary anti-corporate left. Rarely do we conceive of an internationalism on the right.

Few are aware of concrete attempts by Italian fascists in the late 1920s and 1930s to Europeanize and universalize fascism. For them, fascism represented a novel, ultra-nationalist, socialist revisionism and authoritarian synthesis, which could be applied across Europe. Seen in this light, fascism was a *fourth* way that rejected conservative, liberal and communist solutions for Europe's inter-war ills.

Fascist intellectuals such as Enrico Corradini, Ugo Spirito and Sergio Pannunzio proposed a rational, coherent body of thought that sought to provide concrete solutions to Italy's late modernization development woes through corporatist, national syndicalist ideals in the context of a fascist, 'developmental dictatorship' (Gregor 1979; 2000; 2001; 2005). Corradini saw Italy as a 'proletarian nation' in contrast to other 'plutocratic' European colonial powers and Italy too required its 'place in the sun' (Gregor 2005: 18–37). This 'place in the sun' would be achieved under the modernizing aegis of the PNF. This was a 'right-wing' internationalism that rejected left-wing, communist internationalism in favour of an international struggle between *nations* rather than classes.

The attempt to create 'universal fascism' finds its first expression in fascist Italy in the mid 1920s in sections of fascist, 'spiritual' youth culture that sought to radicalize fascism, give it greater coherence, and restore the revolutionary legacy of 1919 inherent in the birth of the PNF. In short, one generation had been responsible for animating the first phase of fascism leading to the March on Rome in 1922, but this generation had now lost its youthful vigour and institutionalized an excessively bureaucratized fascist state 'where young position-seekers came to make their fortunes' (Ledeen 1972: 36). In this context, the doctrine of 'universal fascism' signified a generational revolt, an attempt to transform fascist institutions and a desire to find comprehensive European-wide solutions to the 'crisis of civilization' plaguing the continent.

Despite tensions within the PNF over the notion of 'universal fascism', particularly with leading fascist ideologue Giovanni Gentile, on 7 October 1930 Mussolini declared his support for 'universal fascism': 'Today I affirm that Fascism, as idea, doctrine, and realization, is universal: Italian in its particular institutions, and universal in spirit' (quoted in Ledeen 1972: 63).

Fascist leader Benito Mussolini sponsored the International Conference of Fascist Parties, also known as the Volta Congress, in 1932 as a rival to the Soviet Union's Comintern. The theme of the congress was 'On Europe'. The conference called for 'a kind of spiritual geopolitics which saw Europe menaced by a Soviet-led Africa and Asia on the one hand, and America and England, on the other hand' (Ledeen 1972: 83). The conference stressed Italian guidance of the new universal, pan-European fascism, as well as Mussolini's defeat of the 'Bolshevik menace' (Ledeen 1972: 83). In Italy, the conference was received with intoxicating delight by younger fascist circles and led to a fascist 'Young Europe' movement in 1933, which deplored the biological racial anti-Semitism of Nazism and warned of Hitler's desire for an expansionist, homogeneous German state (Ledeen 1972: 84).

The 1934 Fascist International Congress at Montreux in Switzerland, which included among the participants Marcel Bucard, Vidkun Quisling and General Eoin O'Duffy, was the heyday of 'universal fascism'. Thirteen countries were represented. A fascist Englishman, James Strachey Barnes, led the International Congress, although Italian Fascist authorities financed it. Barnes wrote *The Universal Aspects of Fascism* in 1928 in which he argued that *youth* was the essence of the fascist worldview (Barnes 1929: 164). His *Centre International d'Études sur le Fascisme* (CINEF) was based in Lausanne, Switzerland. Its primary goal was to distribute fascist propaganda throughout Europe and to encourage fascist solutions as an antidote to liberal, conservative and communist solutions (Griffiths in Blamires 2006: 339–40). One such solution was the corporate state. The other 'universal' solution was to reject biological racism and anti-Semitism of the Nazi type, although not all delegates could agree on this point. Owing to Italian fears of revolt, no open declaration of a rejection of anti-Semitism occurred at the Congress.

It is also true that Mussolini's regime financed foreign fascist movements, including the Austrian *Heimwehr* and Belgian Rexists (Ledeen 1972: 99–100). In addition, Mussolini created the *Comitati d'Azione per l'Universalità di Roma* (CAUR – the Action Committees for Roman Universality) in 1933 to bring independent groups pining for 'universal fascism' under tighter state control. CAUR would guarantee the independence of local European fascisms, while seeking to loosely unite European-wide fascist organizations that paid lip service to the greatness of Mussolini and Italian fascism as the leader of the fascist struggle (Ledeen 1972: 109–10).

Yet, there were problems looming on the horizon for 'universal fascism', especially the ascendancy of Nazi Germany. This meant that the notion of 'universal fascism' would become a dead letter; an 'incomplete revolution'. By 1936, Mussolini was working towards a *rapprochement* with Nazi Germany.

'Universal fascism' also implied that fascist movements throughout Europe called for similar ultra-nationalistic, authoritarian and corporatist solutions. By 1933 they had different fascist models in Nazi Germany and fascist Italy. The former model was more vigorous, youthful, virile and soldierly for many younger fascists, and certainly more anti-Semitic at its core. The pan-European SS Brigades highlight the ascendancy of the Nazi model in a universal fascist movement that once saw Rome as opposed to Berlin as its model (for the contemporary transnational dimension of Nazism see Virchow in this volume).

Yet, the only concrete and serious attempts to create a pan-European fascist framework came in fascist Italy from the mid 1920s to mid 1930s. This is not to say that others in Europe did not share in the pan-European fascist dream (Griffin 1995: 66–8; 200–2).

As a footnote to 'universal fascism', potent fascist movements existed in Brazil, Chile, Argentina, South Africa and Japan in the inter-war years (Griffin 1995: 228–44). For Payne, Peronism in Argentina had some though not all the prerequisites of fascism, while outside Europe Saddam Hussein's Ba'athist Iraq came closest to mimicking the full-fledged, European-style fascist regimes of the inter-war years (Payne 1995: 516).

The centrality of European identity in early post-war fascism

If pan-European identity was important to historical fascism, it increasingly shaped post-war fascism. The ND's European turn was presaged by Bardèche, the brother-in-law of executed fascist writer Robert Brasillach. In the late 1950s and early 1960s, Bardèche argued that for the revolutionary right to reinvigorate itself in the context of the official defeats of fascism and Nazism in 1945 it would have to turn more European rather than strictly nationalistic. It would look for inspiration to the short-lived RSI. For post-war neo-fascists such as Bardèche, the RSI represented a radical, 'left-wing' thrust, which resembled Mussolini's 'movement fascism' as opposed to the more corrupt 'regime fascism' of the PNF. In his neo-fascist text *Qu'est-ce que le Fascisme?* (*What is Fascism?*) (1961), Bardèche urged a radically new tactical approach to fascism: dropping the leadership principle, totalitarian single party, secret police and militaristic 'fascist style' (Bardèche 1970: 175–6). In the post-1968 period, the ND under de Benoist learned its lessons from Bardèche's metapolitical, pro-European fascist turn.

Bardèche's pro-Europeanism began earlier than 1961. At the Congress of Malmö in 1951, Bardèche led a French delegation that sought to Europeanize fascism by erecting a pan-European fascist movement. This conference brought together fascists from fourteen countries and founded the 'Malmö International' or European Social Movement, which included sixteen national movements (Griffin 1995: 342). Like the universal fascist movement, the conference disagreed about issues such as anti-Semitism or the degree of racism necessary for post-war fascism, but there was unanimous agreement by delegates about the idea of a regenerated Europe battling against the two 'materialist' superpowers. The Malmö Manifesto enshrined the idea of Eurofascism as opposed to insular nationalisms (Griffin 1995: 342). In clause 2, it called for the erection of a 'European Empire'. In clause 3, prices and salaries were to be controlled and regulated by the 'European Empire'. In clause 4, the armed forces of all the nations of Europe were to be put 'under the control of the central government of the Empire'. Clause 5 argued for 'the right of colonial peoples to enter the Empire once they have attained a certain educational and economic level'. The Malmö Manifesto shaped the pan-European rather than nationalist orientation of the ND under de Benoist.

Yet, it is Bardèche's *Que'est-ce que le Fascisme?* that most explores the European and universal dimensions of post-war neo-fascism. Despite his warning in the first page that he is 'a fascist writer' (Bardèche 1970: 9), Bardèche's text might not be recognizable to a Mussolini or Hitler because it focuses on revising fascism tactically. If fascism is reborn, insisted Bardèche, it would be pan-European and its face might no longer be recognizable.

For Bardèche, Italian Fascism strayed from its syndicalist–socialist roots best embodied in *The Charter of Work* (1919), D'Annunzio's *Constitution of Fiume* (1920) and the *Verona Charter* (1944) of the RSI (O'Sullivan 1983: 193–206). It is in the *Verona Charter*, argues Bardèche, that exists the 'true fascism', which Mussolini should have struggled for in the course of Italian Fascism (Bardèche 1970: 20). This 'true fascism', Bardèche adds, has a European-wide destiny.

Bardèche holds the pro-Nazi RSI as his 'model fascism'. He goes further by arguing the Nazi SS represents a 'permanent preoccupation of fascism': a warrior elite incarnating the national-socialist ideal (Bardèche 1970: 35–7). Bardèche claims the SS should have been more regulated by the state (Bardèche 1970: 53–4). The implication being that fascism made 'errors', but the 'true fascism' of the people will be reborn under a pan-European sky.

Bardèche's work is designed to weed out 'good' from 'bad' fascisms in order to allow fascism to be reconstituted along a pan-European path. Fascism is not extermination camps or racial legislation, Bardèche insists, but a legitimate national socialist project with concrete solutions for post-war European ills (Bardèche 1970: 87–8). Yet, as he puts it, 'We search in vain for the book of fascism: This Bible does not exist' (Bardèche 1970: 89). If the doctrine of fascism does not exist, it must be continuously revised.

Bardèche's European path to post-war fascism is unambiguous. If fascism is reborn, it will be out of crisis where the nation or Europe is in existential danger and authoritarian solutions are necessary (Bardèche 1970: 174–5). He argues that Hitler's government 'spoke of Europe' rather than strictly Germany as the destiny of the continent (Bardèche 1970: 175–6). This European fascism will establish a 'third order' against the 'materialism' of the US and Soviet Union (Bardèche 1970: 177).

Most importantly, European fascism of the future will jettison the character-istics of historical fascism. In a key orientation that would influence the ND's metapolitical turn, Bardèche writes that 'the famous fascist *methods* are constantly revised' (Bardèche 1970: 182). In an argument that influenced the ND's anti-multicultural orientation, Bardèche rejects the 'mixing of blood' and the creation of an 'adulterous race', which is the real 'genocide' of modern democracies (Bardèche 1970: 185). Bardèche cryptically ends his neo-fascist text by arguing that fascism will return with 'another name, another face' (Bardèche 1970: 195).

It will certainly be a more European fascism and might even be a fascism that waves the 'post-fascist' or even 'anti-fascist' banners (Bar-On 2007b: 20).

Bardèche was not alone in shifting the discourse of post-war neo-fascism on the European continent. The Belgian Jean-François Thiriart founded *Jeune Europe* in 1960 with branches in numerous European countries from Italy to Belgium. Thiriart's orientation was pan-European rather than strictly national (Macklin 2005: 320–1). Although he claimed to be on the political centre, Thiriart sought to create political alliances with radical ultra-nationalist and left-wing movements and regimes, and even espoused a revolutionary, National-Bolshevik orientation with committed 'European political soldiers'. This tendency influenced Pino Rauti's extra-parliamentary formation *Ordine Nuovo* (New Order) in Italy, as well as elements of the parliamentary-based MSI (Mammone 2007). In 1962, Thiriart launched the unsuccessful National Party of Europe in conjunction with Mosley, which sought to create a European parliament, an alternative economic system to capitalism and communism, and to get rid of Soviet and North American influences in Europe.

The ND's pan-European revisionism

When Bardèche said that fascism would return with 'another name, another face', he found a welcome ear in ND leader de Benoist. Although the latter did not *explicitly* work from the fascist tradition and favoured a slow transformation of hearts and minds, his long list of negations (i.e. anti-capitalism, anti-communism, anti-liberalism, anti-conservatism and anti-parliamentarism), indebtedness to the CR tradition and pan-European framework echoed fascism (Payne 1995: 7) (but on this see also Antón-Mellón and Wolfreys). From a Paris university student who embraced French Algerian colonialism in the early 1960s, de Benoist moved towards radical ethnic pluralism and defence of particular cultures worldwide in the 1970s and 1980s. He was for yellow, black, red and white power with equal ardour; for an Algeria for the Algerians, as well as a France for the French (de Benoist 1979: 156). Echoing a tradition on the conservative right in favour of regionalism, he longed for a 'Europe of a Hundred Flags' against assimilationist state and corporate engineering (Fouéré 1968). Like Bardèche, de Benoist sought the revival of the ND along pan-European lines, while claiming to be anti-racist, anti-totalitarian and anti-fascist. Some critics asked the question whether de Benoist had resurrected a fascism that masked itself as a synthetic, revitalization movement with 'another name, another face' (Griffin, 'Foreword' in Bar-On 2007b).

With Bardèche's fascist revisionism as an inspiration, the ND attempted to distance itself from official variants of fascism, overt racism and anti-Semitism and the charismatic leadership principle. Nonetheless, one scholar demonstrated how a defence of cultural particularism has been a consistent thread of the ND's worldview from a support for French colonialism and the 'white race' in the 1960s; biological conceptions of race in the 1970s; and cultural formulations such as the 'right to difference' in the 1980s (Taguieff 1990; 1994). The 'right to difference' can be used for diametrically opposed purposes: liberal, republican anti-racism and racist separatism (Taguieff 1993–4: 160).

In addition, the ND refused to *sever* links with the CR milieu, which nourished the fascist and Nazi regimes (Taguieff 1993–4: 160). Nonetheless, in seeking to escape the ghetto milieu of the revolutionary right, the ND has been successful owing to the following factors: the passage of time, its pan-European intellectual networks, the virtual collapse of the communist left, disaffection with established parties and movements, increasing acceptance of issues such as immigration across political formations (Schain 2006) and cooperation with extreme-right political parties. In 2000, the extreme-right Freedom Party shocked the international community by joining Austria's ruling conservative national coalition. The neo-fascist MSI, which became the National Alliance in 1995, and extreme-right Northern League (LN – Lega Nord) joined the ruling Forza Italia (Go Italy) government coalition first in 1994 and in 2001 and 2008.

Despite its origins in the revolutionary right, the French ND influenced diverse European and international movements: the New Right in the United Kingdom, Neue Rechte in Germany, Nieuw Rechts in the Netherlands and Belgium, Nuova Destra in Italy, Imperium Europa in Malta and the New Right of Paul Weyrich and the Free Congress Foundation of the United States (Minkenberg 2000: 170–88). One scholar highlighted the 'multinational' character of the ND's major think tank GRECE (Duranton-Crabol 1991: 68–73). The German *Neue Rechte* is modelled after GRECE and its first journal, *Elemente*, is named after its French sister publication *Éléments*. The Italian Nuova Destra was created in 1974 after contacts were established and guidance given from the French ND (Sacchi 1993–4: 73). The French ND and GRECE's influence are noticeable in diverse publications such as *Punto y coma* and *Hespérides* in Spain and Michael Walker's *The Scorpion* in England. *Tekos*, *Vouloir* and *Orientations* mimic the concerns of the French ND in Holland and Belgium. Alexander Dugin's Russian New Right journal *Elementy* is modelled on its French counterpart *Éléments* and de Benoist briefly served on its editorial board. Moreover, the ND influenced the 'post-fascist' discourse shifts of neo-fascist and extreme-right parties in the 1980s and 1990s such as the French FN, Italian MSI and Lega Nord, which has arguably assisted in the *legitimization* and popular success of these parties within European party systems (Ignazi 2006).

The ND's pan-Europeanism of many flags

Like Bardèche before him, ND leader de Benoist longed for an imperial Europe that was a *third way* between the 'materialist' superpowers of the Cold War era. In the post-9/11 climate, the US was the sole remaining superpower and became 'enemy number one'. Within Europe, de Benoist called for hundreds of independent regions under an independent, re-spiritualized, secular, hierarchical, pan-European framework. Yet, the communities he longs for are *homogeneous* communities in which popular, direct democracy erodes 'abstract' liberalism and multiculturalism, which are seen as 'genocidal' for rooted cultural communities (de Benoist 1982; Faye 2003).

Despite de Benoist's vindication of inequality and support for elitist, hierarchical, organic societies, there is an appeal to the white 'silent majority', which rejects multiculturalism and would vote in referenda to block immigration and preserve local, European cultures against the homogenized 'steamrollers' of Americanization, Westernization and globalization.

Yet, the ND's 'democratic' turn from the 1980s into the new millennium can be interpreted as a by-product of its primordial desire to return to a world of relatively stable homogeneous, European ethnic communities within the context of a 'heterogeneous' world. Moreover, the ND's ultimate goal was the union of homogeneous ethnic community belonging (*ethnos*) and rule by the people (*demos*) in a framework that masked a more exclusionary political project (Bar-On 2007a). One astute observer of the ND does not take de Benoist's pro-democracy, intellectual makeover in recent years at face value and insists the ND promotes 'ethnic diversity within a federation of European ethnicities, banned to non-Europeans' (Spektorowski 2003: 61).

The ND's pan-European project connects it to elements in historical fascism and early post-war neo-fascism. Yet, what is unique about the ND's pan-Europeanism is its regional thrust that longs for homogeneous, regional communities in the context of a hierarchical, united Europe. In a spirit akin to 'modern populist' discourse that pits the people against elites, the ND sought to cause a rupture between the people and leaders and cultural elites on questions related to cultural identity, multiculturalism, immigration and notions of belonging. It attempts to undermine liberal multicultural notions of community and assist in the collapse of a blocked, 'totalitarian' system (de Benoist 1979b: 250–9). These 'people' that de Benoist is largely concerned with are the 'silent majority' of white Europeans that face supposed 'cultural extinction' as a result of uncontrolled immigration, globalization and the multicultural, egalitarian politics of a Europe dominated by the liberal-left (Raspail 1994; 2004).

Despite de Benoist's 'opening to the left' in the 1990s, even his writings in a former NL journal such as *Telos* demonstrated his commitment to a pan-European political project based on the centrality of a *homogeneous ethnos* within the context of an ancient Athenian *demos* in which 'cultural cohesion and a clear sense of shared heritage' prevailed (de Benoist 1995b: 75). In short, the ND longs for an *ethnocracy* in which 'original' white Europeans are favoured above immigrants (including citizens) by the state politically, legally, culturally and socio-economically.

The aim of de Benoist was to distance the people from their leaders and cultural representatives in the context of support for a liberal, multicultural Europe. This trend was evident in the ND manifesto published in *Éléments* in 1999. This is the most comprehensive ND manifesto since its foundation in 1968. What is striking about the manifesto is its concern for a pan-European political framework and obsessive desire for rooted, homogeneous communities. For the ND, the only authentic *demos* is one that is representative of the majority *ethnos* within a given state or region. The authors of the ND manifesto, de Benoist and Charles Champetier, argue for a multipolar civilization-based model rather than a strictly national or regional framework to counter US superpower hegemony (de Benoist and Champetier 1999).

The ND continues the pan-European project of Bardèche and Italian fascists sympathetic to 'universal fascism' from the mid 1920s to mid 1930s. In an age of global telecommunications when increasingly 'corporations rule the world' (Korten 2001), to use the language of one popular anti-corporate tract, nation-states become less relevant. The nation-state so valorized by fascists from George Valois to Giovanni Gentile is rejected as outmoded by the ND in section three of its manifesto: 'The nation-state is now too big to manage little problems and too small to address big ones.' The ND clearly understands that a pan-European framework will be necessary because historical fascism was too narrowly conceived and a failure, while changes in global economic and technological structures, ideological possibilities and mentalities necessitates a novel right-wing framework. Section 2, clause 8 of the manifesto argues that belonging will be more European in nature, as well as federal and regional, but ultimately rest on ethno-cultural foundations of '*common origins*'.

Like extreme-right political parties, the ND's other major pan-European concern is the inability of Europeans to control their borders from 'inassimilable' immigrants, particularly from the Muslim world. The restrictive immigration calls in the manifesto are similar to the French FN as they combine an anti-capitalist mantra with a desire to curtail non-European immigration to the continent. In section 3, clause 3, like the FN, the ND argues that restricting immigration will benefit immigrant and host societies alike since both will be able to maintain traditional homogeneous ethnic communities and ways of life.

The ND is realistic. Immigrants throughout Europe will not suddenly leave. Instead, the ND calls for a '*dissociation* of citizenship from nationality'. The attempt to link citizenship to nationality and blood eerily mimics Vichy or fascist Italy's race laws. It represents the ultimate triumph of homogeneous, populist ethnic belonging over democratic rights-based considerations of a liberal multicultural society. It also embodies a closed, ethnic conception of citizenship against a civic, republican model.

It is significant that Europe as a federalized, sovereign power bloc would be tied with Russia against the US, the key representative of liberalism. The latter is viewed by the ND as 'the main enemy'. This is an attempt to weaken the US as a global superpower, while the alliance with Russia has historical echoes of the Nazi–Soviet Non-Aggression Pact (1939) and Ernst Niekisch's National Bolshevism that sought to unite a re-spiritualized, worker-centred Germany and Stalinist Soviet Union in order to destroy the 'materialism' of Western civilization.

In what is arguably the key line of the manifesto in section 3, clause 7, the authors unite *ethnos* and *demos* in a political potion that synthesizes 'totalitarian democracy' (Talmon 1952) in the mould of Robespierre with an ethnic conception of belonging that closely mimics fascism: 'The essential idea of democracy is neither that of the individual nor of humanity, but rather the idea of a body of citizens politically united into a people.' This people is not the entire *demos* along liberal or left-wing lines, but a homogeneous people rooted in pan-European, ethnic communities.

Conclusion

It has been my central argument that despite the narrow ultra-nationalist model offered by historical fascism, it also had a pan-European dimension. The attempt to create 'universal fascism' within the PNF was a concrete expression of the pan-European dimension of fascism. Right-wing authoritarian and fascist solutions impregnated the European continent from the 1920s to 1940s. Fascism was a revolutionary, synthetic, totalitarian and pan-European response to an epoch of multiple crises: military, political, socio-economic and cultural-ideological (Mann 2004).

When fascism came crashing down in 1945, Bardèche reinforced the pan-European dimension of fascism. An early post-war neo-fascist, he organized fascists from different countries in the Malmö Conference in 1951 and argued for a Europeanized fascism to combat both the Soviet Union and the US. Bardèche's successor was de Benoist. His major innovation was the Gramscian, metapolitical struggle that borrowed from the NL. In his rejection of egalitarianism, de Benoist remained more on the right than left. De Benoist further cemented the pan-European turn of the ND by building think tanks and influencing right-wing political parties throughout Europe. The ND sought to change hearts and minds on crucial issues such as multiculturalism, immigration, nationalism and regionalism. The ND's distance from extreme-right parliamentary forces and violent extra-parliamentary politics gave his movement some legitimacy, although for others de Benoist's 'left' turn in the late 1980s harkened back to the 'neither right, nor left' fascist synthesis.

What is fascinating about historical fascism, early post-war neo-fascism and the ND is how they remained true to the pan-European task of 'saving the continent' from the 'materialist' ideologies of the day. All three forces rejected the liberal, conservative or communist alternatives for Europe, while seeking a reborn, pan-European empire to 'liberate' the continent from the cultural 'genocide' of its rooted, homogeneous ethnicities. De Benoist, like Bardèche and Evola before him, rejected the 'Europe of the politicians' and liberal elites. Like extreme-right political forces, de Benoist rejected the EU because it was an 'anti-Europe Europe'. That is, the EU does not represent the desire of the majority of white Europeans for a hier-archical Europe free of superpowers and one that is internally homogeneous in the contexts of different flags.

Our travels through the revolutionary right-wing milieu in three epochs raises questions of definitional issues over what constitutes fascism, whether it was epochal and whether fascism is about core ideological goals, a set of negations and specific style and organizational framework (Payne 1995: 7). The ND, in com-bination with anti-immigrant parties such as the FN, has been instrumental in shifting

European discourse against immigration, immigrants, minorities, multiculturalism and liberalism. This is especially true about non-European immigration, as the discourse of many conservative, right-wing parties demonstrated in respect of Turkey's proposed entrance into the EU. The ND sought to create a new rights framework in which the *collective* rights of European ethnic groups trumps individual rights, as well as the rights of the *demos* as a whole. Had Bardèche or the Italian activists of 'universal fascism' been alive today they might have found a 'spiritual home' in the ND.

References

Bardèche, M. (1970) *Qu'est-ce que le Fascisme?* (Paris: Les Sept Couleurs).

Barnes, J.S. (1929) *The Universal Aspects of Fascism* (London: Williams and Norgate).

Bar-On, T. (2001) 'The ambiguities of the Nouvelle Droite, 1968–1999', *The European Legacy* 6 (3), 333–51.

Bar-On, T. (2007a) 'The triumph of ethnos over demos in the Nouvelle Droite's worldview', paper presented, Immigration, Minorities and Multiculturalism in Democracies Conference (Montreal 25–27 October).

Bar-On, T. (2007b) *Where Have All the Fascists Gone?* (Aldershot: Ashgate).

Bar-On, T. (2011) 'Transnationalism and the French Nouvelle Droite', *Patterns of Prejudice* 45 (3), 199–223.

Bastow, S. (2006) 'Alain de Benoist', in Blamires, C. (ed.), *World Fascism: A Historical Encyclopedia* (vol. 1) (Santa-Barbara, CA: ABL-CLIO).

Bellamy, R. (2003) 'Conservatism', in Eatwell, R. and Wright, A. (eds), *Contemporary Political Ideologies* (London: Continuum).

Blamires, C. (ed.) (2006) *World Fascism: A Historical Encyclopedia* (vol. 1) (Santa-Barbara, CA: ABL-CLIO).

Bobbio, N. (1996) *Left and Right: The Significance of a Political Distinction* (Allan Cameron, trans.) (Chicago: University of Chicago Press).

de Benoist, A. (1979a) *Vu de droite* (Paris: Copernic).

de Benoist, A. (1979b) *Les Idées à l'endroit* (Paris: Libres-Hallier).

de Benoist, A. (1982) *La cause des peuples* (Paris: Labyrinthe).

de Benoist, A. (1986) *Europe, Tiers monde, même combat* (Paris: Robert Laffont).

de Benoist, A. (1993–4) 'The idea of empire', *Telos* 98–9 (Winter–Spring), 81–98.

de Benoist, A. (1995a) 'The end of the left–right dichotomy: The French case', *Telos* 102 (Winter), 73–90.

de Benoist, A. (1995b) 'Democracy revisited', *Telos* 95 (Spring), 65–75.

de Benoist, A. (1996) 'Confronting globalization', *Telos* 108 (Summer), 117–38.

de Benoist, A. (1998) 'Hayek: A critique', *Telos* 110 (Winter), 71–104.

de Benoist, A. (1999) 'Johannes Althussius (1557–1638)', *Krisis* 22 (March), 2–34.

de Benoist, A. (2001) 'Jihad versus McWorld', *Padania* (19 September).

de Benoist, A. (2007) *Demain, la décroissance! Penser l'écologie jusqu'au bout* (Paris: Édite).

de Benoist and Champetier, C. (1999) 'La nouvelle droite de l'an 2000', *Éléments* 94 (February), 11–23.

de Caprariis, L. (2000) 'Fascism for export? The rise and eclipse of the Fasci Italiani all'Estero', *Journal of Contemporary History* 35 (2) (April), 151–83.

Duranton-Crabol, A.-M. (1991) *L'Europe de l'extrême droite: de 1945 à nos jours* (Brussels: Editions Complexe).

Eatwell, R. (1996) *Facism: A History* (London: Vintage).

Faye, G. (2003) 'The cause of peoples?', *Terre et Peuple* 18 (Winter).

Fouéré, Y. (1968) *L'Europe aux cents drapeaux* (Paris: Presses d'Europe).

GRECE (1998) *Le Mai 68 de la nouvelle droite* (Paris: Labyrinthe).

Gregor, A.J. (1979) *Italian Fascism and Developmental Dictatorship* (Princeton, NJ: Princeton University Press).

Gregor, A.J. (2000) *The Faces of Janus: Marxism and Fascism in the Twentieth Century* (New Haven, CT: Yale University Press).

Gregor, A.J. (2001) *Fascism in Our Time* (New Brunswick, NJ: Transaction).

Gregor, A.J. (2005) *Mussolini's Intellectuals* (Princeton, NJ: Princeton University Press).

Griffin, R. (1993) *Europe for the Europeans: Fascist Myths of the New Order 1922–1992* (Oxford: Oxford Brookes University Humanities Research Centre).

Griffin, R. (ed.) (1995) *Fascism* (Oxford: Oxford University Press).

Griffiths, R. (2005) *Fascism* (London: Continuum).

Griffiths, R. (2006) 'International fascism', in Blamires, C. (ed.), *World Fascism: A Historical Encyclopedia* (vol. 1) (Santa-Barbara, CA: ABL-CLIO).

Huntington, S. (1998) *The Clash of Civilizations and the Remaking of the World Order* (New York: Touchstone).

Ignazi, P. (2006) *Extreme Right Parties in Western Europe* (Oxford: Oxford University Press).

Korten, D.C. (2001) *When Corporations Rule the World* (San Francisco, CA: Kumarian Press).

Ledeen, M.A. (1972) *Universal Fascism: The Theory and Practice of the Fascist International, 1928–1936* (New York: Howard Fertig).

McCulloch, T. (2006) 'The Nouvelle Droite in the 1980s and 1990s: Ideology and entryism, the relationship with the Front National', *French Politics* 4 (2) (August), 158–78.

Macklin, G.D. (2005) 'Co-opting the counter culture: Troy Southgate and the national revolutionary faction', *Patterns of Prejudice* 39 (3), 301–26.

Mammone, A. (2007) 'The black-shirt resistance: Clandestine fascism in Italy, 1943–50', *The Italianist* 27, 282–303.

Mann, M. (2004) *Fascists* (Cambridge: Cambridge University Press).

Minkenberg, M. (2000) 'The renewal of the radical right: Between modernity and anti-modernity', *Government and Opposition* 35 (2), 170–88.

Mudde, C. (2004) 'Globalisation: The multi-faced enemy?', Melbourne, Australia: CERC Working Papers Series No. 3, pp. 1–22.

O'Sullivan, N. (1983) *Fascism* (London: J.M. Dent and Sons).

Payne, S. (1995) *A History of Fascism, 1919–1945* (London: UCL Press).

Piccone, P. (1993–4) 'Confronting the French New Right: Old prejudices or a new political paradigm?', *Telos* 98–99 (Winter–Spring), 3–23.

Raspail, J. (1994) *The Camp of the Saints* (trans. Norman Shapiro) (Petoskey, MI: The Social Contract Press).

Raspail, R. (2004) 'The fatherland betrayed by the republic', *Le Figaro* (17 June).

Sacchi, F. (1993–4) 'The Italian New Right', *Telos* 98–99 (Winter–Spring), 71–80.

Schain, M. (2006) 'The extreme-right and immigration policy-making: Measuring direct and indirect effects', *West European Politics* 29 (2) (March), 270–89.

Schmitt, C. (2002) 'Donoso Cortés: A pan-European interpretation' (Mark Grzeskowiak, trans.), *Telos* 125 (Fall), 100–15.

Spektorowski, A. (2000) 'Regionalism and the right: The case of France', *The Political Quarterly* 71 (3) (July), 352–61.

Spektorowski, A. (2003) 'Ethnoregionalism: The intellectual New Right and the Lega Nord', *The Global Review of Ethnopolitics* 3 (March), 55–70.

Sternhell, Z. (1994) *The Birth of the Fascist Ideology* (Princeton, NJ: Princeton University Press).

Sunic, T. (1990) *Against Democracy and Equality: The European New Right* (New York: Peter Lang).

Taggart, P. (2000) *Populism* (Philadelphia, PA: Open University Press).

Taguieff, P.-A. (1990) 'The new cultural racism in France', *Telos* 83 (Spring), 109–23.

Taguieff, P.-A. (1993–4) 'An interview with Pierre-André Taguieff', *Telos* 98–9 (Winter–Spring), 159–72.

Taguieff, P.-A. (1994) *Sur la nouvelle droite: jalons d'une analyse* (Paris: Descartes et Cie).

Talmon, J.L. (1952) *The Origins of Totalitarian Democracy* (London: Secker and Warburg).

Woods, Roger (2007) *Germany's New Right as Culture and Politics* (New York: Palgrave Macmillan).

5

GLOBALIZATION, CLASS CRISIS AND THE EXTREME RIGHT IN FRANCE IN THE NEW CENTURY

Gabriel Goodliffe

Nicolas Sarkozy's victory in the April 2007 French presidential election was widely touted in France and abroad as heralding the demise of the Front National (FN). Having obtained only 10.4 per cent of the vote and seen its electorate shrink by nearly a million votes compared to April 2002, the FN suffered its first electoral reversal in a presidential election and recorded its worst result since its initial breakthrough in the early 1980s. This slide appeared to be confirmed by the June 2009 European parliamentary elections, in which the party received only 6.3 per cent of the vote and garnered less than a third the number of votes it had obtained in the 2007 presidential election and more than half a million votes less than it had received in the previous European parliamentary election of 2004 (Abonneau 2010; Ministère de l'Intérieur 2011). According to many observers, these electoral results saw the 'crowding out' of the FN owing to the resumption of a traditional right-wing position by the mainstream French right, notably through Sarkozy's co-optation of the themes of restoring social order and controlling immigration. For them, the FN's electoral decline marked a return to the bi-partisan structure of political competition that it had obtained in France during the 1960s and 1970s, and that characterizes most other 'post-industrial' Western democracies. From this viewpoint, the FN was to be seen as essentially an aberration, a bad dream from which the country had (finally) roused itself as the 'normal' dynamics of electoral competition reasserted themselves and the extreme right was shut out of political contention.

The FN's electoral resurgence in the March 2010 regional elections and the March 2011 local elections has put paid to this optimistic prognosis.[1] Similarly, the emergence of Marine Le Pen as an able successor to her father as the party's leader, combined with her growing popularity in the run-up to the 2012 elections, appear to further confound predictions of the FN's passing.[2] Of course, such predictions are nothing new. Similar prognoses were ventured in the wake of the party's poor showing in the 1999 European parliamentary elections following the defection of Bruno Mégret, formerly Le Pen's closest lieutenant, that same year, as well as in 1988, when the FN's thirty MPs – elected thanks to the introduction of proportional representation in the run-up to the 1986 parliamentary elections – were wiped out owing to the re-establishment of majority voting by the new Chirac government. Much as with the 2007 electoral post-mortem, underlying these predictions was a reductive, monocausal bias that persisted in portraying the FN as a marginal anti-system protest party that was slated to disappear as the issues and concerns it had tapped into were addressed by the mainstream right.

A first raft of explanations settled around structural social and economic factors to explain the party's breakthrough in the early 1980s, focusing in particular on the coincidence of non-European immigration with rising unemployment in order to account for its burgeoning appeal among the autochthonous French population (Mayer 1989; Perrineau 1989). In turn, spatial electoral accounts portrayed the FN as having occupied the political space vacated by the mainstream right follow-ing the latter's attempt to secure the support of undecided voters (Ignazi 1992), while others conceived of the FN as a post-materialist political by-product of the country's transition from an industrial to a post-industrial society (Kitschelt 1995; Minkenberg 1998, 2000). Most recently, some scholars have moved away from these broad socio-structural and institutional explanations and focused instead on the party's internal discursive and organizational capacities in attracting discontented voters and transforming them into a loyal base of support. In particular, they analyse the FN's ability to disseminate its nativist ideology as a function of the persistence of a large non-European immigrant population in France as well as the pressures of global economic competition and European integration, thus restoring immigration to the fore of scholarly debate on the French and European extreme right (Mudde 2007).

These interpretations are not without their problems. At a socio-structural level, a direct causal link between such factors as immigration and unemployment on the one hand and support for the FN on the other is not so easily established. Most troubling for initial and recent immigration-based explanations, census figures show that the proportion of immigrants in the total French population has not substantially changed since the mid 1970s, invalidating the direct causal relationship inferred by many researchers between the FN's electoral breakthrough in the mid 1980s – that is, a full decade after the great immigration wave that was experienced by the country from 1956 to 1973.[3] Likewise, beyond the difficulty of empirically linking macroeconomic processes and the micro processes of electoral choice (Mudde 2007: 206–7), it is not clear why unemployment should have been of particular benefit to the FN as opposed to anti-system parties of the extreme left who explicitly campaigned on socio-economic issues.[4] At the very least, it seems that a crucial intervening variable – such as political culture – is missing in order to explain why people's real or perceived socio-economic distress would have driven them to vote for the FN.

In turn, similar problems plague the spatial and post-materialist politics inter-pretations of the rise and persistence of the latter. For one thing, as we have seen, these are unable to account for why far left or 'left libertarian' parties have failed to achieve the same level of popularity as the extreme right in France. More broadly, since the transition from an industrial to a post-industrial society is considered to hold similar political consequences across advanced capitalist countries, the question perforce arises of why extreme-right parties have failed to take root in a substantial number of them. Additionally, shunning the socio-structural and cultural context and focusing instead on the FN's discursive and organizational capabilities, internal 'supply side' explanations are unable to satisfactorily account for variations in the party's electoral fortunes over its thirty-seven-year history. Though the FN's organizational and propagandistic capacities were certainly not as evolved in the 1970s compared to what they would become in the 1980s and 1990s, it seems far-fetched to believe that the party's breakthrough and subsequent consolidation had nothing to do with the social costs engendered by the transformation of the French economy as a result of global competition and European integration.

Finally, and more broadly, these different accounts of the FN's evolution im-plicitly or explicitly view it as a historically discrete phenomenon reflecting political and economic conditions unique to late twentieth-century French politics and society. Though this is obviously true to a degree, it does not necessarily follow that we have nothing to learn from comparing the FN with previous formations of the French extreme right or from studying the sociopolitical conditions that respectively produced them. Indeed, far from representing a temporally circum-scribed phenomenon, the FN presents ideological and sociological likenesses with previous political movements and parties that highlight the continuing salience of certain social identities and interests that sustained the extreme right in France historically.

At an ideological level, the FN combines political anti-liberalism, in the guise of an exclusionary or 'ethnocentric' authoritarianism, with economic anti-liberalism, in the form of protectionism and 'welfare chauvinism' (Bastow 1997; Taguieff 1998). As such, it represents the latest incarnation of an extreme right–wing tradi-tion that first appeared in France at the end of the nineteenth century and then re-emerged during the inter-war period. (For contributions on the ideology of the FN, notably its adaptation of the discourse of the Nouvelle Droite and moulding of the French extreme right-wing ideology to post-war political realities, see the respective chapters by Bar-On and Wolfreys in the present volume.) At a socio-logical level, the FN has enlisted its principal support among those strata most threatened by the processes of economic and social modernization. Through the 1980s, these have included the traditional middle classes, the principal base of support for the extreme right historically. Composed of *petits indépendants* – shopkeepers, artisans, small family firm owners[5] – these strata saw their economic function increasingly displaced and material and social well-being progressively eroded as a result of the country's accelerating industrial and commercial rationalization throughout the post-war period. In turn, since the early 1990s, the FN has attracted significant support among industrial workers, so that by the end of the decade it had become the leading recipient of the French labour vote.[6] As in the case of the *petits indépendants*, the FN's newfound appeal among working-class voters coincided with the growing professional and socio-economic marginalization of the latter as a function of the spread of deindustrialization and intensifying international competition under the aegis of globalization.[7]

These social bases of support suggest that class appurtenance remains a crucial factor in accounting for the FN's political fortunes and that collective economic interests are better predictors of its performance than post-materialist issues and values. In the following, the class factors for the emergence of the FN will be analysed and the argument made that these obviate current predictions of the party's demise. First, it shall be shown that, as a function of the domestic and global dynamics of capitalist modernization, *petits indépendants* and industrial workers experienced worsening structural and cultural crises on which the FN was poised to capitalize. Second, it will be argued that these crises did not lessen under Sarkozy but, if anything, worsened the composition of his electoral coalition, making it near impossible for him to improve the situation of French *petits indépendants* and industrial workers while pursuing the agenda of economic reform and social deregulation on which he was elected. In short, it was premature to interpret the electoral reversal suffered by the FN in the 2007 presidential election as marking the end of the extreme right in France. Rather, on the eve of the 2012 election, the FN continued to fulfil the historical role of the latter as the principal political refuge for the 'losers' of economic and social modernity by harnessing the fears and frustrations of French middle- and working-class voters who have been adversely impacted by globalization.

Explaining the appeal of the FN – a structural and cultural analysis

The petit bourgeois–labour synthesis achieved by the FN can be explained in terms of the similar conditions of crisis to which *petits indépendants* and industrial workers have respectively found themselves exposed in advanced capitalist society. At a first level, this crisis is structural in nature, the result of the growing functional incongruity of *petits indépendants* and workers within the process of capitalist production and the consequent erosion of their economic and social position in modern society. At a second level, this crisis is also 'cultural', reflecting the sense of alienation felt by individual members of these groups within a society to whose dominant structures and values they are increasingly incapable of relating.[8] Such a subjective conception of crisis places the onus on understanding the cultural 'worldviews' of crisis-ridden *petits indépendants* and industrial workers. Most importantly, the norms and values they developed as a function of their respective roles in the economy and society on the one hand, and sociopolitical experiences – notably their relationship to the republican state – on the other, were key in shaping the nature and direction of their political radicalization. As the economic and social structures that underlay their sociocultural norms progressively eroded, and their needs and concerns went increasingly unaddressed by the French state, these groups fastened onto the FN's authoritarian and xenophobic message. By positing the return to an orderly and harmonious past, offering a powerful and exclusive basis of identity, and designating scapegoats on whom their decline could be blamed, the FN restored a sense of collective purpose to these structurally and culturally embattled constituencies. (For an analysis of the socio-psychological dynamics attending the identification of members of these groups with the extreme right, see the chapter by Birgitta Orfali in the present volume.)

Artisans, shopkeepers and small firm owners have constituted the principal source of support for extreme-right movements and parties in France historically. Up until the 'proletarianization' of the Front National during the 1990s, these strata have made up the bulk of support for the extreme right during the three periods in which it achieved its greatest support: the late 1880s through the 1890s, the inter-war period, and the 1980s. In addition, they fed movements of *petit bourgeois* protest such as the *Fédération des contribuables* in the 1930s, Pierre Poujade's *UDCA* in the 1950s, and the *CID-UNATI* and *SNPMI* in the 1970s and 1980s, whose anti-parliamentary activism and verbal violence dovetailed with the extreme right's own methods and rhetoric (Berger 1986: 232; Mayer 1984: 672; Milza 1987: 308).

At a structural level, *petits indépendants'* historic support for the extreme right reflected the combination of economic crises and technological and social changes that disproportionately impacted these strata from the end of the nineteenth century on. Even prior to their post-war decline, successive bursts of commercial and industrial concentration in the 1860s and 1870s and then after the First World War and through the 1920s ensured that traditional shopkeepers and artisans suffered most from the Depressions of the 1880s–90s and the 1930s. Yet it was in the post-war era, which presided over the most sweeping economic modernization and rationalization the country had experienced to date, that *petits indépendants* underwent their most significant economic and social decline. In the artisanal sector, the number of industrial firms counting from zero to four employees, excluding the commercial and service *artisanat* (bakers, butchers, café and restaurant owners etc.) fell from 757,000 in 1954 to 533,000 in 1975, a roughly 30 per cent decline. In turn, following a temporary resurgence in the late 1970s, the number of artisanal enterprises (excluding the commercial *artisanat*) fell from 584,000 in 1983 to 547,000 in 1998 (Estrade and Missègue 2000: 160; Mayer 1984: 96, 108–9, 111). This dynamic of concentration was even more pronounced in the commercial sector. The spread of supermarkets and *hypermarchés* precipitated a rapid decline in the number of shopkeepers (including family aides) from 1,252,000 in 1954 to 913,000 in 1975, a fall of 27 per cent (Mayer 1984: 96). In turn, after remaining basically constant in the 1980s, this decline resumed in the 1980s, the number of *commerçants* (including family aides) falling to 621,000 in 2001 (Blanpain and Rouault 2002: 428). In short, by the close of the twentieth century *petits indépendants* had gone from constituting the dominant economic and social actors in the country to representing a dying breed in post-war French society. Incapable of competing with more concentrated forms of production and commerce, they became more and more vulnerable to economic crisis and hence, a significant potential reservoir of political discontent.

At the same time, the transformation of production and the social changes it heralded contributed to a crisis of identity among *petits indépendants*. The cultural model of *indépendance* which they historically evolved as a function of their simultaneous roles as small property owners and workers rendered them particularly ill-suited to the principles and processes of modern industrial capitalism. Enshrining the ideals of economic autonomy, craftsmanship and the familial working of property, this cultural model translated into an 'archeo-liberal' or 'Malthusian' economic mindset dramatically at odds with the imperatives of rationality and efficiency that underlay advanced industrial production (Mayer 1984: Part II). Similarly, this model of *indépendance* implied a paternalistic and repressive morality which condemned the consumerism, loose mores, and cultural pluralism of modern society, calling instead for the return to a traditional disciplined and homogeneous social order.

One cannot but be struck by the commonalities between *petits indépendants'* sociocultural model of *indépendance* on the one hand, and the discourse of the extreme right on the other. Both place the same emphasis on the family as the fundamental social unit at the centre of their respective worldviews. Each professes a common attachment to an 'archeo-liberal' conception of economics based on the sanctity of private property, loyal competition and limited state intervention. Finally, each posits a traditionalist ethic and rigorist morality while evincing a common aversion to modern industrial society. In many ways, the cultural model of *petits indépendants* and the discourse of the extreme right reflect one another, explaining the frequency with which the former have identified with the latter since the late nineteenth century.

In turn, at the level of their cumulative political experience, the primordial republicanism of *petits indépendants*, rooted in a small-property-based conception of society and democracy, increasingly put them into conflict with the process of capitalist modernization and the republican state charged with overseeing it. As this process progressed and *petits indépendants* saw their influence over the representative and administrative instances of the state erode vis-à-vis rival socio-economic interests, their hostility grew towards the institutions and personnel of the republican state. These were seen to have betrayed the primordial republican compact according to which, in exchange for their support, small producers and traders enjoyed the state's protection (Barral 1968). Thus, *petits indépendants* grew increasingly resentful of policies that ran counter to their interests, and this sometimes boiled over into a wholesale rejection of the republican regime and liberal democracy.

As the cultural crisis afflicting *petits indépendants* worsened and their ambivalence towards the republican state and democracy grew, the extreme right – most recently under the auspices of the Front National – was well placed to harness their anxieties and frustrations. It affirmed the economic, social and moral primacy of the ideal of *morcellement* which underpinned the cultural and political worldview of *petits indépendants*, investing it with a primal conception of communal identity and identifying the 'anti-French' agents on whom their decline could be blamed. By replicating the tropes of *indépendance* and casting them in terms of an exclusive collective appurtenance, the extreme right shored up *petits indépendants'* social identity and held out the reassuring – if illusory – prospect of escaping the passage from an early to an advanced capitalist society.

Up to this point, the analysis has focused on *petits indépendants* as the historic wellspring of the extreme right. This pattern held through the 1980s, in which they outstripped every other constituency in their support for the Front National. However, from the early 1990s on, a seminal shift occurred in the composition of the party's electorate as *petits indépendants* were supplanted by industrial workers as its principal base of support. This would suggest that the social situation of French workers over the last quarter century also needs to be taken into account. In particular, we need to explain how the FN came to eclipse the Communist Party (PCF) as the leading recipient of working class votes during this period.

This shift of French workers to the extreme right has gone hand in hand with the profound social crisis that has engulfed the working class as a result of the far-reaching transformation of the French economy since the late 1970s and early 1980s. As in the case of *petits indépendants*, this crisis presents both structural and cultural dimensions. In the first place, it reflects the deteriorating socio–economic situation of French workers as a function of the growth of manufacturing unemployment and the consequent erosion of workers' living standards over the past quarter century. After spiking at 12.5 per cent in 1995, by the turn of the millennium the country faced an aggregate unemployment rate of between 9 per cent and 10 per cent. Industrial workers were hit harder than any other occupational group, unemployment peaking among them at nearly 16 per cent (versus 14.4 per cent for service sector *employés*, the second-worst affected group) in March 1997. Worst affected were unskilled workers who were also most likely to be unemployed the longest (Amossé and Chardon 2002: 216; Gonzalez-Demichel *et al.* 2002: 178). In turn, partly as a result of the effect of higher unemployment, the living standards of French workers declined dramatically beginning in the 1980s. Assuming a median income level of 100 for the workforce as a whole, the average yearly salary of French workers fell from 79 in 1983 to 76 in 1991. And despite a slight improvement during the second half of the 1990s, this rise was offset by the loss of earnings occasioned by the increase in worker unemployment, particularly among younger workers (Chenu 1993: 482; Chevalier *et al.* 2005: 448–9).

The rise of worker unemployment and deterioration of workers' incomes over the last quarter century can be largely attributed to the campaign of *déplanification* and deregulation that was pursued by the French state in order to meet the challenge of intensifying global competition and prepare the country for European Monetary Union. At the macroeconomic level, this entailed privatizing nationally owned firms or subjecting them to market competition, while discarding the Keynesian emphasis on growth and full employment in favour of monetarist policies to maintain the country in the European Monetary System and make it attractive to foreign investment (Levy 2005: 105). At the microeconomic level, price, wage and credit controls were lifted, restrictions on layoffs and temporary and part-time employment were eased, and work safety laws and worker participation rules were ignored in order to force businesses to reduce their labour costs (Beaud and Pialoux 1999: 423–4; Cézard and Dussert 1993). The resulting wage de-indexation and subsequent efforts by firms to maximize profits by cutting labour costs significantly eroded workers' living standards during the 1980s and 1990s. At the same time, greater flexibility in hiring and firing opened the door to mass layoffs and increased the capacity of employers to drive down wages. Finally, the dramatic increase in capital flows, combined with access to cheap labour and minimal taxation and regulation abroad, accelerated the outsourcing of French manufacturing. In short, coinciding with the country's deindustrialization and its shift to a services-based economy, the economic liberalization of the 1980s and 1990s underscored the functional redundancy of French workers in the new, 'post-industrial' economy. It spelled the end of the Fordist compromise that, built on the 'virtuous cycle of mass consumption fueling mass production', had underpinned the post-war social contract and guaranteed lifetime employment, improving living standards, and comprehensive social protections and benefits to French workers (Howell 1992: 71).

However, as in the case of the *petits indépendants*, this crisis of the French working class cannot be apprehended at a purely structural, socio-economic level. It is also cultural in nature, reflecting the profound crisis of identity afflicting growing numbers of French workers as well as the erosion of the principal 'loci' or institutions that reproduced and sustained that identity. Posited in contradistinction to the onerous conditions of industrial labour within capitalist society, industrial workers staked out an oppositional collective identity based on the affirmation of class consciousness and solidarity (Verret 1996: 185). The two institutions that sustained this class identity historically were the trade unions – especially the Confédération générale du travail (CGT) and, to a lesser degree, the Confédération française démocratique du travail (CFDT) – and the Communist Party. These organizations served complementary roles as socializing agents for the French working class. By respectively defending their interests in the workplace and the political arena, the unions and PCF strove to improve workers' social and political standing in French society and made it possible for them to occupy economic, political, social and cultural fields of activity from which they had been formerly excluded. Thus, they served as ideological and cultural agents of class consciousness, imbuing French workers with an interpretive framework by which to apprehend and relate to the broader society while impressing upon them the sense of belonging to a historically foreordained and normatively superior collectivity.[9]

At the same time, despite their oppositional – and in the case of the PCF and CGT, ostensibly revolutionary – vocations, these institutions reconciled the French working class to capitalism and liberal democracy. The trade unions facilitated informal, firm-level negotiations and conflict resolution in the workplace, a role that was substantially reinforced by the creation of *comités d'entreprise* (CEs) after the Second World War and the mandating of union representation in the latter following the 1968 Grenelle Accords. For its part, the PCF served an essential 'tribunary function' that served to co-opt French workers into the parliamentary process. By providing a source of catharsis that allowed them to vent their economic and political frustrations, the PCF fulfilled the workers' need 'for a dream, a utopia, for radical solutions' while limiting its expression to the ballot box (Lavau 1981: 36). In this sense, by the end of the *trente glorieuses*, the labour movement and PCF had become crucial agents of social and political stability within the country.

The transformation of the French economy since the 1970s has eroded these twin loci of working-class socialization and identification. From a peak of 35 per cent in 1949, the unionization rate inexorably declined to 24 per cent in 1970, 19 per cent in 1980, 11 per cent in 1990, and only 8 per cent in 2003 (Andolfatto 2005: 232; Labbé 1996: 132). Similarly, the PCF vote in successive parliamentary elections (held to constitute the truest barometer of voters' political beliefs) fell from nearly 50 per cent in the early 1950s to 24 per cent in 1981, 14 per cent in 1993, 6 per cent in 2002, and a lowly 2.5 per cent in 2007 (CEVIPOF 2007; Mayer and Cautrès 2004: 150–2; Verret 1996: 235). At one level, the decline in the unionization rate and communist vote reflects the process of deindustrialization and shift to a service economy whereby industrial workers went from representing roughly four in ten members of the total workforce in the late 1960s and early 1970s to less than one in three in the late 1990s (Mayer 1996: 111). Yet deindustrialization cannot be the sole nor even the principal explanation for the decline of the unions and PCF, since the proportional fall in their memberships has far outstripped the decline in the size of the working-class population over the past quarter century. Equally important has been the fundamental transformation of industrial production since the 1970s, which obliterated the socio-structural conditions that had formerly facilitated worker organization in the workplace. The increasing unwieldiness of large productive units in the global economy, combined with the individualization of consumer tastes in advanced industrial society, encouraged a movement away from the highly concentrated and rigidly organized factories of the Fordist era. This development heralded the arrival of diffuse or flexible factories featuring unparalleled automation and organized according to adaptable flow-process models of production, a reliance on just-in-time inputs and outputs, greater subcontracting of productive tasks, and increasingly sophisticated monitoring of worker performance (Beaud and Pialoux 1999: Ch. 1; Bihr 1990: 8–15). These new methods and technologies have profoundly impacted the industrial workforce, devaluing unskilled labour in the new 'post-industrial' economy and greatly reducing the need for the kinds of workers who comprised the bulk of the manufacturing labour force under Fordism. Consequently, industrial employment has become much more insecure and contingent, with atypical forms of employment, such as part-time and short-term contracts, increasing dramatically among these workers (Capdevielle 2001: 23).

Third, this transformation of productive structures and processes has been supported by a juridical framework that codified the shift to more flexible, adaptive modes of production. Legislation such as the Auroux Laws, which gave firm-level labour contracts priority over branch and national contracts, and the 35-hour work week, have substantially enhanced the leverage of employers over their workers. Combined with the abrogation of wage indexation, the exemption of firm-level contracts from the minimum wage and lackadaisical enforcement of worker participation and safety rules, the cumulative effect of this legislation has been a labour market reform 'equivalent to a particularly brutal form of flexibility' (Beaud and Pialoux 1999: 422–4; Howell 1992: 87, 90).

The transformation of production within the firm and corresponding development of an enabling legal framework to increase labour market flexibility had the effect of fracturing the industrial workforce and eroding the solidarities that had bound workers to a shared collective identity and purpose. Growing numbers of them were unable to recognize themselves in trade unions and a Communist Party that had appealed historically to the Fordist 'labour aristocracy' concentrated in large factories and traditional heavy industry.[10] Their ephemeral professional competencies and identities, not to mention heightened professional and material vulnerability, effectively precluded their identifying with one another or risking losing what employment they did have by seeking to organize economically and politically. From this standpoint, the process of capitalist restructuring during the 1980s and 1990s induced a profound crisis of representation within the unions and PCF. As these institutions which had sustained their class identity for the greater part of a century grew increasingly powerless to redress their grievances, French workers sought out new sources of identification with which to replace them.

In short, deprived of their traditional corporative and collective markers of identity and viewing the unions and the Left as unwilling or unable to defend their social *acquis*, French workers turned in growing numbers to the Front National. As in the case of *petits indépendants* before them, the FN crystallized their fears and resentments, identifying recent immigrants as ready scapegoats on whom they could blame their social and economic decline. At the same time, it offered the countervailing myth of a 'pure' or 'authentic' France in which workers remained secure as producers and vital to the economic and social life of the nation. This positing of a primordial France was coupled with policy proposals specifically designed to appeal to a working-class audience. These included 'welfare-chauvinist' measures that promised to improve the material situation of French workers while threatening to repatriate the non-European immigrants who competed for jobs and benefits with them (Bastow 1998). As their class consciousness and the institutions that sustained it dissolved, the exclusionary conception of national identity cultivated by the FN became a ready basis of identification for growing numbers of French workers on the eve of the twenty-first century.

The French extreme right under the Sarkozy presidency

Nicolas Sarkozy's election in April 2007, based in large part on the support of former Le Pen voters, appeared to mark the electoral unravelling of the FN or at least to herald its definitive ebb. Many of these voters issued from the ranks of *petits indépendants* and industrial workers, the party's principal class constituencies, suggesting that its appeal among the 'losers' of modernization and globalization was eroding (Mayer 2007: 436–7; Strudel 2007: 461). In retrospect, much more caution was warranted in interpreting these results. The FN continued to account for roughly four million votes and some of its ideas, particularly the conflation of immigration, criminality, and Islam, remained broadly accepted beyond its own electorate. Similarly, there were good short-term political as well as longer-term economic reasons to doubt that Sarkozy – or, for that matter, his opponents on the Left – would be able to successfully resolve the profound social crisis that had fuelled the party's ascendancy in the first place.

Politically, the divergent bases of Sarkozy's electoral coalition have made it exceedingly difficult for him not to disappoint erstwhile FN voters while catering to the other interests that helped to get him elected. On the one hand, second-round Sarkozy voters who first cast their ballots for the centrist François Bayrou tended to be much more culturally liberal and socially tolerant than FN voters, who presented the highest indices for intolerance, ethnocentrism, and repressiveness of any segment of the electorate (Mayer 2007: 443). From this standpoint, initiatives to crack down on immigration or that singled immigrants out as a foreign and nefarious presence in French society – the attempt to institute DNA testing as a precondition for reuniting immigrant families; the inauguration of a 'debate' on immigration and nationality; proposals to strip immigrants or their children who are convicted of certain crimes of the French nationality and to create a probationary period during which the nationality of naturalized immigrants could be revoked; the banning of the burqa and niqab in public spaces; the stepping up of deportations of *sans papiers* – was always likely to drive a rift between the more liberal and repressive wings of Sarkozy's electorate (Nau 2007; Weil 2010; Lichfield 2010). On the other hand, potential conflicts loom between many Sarkozy voters and *lepéno-sarkozystes* over economic issues. The economic liberalism of Sarkozy voters who were linked to the advanced sectors of the French economy was always likely to clash with the traditional *petits patrons* and working-class voters he managed to siphon off from the FN. In particular, the new government's liberalization agenda, which is supported by the former and aims to reduce the fiscal burden on French firms and the wealthy by shifting a part of their social security obligations to consumers through a *TVA sociale*, increasing the *bouclier fiscal* (the proportion of total income not subject to taxation), and raising the retirement age for public sector workers in line with those of the private sector, is sure to clash with the welfarist proclivities of many erstwhile FN voters and Bayrouistes (Mayer 2007: 443–4; Monnier 2009).

Sarkozy has so far proven unsuccessful in his bid to satisfy these different constituencies and to pursue his mandate of economic reform while trying to keep erstwhile Le Pen voters 'on side'. This failure is borne out by his party's poor showing in the 2010 regional and 2011 local elections, which marked the return to the FN of large numbers of *déçus du sarkozysme* (Abonneau 2010; Abonneau 2011).

In turn and perhaps more significantly, the longer-term transformation of the French economy as a result of globalization has intensified the structural and cultural crises that fuelled the FN's rise in the first place. In order to remain internationally competitive, the country has been forced to continue pursuing policies of market liberalization and price deflation, while dismantling the costly 'social anesthesia state' put in place in the 1980s and 1990s to dampen the pain of *déplanification* (Levy 2005). Accordingly, Sarkozy's advocacy of limited trade protections and capital controls in order to safeguard French jobs – notwithstanding the fact that they would require overturning the current EU trade and financial regimes – would most likely backfire in an integrated global marketplace in which French firms have increasingly outsourced their operations and French consumers have grown dependent on cheap consumer durables from outside the EU (Lemaître 2007). Furthermore, the policies of budgetary austerity to which the country has pledged itself in order to defend its participation in the euro in the wake of the European sovereign debt crisis of 2010–11 is likely to prolong and deepen the socio-economic crisis afflicting a growing segment of the French population, in particular industrial workers and an expanding swathe of the middle class, as a result of the global recession that began in 2009.

From this standpoint, the austerity package proposed in August 2011 by the Fillon government, which seeks to reduce government expenditures by €1 billion in 2011 and €11 billion in 2012, is set to accelerate the course of fiscal retrenchment and state disengagement from the provision of social services that was embarked upon by Sarkozy following his election, and which is bound to disproportionately affect those hardest hit by the economic and social crisis (*Le Monde* [online] 2011a; Kahn 2011: 24). Finally, and more generally, by disarticulating the workplace and eroding its associated social identities on an unprecedented scale, the sweeping socio-structural changes wrought by globalization have begun to threaten formerly unaffected professional and social groups, including service-sector employees, members of the 'intermediary' professions, and even the previously secure category of *cadres* (Capdevielle 2001: 171).[11] Like *petits indépendants* and industrial workers before them, these new losers from globalization are also likely to latch onto the forceful and exclusionary forms of sociopolitical identity that held out by the extreme right. From this standpoint, the reversal suffered by the FN in the 2007 presidential and 2009 European parliamentary elections appear to represent only a temporary setback for the latter in France, rather than an irreversible defeat.

By the same token, speculation that the party would not survive the passing of its founder from the political stage has not been borne out. In January 2011, the reins of the party leadership were successfully transferred to Marine Le Pen without provoking the internecine divisions that had been predicted. She has shown herself to be a strategically adroit and media-savvy politician, marrying a discourse advocating economic interventionism and protectionism in order to comfort those hardest hit by globalization with the party's traditional appeals to limiting immigration, suppressing crime and asserting *la préférence nationale* as a basis for directing state services and social spending.[12] This discourse is presented in a more palatable guise, shorn of the rhetorical *dérapages* in which her father regularly indulged. In particular, Le Pen *fille* has publicly disavowed the anti-Semitic outbursts that characterized the FN's propaganda in the past, and she even appears at times to soft-pedal its anti-immigration programme. The latter is no longer presented under the light of racial *différencialisme* but instead as a practical necessity imposed by the burdens of globalization as well as in defence of the foundational republican principle of *laïcité*. Through this attempt to normalize the party by curbing its rhetorical excesses and resituating it in the French republican tradition – a strategy facilitated by President Sarkozy's own willingness to play on the issue of immigration for electoral gain and tie it, as the FN has since its inception, to the themes of criminality and *délinquance* – Marine Le Pen has sought to move the FN beyond the status of anti-system or protest party that was formerly embraced by her father and to recast it as a responsible *parti de gouvernement*.[13] When combined with her full-throated defence of French industry and state intervention in the face of the worsening economic and social crisis, it is no wonder that, given this new veneer of respectability, nearly half – 42 per cent – of French workers claimed in June 2011 that they would vote for Marine Le Pen in the upcoming presidential election – double the proportion attained by any of the prospective Socialist candidates (Dély 2011).[14]

In sum, the present resurgence of the FN, as well as its initial breakthrough and entrenchment over the past quarter century, suggest that the break-up of the Fordist economic and social model has had a particularly profound impact in France, where it has proved more politically destabilizing than elsewhere in Europe, let alone the US. Capitalizing on the fears and uncertainties raised by the new post-Fordist economic realities, the FN has succeeded in combining the extreme right's age-old appeal among *petits indépendants* with a politics of 'welfare chauvinism' directed to the working class. Accordingly, it has accomplished what its predecessors on the extreme right could only dream of: forging an alliance between the *petite bourgeoisie* and the working class to combat the evils of monopoly capitalism and socialist collectivism on the one hand and bring about purification and renewal of the nation on the other.[15] More broadly, deepening economic globalization and the corresponding failure of the country's political elites to alleviate the social crisis currently engulfing these strata would suggest that, over the medium to long term, there is little to keep growing numbers of working- and middle-class voters from gravitating to the FN or a similar successor. On the contrary, the extreme right is likely to remain the principal refuge for the losers of globalization in France for the time to come.

Notes

1 After obtaining 11.4 per cent of the vote in the first round of balloting in the 2010 regional elections, the FN garnered an average of 17 per cent in the twelve three-way races in which its candidates were involved during the second round, recording its strongest performance in such an election since 2004. Suggesting that the party may be recovering the electoral ground it had lost in 2007, the party achieved its highest scores in its traditional southern and eastern strongholds (recording a high of 22.9 per cent in Provence-Alpes-Côte d'Azur), as well as in the Nord-Pas-de-Calais (22.2 per cent), where Jean-Marie Le Pen's daughter Marine headed the party list. In turn, in the 2011 local elections, the FN won 15.6 per cent of the vote in the first round – a 3 per cent increase from the 2004 local elections. And although the party won only two seats and 12 per cent of the national vote in the second round of voting, in the 403 cantons in which its candidates acceded to the run-off, it achieved an average electoral score of 40 per cent. Most disquieting about these results was that the FN's progression was not limited to its traditional electoral bastions of the northeast, Rhône-Alpes and Mediterranean coast, but could also be seen in western, more rural areas of the country that had historically been impervious to its entreaties (Perrault 2010; Piquard 2011; *Economist* [online] 2011b; *Le Monde* [online] 2011b).

2 Indeed, a growing number of French political pundits have begun to view Le Pen *fille* as a viable candidate for the 2012 presidential election, particularly in the wake of a series of opinion surveys in the spring and summer of 2011 which had her receiving between 19 per cent and 24 per cent of the vote in the first round, sufficient to finish ahead of Mr Sarkozy and, in some scenarios, the Socialist Party candidate as well (*The Economist* 2011c; Chrisafis 2011). This has prompted fears of a repeat of the nightmare scenario of April 2002, whereby she might be able to capitalize on a divided field of candidates on the Right in order to accede to the second round run-off (*The Economist* [online] 2011a; Laurent and Nunès 2011). Even in the wake of the July 2011 Utøya massacre and Oslo bombing by a right-wing extremist which cast a new pall on extreme right-wing parties throughout Europe – a perception made worse by comments on the part of an FN committee member as well as her father that Norway's immigration policies were fundamentally to blame for the massacre – as of September 2011 20 per cent of the electorate continues to back her for president (as measured by the criterion of 'hoping to see her play an important political role in the months and years ahead'), enough for her to still accede to the second round run-off in the 2012 presidential elections according to certain electoral scenarios (TNS-Sofres 2011).

3 Census figures indicate that the proportion of immigrants in the total population remained essentially steady at 7.4 per cent of the total population from 1975 to 1999. Interestingly, the previous period of large-scale immigration, lasting through the 1920s and reaching a peak of 6.6 per cent of the population in 1931, also failed to coincide with the surge in the political strength of the extreme right. It was only during the following decade, as immigration rates paradoxically fell off, that movements of the extreme right gained political traction (Daguet and Thave 1996; Barou 2005).

4 The combined score of 10.5 per cent attained by the Trotskyist party candidates in the first round of the 2002 elections, followed by the mass mobilization of left-wing voters to help defeat the referendum on the EU Constitution in May 2005, appeared to suggest that a substantial movement was constituting itself on the far left in France, and that such a movement might provide a durable alternative source of political identification for the 'losers' of globalization to the FN. However, successive electoral declines recorded in the 2007 presidential race, 2009 European elections, 2010 regional elections, and 2011 local elections, punctuated by factional divisions among and within the various left-wing parties, raised doubts about the sustained electoral viability of this alternative and its ability to contest the extreme right's influence among these voters over the longer term (Wolfreys 2008: 71, 72–5, 79–80; Zappi 2009; Ministère de l'Intérieur 2011).

5 These strata are distinct from other socio-professional categories in that they denote individuals who simultaneously own and 'work' their instruments of production. According to François Gresle:

> Notwithstanding agricultural producers, *indépendants* can be defined as non-salaried producers registered with the board of commerce, the board of trades or both, who exercise on their own account an artisanal or commercial profession, employ a restricted number of salaried workers, and personally control the finances and manage the affairs of their businesses.
>
> (Gresle 1980: 227)

6 The party polled 17 per cent of the shopkeeper and artisan vote in the 1984 European elections (versus 9 per cent for workers), a proportion that nearly doubled to 31 per cent in the 1988 presidential election (versus 16 per cent for workers). From thereon in, the proportion of *petits indépendants* who voted for the FN remained constant at around 20 per cent, while the percentage of workers who did so dramatically increased – attaining a high of 30 per cent in the 1995 presidential election – before levelling off at around 25 per cent by the end of the 1990s and early 2000s (Perrineau 1997: 102; 2002: 210).

7 The political provenance of working class support for the FN has been the subject of some debate. While some have argued that it was mostly constituted of former left-wing voters (Perrineau 1997: 108–10, 218–19), others have contended that the proletarianization of the FN vote is the expression of the broader depoliticization of French workers (Mayer 2002: 98–103, 124–6). Both of these views, however, are compatible with the argument that is advanced below: that this upsurge in worker support for the party coincided with the collapse of the Communist Party and union movement as the historic vehicles of political socialization and acculturation of the French working class – regardless of whether these new FN voters had actually voted on the left in the past.

8 This conception of cultural crisis implies a general dislocation of the individual's perspectives on the world and a fundamental questioning of his or her place and significance within it. It helps to explain how, as a function of their culturally defined social identities and outlooks, members of 'anti-modern' social groups conceive and react to their increasingly unsustainable economic role and marginal social position in advanced capitalist society (Bihr 1998: Ch. 4; Lecœur 2003: Ch. 8).

9 Writing with respect to the Communist Party, Marc Lazar places particular emphasis on the deliberate nature of this project:

> pursued by leaders at all levels of the party . . . to diffuse the ideology, mould the imaginary and mythical representations, define the collective beliefs, impose the values, organise the distribution of material and symbolic rewards, determine what in the past could be useful in advancing [workers'] immediate interests, [and] elaborate the representations of a [working class] social and cultural milieu, in order to found a properly French communist tradition.
>
> (Lazar 1994: 16)

10 It is no surprise that the socializing institutions of the working class – and the strong sense of class consciousness they instilled among their members – were most deeply ingrained in traditional heavy industrial sectors such as mining, steel, and metallurgy whose workers were subject to a highly uniform experience of work, greatly facilitating their socialization by the unions and the *PCF*.

11 This is suggested by the fact that, as of June 2011, service sector employees (*employés*) had overtaken *petits indépendants* as the socio-professional category most likely to vote for Marine Le Pen after industrial workers, with 35 per cent of *employés* surveyed saying they would cast their vote for her versus 30 per cent for shopkeepers and artisans and 42 per cent for industrial workers (Weill 2011; Dély 2011).

12 Of particular note has been Marine Le Pen's advocacy of reinforcing the tutelary economic role and welfarist capacities of the state in order to assist those Frenchmen (defined

according to the exclusionary criteria of national preference) hardest hit by the current economic crisis, as well as her advocacy of pulling France out of the euro and readopting the franc as a means of reasserting the country's economic sovereignty and autonomy in dealing with external economic disruptions. In this way, she has been able to present the FN as the only major French political party opposed to the process of European integration, which she in turn portrays as a project of economic liberalization of benefit to the country's financial elites and the politicians who defend them while condemning France's industrial base and public sector – and the millions of industrial workers, *employés* and *fonctionnaires* who depend on them – to economic and social oblivion (Fay 2011; Kahn 2011).

13 The extent of this shift must not be exaggerated, however. Anti-immigrant and particularly anti-Islamic racism and xenophobia still occasionally show through the new FN chief's rhetoric. (See, for example, her comparison of mosques spilling their faithful into the street in some cities during Friday prayers to the Nazi Occupation of the Second World War, or her assertion that the serving of hamburgers made from *halal* meat in some immigrant neighbourhoods by the Quick fast-food chain is tantamount to the 'Islamization' of the country.) This in turn raises the question of the intentionality of such slippages. Specifically, such expressions of anti-Muslim xenophobia can be seen to assume the symbolically mobilizing role that anti-Semitism used to play in the FN's discourse by signalling to the party's ideologically committed core of activists that it has not abandoned them, while simultaneously presenting a euphemized discourse to the broader public and portraying itself as a potential party of government. On this dualistic rhetorical strategy developed by the FN in targeting different components of its electorate, see Fysh and Wolfreys 1998: 107–8.

14 Other surveys, though less stark in recording this upsurge of working class support for the FN's new leader, nevertheless underscored the substantial inroads achieved by the party among those groups most threatened by economic and social upheaval. For example, another survey from May 2011 recorded that between 24 per cent and 29 per cent of industrial workers would vote for Marine Le Pen in the upcoming presidential election followed by 22 per cent to 23 per cent of service sector workers (*employés*), an increase of 8–13 per cent and 10–11 per cent respectively for each of these categories compared to the 2007 presidential election (Abonneau 2011; Mayer 2007: 436). Confirmation of this trend was also to be seen in the geographic distribution of the vote in the 2010 regional and 2011 local elections, the FN achieving its best results in the north and northeast, the Rhône valley, the Mediterranean coast, and the greater Paris periphery, the areas hardest hit by deindustrialization, unemployment and poverty (Abonneau 2010; 2011).

15 The substantial working-class support garnered by the *Front National* since the late 1980s marks the first time an extreme right-wing party has been able to garner a significant following among French workers since the late nineteenth century, when large numbers of them turned out for General Boulanger. Yet, whereas *boulangisme*'s hold on workers failed to outlast the 1885–90 election cycle, the FN has been able to sustain its working-class support for nearly two decades, underscoring its ability to harness the anxieties and resentments of a working class hard-hit by economic restructuring and deprived of its traditional corporative and partisan attachments.

References

Abonneau, J. 2010. 'Front national: un regain de vitalité fragile', *Le Figaro*, 4 May: 18.
—— . 2011. 'Front national: un retour en force?', *Le Figaro*, 29 March: 18.
Amossé, T. and O. Chardon. 2002. 'La carte des professions (1982–1999): le marché du travail par le menu', in *Données sociales: La société française 2002–2003*. Paris: INSEE, pp. 1–4.
Andolfatto, D. 2005. 'Syndicalisme', in S. Cordellier and E. Lau (eds) *L'État de la France 2005–2006: Un panorama unique et complet de la France*. Paris: La Découverte, pp. 231–4.

Barou, J. 2005. 'Immigration. Grandes tendances', in S. Cordellier and E. Lau (eds) *L'État de la France 2005–2006: Un panorama unique et complet de la France*. Paris: La Découverte, pp. 39–40.

Barral, P. ed. 1968. *Les fondateurs de la Troisième république*. Paris: Armand Colin.

Bastow, S. 1997. 'Front National economic policy: From neo-liberalism to protectionism', *Modern and Contemporary France* 5(1): 61–72.

——— . 1998. 'The radicalisation of Front National discourse: A politics of the "Third Way"?', *Patterns of Prejudice* 32(3): 55–68.

Beaud, S. and M. Pialoux. 1999. *Retour sur la condition ouvrière: Enquête aux usines Peugeot de Sochaux-Montbéliard*. Paris: Fayard.

Berger, S. 1986. 'The socialists and the *patronat*: The dilemmas of coexistence in a mixed economy', in H. Machin and V. Wright (eds) *Economic Policy-Making under the Mitterrand Presidency*. London: Frances Pinter, pp. 225–44.

Bihr, A. 1990. 'La fragmentation du prolétariat', *L'Homme et la société* 24(4): 5–20.

——— . 1998. *Actualité d'un archaïsme: La pensée d'extrême droite et la crise de la modernité*. Lausanne: Page Deux.

Blanpain, N. and D. Rouault. 2002. 'Les indépendants et dirigeants dans les années quatre-vingt-dix', *Données sociales: La société française 2002–2003*. Paris: INSEE, pp. 427–38.

Capdevielle, J. 2001. *Modernité du corporatisme*. Paris: Presses de Sciences Po.

CEVIPOF. 2007. 'Résultats des élections législatives des 10 et 17 juin', *Baromètre politique français. Elections 2007* [online]. Available from: www.cevipof.msh-paris.fr/bpf/index.htm, accessed March 2011.

Cézard, M. and F. Dussert. 1993. 'Le travail ouvrier sous contrainte', *Données sociales 1993*. Paris: INSEE, pp. 202–11.

Chenu, A. 1993. 'Une classe ouvrière en crise', *Données sociales 1993*. Paris: INSEE, pp. 476–85.

Chevalier, P., O. Guillemin, A. Lapinte and J.-P. Lorgnet. 2005. 'Les évolutions du niveau de vie entre 1970 et 2002', *Données Sociales 2006*. Paris: INSEE, pp. 445–59.

Chrisafis, A. 2011. 'Marine Le Pen emerges from father's shadow', *The Guardian* [online]. Available from: www.guardian.co.uk/world/2011/mar/21/marine-lepen-defends-republic, accessed March 2011.

Daguet, F. and S. Thave. 1996. 'La population immigrée. Le résultat d'une longue histoire', *INSEE Première* 458: 1–4.

Dély, R. 2011. 'Dossier: Pourquoi elle est si dangereuse; Un défi pour la gauche', *Le Nouvel Observateur*, 23 June: 59.

The Economist. 2011a. 'France's far right: A respectable front' [online]. Available from: www.economist.com/node/17905837?story_id=17905837, accessed January 2011.

The Economist. 2011b. 'French politics: Giving the UMP the hump' [online]. Available from www.economist.com/node/18485957?story_id=18485957, accessed May 2011.

The Economist. 2011c. 'France's Far Right: They can't keep her down', March 19: 59–60.

Estrade, M.-A. and N. Missègue. 2000. 'Se mettre à son compte et rester indépendant: Des logiques différentes pour les artisans et les indépendants des services', *Économie et statistique* 337–8: 159–81.

Fay, S. 2011. 'Dossier: Pourquoi elle est si dangereuse: Si Marine Le Pen prenait Bercy', *Le Nouvel Observateur*, 23 June: 66–7.

Fysh, P. and J. Wolfreys. 1998. *The Politics of Racism in France*. London: Macmillan.

Gonzalez-Demichel, C., E. Nauze-Fichet and S. Seguin. 2002. 'Les performances du marché du travail au tournant du XXIe siècle', *Données sociales 2002–2003*. Paris: INSEE, pp. 173–81.

Gresle, F. 1980. 'Indépendants et petits patrons: pérennité et transformation d'une classe sociale', Ph.D. dissertation, Université de Lille III.

Howell, C. 1992. 'The dilemmas of post-Fordism: Socialists, flexibility and labour market deregulation in France', *Politics and Society* 20(1): 71–99.

Ignazi, P. 1992. 'The silent counter-revolution: Hypothesis on the emergence of extreme right-wing parties in Europe', *European Journal of Political Research* 22(1): 3–34.

Kahn, J.-F. 2011. 'Le séisme Marine Le Pen menace d'écroulement la droite et la gauche', *Marianne*, 12 March: 22–6.

Kitschelt, H. 1995. *The Radical Right in Western Europe: A comparative analysis.* Ann Arbor, MI: University of Michigan Press.

Labbé, D. 1996. *Syndicats et syndiqués en France depuis 1945.* Paris: L'Harmattan.

Laurent, S. and E. Nunès. 2011. 'PS et UMP face au "piège" Marine Le Pen', *Le Monde* [online]. Available from: www.lemonde.fr/politique/article/2010/12/13/ps-et-ump-face-au-piege-de-marine-le-pen_1452594_823448.html, accessed January 2011.

Lavau, G. 1981. *À quoi sert le Parti communiste français?* Paris: Fayard.

Lazar, M. 1994. 'L'invention et la désagrégation de la culture communiste', *Vingtième siècle* 44: 9–18.

Lecœur, E. 2003. *Un néo-populisme à la française: trente ans de Front national.* Paris: La Découverte.

Lemaître, F. 2007. 'Analyse: L'économie rattrape Nicolas Sarkozy', *Le Monde*, 16 August: 2.

Levy, J. 2005. 'Redeploying the state: Liberalisation and social policy in France', in W. Streeck and K. Thelen (eds) *Beyond Continuity: Institutional change in advanced political economies.* New York: Oxford University Press, pp. 103–26.

Lichfield, J. 2010. 'France's highest legal authority removes last obstacle to ban on burqa', *The Independent* [online]. Available at: www.independent.co.uk/news/world/europe/frances-highest-legal-authority-removes-last-obstacle-to-ban-on-burka-2101002.html, accessed October 2010.

Mayer, N. 1984. 'Les classes moyennes indépendantes dans la vie politique: le cas des petits commerçants français', Ph.D. dissertation, Institut d'Études Politiques de Paris.

——. 1989. 'Le vote FN de Passy à Barbès', in N. Mayer and P. Perrineau (eds) *Le Front national à découvert.* Paris: Presses de la Fondation Nationale des Sciences Politiques, pp. 249–67.

——. 1996. 'Du communisme au Front National', *L'Histoire* 195: 110–13.

——. 2002. *Ces Français qui votent Le Pen.* Paris: Flammarion.

——. 2007. 'Comment Nicolas Sarkozy a rétréci l'électorat Le Pen', *Revue française de science politique* 57(3–4): 429–45.

Mayer, N. and B. Cautrès. 2004. Les métamorphoses du vote de classe', in N. Mayer and B. Cautrès (eds) *Le nouveau désordre électoral: les leçons du 21 avril 2002.* Paris: Presses de Sciences Po, pp. 145–59.

Milza, P. 1987. *Fascisme français, passé et présent.* Paris: Flammarion.

Ministère de l'Intérieur [online]. 2011. Available from: www.interieur.gouv.fr/sections/a_votre_service/elections/resultats, accessed September 2011.

Minkenberg, M. 1998. *Die neue radikale Rechte im Vergleich: USA, Frankreich, Deutschland.* Opladen: Westdeutscher.

Minkenberg, M. 2000. 'The renewal of the radical right: Between modernity and anti-modernity', in *Government and Opposition* 35(2): 170–88.

Le Monde. 2011a. 'Fillon dévoile un plan de 11 milliards d'euros de réduction des déficits' [online]. Available from: www.lemonde.fr/politique/article/2011/08/24/francois-fillon-devoile-son-plan-de-11-milliards-d-euros-de-reduction-des-deficits_1563069_823448.html, accessed September 2011.

——. 2011b. 'Le FN progresse partout, dans ses bastions et au-delà' [online]. Available from: www.lemonde.fr/politique/article/2011/03/21/le-fn-progresse-partout-dans-ses-bastions-et-au-dela_1496462_823448.html, accessed May 2011.

Monnier, J.-M. 2009. 'Politique fiscale: Une mise en perspective', in E. Lau (ed.) *L'État de la France 2009–2010. Un panorama unique et complet de la France*. Paris: La Découverte, pp. 182–92.

Mudde, C. 2007. *Populist Radical Right Parties in Europe*. New York: Cambridge University Press.

Nau, J.-Y. 2007. 'Analyse: l'ADN, la biologie et l'éthique', *Le Monde*, 3 October: 2.

Perrault, G. 2010. 'Le Front national confirme son redressement', *Le Figaro* [online]. Available from: www.lefigaro.fr/politique/2010/03/22/01002–20100322ARTFIG00019- le-front-national-confirme-son-redressement-.php, accessed March 2011.

Perrineau, P. 1989. 'Les étapes d'une implantation électorale (1972–1988)', in *Le Front National à découvert*. Paris: Presses de la Fondation Nationale des Sciences Politiques, pp. 37–62.

——. 1997. *Le symptôme Le Pen. Radiographie des électeurs du Front national*. Paris: Fayard.

——. 2002. 'La surprise lepéniste et sa suite législative', in P. Perrineau and C. Ysmal (eds) *Le vote de tous les refus. Les élections présidentielle et législatives de 2002*. Paris: Presses de Sciences Po, pp. 199–222.

Piquard, A. 2011. 'Le FN progresse partout, dans ses bastions et au-delà', *Le Monde* [online]. Available from: www.lemonde.fr/politique/article/2011/03/21/le-fn-progresse-partout-dans-ses-bastions-et-au-dela_1496462_823448.html, accessed March 2011.

Strudel, S. 2007. 'L'électorat de Nicolas Sarkozy: "rupture tranquille" ou syncrétisme tourmenté?', *Revue Française de Science Politique* 57(3–4): 459–74.

Taguieff, P.-A. 1998. 'Biopolitique de l'identité et ordre moral: l'orthodoxie du Front National', *Raison présente* 127: 37–63.

TNS-Sofres. 2011. 'Le baromètre politique Figaro Magazine: Septembre 2011' [online]. Available from: www.tns-sofres.com/_assets/files/2011.09.01-baro-figmag.pdf, accessed September 2011.

Verret, M. 1996. *La culture ouvrière*. 2nd edn. Paris: L'Harmattan.

Weil, P. 2010. 'Les quatres piliers de la nationalité', *Le Monde* [online]. Available from: www.lemonde.fr/idees/article/2010/08/23/les-quatre-piliers-de-la-nationalite-par-patrick-weil_ 1401781_3232.html, accessed October 2010.

Weill, C. 2011. 'Dossier: Pourquoi elle est si dangereuse; Qui vote Marine Le Pen?', *Le Nouvel Observateur*, 23 June: 58.

Wolfreys, J. 2008. 'Regroupment and retrenchment on the radical left in France', *Journal of Contemporary European Studies* 16(1): 69–82.

Zappi, S. 2009. 'Des cadres du NPA démissionnent au lendemain d'un scrutin européen qui n'a pas répondu à leurs espoirs', *Le Monde*, 28 June: 8.

PART II

Mobilizing old and new passions

6

THE EUROPEAN EXTREME RIGHT AND RELIGIOUS EXTREMISM

Jean-Yves Camus

The ideology of the extreme right in Western Europe is rooted in Catholic fundamentalism and counter-revolutionary ideas while at the same time the extreme right, like all other political families, has had to adjust to an increasingly secular society. The old link between religion and the extreme right has thus been broken and in fact this was already the case when fascism overtook Europe: in its essence, fascism was secular, sometimes even anti-religious. Although Catholic fundamentalists still retain strong positions within the apparatus of several extreme-right parties (the French Front National; the Italian Forza Nuova; the various Spanish Falangist groups), the vote for the extreme right is generally weak among regular churchgoers and strong among non-believers. In several countries, the vote for the extreme right is stronger among Protestant voters than among Catholics, since the Christian-Democratic parties there are acting as a bulwark against the Catholics' vote for extremist parties. Presently, it also seems that Paganism is becoming the dominant religious creed within the extreme right. In a multicultural Europe, non-Christian forms of religious fundamentalism such as Islamism also exist and display similarities with extreme-right ideology, but this is not sufficient to categorize Islamism as a form of fascism. Some Islamist groups seek alliances with the extreme right on the basis of their common dislike for Israel and the West, globalization and individual freedom of thought.

Introduction

The extreme right in Europe is often associated with religious extremism, especially with the theocratic ideas of the fundamentalist Catholic thinkers and, in parts of Eastern Europe and the Balkans, with a blend of chauvinistic nationalism, xenophobia and orthodox mysticism. Indeed, the counter-revolutionary school of thought that opposed the ideas of the Enlightenment and the French Revolution of 1789 was deeply linked to the fundamentalist wing of the Catholic Church in countries such as France, Spain, Portugal and Italy, at least until the 1960s. However, the growing secularization of Western societies and changes within the Catholic Church itself after the Second Vatican Council, have marginalized the political influence of fundamentalism. The extreme right has become mostly secular, to the extent that, at least in Western European democracies, those who vote for the ultra-nationalist and xenophobic parties are often citizens who are not affiliated with any church and do not declare themselves to be practising believers. There is, therefore, a new phenomenon in the emergence of 'free-thinking' extreme-right voters and activists, and an important change is the widening gap between parties/groups still influenced by Catholicism and parties/groups invoking the pagan heritage of Europe. As the philosophy of the New Right shows (see Bar-On and Mellón in this volume), there has been a real renewal of Paganism within the European extreme right.

The extreme right is sometimes open to modernity, and even tries to be a vanguard of modernity (see the various chapters on identity, socialization and mobilization in this book), but it is also sometimes nostalgic about the past, especially when it comes to religion. The imprint of Christian values (or rather, of values interpreted as such by the extremists) is still strong in many European extreme-right parties, which even though they do not ground their policies on religion, refer to Europe as a 'Christian', or 'Judeo-Christian' continent. Therefore, one of the major topics of discussion within the extreme right today, is how to react to the presence of 'non-European' religions on European soil. This is a complex problem simultaneously involving the extreme right's marked hostility to Islam (see Rosenberger and Hadj-Abdou's chapter) and the long tradition of anti-Semitic prejudice in this ideological family (see my other contribution to this volume). As we will demonstrate, the extreme right today is divided between a faction that first and foremost promotes hostility to Islam and even finds itself capable of supporting Israel and the Jews as 'bastions of Western civilization'; another faction that, on the contrary, sees Islam, and even political Islam, as an ally in the fight against 'US imperialism', Israel and 'Zionism'; and a third faction that does not take sides but combines a staunch anti-immigration and anti-Muslim agenda with solid, if sometimes veiled, anti-Semitism. In any case, those who take sides are often motivated by something other than ideology: several extreme-right groups have become tools of 'rogue state' propaganda, most notably on behalf of Iran, Libya, Syria and, formerly, Saddam's Iraq.

Finally, some political movements grounded in non-Christian, non-European religions, are problematic as it is difficult to ascertain their political nature: whether they deserve to be labelled as belonging to the 'extreme right', is debatable. In the post-9/11 controversy on radical Islam, several authors have argued that Islamism is indeed a new brand of fascism, and coined the term 'Islamofascism' (Ruthven 1990; Hitchens 2001; Schwartz 2001), or even 'Nazislamism'. There are political groups today in Europe having noticeable relays within immigrant communities which display tendencies usually associated with extreme-right movements: the

Turkish nationalist 'Grey Wolves', the most radical faction of the Hindutva movement or, arguably, small Jewish self-defence groups with a racist anti-Arab agenda.

The marginalization of the Catholic fundamentalist movement

In the years 1990–2000, parties of the 'third wave' of ultra rightist movements (von Beyme 1988) succeeded in escaping from the narrow political ghetto of fringe groups to which the rejection of fascism, National Socialism and right authoritarian models had confined them after 1945. In order to do so, they were obliged to change their style and, at least in public discourse, their ideology, since it was necessary for them to adapt to the context of a modern, post-industrial society. One of the major changes between the pre-Second World War era and the post-1945 era is secularization: the proportion of citizens affiliated with a Church and, more importantly, the number of voters who cast their ballot according to the teachings of their religious hierarchy, has been continuously dwindling. Therefore, parties that have an agenda heavily influenced by an authoritarian, anti-pluralistic, theocratic or at least anti-democratic version of Catholicism have been unable to emerge or retain their past influence, because counter-revolutionary ideas and the ideal civilization of the pre-Enlightenment era they refer to, seem outdated even to an extreme right that is trying to adapt to modernity. If one searches the map of Europe for countries with no, or only marginal, extreme-right parties, Portugal and Spain stand out immediately, and these are precisely the countries where the nostalgic extreme right failed to get rid of its outdated fundamentalist rhetoric at the time of the 'democratic transition' (1974–6). In the two former dictatorships, the extreme right has clung to the fundamentals of the Franco and Salazar era, eventually becoming no more than 'cult movements' worshipping the defunct national corporatist state. In Spain, the strong Catholic fundamentalist flavour of Fuerza Nueva, led by Blas Pinar, and of the so-called 'bunker' Falangists was totally out of tune with the expectations of the Spanish electorate. Conversely, the more pragmatic former Franquists, usually found on the technocratic Right, had the wisdom to accept democracy and launch new parties such as Manuel Fraga's Aleanza Nacional, which later became Partido Popular (Rodriguez Jimenez 2000; Casals Meseguer 2003). The same process took place in post-Salazar Portugal, where many supporters of Estado Novo switched to Partido Popular and CDS (the Christian-Democratic Party). This explains the bad fortunes of the extreme right in those countries: in the 2009 general election, the Partido Nacional Renovador polled 11,628 votes (0.2 per cent) and, in 2008, the eight extreme right parties that took part in the Spanish general election polled 40,000 votes (less than 0.5 per cent).

It is also clear from the experience of Ireland and Poland that, in those countries where the Catholic Church retains a strong influence over the people's daily life, the more conservative and even extremist Catholic voters cast their vote for a mainstream conservative party, because their vote is not a protest but rather an affirmation of values shared by many and supported by an important part of the Church hierarchy. Significantly, the 2007 general election in Poland saw the League of Polish Families (LPF) losing its parliamentary representation, and the influential Radio Maryja gave its backing to Prawo i Sprawiedliwosc (PiS), the Eurosceptic, Catholic-inspired but mainstream conservative party led by the Kaczynski brothers, not the LPF. Furthermore, conservative Catholics who want to influence the political agenda, especially on pro-life or other moral issues, tend to form their own caucus within or alongside a mainstream party of the right. Such is the case in France of Christine Boutin's Parti Chrétien-Démocrate (an ally of the Union pour un Mouvement Populaire) or in Germany of Martin Lohmann's Arbeitskreis Engagierter Katholiken within the CDU–CSU (*Junge Freiheit*, 27 November 2009). This choice is probably a consequence of the doctrine of the Church which recommends obedience to the temporal powers. Whereas fundamentalists who are not afraid of straying away from the Vatican also accept to be politically marginal, conservatives defend a more pragmatic approach. The fact that Catholic fundamentalism hampers the chances of a party becoming successful does not mean, however, that voters for extreme-right parties are never motivated by their religious beliefs. There is an ongoing debate among political scientists as to whether being a devout Catholic restrains citizens from voting for the extreme right or not, and the situation seems to vary from country to country. For example, according to Jaak Billiet, in Flanders, regularly practising Catholics are less likely to have highly negative feelings towards Muslim immigrants (Moroccans and Turks) than marginal members of the Church and some categories of non-Catholics' do (Billiet 1995). In France, Nonna Mayer has shown that the relation between being a Catholic and voting for the FN depends on a variety of factors: the context (when the Catholic hierarchy warns against FN ideology, as in 1988–97, the FN vote among Catholics drops below average); the level of religious practice (regular worshippers are less prone to vote for the FN than irregular worshippers, while fundamentalist worshippers vote heavily for the FN); and the regions of France, those with a strong Catholic culture, such as Brittany or Vendée, being less receptive to the ideas of FN (Mayer 1999).

The Protestant faith and the extreme right

The common belief is that while there is a structural link between Catholic fundamentalism and the extreme right, worshippers of the various Protestant denominations are immune from voting for extremist, national-populist and xenophobic parties, because of their belief in freedom of conscience, their rejection of dogmatism and their concern for individual rights. And yet, the fact that populist, xenophobic and nationalist parties of the Right are particularly strong in Denmark, Norway and Switzerland, suggest that the reality is more complex. First of all, in his seminal study of the Conservative Revolution, Armin Mohler (Mohler 1993) demonstrated the presence of a strong Protestant component in this intellectual movement and attributed this to the Lutheran conception of the authoritarian state, that derives from the Two Kingdoms theory (*Zweireichelehre*); to the existence of a Christian-Social movement in the Protestant churches and to the existence of a Protestant wing of the Jugendbewegung, as well as to the emergence of the Deutsche Christen, who promoted a *völkisch*, ethnic German Christianity.[1] The authoritarian interpretation of Protestantism may also explain the values that influenced the Schweizerische Volkspartei leader, Christoph Blocher, who is the son of a Swiss parish minister, or those of the vice-president of the Hungarian Party of Justice and Life (Magyar Igazság és Élet Pártja, MIÉP), Lorant Hegedus, a Calvinist minister. Nevertheless, these are individual cases of militancy: the reality is that there is not a single case of a Protestant extreme-right political party anywhere in Europe, although in 1987–9 the Ulster Unionist Party Euro-MP, John Taylor, was a member of the European Right Group, possibly because he was attracted to the strongly anti-EU stance of the group, under the guidance of the French Front National. What is remarkable is not that Protestants as individuals can play a role in extreme-right parties, but that wide segments of the Protestant electorate can vote for such parties in a proportion exceeding that of their Catholic fellow citizens. The explanation for this phenomenon has been given by Bernard Schwengler (2005) in his comparative study of the Catholic and the Protestant vote in religiously mixed areas of the Alsace region (France), in Switzerland and in the land of Baden-Wurttemberg in Germany. Schwengler explains that Catholic voters in these areas can cast a kind of 'vote in group' as well as Christian-Democratic parties such as the French Centrist parties, the Swiss Christlichdemokratische Volkspartei and the German CDU. Protestant voters, on the other hand, do not have such a confessional party to vote for and consequently split their vote ('fragmented vote') between various competing parties, which means that those who support the Right are not restrained from voting for the extreme right. Schwengler shows that in Alsace the Front National, in Switzerland the Schweizerischer Volkspartei and in Germany the Republikaner are supported by Protestants more than by Catholics. Finally, there are two mistakes that are frequently made regarding the relationship between the Protestant denominations and the extreme right. The first is to label 'extremist' those parties that derive their ideology from an arch-conservative reading of the Holy Scriptures. Such parties exist in the Netherlands, where the Staatkundig Gereformeerde Partij (SGP) is a theocratic movement that represents an anachronic segment of society, but does not belong to the extreme right because it stresses the importance of parliamentary discussion, supports freedom of conscience and does not promote ethnic discrimination (Fieret 1990), and in Switzerland where the Union Démocratique Fédérale, despite having co-sponsored the 2009 referendum on Muslim minarets, does not qualify as extremist, because it promotes democracy, freedom of opinion, equality before the law and free-market economy. The second misconception involves the few attempts at building Protestant pressure groups in line with the ideology of the American Moral Majority, such as the Christian Institute or the Conservative Christian Fellowship in the United Kingdom. The Moral Majority may be criticized as reactionary; part of it promotes the kind of bigotry that may even at times lead to intolerance. Yet, in America, the Moral Majority is a pressure group lobbying the Republican Party and not a faction of the extreme right, the same being true of the aforementioned British groups vis-à-vis the Conservative Party or of the religious right that influenced Australian Premier John Howard (Maddox 2005).

Is Paganism the new religious creed of the extreme right?

The decline of monotheistic faiths has created a vacuum partially filled by 'New Age' philosophies, the growth of conversions to Buddhism or Hinduism and by the renewal of Paganism. This phenomenon is more visible in the extreme-right subculture, where pagan creeds are often mixed with ethnocentric or even racist ideas. The consequence is that the major rift within the extreme right in Europe is perhaps the one between neo-pagan '*völkisch*' nationalists and Catholic-inspired nationalists (the former, supporting the idea of a European federation of ethnic states; the latter clinging to the concept of the multi-ethnic nation-state). This difference explains, for example, the fact that the French 'Terre et Peuple' movement has decided to go away from the Front National.

The relationship between Paganism and the extreme right is a complex one. On the one hand, as Stéphane François shows, only a minority of pagan movements are oriented towards the extreme right, as many are influenced by anarchism, ecology and alternative thinking (François 2007). On the other hand, it is obvious that many extreme-right groups promote Paganism as a European ethnic creed, an anti-egalitarian view of the world, and as a tool in their fight against the universal ideas of Christianity, which is described by many extreme-right pagans as having 'Jewish' roots. This is obvious in the ideology of the Identity Churches or the World Church of the Creator, which were established in the United States and later became popular among the European neo-Nazis, including the skinheads. Paganism is also the core of the ideology of the 'New Right', a movement that began with the French think tank, GRECE (*Groupement de Recherches et d'Études pour la Civilisation Européenne*: on this see also both Antón-Mellón and Bar-On in this volume). Launched in 1968, it later spread across Western Europe. For the New Right, the rebirth of authentic European values is only possible if the peoples of the continent go back to their roots, by refusing multiculturalism and repudiating the Christian values that were imposed upon them, without totally reverting to the pagan customs that still live among the unspoiled 'folk'. Nevertheless, the New Right is not an ethnic supremacist movement: rather it strives for ethno-pluralism and respects non-European philosophies and creeds, insofar as they are interpreted as being a facet of the perennial tradition.

Who exactly are the extreme-right pagans? The ethnologist and national revolutionary thinker, Christian Bouchet, defines six sub-categories within Paganism (Bouchet 1998): the denominational and non-denominational; the reconstructionist and the creationist, the *völkisch* and the universalist. According to him, the pagan right-wing extremist movement is to be found among the non-denominationalists, that is, among those for whom Paganism is a philosophy rather than a cult. This is supported by the fact that as a cult, the Asatrufelagid in Iceland is an ecologist, alternative movement recognized by the state whereas pagan, *völkisch* philosophers such as Pierre Vial and the late Jean Mabire in France are key figures of the extreme right. Yet one can argue that it would be difficult to revive the ancient pagan cults, but as a parody. Paganism nowadays is a postmodern reaction, in the context of high secularization, against what remains of Christianity, a kind of quest for a 'Golden Age' that is more fictional than based on historical truth. This can also be said of another trend within the extreme-right spectrum: the interest in the occult, the paranormal and even in Satanism (Goodrick-Clark 2002: 215–17). Contrary to the widespread belief that Satanism is a religion, it is rather a materialistic philosophy, very modern in essence and popular among the youth, who are trying to build their personality upon the rejection of social norms (Walzer 2009). The major 'Satanist' group, the Church of Satan, is inspired by hedonism, social Darwinism and an anarchistic conception of life, which seems more related to the American counter-culture of the 1970s than inspired by the extreme right: it does not even believe in Satan as a real deity.

What is often referred to mistakenly as 'neo-Nazi Satanism' is in fact more aptly named 'occult neo-Nazism', that is, the belief in the occult roots of German National Socialism, and the quasi-divine nature of Adolf Hitler as a kind of Aryan Messiah. Such a philosophy was disseminated by David Myatt in the United Kingdom, and by Savitri Devi Mukherjee (aka Maximiani Portas, a French citizen), and once by Raymond Kerry Bolton in New Zealand. Its major exponent was the Chilean diplomat and writer, Miguel Serrano (1907–2009), who, together with Mukherjee, believes that Hitler was an avatar of Vishnu, that he came on earth to oppose the Kali-Yuga (Ars Magna 2003). Finally, one should mention the long-lasting interest by many extreme-right activists, in the writings and lifestyle of the British occultist, Aleister Crowley (Pasi 2006). Whether it be Satanism, Nazi occultism or Crowleyan philosophy, this interest is a result of the neo-Nazis' failure to achieve any political significance, thus leading them to move away from political activism and take refuge in cults that are accessible only to an elite of cognoscenti. For example, a way to retract from active politics and take refuge in a mix of philosophy and religion is to follow the traditionalist school of thought, which refers to René Guénon and Julius Evola (Boutin 1992; Sedgwick 2004). Traditionalism, which is popular among the national-revolutionaries and some segments of the New Right, is a doctrine premised on the decline of the West. Traditionalists are very critical of progress and of democracy, which they despise as being the rule of the mob, the average man who lacks access to the knowledge of the 'hidden truths'. They also think that the West has been in a continuous process of decadence since, at least, the period of the Enlightenment, and perhaps since the end of the Middle Ages. In the religious sphere, they pursue the quest for the perennial 'tradition', that is, a set of beliefs that include the cyclical evolution of world history; the necessity of a government of knights and priests; a caste conception of social hierarchy. The traditionalists usually repudiated Christianity as a religion infected by modernism, which is the vehicle for a lower spirituality, an offspring of Judaism. Instead, they are fascinated by Islam and Hinduism, to which many of them converted, while others promote various brands of theosophy. In all cases, the fascination of a segment of the extreme right for those traditionalist philosophies can be interpreted as a repudiation of political activism and as isolation from the reality of a world they feel no longer able to change by means of politics. In some cases, they do not even want to change it yet, because they believe that a New Order can only be established after the complete collapse of the present order. Traditionalism is the absolute anti-modern wing of the extreme right.

Is Islamism a fascism? Can Islamism be an ally of the extreme right?

Since the start of the second Intifada in 2000 and the terrorist attacks of 11 September 2001, a new polemical concept has emerged in the media and in would-be scholarly research: that of 'Islamo-fascism' or 'Nazislamism'. It is not the subject of this chapter to explain why the use of these terms is not relevant to describe the content of Islamist ideology: Islamism, namely the political project of fundamentalist Muslims to build an Islamic state ruled by the Sharia, lacks most of the criteria selected by serious scholars in order to characterize a movement as 'fascist'. Islamism does not strive to impose a state-regulated economy and is not hostile to free-market economics, nor is it anti-conservative, so it does not match Stanley Payne's definition (Payne 1983). It is not a palingenetic enterprise, seeking the rebirth of an ethnic nation, as characterized by Roger Griffin (1993), nor is it a 'sacralization of politics' by totalitarian methods, to echo Emilio Gentile (2004). The list could go on and on. However, this is not to say that Islamism is not totalitarianism, nor does it mean that Islamism has nothing in common with extreme-right ideology, in fact it is quite the opposite, as we will see.

There are several similarities: the Islamist parties want to build a state that, without ethnic discrimination, nevertheless grants different and unequal rights to people on the basis of their religion, and discriminates against non-Muslims and women, who, in a Sharia-state, are second-class citizens; the Islamists refuse secularism and are very suspicious of democracy; they despise the West and its values, to the extent that the Islamic thinker, Sayid Qutb built his political system after a stay in the United States, where he lamented the corrupt mentality, materialism and evilness of everything non-Muslim. In line with the anti-Semitism of the extreme right, most Islamists believe that Jews are evil and support anti-Jewish conspiracy theories which are used to explain the fate endured by the Palestinians, the terrorist attacks of 9/11, the war in Iraq and even the spreading of AIDS. These conspiracy theories are built on such prejudices as anti-Americanism, opposition to Freemasonry, the belief in a 'Zionist plot' (as exposed in the Protocols of the Elders of Zion) – in all, Islamism and the extreme right share what Richard Hofstadter (1965) called 'the paranoid style' in politics.

There have been attempts at launching Islamist political parties in Eastern Europe and although they have remained at the fringe of politics, several of them have tried to achieve an alliance with the extreme right, mostly on the common grounds of radical 'anti-Zionism' and opposition to the influence of the United States in Europe. The best-known example is the Parti Anti-Sioniste, which polled 1.5 per cent in the Paris area when it contested the 2009 European election, and which is a coalition of pro-Iran Islamists, far-left anti-globalization activists and national-revolutionary militants (Mercier 2009). Joint actions between the extreme right and political Islam can be dated from the immediate post-9/11 era. In February 2003, a delegation visited Iraq in order to show its support for Saddam Hussein. It included Mohamed Latrèche, chairman of the Parti des Musulmans de France; Hervé Van Laethem, the leader of the Belgian nationalist group 'Nation'; as well as French and Italian members of the Réseau Radical. What do these contacts between Islamists and extreme-right activists prove? Some authors such as Alexandre Del Valle (2002) have suggested that there exists a 'red–brown–green' alliance of the extreme left, extreme right and Islamists, based upon a common hatred of Israel and the Jews, rejection of liberalism and the United States, and of the West in general. Such a concept contains some truth, if one is cautious enough to say that such an alliance does not include all groups and individuals belonging to the aforementioned political families, that it is not a permanent alliance, indeed it is an ideological convergence rather than an alliance, because an alliance means that the allies conclude a pact, set common goals and common means to achieve them, something that is not the case here. Nevertheless, relations with Islam have become a point of conflict within the extreme right and are worth the study for their own sake. To be succinct, the European extreme right today is divided into three opposing 'families'. One considers Islam to be an ally in the fight against the West (but the *ultima ratio* of this attitude is in fact, opposition to Israel and the Jews, which are seen as controlling the United States and other countries); another family is strongly Islamophobic and therefore considers Israel and the Jewish communities in the Diaspora as allies in the fight against the threat of what they imagine to be the Muslim takeover of Europe; and a third group thinks that the interests of both Islam/the Muslim world and those of Israel/Judaism are alien to those of Europe. This attitude is best exemplified by the French Bloc Identitaire, whose slogan is 'Neither keffieh, nor kippa'. The rift between those tendencies within the extreme right is certainly most acute in France, because of the country's colonial past in the Arab world and the presence of important Jewish and Muslim communities. Today, most extreme-right political parties in Western Europe are more anti-Islamic than anti-Jewish. This is one of the themes that clearly separate the Italian Lega Nord, the Alleanza Nazionale and the neo-Fascist Movimento Sociale–Fiamma Tricolore or the Rome newspaper, *Rinascita*: the Lega Nord is very strident against Islam and is not anti-Jewish; the AN has largely repudiated anti-Semitism and is not opposed to legal immigration from Muslim countries, whereas MS–FT and *Rinascita* are anti-Semitic, anti-Israel and pro-Arab, but stand firmly against immigration, legal or illegal. Other parties, such as the French Front National and the Flemish Vlaams Belang, still tolerate anti-Jewish and anti-Israeli prejudice but at the same time, given the respective impact of anti-Semitism and

Islamophobia on their voting constituency, have chosen to approach the Jewish community in their country with gestures of goodwill, with very limited success. A few extreme-right parties that are not linked to the pre-Second World War fascist movements but are on the fringe of the extreme-right party family (such as the Norwegian Fremskrittspartiet) may even appear to be genuinely free of anti-Semitic prejudice. The more one moves towards the fringe of the neo-Nazi or National-Revolutionary extreme right, the more one is likely to find parties that are totally committed to anti-Semitism and to supporting militant Islam, such as the German Nationaldemokratische Partei Deutschland (NPD). In fact, one of the less known aspects of German neo-Nazi ideology is that it has influenced the current Iranian government campaign in support of Holocaust denial. Mohammad Ali Ramin, President Ahmadinejad's adviser in charge of organizing the Holocaust-denial conference in Teheran in December 2006 was educated in Germany, spent seventeen years there and befriended the NPD activist Benedikt Frings. Ramin frequently refers to a pamphlet published in 1974 as source material. This pamphlet was written by the neo-Nazi Hennecke Kardel, and refers to Hitler's alleged Jewish origin (Kardel 1974). This kind of connection between the neo-Nazi extreme right and the Muslim world is nothing new: in the 1980s, members of the Wehrsportsgruppe Hoffmann and other German Nazis fought alongside the Palestine Liberation Front, clearly motivated by their hatred of the Jews (Winterberg 2004).

However, what is new since the beginning of the Second Intifada is that the extreme right supports religious fundamentalist movements, both Sunni and Shia, whereas before it supported secular, Arab nationalist movements or states, such as Saddam's Iraq, Ghaddafi's Libya, the various factions of the Palestinian resistance, the Baath Party or the Syrian Social Nationalist Party. This has become even more obvious since Hamas came into control of the Palestinian Government (in January 2006) and Hizbullah confronted the Israeli army (July 2006). There are reasons to believe, however, that the radical extreme right does not much care about the subtleties of the Arab world: in its quest for alliances, it simply pursues the old goal of helping whomever may contribute to the destruction of Israel, to harm the Jews and undermine the Western world, which it sees as 'Jewish-ruled'. In conclusion, it may be said that the extreme right has little interest in Islam or Judaism as such. Supporting or opposing one or the other is merely a way of taking sides in the two major battles that, it argues, will shape Europe's future: the fight against Muslim immigration and that against Jewish conspiracy theory, in its various guises, such as the 'One-World Government' scheme, the fight against the 'Zionist Occupation Government' or the domination of the United States.

Is there an extreme-right movement among religious/ethnic minorities in Europe?

A panorama of the relations between the European extreme right and religious fundamentalists would not be complete without asking the following question: are there religious fundamentalist movements other than Islamist and Christian ones, which are active within the ethnic and religious minorities now present in Europe, and which may be legitimately defined as 'fascist' or belonging to the extreme-right family? In other words, do we have reason to think that the old paradigm equating the extreme right with Christian fundamentalism and the newer paradigm equating fascism with Islamism are only partially relevant? There are different answers to this question. First of all, there are, within some of the ethnic immigrant groups now residing in (mostly Western) Europe, imported ideologies with a distinct religious and totalitarian orientation and that have some connections with the extreme right. This is true of the Hindutva movement which is active among Indian expatriates of Hindu religious/ethnic stock, and which is represented in Europe by the Rashtriya Swayamsevak Sangh (RSS) or the Vishva Hindu Parishad (VHP). These groups, active in the UK, the Netherlands and Germany, are nationalist, rabidly hostile to Islam and follow a strictly communal, sectarian and religious agenda. Both have raised an interest within the circles of the extreme right, mostly because of their anti-Islamic agenda. One of the major propagandists of Hindutva in the Western world is a Flemish extreme-right activist, Koenraad Eelst, a would-be scholar who is popular in India and who was an editor of the New Right Flemish journal, *Teksten, Kommentaren en Studies* between 1992 and 1995.

Another much discussed topic is that of the existence of a Jewish extreme right. In Israel, there exist several parties and movements displaying strong extreme-right features, including an ethno-nationalist conception of identity and state, the use of violence, contempt for democracy and sometimes an outright racist agenda calling for the deportation of Arabs. The outlawed Kach Party, founded by the late rabbi Meir Kahana, fits exactly into this category (Epstein 1994). However, the most extreme nationalist parties in Israel have an ethnic conception of Jewishness that does not always carry a religious ideology: Avigdor Lieberman's Israel Betainu Party, for example, is strictly secular, while the Ihoud HaLeumi (National Union) Party, led by Benny Elon, is a strange mix of national-religious Zionism and secular nationalism, advocating the transfer by force of the Palestinian population to neighbouring Jordan.

All Israeli political parties have more or less permanently organized groups of activists in European countries with sizeable Jewish communities. The same alliance between religious Zionists and secular nationalists does exist in the Diaspora: the National Religious Party (Mafdal) has increasingly moved to the right, and so has the Likud, but small activist groups, which have emerged to the right of those parties as a result of the resurgence of anti-Semitism after 2000, are mostly set up by secular Jews. For instance, the Jewish Defense League, founded in the United States and which has achieved media fame in France under the name Ligue de Défense Juive, is a self-defence organization led by non-religious people who have left the Likud's youth movement (named Betar) and whose only concession to religious observance is that they do not stage activities on Saturday (the Jewish Shabbat). This may not seem very coherent, but it is very much an expression of the difficulty faced by Jews who are active in the life of the Jewish community when it comes to defining themselves as either an ethnic/minority group or a religion. In any case, it must be remembered that in the context of the sometimes hysterical controversy surrounding the Middle-East issue, the existence of very tiny movements of Jewish extreme-right activists, mostly in France, has provided an excuse for the extreme left and part of the pro-Palestinian movement to label the entire Jewish right as 'fascist', and to equate Zionism with fascism. This is a misconception: the only serious, although marginal, attempt at finding common ground between Jews and the extreme right has come from ultra-Orthodox, anti-Zionist fringe groups, who believe in the separation of races and of religious or ethnic groups, and who are opposed to the very existence of Israel. As such, they are ready to build bridges with the black separatist, Muslim fundamentalist and white supremacist movements.

One key figure in this attempt is the American rabbi Mayer-Schiller, a teacher at Yeshiva University in New York, whose first contact with the extreme right goes back to his association with the British Third Way movement at the beginning of the 1990s, and who summarized his thinking in an interview with the *Ulster Nation* national-revolutionary magazine:

> There are two things that threaten the West. One is liberalism, which is the destruction of faith and values and culture. The other is multi-racialism or multi-culturalism, which is essentially a peaceful invasion and takeover of these countries. Both of these things are hard to turn back the clock on once they have been done.
>
> (*Ulster Nation* 32, July 2000)

Needless to say, this odd alliance has never borne fruit, although some segments of the European extreme right have presently an interest in the Neturei Karta sect, some of whose London- and Vienna-based dissident members attended the Holocaust denial conference in Tehran, in December 2006.

Finally, the extreme right is also present within Turkish immigration in Europe. This is a very interesting case of ethnic ultra-nationalism blending with religion (in this case, Islam). There are two Turkish extreme-right political parties: the Milliyetçi Hareket Partisi (MHP) and its youth wing, Bozkurtlar (Grey Wolves), and the Büyük Birlik Partisi (BBP), led by Muhsin Yazicioglu. The former, which is very active in Belgium, the Netherlands and Germany, and to a lesser extent in France, is secular and mostly concerned about the ethnic essence of the Turkish nation, although some experts within the German Verfassungschutz believe that there is one 'Turkish nationalist' and one 'Turkish–Islamist' wing within MHP (Verfassungsschutz des Landes Nordrhein-Westfalen 2004). The latter split from MHP in 1993 precisely because it felt the party's Islamist credentials were 'weak'. It received 1.02 per cent in the 2003 general election and did not contest the 2007 election. It operates in Europe under the name of Avrupa Tûrk Birligi, or Verband der Turkischen Kulturvereine E.V. in Europa, and promotes a mix between the Atatürk tradition of nationalism and the Koran. Whereas in the 2007 general election, the MHP has become Turkey's third political force with 14.29 per cent of the vote, the BBP seems to have failed politically. Yet it is worth monitoring, because of its extreme anti-Kurdish and anti-Armenian propaganda, and also because of its alleged involvement in violent activities.

Conclusion

Historically, in Western Europe, the extreme right takes its roots in the alliance between the Roman Catholic Church and the counter-revolutionary ideology inherited from opponents to the Enlightenment: this extreme-right family remains active in Latin countries. Yet, today, the extreme right in general is a largely secular movement. Fascism, with a few exceptions such as Falangism, the Iron Guard and Rexism, was secular. National Socialism was predominantly anti-Christian. And if one tries to find a connection between Christian values and politics today, one would be more likely to find it within the conservative, democratic right and the progressive left, both differently inspired by the Gospels.

The extreme right retains an interest in religion, because it considers it as one of national identity's core components; even more since the presence of Islam in Europe has become the major concern of most extreme-right political parties with significant electoral success. So, on the issue of religion, the present-day extreme right may be split into three families. One, best exemplified by the late Dutch politician, Pim Fortuyn, seeks to defend freethinking and libertarian values from what it perceives as the assault of Islam on the European tradition of separating church and state. Another, by contrast, promotes 'European civilization' against the threat of Islamization and immigration, and although it is not theocratic, it sees Christianity as a cultural cornerstone of European civilization. This family, which lies at the crossroads of the ultra-conservative right and the extreme right, is opposed, within the extreme right, by another family, which has totally set aside any reference to religion and promotes a European identity based upon ethnicity and 'racial awareness'. This is just another variation of the old controversy opposing the 'pro-Western' and the 'Third Way' extreme-right families.

Note

1 Mohler also points to the support given by many Protestant church ministers to the Deutschnationale Volkspartei (DNVP), which became an ally of the Nationalsozialistische Deutsche Arbeiterpartei (NSDAP).

References

Ars Magna (ed.) 2003. *Miguel Serrano, un Ésotérisme hitlérien*. Nantes: Ars Magna.
Billiet, Jaak B. 1995. 'Church involvement, ethnocentrism, and voting for a radical right-wing party: Diverging behavioural outcomes of equal attitudinal dispositions', *Sociology of Religion*, 56, 3: 303–26.
Bouchet, C. 1998. *BA-BA Néo-paganisme*. Puiseaux: Éditions Pardès.
Boutin, C. 1992. *Politique et tradition. Julius Evola dans le siècle (1898–1974)*. Paris: Kimé.

Casals Meseguer, X. 2003. *Ultrapatriotas*. Barcelona: Critica.

Del Valle, A. 2002. *La convergence des totalitarismes, ou les nouveaux visages rouge-bruns-verts de l'antisémitisme*. Paris: Observatoire du monde juif.

Epstein, S. 1994. *Les chemises jaunes*. Paris: Calmann-Lévy.

Fieret, W. 1990. *De Staatkundig Gereformeerde Partij 1918–1948. Een bibliocratisch ideaal*. Houten: Den Hertog.

François, S. 2007. *Le néo-paganisme. Une vision du monde en plein essor*. Apremont: MCOR La Table d'Émeraude.

Gentile, E. 2004. *Qu'est-ce que le fascisme?* Paris: Gallimard.

Goodrick-Clark, N. 2002. *Black Sun: Aryan cults, esoteric Nazism and the politics of identity*. New York: New York University Press.

Griffin, R. 1993. *The Nature of Fascism*. Abingdon: Routledge.

Hitchens, Christopher. 2001. 'Against rationalization', *The Nation*, 8 October.

Hofstadter, R. 1965. *The Paranoid Style in American Politics*. New York: Knopf.

Kardel, H. 1974. *Adolf Hitler, begründer Israels*. Geneva: Verlag Marva.

Maddox, M. 2005. *God under Howard: The rise of the religious right in Australian Politics*. Crows Nest: Allen & Unwin.

Mayer, N. 1999. *Ces français qui votent FN*. Paris: Flammarion.

Mercier, A.-S. 2009. *Dieudonné démasqué*. Paris: Seuil.

Mohler, A. 1993. *La Révolution conservatrice en Allemagne 1918–1932*. Puiseaux: Pardès.

Pasi, M. 2006. *Aleister Crowley und die Versuchung der Politik*. Graz: Ares Verlag.

Payne, S. 1983. *Fascism: Comparison and definition*. Madison, WI: University of Wisconsin Press.

Rodriguez Jimenez, J.-L. 2000. *Historia de la Falange Espanola de las JONS*. Madrid: Alianza Editorial.

Ruthven, Malise. 1990. 'Construing Islam as a language', *The Independent*, 8 September.

Schwartz, Stephen. 2001. 'Ground Zero and the Saudi connection', *The Spectator*, 22 September.

Schwengler, B. 2005. 'Le clivage électoral catholique-protestant revisité', *Revue française de science politique*, 55, 3: 381–413.

Sedgwick, M. 2004. *Against the Modern World: Traditionalism and the secret intellectual history of the twentieth century*. Oxford: Oxford University Press.

von Beyme, Klaus. 1988. 'Right-wing extremism in post-war Europe', *West European Politics*, 11, 2: 1–18.

Walzer, N. 2009. *Satan profane. Portrait d'une jeunesse enténébrée*. Paris: Desclée de Brouwer.

Winterberg, Y. 2004. *Der Rebell. Odfried Hepp. Neonazi, Terrorist, Aussteiger*. Köln: Lübbe.

7

THE FRENCH EXTREME RIGHT, ANTI-SEMITISM AND ANTI-ZIONISM (1945–2009)

Jean-Yves Camus

In a recent essay on the French extreme right under the Fifth Republic, Nicolas Lebourg writes:

> Radical extreme-right groups are forced to act according to a complex *pas de deux*, because they set for themselves a twofold mission: 1) to fight against subversion, which at times leads them to support a stronger state; 2) to engage in subversive activities aimed at toppling the state and constructing a new order.
>
> (Lebourg 2009: 310)

We will show that within the French extreme right, the divide between the pro-Zionists and the pro-Israelis on the one hand, and the anti-Zionist/anti-Israelis on the other hand, is an old phenomenon that is not solely the result of diverging geopolitical analysis. The fierce opposition between these two factions of the extreme right has become more acute in the context of the rise of political Islam and the transformation of extreme anti-Zionism into the main purveyor of anti-Semitism in Europe. However, the core issue at stake here is that of subversion, because the extreme right believes that the French state is in the hands of the Zionists. Therefore, the more radical an extreme-right movement is in its denunciation of the state, the elite and the dominant world order, the more it will espouse extreme anti-Zionist and anti-Israeli views. Conversely, more moderate extreme-right movements (on this, see also Jamin's chapter) that aim at becoming mainstream players in the political field think that French society is subverted by Islam, and as a consequence, they have softened their anti-Jewish, anti-Zionist rhetoric. Whether this is genuine or merely a tactic is a matter of debate. The emergence of an anti-Zionist extreme right is the result of a new division between centre and periphery. Pro-Israeli and pro-Zionist parties of the extreme right tend to present themselves as supporters of the Western world in the struggle against the 'Axis of Evil', and their newly proclaimed support for democracy is supposed to increase their political respectability. Anti-Zionist/anti-Israeli groups consider the West, globalization and the so-called New World Order as the ultimate evil, and they also reject any kind of compromise with democracy. This division within the extreme right, is consistent with the fact that since 1945, anti-Semitism and racism are not tolerated by mainstream democratic political parties.

Before the Second World War: an anti-Semitic, pro-Zionist extreme right

Under the Third Republic, anti-Semitism was politically and socially acceptable, in the sense that it was not confined to the extreme right. Although it was rabidly anti-Semitic, the extreme right was rather positive about Zionism. Those who believed, with Charles Maurras, in a Jewish international conspiracy supposedly taking hold of France, described the Jews as 'a state within the state'. Their anti-Semitic prejudice was a mix of Catholic theological teachings, belief in the superiority of the Aryan (and French) 'race', and anti-capitalist stereotypes that associated the Jews with money and modernity. When they wrote about Zionism, anti-Semites often saw it as a way to get rid of the 'Jewish problem', an idea supported by Edouard Drumont (Kaufmann 2008: 317–19) and Louis-Ferdinand Céline (Birnbaum 2006: 161–74). Among French nationalists, there were also diverging positions on Zionism according to foreign policy issues. For example, anti-British sentiment was then a constant feature of the French extreme right and it justified opposing Zionism on the ground that the Balfour declaration reflected British–Zionist connivance. Conversely, it was also possible to support Zionism because Zionist fighters were seen as undermining British imperialism, a position that became popular after 1920, when France was given a mandate over Lebanon and Syria. However, Zionism was not the major concern of the extreme right, which focused its vitriolic attacks on the *Juifs d'État*, that is, those Jews who had achieved prominent status as senior civil servants or politicians, and who often belonged to the socialist Section Française de l'Internationale Ouvrière (SFIO) or centre-left parties. True to their anti-Semitic ideology, the Ligues, the *Action française* and the pro-fascist groups that wanted to overthrow the Republic, tried to discredit it by pretending that it was 'Jewish'.

A pro-Arab extreme right also emerged in the 1930s, when some anti-Semitic movements realized that Jewish immigration to Palestine was strongly resented by the then awakening Arab nationalist movements in French North Africa, particularly in Algeria, where the extreme right was very active. This is why Jacques Doriot asked his Parti Populaire Français (PPF) to set up a branch there and campaign for the revocation of the Crémieux decree, which in 1870 had granted full citizenship to the Jews of Algeria, but not to the Muslims. This enabled the PPF to recruit among the Muslim population as well as among the French settlers (Stora 2006: 80) and in March 1942, the party held a public meeting in Paris, with two

Algerian nationalist leaders, Mohamed Bouali and Hadj Mostaf Bendjemaa as speakers. This first example of the emergence of a pro-Arab extreme right is still very controversial. In the 2000s, because of the rise of political Islam, the anti-Zionist and pro-Arab faction of the French extreme right (such as the *Réseau Radical*, led by Christian Bouchet) edited brochures eulogizing the 'Arab volunteers of the Third Reich' (Fabei 2005) while pro-Zionist, anti-Islam extreme-right militants supported the idea that present-day Islamic anti-Zionism has its roots in the Arabs working hand in hand with the Third Reich and the alliance between Hitler and the then Mufti of Jerusalem-Al Qods, Haj Amin al Husseini (Landau 2005).

In the 1930s, another extreme-right faction was both anti-Semitic and anti-Zionist, namely the Catholic fundamentalist movement. From this perspective, Zionism was an evil creation, promoted by the Jews in order to achieve world domination through a war that would start in the Middle East and then spread over the world. This theory was promoted by Bishop Ernest Jouin's *Revue Internationale des Sociétés Secrètes* (RISS, published in 1912–39), which described Zionism as 'the 1898 Zionist prophecy'. The Catholic fundamentalist movement is nowadays embodied in the St Pius X Society, founded by the late Bishop Marcel Lefebvre. The controversy that erupted in 2009, when one of its bishops, Richard Williamson, publicly denied the existence of the Nazi genocide, proves that the Catholic fundamentalist movement is still tainted by anti-Semitism. It is also opposed to the Jewish state and after 2001, the RISS was re-published by the sedevacantist[1] *Éditions Delacroix*, with the goal of showing that the existence of Israel will lead to a third world war (on Catholic fundamentalism, see my other chapter on the 'Extreme right and religious extremism' in this volume). Catholic fundamentalists are also opposed to Islam, which according to them is a false religion trying to subjugate Christianity, and they have a tradition of explaining that Islam is a Jewish invention (Zakarias 1955; Bertuel 1981).

The Algerian War and the Suez crisis: a turning point

After 1945, the French extreme right was marginalized and the public expression of anti-Semitism became almost impossible. What remained of the extreme-right primarily focused its attacks on de Gaulle, the communists and the post-war purges, so that the creation of Israel in 1948 did not attract open criticism. Extreme-right periodicals such as *Écrits de Paris* and *Aspects de la France* (whose publication had been legally authorized in 1947), rehashed the same ideas about the Jews as they had done before and during the Vichy regime. The creation of Israel did not change an argument inspired by the *Action française* and a devout faithfulness to Pétain: the Jews were attacked because of their 'cosmopolitanism', their alleged lack of patriotism, their 'treachery' and their support for communism, socialism or Gaullism.[2] As *Rivarol* (*Rivarol*, 20 September 1951) put it:

> The Jews will now legally have two identity cards in their pockets: that of Israel and that of the country where they camp. We will be the last to reproach

them to be faithful to their nation. But precisely, we ask the question: can one serve two masters?

This accusation of 'dual loyalty' became a weapon against the Jews, but it was not a weapon against Zionism: after 1945, Xavier Vallat, the former Commissioner for Jewish Affairs in the Vichy government, supported Israel and Zionism, not because he had changed his mind about the Jews, but because he believed the Jews were not French and had to live in their 'motherland'.

There was no pro-Arab movement on the extreme right at that time, but this does not mean that the seeds of anti-Zionism had not yet been planted. In October 1948, Maurice Bardèche published *Nuremberg ou la terre promise*, which is the first Holocaust-denial essay in history (Igounet 2000: 37–60). Bardèche explained that the Nuremberg trial was the 'promised land' of the Jews, providing Israel and the Diaspora with legal grounds to blackmail Germany and extort money from the German people in order to finance the new Israeli state. This idea remains the cornerstone of Holocaust denial even today, except that in 1948 the neo-fascist deniers were not in contact with the propaganda apparatus of the Arab world, nor did they pay much attention to the situation in the Middle East. Contacts with Arab countries were initiated by former German Nazi propagandists who were employed by the information service of Nasser's government in Egypt. Bardèche came into contact with Egypt in the mid 1950s, through the German Nazi, Karl-Heinz Priester, with whom he sat on the board of the *European Social Movement*. Likewise, Rassinier came into contact with Johann Von Leers, Goebbels' former aide, at the beginning of the 1960s (Fresco 1999: 40).

On the other hand, the event that triggered the alliance between part of the extreme right and Israel is the 1956 Suez expedition. In the context of the Cold War, Nasser was considered a pro-communist dictator by the extreme right, which also hated him for supporting the Algerian independence movement. So, even among those who were not friendly to the Jews, many came to see Israel as an ally of the West against the possible communist takeover of the Middle East. This idea was especially popular among extreme-right officers who took part in the Suez expedition and has to be understood in the broader context of the fight between subversion and the 'free world'. Many officers in the Army who had fought communists in Indochina, experienced in counter-insurgency tactics and now serving in Algeria, were persuaded that it was necessary to overthrow Nasser by marching on Cairo. They interpreted the decision to stop the Suez expedition as another confirmation of Western weakness, in sharp contrast to Israeli determination. Such were the views of Colonel Pierre Chateau-Jobert, a high-ranking officer and Resistance hero, who led the Second Paratroopers Commando unit at Suez. A follower of the fundamentalist Cité Catholique, he became a leader of the Organisation Armée Secrète (OAS) and confessed his admiration for the Israelis because Israel was 'a nation in arms', a country where every citizen is also a fighter for his people's very existence. Returning from Suez, Chateau-Jobert stayed in contact with the Israeli Army and in 1961, as the head of the OAS in Constantine (Algeria), he wrote to the Israeli Embassy in Paris, asking it to 'send some Israeli boys and girls to Algeria, who need to be particularly resolute, active and selected', so that they could 'give hope to the [local] Jewish community and organise its self-defence' (Haroun 2005: 156).

The war in Algeria also contributed to convince a part of the extreme right that Israel was a bulwark against Soviet-sponsored Arab nationalism. Two Poujadist members of parliament, Jean-Marie Le Pen and Jean-Maurice Demarquet, served as paratroopers during the Suez expedition and both wished for an Israeli victory, although the Poujade movement was known for its anti-Semitic attacks against Pierre Mendès-France. However, others were genuine friends of Israel and Zionism: the OAS, especially in Oran (Algeria), maintained good relations with the local Jewish community and recruited Jews. Lieutenant Roger Degueldre, the leader of an OAS death-squad, wanted to initiate an uprising of the European population in Algeria 'like that of Budapest' and wanted to draft them into a 'popular army' modelled on the Haganah (Dard 2005: 76). Later, when prominent figures from the Christian Democratic Party (Georges Bidault), the Gaullist movement (Jacques Soustelle) and army officers without extreme-right connections such as Pierre Sergent rallied to the OAS, the pro-Israel leanings of the organization became even stronger. Soustelle was very popular among the Jewish community because of his involvement in the Comité de Vigilance des Intellectuels Antifascistes and later in the anti-Nazi *résistance*, remained close to the Jews and Israel until he left politics in the mid 1970s. Sergent, also a former *résistance* fighter, later joined the Front National (FN). Together with another OAS activist, Pierre Descaves, who had become a FN branch leader, he travelled to Jerusalem in 1987 and tried to meet with members of the Knesset belonging to the Likud Party, in order to convince it that the FN was not anti-Semitic and that it was a potential ally against Arabs. Their attempt failed.

The Six-Day War: the revenge for the loss of Algeria

In 1967, five years after the loss of Algeria, often lived as a national trauma, the extreme right rejoiced at the Israeli victory against its Arab neighbours. For the French nationalists, this was the revenge of the West against the Arabs. The fact that de Gaulle had become increasingly hostile to Israel made it easier for a part of the extreme right to openly support the Hebrew state. Colonel Jean Thomazo (a leading supporter of Algérie française) and Jean-Louis Tixier-Vignancour (a former member of the Pétain cabinet) took part in a pro-Israel demonstration in Paris during the 1967 war. Anti-Semites such as Xavier Vallat, Lucien Rebatet and Henri Lèbre, who had been at the forefront of anti-Jewish propaganda in 1940–5, voiced their support for Israel, as did *Rivarol* and *Aspects de la France*, although neither newspaper repudiated anti-Semitism and *Rivarol* even questioned the reality of the Holocaust, both before and after 1967. Vallat supported Zionism because he believed it was the most effective mean of convincing the Jews to leave France for Israel. Lèbre, a former columnist in the pro-Nazi weekly *Je suis partout*, held the view that because the Arab population in Israel and in the Arab countries had a much higher birth rate than that of Israeli Jews, the latter would be overwhelmed. He supported Israel because he believed the Arabs were pro-communist and hostile to the West.

Such pro-Israeli conversions were tactical, but other people genuinely changed their mind. The best example is the philosopher Pierre Boutang, the editor of the royalist weekly *La nation française*. Although Boutang had been an anti-Semite, he later came to admire Zionism, which for him meant the regeneration of the Jewish people, who had finally been restored to the biblical land of Israel. Boutang wrote that 'the European man does not live in Europe, where the peoples are not awake. He lives – this is a paradox and a scandal – in Israel' (*La nation française*, 1 June 1965). He went on to say that 'the creation of the state of Israel is the only payoff, the only positive' result of the Second World War. A devout Catholic, he saw 'something sacred' in the Jewish state although, in accordance with his Catholic beliefs, he wished the creation of Israel would later bring back the Jews to the 'true faith'. His opinion was shared by the Swiss reactionary intellectual and long-time anti-Semite, Marcel Regamey, who wrote about 'the legitimacy of the state of Israel' (*La nation française*, 13 July 1967).

The Six-Day War also reinforced the anti-Zionist extreme right. The rallying point of this faction was the quarterly *Défense de l'Occident*, edited by Bardèche, who supported a 'third way' between capitalism and communism that would free Europe from the domination of the superpowers. From this perspective, Israel was a mere tool of the United States. Together with the periodical *Lectures françaises* (edited by Henry Coston), Bardèche exposed the alleged plans of the United States and the multinational corporations for securing oil supply by dominating the Arab countries.[3] He refuted the assimilation policy of the Arabs, promoted by the '*Algérie française*' movement, because he believed this would lead to race mixing and Arab immigration to the French mainland. For those reasons, Bardèche supported independence for Algeria, and professed a keen interest in the remnants of fascism he found in the Syrian Baath Party and the personality of Nasser. In June 1967, *Défense de l'Occident* took a decisive turn by publishing a special issue entitled *The Israeli aggression*. It featured an article by Rassinier and another one by the fascist historian François Duprat, a leader of *Occident*, *Ordre Nouveau* and the FN until his mysterious assassination in 1978. This milestone issue was at the crossroads of anti-Semitism, anti-Zionism and Holocaust denial. From then on, Bardèche and Duprat became the theoreticians of the pro-Arab extreme right, which was also influenced by the Belgian Jean Thiriart and the American-born Francis Parker Yockey.

Within the reactionary extreme right, there were also two diverging appreciations of the Middle-East conflict. Those who believed France should be an ally of the United States and a partner in the fight of 'the West' against the communist camp became more positive towards Israel, seen as a citadel of the free world standing against Arab countries backed by the USSR. On the opposite, some disciples of Maurras believed that France could remain a world power only by forming an alliance with the Arab world against American domination. They identified themselves with the Gaullistes de Gauche who after 1967 identified themselves with the 'third way' foreign policy of the French government. As a consequence, they became propagandists for the Arab/Muslim countries, which denied Israel the right to exist. The Gaullistes de Gauche, who drew on the works of the former collaborationist historian, Jacques Benoist-Méchin, are best exemplified by the bimonthly *La pensée nationale* (Special issue: *La France et le monde arabe*, 1974) published by Charles Saint-Prot. Another key figure is Gilles Munier, one of Thiriart's disciples, who became the general secretary of the Association des amitiés franco-irakiennes, a pro-Saddam Hussein lobby linked to the mainstream conservative right. However, one must not overrate the influence of this faction. The reality is that support for Palestine is widespread in France, and thus the extreme right only played a marginal role in the pro-Palestine lobby: the Rassemblement pour la Libération de la Palestine, initiated in 1967 by Duprat, was a one-man attempt, despite the links he had with al Fatah, the Popular Front for the Liberation of Palestine, the pro-Syrian al Saika and the Syrian Social Nationalist Party. Nevertheless, various Arab governments or parties have, mostly in times of acute international crisis, supported extreme-right groups, and even financed them. In the 1990s, the leadership of Nouvelle Résistance was invited to the annual 'anti-imperialist university' in Libya. There is proof that, in the same period, the neo-Nazi publisher Ogmios received money from an Iranian diplomat in Paris (Ferjani 1991: 35) and that the Syrian Minister of Defence, Mustafa Tlass, financed the neo-fascist student movement GUD (*Libération*, 20 November 2006).

The extreme right can support the Arab world against the Jews and at the same time oppose Arab immigration, but there can be other reasons for its interest in this region: for example, the Nouvelle Droite (whose ideology is studied by Bar-On and Mellón in this volume) and the followers of Julius Evola and René Guénon, acknowledge Islam as a part of the perennial tradition[4] that opposes materialism and democracy. Others simply see the Arab/Muslim countries as the spearhead of the 'anti-Imperialist' struggle. Consequently, they chose the Arab country/faction they support according to those criteria: the Parti Communautaire National-Européen (PCN) supported Libya, then Iraq; Nouvelle Résistance/Unité Radicale/Réseau Radical supported Iraq, then Iran after the downfall of the Saddam regime. The French extreme right also tries to build an axis of all the extremisms against Western political and cultural domination and liberal values. What some call the 'red–brown–green'[5] alliance (Del Valle 2002) gathers those who use anti-Zionism as a disguise for anti-Semitism, and who use anti-imperialism to mask their hatred for the alleged domination plan of ZOG (Zionist Occupation Government). It is usually used, in the European context, to describe the fact that militants from the extreme left, militants from the extreme right and Islamists marched together in Paris on 24 January 2009 against the Israeli strike in Gaza, some of them under the motto: 'United front against Zionism'.[6]

The extreme right, anti-Semitism and Zionism in the post-9/11 era

The Front National is a party whose 'modernist' wing wants to be considered 'mainstream' but many of the party leaders have been schooled in traditional extreme-right values: open anti-Jewish prejudice is still rife among its leaders. From 1972 until 1982, the FN included two factions that were outspokenly anti-Jewish and anti-Israeli: the Groupes Nationalistes Révolutionnaires, led by Duprat, and the militant faction, led by former French Waffen SS volunteers. In 1986, Le Pen succeeded in attracting several Gaullist and conservative elected officials to his party, but ultimately this failed, because these newcomers defected when Le Pen declared that the Holocaust was 'a detail in the history of the Second World War'. Because the FN is an umbrella organization that strives to unite different and often conflicting factions of the extreme right under the same banner, Le Pen has tried to prevent these different factions from overly debating this subject, fearing that this sort of intra-party conflict would dramatically damage the fortunes of the FN.

What is certain, however, is that low-key anti-Semitism is a constant feature in the ideology of the different factions. The core of this anti-Semitism is a shared paranoid vision of French politics and the belief in a conspiracy of the left, the conservative right and the institutions of the Jewish community, in order to keep Le Pen and FN away from power, and even to persecute them by legal means. On 11 August 1989 in the Catholic traditionalist daily newspaper *Présent*, Le Pen denounced 'the big trans-national lobbies, including the Jewish International, [which] is playing a significant role in stirring up the anti-national spirit'. Other officials of the party have identified even more precisely the core of this 'Jewish conspiracy': the editor of *Présent*, Jean Madiran, published a brochure entitled 'Ce que l'on vous cache: comment a été imposé l'interdit: ne s'allier en aucun cas avec le Front national' (Madiran 1986) and it targeted the Freemason-like Jewish organization, Bnai Brith. In his book, *L'Adieu à Israël*, Madiran (Madiran 1992) also explained that he became a supporter of Israel because he admired the rebirth of the Jewish nation, but that he later reverted to his former anti-Jewish prejudice, because he felt betrayed by the staunch opposition of the Jewish institutions such as CRIF (Conseil Représentatif des Institutions Juives de France) to the FN.

Sometimes, the feelings of the extreme-right militants towards the Jews are much more mixed and even those nostalgic for National Socialism may show a veiled admiration for them and for Israel. For example, many members of the FN youth wing, Front National de la Jeunesse, have been politically educated by reading the works of Saint-Loup (aka. Marc Augier). A former political officer of the French Waffen SS, Saint-Loup wrote numerous novels in apology for the Division Charlemagne, such as *Les Hérétiques* (Saint-Loup 1965). In the third chapter of this book, entitled 'Les Macchabées', he tells the half-authentic story of a so-called 'pan-European faction' within the Nazi SS. In his version, the defeat of the Third Reich was caused by its narrow-minded German nationalism: the pan-European faction, on the other hand, stood for a united White Europe. Members of the faction refuted the 'pseudo-scientific and imperialist racism' of the Nazis and stood 'for apartheid on a worldwide scale, under the motto of happiness for every man, within his own biologically defined ethnic group'. The heroes of Saint-Loup believe that after 1945 the Nazis will be 'dispersed and persecuted the way Israel was'. Saint-Loup also wrote that after 1945 history will be 'a dialogue between Israel and us, exclusively'. The commanding officer of these soldiers read to them the story of the Maccabees, in order to show them that the fate of the post-1945 Nazis would be similar to that of the Jews who, after having defeated the Seleucids, had set up a dynasty that reigned over a sovereign Jewish state. This veiled admiration for the Jews did not mean that Saint Loup was not an anti-Semite: he also wrote a book suggesting that the *Protocols of the Elders of Zion* were authentic (Saint-Loup 2007).

This ambivalent discourse is an exception: the neo-Nazi extreme right is crudely anti-Semitic. It stands for the extinction of Israel as a state and some movements have been linked to Palestinian terrorist factions: in the early 1980s, the Fédération d'Action Nationale et Européenne (FANE) was in contact with the German neo-Nazi, Odfried Hepp, who had enlisted in the Palestine Liberation Front in Lebanon (Winterberg 2004). Most neo-Nazis have no interest in understanding Middle-Eastern politics, Jewish history or geopolitics: they simply hate the 'eternal Jew'. For them, the Jews aim at securing total control of every country in the world and this is the reason every government in the world that they believe is dominated by the Jews must be destroyed by any means, including terrorism.

This hatred found new grounds and new channels after 2001, when anti-Semitic incidents reached their highest level since 1945. The novelty lies in the fact that the overwhelming majority of these incidents are perpetrated not by the extreme right, but by second-generation immigrants from the Maghreb and West Africa, who feel a sense of solidarity with Palestine and do not distinguish between Jews, Zionists and Israelis. The most radical elements of the extreme right, especially the national-revolutionaries, see this situation as an unexpected opportunity: if immigrants are ready for anti-Semitic action, maybe the nationalists, with appro-priate propaganda, can convince them to join in a united front against Israel and the Jews. This option is also possible because since 9/11 and the controversy over the Danish cartoons of Muhammad, some French Muslims think their religion is under attack in Europe and because they believe in conspiracy theories that seek to expose the alleged Israeli involvement in everything that is going wrong in the Muslim world. These theories are shared by a segment of the far left, part of the extreme right and part of the Islamic movement, resulting in a vivid controversy within the extreme right, between pro-Arab and pro-Israeli factions. On the other hand, the decrease in anti-Semitic violence originating in extreme-right milieu can be attributed to the widespread feeling that Islam is the main enemy and that in this context the Jews and Israel, while not exactly friends, may at least be allies in the alleged clash of civilizations. At the same time, the number of attacks on

French Muslim individuals, places of worship, graves and symbols, is growing, and many such incidents originate in the extreme right.

As a result too, several extreme-right groups have toned down their anti-Zionist/anti-Jewish rhetoric. The Mouvement National Républicain (MNR) claims that it strives for 'an understanding with the Arab world', but at the same time affirms that 'several countries in the Middle East are now a potential danger for France and Europe, a danger that has already taken shape in the existence of terrorism and a certain kind of immigration' (Megret and Dupont 2000). As a symbolic gesture, this declaration was made on 30 September 2001 in the city of Poitiers, where in 732, Charles Martel defeated the Arabs.

The FN has mixed feelings on this issue. In January 2005 Le Pen said in the weekly *Rivarol* that the German occupation of France 'was not especially inhuman', which in some respect is an anti-Semitic comment. Several party officials openly voiced their anti-Jewish prejudice or endorsed a revisionist agenda, denying the Holocaust. For example, a former FN regional councilman, Georges Theil, published under the alias Gilbert Dubreuil a Holocaust-denial booklet entitled *Un cas d'insoumission, comment on devient révisionniste* (Dubreuil 2002). The party's second-in command, Bruno Gollnisch, said at a press conference in 2004: 'There is no longer any serious historian who supports the findings of the Nuremberg trials.' At his 2006 trial, Gollnisch finally recognized that the genocide actually took place, but the 2007 programme of FN still calls for 'the restoration of freedom of opinion and freedom of speech [in academic research]', which means toleration of Holocaust denial. There is also no doubt that the FN remains prejudiced against Israel: commenting on his book *Israel–Palestine, assez de mensonges* the party vice-president, Roger Holeindre, explains that 'Israel is in the hands of the settlers [in the West Bank] who are supported by Mr Bush's friends in the US, and all this may well lead to a Third World War' (Holeindre 2003). However, this anti-Israeli stand is not shared by the whole leadership. Marine Le Pen, the leader of the modernist wing of the party, has rejected her father's anti-Jewish utterances, although she did not formally repudiate anti-Semitism and racism. As part of her efforts to turn the FN into a mainstream party and end the isolation that denies it access to power, she has tried to visit Israel as a member of a Euro-Parliament delegation in 2006, but the Israeli Government denied her access.

Conversely, extreme-right groups which reject any kind of inclusion into the democratic process have been further radicalized by the events of 9/11 as well as by the second Intifada. They have built links with groups from the far left and the Islamist movement, thus giving some kind of justification to the 'red–brown–green' alliance' theory. Alain Soral, a former FN *idéologue*, denounced the Israeli strike over Gaza. On 24 January 2009 with his movement Egalité et Réconciliation, he marched under the banner 'United Front against Zionism', together with pro-Iran, Shia activists from the Parti Anti-Sioniste. Likewise, Christian Bouchet, leader of the movement Les Nôtres, writes: 'One should never target the wrong enemy and find the causes at the roots of evil. And the evil, at the beginning of this 21st century, is not Islam but the consumerist society, the liberal system' (Bouchet, www. voxnr. com. 11 September 2007). On his blog, Boris Le Lay, a rabid neo-Nazi anti-Semite, features a video of the speech given by sheikh Hassan Nasrallah, to commemorate the 'anniversary of the victory of *Hezbollah* over the Zionist entity' (http://borislelay.blogspot.com/2008/08/commmoration-de-la-victoire-du.html).

Confirming the general rule for extreme-right groups, that the less radical they are the less anti-Zionist they are likely to be, the 'Identity' movement embodied into the Bloc identitaire, adopts a very interesting position on the Middle-East conflict. When it was still a violent extra-parliamentary group, it used to stand against Zionism and support the Palestinians, in what they saw as the fight between 'the system' and those who rose against the New World Order. Now that it has become a political party contesting elections, it argues that nationalists should not take sides in the conflict opposing the Jews and the Arabs and its motto reflects this position: 'Ni keffieh, ni kippa', neither (Palestinian) keffieh, nor skullcap. The 'Identity' movement is supporting the concept that each ethnic group should be homogeneous and live on its own soil. It targets Islam and Muslims as being the major threat to French and European ethnic stock and culture. One of the 'Identity' ideologues, Guillaume Faye, holds the controversial view that a racial war between 'White people' and Islam is imminent in Europe, and that in this conflict, the Jews are on the side of the 'Whites'. This idea, which he promoted in his book *La nouvelle question juive* (Faye 2007) has been denounced by the New Right thinker, Alain de Benoist, as 'strongly racist' (Area Editoriale, March 2000) and by Christian Bouchet as 'national-Zionism' (www. voxnr.com, 11 September 2007).

After 9/11, ideological stances that had previously been characterized by their polar opposition found between themselves sufficient areas of agreement to form a determined anti-Jewish alliance. When *L'autre visage d'Israël* was published in 2005 by the Jewish-Israeli anti-Semite Israel Shamir, the publisher was the Paris-based Islamist *Éditions al Qalam* and its lawyer was Eric Delcroix (1994), a former elected official of the FN and the MNR as well as a well-known Holocaust denier. When in September 2006, the comedian Dieudonné M'Bala M'Bala, who is of African origin, travelled to Lebanon and met with *Hezbollah*, two individuals were by his side: Thierry Meyssan, a conspiracy theorist from the Left and Frédéric Chatillon, the former leader of the neo-Fascist Groupe Union Défense (GUD). Finally, the anti-Jewish bias of the most extreme nationalist groups is so strong that in 2007–8 some of them decided to build a coalition with black supremacists, against what they perceive to be the 'Zionist grip' on the media, the economy and politics. The groups Droite Socialiste and Renouveau français united with the Mouvement des Damnés de l'Impérialisme (MDI). The MDI was a coalition of White and black supremacists, which also included people of Arab origin as well. The rationale was a common rejection of a multicultural society, the shared belief in ethnic supremacy and above all, a strident anti-Semitism under the guise of radical anti-Zionism.

Conclusion

Since the 1960s, the issues of Zionism, the Arab world, and the attitude to adopt both towards Jews and Muslims have deeply divided the extreme-right family. The groups, which seriously aspire to become mainstream political parties, do not campaign on the issues of anti-Semitism and Holocaust denial. They have also softened their anti-Israel rhetoric, although anti-Semitism is still part of the doctrinal corpus of many party activists, such as in the Front national. One reason is that those ideas do not appeal to their potential voters, so they focus their agenda on the critique of Islam and multiculturalism. Another reason is that anti-Semitism, apart from being a cause for social marginalization, is a criminal offence and the laws against it are seen in most European countries as a symbol of the political consensus on democratic values. Therefore, adhering to this consensus implies that one refrains from subverting the state by promoting a prejudice, which sets a divide between what is morally acceptable and what is not. On the other hand, the extreme right, which prefers to remain on the fringe of the political spectrum and is content with bearing testimony to the past, adheres to a sub-culture composed of various conspiracy theories in which the Jews and Israel play a pivotal role. In its rhetoric, 'Zionism' is often a code-word for 'Jewish' and this enables it to link with Arab nationalists and Islamists, with whom it shares a common contempt for Western civilization and liberal values. By adhering to anti-Semitism, it clearly proves its commitment to subverting the democratic system, while also walking into the steps of the fascist movements.

Notes

1 Sedevacantism is the position held by a tiny minority of Catholic traditionalists, who believe that the Holy See has been vacant since the second Vatican Council, as succeeding Popes have supported the modernist reforms such as interfaith dialogue, religious freedom or ecumenism. The main European sedevacantist group, Institute Mater Boni Consilii, is based in Italy. Its bulletin, *Sodalitium*, promotes the conspiracist theory that the Catholic Church is undermined by a Jewish–Freemason subversion plan.
2 Paul Rassinier (1906–67) was a member of the pacifist wing of the French Socialist Party. Because of his activity in the Résistance, he was deported to Buchenwald by the Nazis and became a Member of Parliament in 1946. After the war, he was one of the first Holocaust deniers and, while he remained active in the anarchist movement, he became increasingly involved into the extreme-right anti-Semitic scene.
3 Henry Coston (1910–2001) was the French correspondent of the infamous Nazi foreign propaganda service, the Weltdienst. An 'anti-Jewish' candidate to the 1936 elections in Algiers, in 1941 he founded the Centre d'Information et de Documentation, a pro-Nazi 'research centre' fighting the Jews and Freemasonry. He remained the most influential figure of the conspirationist extreme right until his death.
4 Tradition refers to the concept of a fundamental set of values present in all religions or forms of society that are based upon an aristocratic, elitist structure. The word 'tradition' refers to any set of beliefs or customs taught by one generation to the next, often orally.
5 In that case, green refers to the traditional colour of Islam.
6 Interview on RTL Radio, 13 September 1987.

References

Bertuel, J. 1981. *L'islam, ses véritables origines*. Paris: Nouvelles éditions latines.

Birnbaum, P. 2006. 'The French radical right: from anti-Semitic Zionism to anti-Semitic anti-Zionism', *Journal of Israeli History*, 25(1): 161–74.

Dard, O. 2005. *Voyage au cœur de l'OAS*. Paris: Perrin.

Delcroix, E. 1994. *La police de la pensée contre le révisionnisme: du jugement de Nuremberg à la loi Fabius-Gayssot*. Colombes: Revue d'Histoire Révisioniste.

Del Valle, A. 2002. *Le totalitarisme islamiste à l'assaut des démocraties*. Paris: Éditions des Syrtes.

Dubreuil G. 2002. *Un cas d'insoumission. Comment on devient révisionniste*. Samizdat Publications.

Fabei, S. 2005. *Les arabes de France sous le drapeau du Reich*. Nantes: Ars Magna.

Faye, G. 2007. *La nouvelle question juive*. Chevaigne: Éditions du Lore.

Ferjani, M.C. 1991. *Islamisme, laïcité et droits de l'Homme*. Paris: Éditions L'Harmattan.

Fresco, N. 1999. *Fabrication d'un antisémite*. Paris: Éditions du Seuil.

Haroun, A. 2005. *Algérie 1962, la grande dérive*. Paris: Éditions L'Harmattan.

Holeindre, R. 2003. *Israël–Palestine: assez de mensonges*. Paris: Éditions Godefroy de Bouillon.

Igounet, V. 2000. *Histoire du négationnisme en France*. Paris: Éditions du Seuil.

Kauffmann, G. 2008. *Edouard Drumont*. Paris: Perrin.

Landau, P. 2005. *Le sabre et le Coran. Tariq Ramadan et les Frères musulmans à la conquête de l'Europe*. Monaco: Éditions du Rocher.

Lebourg, N. 2009. 'La subversion de l'extrême droite radicale face à l'État durant la Vè République'. In F. Cochet and O. Dard (eds), *Subversion, anti-subversion, contre-subversion*. Paris: Riveneuve éditions, pp. 311–23.

Madiran, J. 1986. *Ce que l'on vous cache, sous-titré: Qui a imposé ce diktat: ne s'allier en aucun cas au Front National?* Maule: Éditions Difralivre.

Madiran, J. 1992. *L'Adieu à Israël*. Maule: Éditions Difralivre.

Megret, B. and Dupont, Y. 2000. *Pour que vive la France*. Paris: Éditions Cité-Liberté.

Saint-Loup. 1965. *Les Hérétiques*. Paris: Presses de la Cité.

Saint-Loup. 2007. *Hitler ou Juda? Un second procès de Nuremberg*. Prague: Éditions du Cercle du Chêne.

Stora, B. 2006. *Les trois exils. Juifs d'Algérie*. Paris: Stock.

Winterberg, Y. 2004. *Der Rebell. Odfried Hepp, Neonazi, Terrorist, Aussteiger*. Bergische Gladbach: Luebbe.

Zakarias, H. (aka. Gabriel Théry) 1955. *De Moïse à Mohammed, l'islam, entreprise juive*. Cahors: self-publishing.

8

RIGHT-WING EXTREMISM AND THE INTEGRATION OF THE EUROPEAN UNION

Electoral strategy trumps political ideology

Bénédicte Williams

Parties of the extreme right are usually classified as the prime exponents of Euroscepticism, yet the issue of their position towards European integration and the EU remains under-examined, both in terms of its content and underlying motivations. Historically, 'Europe' has been of concern to nationalist movements of both the inter-war and post-war periods, although not necessarily leading to a rejection of Europe: on the contrary, nationalism did not preclude inter-war fascist parties from developing ideas of pan-Europeanism in which a certain conception of European culture and identity primed (Bar-On's chapter in this volume). Additionally, case studies of extreme-right parties show that party platforms present changes, one of the most visible being that of the Italian Lega Nord, which, in 1998, switched from being a strong supporter of European integration to opposition as expressed by its recent proposition of a referendum against the Lisbon Treaty in May 2008 (Chari *et al.* 2004). Furthermore, the case of the Romanian Partidul România Mare, which officially supported Romanian membership of the EU, highlights the need to go beyond a monolithic understanding of the extreme right as ideologically preconditioned to oppose the EU (Grecu 2006; Johns and Adamson 2008). A closer investigation of the positions of parties of the extreme-right family is required, in order both to determine the nature and content of parties' positions, and to explain why positions are taken and, where change occurs, why it does. In this chapter, I investigate the nature of extreme-right parties' position towards European integration over a twenty-year period (1985–2007), by focusing on two representatives of this party family, which experienced growing electoral success from the 1980s: the French National Front (Front National, FN) and the Austrian Freedom Party (Freiheitliche Partei Österreichs, FPÖ).

This chapter first presents an alternative to the currently accepted classifications of Euroscepticism, which tend to present both the EU and the parties' discourses as one-dimensional and static. Recent efforts to go beyond this one-dimensional classifi-cation include, for instance, distinctions between the principle, the practice, and the future of EU cooperation (Vasilopoulou 2009). The classification of Euroscepticism presented here takes as its point of departure an understanding of the EU as a multi-faceted organization, whose impact as a political, economic or cultural community may cause internally conflicting attitudes. The first section therefore applies the different political, economic and cultural indicators to the two case studies. This classification rests on the application of rigorous content analysis methods to party manifestos for national (parliamentary) and European elections since 1985. The coding was based on the development of a specific coding frame adapted from the Euro-manifestos project to cover the maximum range of possible policy positions.[1]

Second, on the basis of the mapping exercise described above, this chapter proposes an explanation for the changes found in tone, content and direction. Several explanations have been developed in the literature on party systems for change, best summarized with Müller and Strøm's (1999) distinction between the three simultaneous and potentially conflicting motivations of vote-seeking, policy-seeking or office-seeking. I here argue that party competition is the best fitting explanation for the parties' stance and for the changes in it. Ideology, public opinion and party membership all contribute to the overall motivations, but considerations of a party's competitive environment are the factor most likely to influence its placement on the issue of European integration.

From Europhilia to Euroscepticism

The FPÖ and the FN of the 1980s both embraced the EC, with overwhelmingly positive references in their respective 1986 manifestos, although support was motivated by different reasons. In the case of the FPÖ, a positive approach to the EC took place primarily by way of promoting Austria's membership of the EC, since, they said, '[w]e consider Austria's membership of the EC to be essential, in order to further our objective of the greatest possible participation of our country in European integration' (FPÖ 1986: 5). In 1986 and 1990, the FPÖ's pro-integration stance was also justified by reference to events in neighbouring Eastern European countries and fears of the consequences of social and military unrest. Setting aside Austria's neutrality obligations after the Second World War, the FPÖ sought to present the EC as the best protection available to Austria. In France, a founding member of the EC, the FN emphasized France's 'European vocation' and called for the Community to take on more, not less, responsibilities, including a 'common currency', a 'common police' and 'a European judicial space' (FN 1985: 191). From these positive appraisals of European integration and of the EC, both parties switched to opposition to the EC/EU, but at different times in the ensuing years and for different reasons.

For the FN, nascent opposition to the EC already appeared in 1989 by rejecting the idea of 'a European super-state' (FN 1989: 2). The 1994 European election represented one of two peaks of FN opposition to the post-Maastricht EU, with a list clearly named 'Against the Europe of Maastricht – Go ahead France!', although as for many of its manifestos the focus was more on domestic issues with a European gloss than on European issues per se (FN 1994). By contrast, the FPÖ's shift against the EU occurred in 1994: in the June accession referendum and the October parliamentary elections, it became a leading campaigner against Austria joining the EU. Thus, in the parliamentary election of 1995, the party called for an end to the transfer of sovereignty to the EU and for restricting Brussels's competences.

After this switch away from support of European integration, the FN and FPÖ's opposition did not hold constant but, rather, presented varying levels of intensity of opposition. The FN's increasing course of Euroscepticism seemed to culminate in the parliamentary elections of 2002, in which it claimed that the way to 're-establish French sovereignty' was 'to take France out of the European Union' (FN 2002: 23), a position that it did not, however, repeat in its manifesto for the parliamentary elections of 2007. By contrast, explicit opposition to the EU from the FPÖ in 1994 and 1999 was followed, after 2000, by a much more unsettled period in which positive and negative references predominated in turn. In its manifesto for the most recent parliamentary elections (October 2008), the FPÖ thus presented itself as speaking in favour of European unification, although not discarding the possibility of exit from 'an European Union which develops as a centralized state' (FPÖ 2008: 5–6).

This brief overview of the FN and the FPÖ's overall position towards the EC/EU highlights two important features. First, both parties were avowed supporters of integration (in terms of ideal and practice) for most of the 1980s. In neither case was this anything new. Since its formation in 1956, the FPÖ had taken pride in being the only party in Austria to campaign for Austrian accession to the EC, thus implicitly accepting the tenets of European integration (Kramer 1998). As for the FN, its original support for European integration displayed an important degree of historical and ideological similarity with the path laid out by the New Right movement in its claims for a pan-European vocation (Bar-On's chapter in this volume). Second, the increasing levels of opposition to the EU or to some of its features shown since the early 1990s are not reducible to overall opposition to any form of European project. On the contrary, both parties still follow the rallying call of a 'Europe of Fatherlands', taking the shape of cooperation, rather than integration, as their ideal for the EU. Overall, then, both parties show an important degree of continuity in their support for the ideal of European integration, and for their support of a vaguely defined 'Europe of Fatherlands' as the model for translating the ideal into practice. This is accompanied by a drastic change in their appraisal of the EU as a form of European integration. The following section, by mapping out the different components of the parties' discourse, presents a more in-depth assessment of the position of extreme-right parties towards the evolving process of European integration.

For figures comparing the FN and the FPÖ, three sets of election years have been brought together to facilitate comparison. These are: 1989 (FN)/1990 (FPÖ), 1996 (FPÖ)/1997 (FN), and 2006 (FPÖ)/2007 (FN).

Political, economic and cultural indicators: an explanation

Different conceptualizations of Euroscepticism have been evolving since the late 1990s, as a response to the increasing levels of dissatisfaction with the process of European integration displayed by citizens and political actors. Among the plethora of definitions of Euroscepticism, the most advanced is that of Kopecký and Mudde (2002), who present a useful distinction between the idea of integration and its practical implementation, which informs their categorization of Euroscepticism: Europhobes 'do not support or even oppose the ideas of European integration underlying the EU', Euro-pessimists 'do not support the EU as it is at the moment, or are pessimistic about the direction of its development' (Kopecký and Mudde 2002: 301).

As has been seen in the previous sections, such distinctions between the ideals and the practice of European integration can serve to highlight a certain underlying continuity in the extreme-right parties' overall appraisal of the ideal, and rejection of the practice, of European integration. It is, however, the latter area, of the practice of integration, which needs further investigating, as current dichotomies leave unexplored a potentially rich source of differentiation. This section explores ways of expanding and systematizing a framework distinguishing between the political, economic and cultural aspects of these discourses. These three indicators cover a majority of the EU-related references of the two parties considered; in the case of the FPÖ, however, the significant proportion of references related to environmental policies in the 2004 manifesto, which could not adequately be included in any of the three main indicators.[2] These references to the environment and animal rights are therefore not included in the indicators, although their existence should be taken into account when analysing the discourse of the FPÖ.

Political

The first, political category covers a spectrum of party positions, from exclusive support of national institutions, to a preference for intergovernmental cooperation, to wholesale support for the transfer of decision-making powers to supranational institutions. This reflects the fact that the EU differs from most other international organizations because of the extensive (although not uniform) transfer of power from national decision-making centres to a new set of European institutions, with consequences in terms of the pooling of responsibilities on border control, policing, foreign and military policy, judicial decision-making, and in terms of citizen participation and democracy in the EU.

Economic

The second, economic category relates to the EU's character as, originally and primarily, an economic organization, in which transfer to the EU of economic responsibilities can create distinct (perceived) benefits or disadvantages to the member-countries. The development of common economic, financial and monetary rules, and enlargement and the extension of the single market area present a number of challenges to member-states' governments' capacity to implement autonomous national distributive and redistributive policies as well as introducing greater competition in the labour and production markets.

Cultural

The transfers of political and economic sovereignty attached to the development of the EU also have cultural implications, reflected in the cultural category that encompasses concepts of culture and way of life, both national and European. The origins of the EC were influenced by pre-war and contemporary ideas of a community of values, historical, religious and democratic, aspects of European construction that have gained importance in recent years as the EU both deepens (the European Convention on the Future of Europe was the scene of a debate on the inclusion of religious references in the proposed constitution) and widens. In particular, the renewed process of Turkey's application for membership has been accompanied by a politicization of the question of the development of a shared European identity (Hurd 2006), highlighting the extent to which identity can be challenged or strengthened by integration and enlargement.

The Freiheitliche Partei Österreichs

The emphasis placed on the different political, economic and cultural categories of references to the EC/EU in the FPÖ's manifestos from 1986 changed over time, with a shift from a predominance of political issues between 1986 and 1995, to a more diversified set of concerns from 1996: primarily economic in 1996 and 1999, cultural in 2006, and environmental in 2004.

The majority of the FPÖ's pro-accession arguments in 1986 and 1990 revolved around political issues. The FPÖ both called for 'a united Europe' and for a greater Austrian role within it, motivated by what the FPÖ thought Austria could bring to the EC as a 'mediator' between East and West (FPÖ 1986: 5). Concerns for the safety of Austria as a neutral country at the confines of a disintegrating Soviet Union were also used to justify the party's pro-accession arguments. In 1990, however, economic issues also played an important role in the FPÖ's pro-accession arguments: at this point, the FPÖ fully subscribed to the idea that accession was necessary to safeguard Austrian economic growth. In debates carried in and out of the parliamentary chamber since at least 1988, the FPÖ stated that 'only a clear yes to accession into the European Community can open the way into the European domestic market' ('Anfrage' 1988).

Political aspects were also at the forefront of the party's anti-EU rhetoric in the 1994 and 1995 elections, although the FPÖ shifted in these two elections to criticism of the Austrian government for 'mishandling' the negotiation process and accepting Brussels' terms 'without ifs or buts' (FPÖ 1994: 8). But the EU itself was also criticized for, in part, providing another arena for collusion between the two governing parties, the Austrian Social-Democratic Party (Sozialdemokratische Partei Österreichs, SPÖ) and the Austrian People's Party (Österreichische Volkspartei, ÖVP), and, as a corollary, for its lack of democracy.

By contrast, the manifestos for the European elections of 1996[3] and 1999 both emphasize economic concerns. Where pre-accession manifestos had underlined foreseen economic benefits of EU membership, the manifestos of 1996 and 1999 are mostly concerned with the negative economic consequences of Austria's accession, particularly for individual citizens, and the governing parties' poor negotiation records are also blamed for leading to rising levels of unemployment. By 1999, just over half of the manifesto relates to economic factors, this time emphasizing the many implications of the EU's forthcoming enlargement to the East, including threats that Austria's labour market will be 'overrun by cheap labour', particularly agricultural, and that the increased national contributions to the EU budget required in an expanded EU will serve to subsidize corruption both in the EU and in the applicant countries (FPÖ 1999: 1).

Politics is once again the most mentioned category in the 2002 manifesto, referring mostly to the military. Where after 1994 the FPÖ had denounced the capacity of the EU to protect Austria's borders and consequently called for a stronger, independent Austrian military, the party now called for Austrian participation in the construction of a European security and defence system, as a measure necessary to Austria's external security (FPÖ 2002: 12). The two following elections, however, break the pattern of predominance of a combination of political and economic categories in the references to the EU. The manifesto for the 2004 European election is thus characterized by an unusually high level of environmental references, primarily relating to concerns about the pollution resulting from increased freight traffic through Austria after enlargement. By contrast, no mention is made of the environment in the 2006 manifesto, in which the majority of references to the EU relates to cultural or identity aspects of European integration. This peak is all the more noteworthy that it follows a long period during which cultural or identity references were virtually absent from the FPÖ's manifestos, and were only minimally put forward as arguments in favour of the FPÖ's pro-accession rhetoric in the period between 1986 and 1994. Unusually, since the EU is habitually conflated with Europe, the FPÖ introduced a distinction between, on the one hand, a cultural concept ('Europe is more than a geographical concept: It is founded on a Christian and occidental community of values') and, on the other, a purely organizational concept ('the concept of Europe can . . . not be reduced to a supranational organization such as the European Union') (FPÖ 2006: ch. 6). Once again, this is therefore another clear indictment of the EU as a project of European integration that fails to comply with the FPÖ's newly developed vision of a culture-based form of European unity.

The Front National

By contrast with the FPÖ, the FN shows much more continuity in the content of its approach to the EC/EU, which tends to be dominated by political arguments. Anti-communism was, until the 1980s, the FN's prime *raison d'être*, and the EC (or any other form of European project) was seen as the best means of protection against potential assaults from the USSR (Hainsworth 2004). Yet, while this threat was deemed a sufficient justification for the development of a defence component to the EC, the FN of the mid-1980s still put forward a model of integration based on cooperation, not integration, which was valid beyond the field of defence, and was symptomatic of their overall perception of acceptable routes for the development of European integration.

From 1989 onwards, issues of immigration and border control prevailed in the FN's discourse towards the EC/EU, but the tension between national and European borders remained, in the main, unresolved. Thus, in 1997, the FN called for a 'renegotiation of the treaties' and for a rejection of Maastricht and Schengen. Yet, paradoxically, given that the role of Schengen is also to provide for European borders, it also called for 'the reinforcement of European borders against third world immigration' (FN 1997: 4). The same unresolved tension is found with respect to the existence of a European citizenship, particularly where it involves the granting of voting rights in local and European elections to EU nationals residing in other member-states. This is not, however, wholly related to the development of the EU, but rather is used to reinforce the FN's anti-immigration rhetoric: the manifesto for the 2004 European election thus strongly opposed the concept of a European citizenship, not only because of the perceived outcome of the erosion of the primacy of French sovereignty and citizenship, but also because, according to the FN, it would lead to the naturalization of immigrants.

Within this primacy of political issues, however, there was a notable change in 2004, as the FN shifted towards a focus on more 'real' European issues. Thus, while the manifestos after 1989 were almost solely oriented towards issues such as immigration or law and order – the mainstays of the FN's national campaign discourse but presented with a European gloss – the 2004 manifesto suddenly shifted to a much more serious focus on attributes of the EU, most visibly with respect to the role and actions of European institutions.

By contrast with political factors, economic factors tend to be approached through a moderately less negative lens. Most of the economic references are to issues over which the EU has little power: in other words, the FN 'Europeanizes' its campaign themes also for economic factors. This included in particular employment policy and welfare provision, for which the FN sometimes advocated a form of 'European preference', reserving access not only to French nationals but also to citizens of other member-states. Protectionism is mentioned recurrently, the FN being in favour of a 'European protectionism', a European free-trade area in agriculture, trade and employment, and the maintenance of tax barriers and health and safety checks to prevent 'uncontrolled imports' (FN 1997: 4). By contrast, issues relating to the budget or the introduction of a common currency are very little mentioned. The 2007 election manifesto broke this trend by addressing both the role of the European Central Bank (ECB) and the European currency, although at the same time illustrated the party's unresolved stance on European economic policy both calling for an extension of the ECB's powers and equating this institution's existence to 'a loss of [French] monetary sovereignty' (FN 2007: 42).

Throughout the period, culture remained almost absent, with the exception of the 1986 manifesto. Overall, integration is not presented as a threat to national culture, but rather notions of culture are used to distinguish between 'foreigners of European origin, easy to integrate, and those from the third world who are difficult to assimilate by reason of their numerical importance and of their cultural and religious specificity which leads them to refuse assimilation' (FN 1985: 112). Contrary to what might have been expected, the renewed process of Turkish application for membership did not, at least in the manifestos, lead to an association between potential Turkish membership and a threatened national or European cultural identity, beyond quoting the Commission's statement that 'the EU is defined by its values more than by its fixed geographical limits' (FN 2007: 60).

Strategy beats ideology: investigating the impact of ideology, public opinion and party competition on the positioning of extreme-right parties towards the EU

Definitions of the extreme-right phenomenon abound, but most agree on the primacy of the nation-state as a common historical and ideological feature of the extreme-right party family. From this point of view, the two parties' continuity in appraising the ideal of European integration, and its changing views with respect to the practice of integration, beg the key question of whether these are grounded in the broader ideology of the party or are vulnerable to short-term strategic considerations (Kopecký and Mudde 2002: 319). Both parties' original support for the EC hinged on distinct and openly acknowledged instrumental reasons: for the FN, the EC/EU was considered a useful protection against communism, while, for the FPÖ, accession to the EC/EU was linked to concerns about the economic disadvantages for Austria of remaining outside the rapidly developing sphere of European integration, and to concerns about the signs of disintegration of the USSR and the social and political developments in the neighbouring Eastern European countries. By contrast, although both parties stressed at various times their participation in a common European civilization, aspects of common culture or identity have played a comparatively small role throughout the time period considered. Thus, unpacking approaches to European integration points to a major difference between the discourse of contemporary extreme-right parties strategically reacting to the real and existing challenge presented by the European Union, and that of inter- and post-war fascist movements that dreamed of installing a pan-European empire founded on exclusionary conceptions of culture and identity (Bar-On's chapter in this volume).

Of course, the EC/EU itself changes over time, especially with the Maastricht Treaty, and the shift towards supranationalism, contrasting with the preferences of the FN and the FPÖ, both of which privileged more intergovernmental forms of organization. Yet, particularly for the FPÖ, the timing of the change, as will be discussed below, indicates that other factors may have been at work in the party's decision to reverse its long-held pro-accession position. In the following, I will therefore contend that strategy not only 'can', but 'does' play an important role in explaining a party's support for, and opposition to, the EU. This is not to say that ideology does not play any role with respect to extreme-right parties' policy positions in general, or positions towards the EU in particular but, rather, that in some cases ideology can be downplayed in favour of strategic considerations. These considerations differ on the basis of whether the parties are vying for influence on policy, for an increase in their vote returns, or for access to government office. Strategic moves may respond to a number of variables, primarily relating to attempts to match shifts in public opinion in order to maximize voter support, and responsiveness to shifts in patterns of party competition.

Public opinion

A standard explanation for party change is developed from Downs' (1957) account of parties as vote-seekers/maximizers, adapting their programmatic commitments in order to expand their electoral appeal. Public opinion, as an indicator of voter preferences, provides a means for parties to select electoral strategies most likely to attract votes. Research on public attitudes to the EU shows that a variety of factors determine public support for European integration, including citizens' opinion of the national political system, individual socio-economic circumstances, or the presence or absence of a strong European identity (Gabel 1998; Sánchez-Cuenca 2000; Wessels 2007). Yet an explanation that links the two parties' changing position with shifts in public opinion presents only limited systematic validity.

Public opinion in Austria in the run-up to accession was very divided and, particularly in 1993, was not wholeheartedly in favour of joining the EC/EU. The closeness between negative and positive opinions of Austria's membership of the EU, both prior to accession and in the two following years, provides some justification for the party's shift against accession (Table 8.1).

But the FPÖ's position on economic issues shows less parallelism with public opinion. From being one of the countries in which the euro was least popular, Austria made a clear break in favour in 1998, just after the FPÖ's launch of an initiative to try and prevent Austria from joining the EMU, which only met with moderate success (Pelinka 2005). After this, the party's continued opposition to

TABLE 8.1 Personal expectations of outcome from Austria's entry into the EC/EU

	1991	1992	1993 (January– May)	1994	1994 (June)	1994 (December)
Advantages	53	54	47	49	59	54
Drawbacks	34	37	44	34	25	37
No answer	12	9	7	15	–	9

Source: Fessel/GfK, cited in Plasser *et al.* 1994: 349.

Austria joining the Eurozone, arguing that this would result in a loss of national independence as symbolized by the schilling, differed from Austrian public opinion, which showed growing levels of support for the euro (surprisingly, much higher than public opinion support for Austrian membership of the EU).

The same discrepancy between public opinion and party stance, across political and economic aspects, is found for the FN. After the dip in public opinion's positive assessment of France's membership of the EC/EU from 70 per cent to 56 per cent between 1991 and 1993, the FN stood consistently in opposition to public opinion trends, both with respect to assessment of France's membership of the EC/EU, and on the issue of the common currency. In particular, the radicalization of the party's stance in 2002 with the call for France to exit the EU was not paralleled by public opinion indicators: public opinion's positive assessment of France's membership of the EU remained constant around 50 per cent in the early 2000s, with a temporary dip only in 2005, coinciding with the referendum on the proposed European Constitutional Treaty. The radicalization of the FN on this and on the issue of the common currency proved to be in touch neither with the electorate at large, nor with the FN's electorate itself, less than half of which condoned the party's exit line (Mayer 2002).

Party competition

The prospect of coalitions with other parties can act as an incentive for extremist parties to moderate or radicalize their policy stance depending on the potential electoral partners. Not all parties are equally feasible coalition partners: one of the basic assumptions of coalition theory is that ideological closeness is a determining factor as coalition partners seek to minimize the transaction costs of coalition bargaining (Müller and Strøm 1999). An alternative explanation for party change highlights on the contrary the dissenting character of the extreme right. As Kitschelt (1995) argues, the emergence of new radical right parties is the result of the successful exploitation of a window of opportunity in the party political space. A similar argument can be made with reference to specific policy issues such as that of European integration. Taggart (1998: 385) thus refers to party-based Euroscepticism as a 'touchstone of domestic dissent' whereby peripheral and extreme parties will seek to use the EU as a tool of contestation in an overall pro-integration party environment. Parties thus seek to exploit a 'niche' in the party environment by radicalizing their stance in comparison with that of mainstream parties.

Party competition accounts for most of the changes in the parties' strategy from 1986 to the present. Two aspects of party competition explain the differing strategies of radicalization and moderation pursued during this time period. Generally, aggressive strategies were used when changes in the party environment left open gaps that the parties could exploit, or when the emergence of new parties presented a challenge to which the party needed to respond. By contrast, opportunities for office (as a coalition partner) created incentives for moderation.

The FPÖ's shift in the early 1990s towards opposing the EU (by way of opposing Austrian accession to the EU) is clearly motivated by the change in the party environment on the issue of European integration. The FPÖ's original pro-accession position, held from its creation in 1956 until the early 1990s, was structured by opposition to the major parties, exploiting a 'niche' that contrasted with the opposition of the two major parties to opening a process of accession (Kramer 1998). The SPÖ and ÖVP's opposition was not directed at the EC itself, but rather privileged the protection of Austria's neutrality, while the FPÖ sought to emphasize on the contrary that neutrality and membership were not mutually exclusive. Yet the late 1980s and early 1990s revealed that only the socialist party impacted on the FPÖ's change. By the late 1980s, the ÖVP had already launched the process of application for membership, but Haider's FPÖ only changed once the SPÖ joined the ÖVP in its support of accession. The SPÖ's switch to supporting membership of the EU prompted the FPÖ to change in turn, maintaining a populist, opposition stance (Interview: member of the FPÖ's political executive, Vienna, 13.09.2007). Such a move was not devoid of vote-maximizing motivations: changes in the socio-economic composition of the FPÖ's electorate in the early 1990s reinforced the party's strategic choices as the FPÖ sought to extend its electorate at the expense of the SPÖ's blue-collar voters. Middle and working class SPÖ voters' concerns about globalization and European integration proved a growth area for the FPÖ, which successfully used the SPÖ's shift on the issue of European integration to gather some of its alienated electorate (Luther 2007).

The FPÖ's increasingly aggressive anti-accession stance, and the promotion by Haider of a nationalist and anti-immigration rhetoric, also resulted, in 1993, in the creation of the Liberal Forum (Liberales Forum, LiF), by some of the more economically liberal representatives of the FPÖ. The split had the effect of removing from the FPÖ's discourse discussions of the economic benefits for Austria of EU accession, which were replaced in 1994 and 1995 by increased references to the – negative – political aspects of integration. The end of the FPÖ's strongest period of opposition to the EU coincided with the party's accession to government in 2000. Moderation was certainly a prerequisite for the FPÖ to enter government as a coalition partner: although quantitatively the stronger coalition partner by the smallest of margins, the FPÖ lacked the credibility and experience of the ÖVP, and its overall stance was constrained by the 'sanctions' imposed by the EU on Austria and by the coalition agreement imposed by the ÖVP (Merlingen et al. 2001).

In turn, the European elections presented an environment freer of governmental constraints for the FPÖ, which, in 2004, returned to a higher level of opposition to the EU than that known either in 2002 or 2006.

By contrast with the FPÖ, party competition was much less of an incentive for the FN in the late 1980s and 1990s, both before and after its change to opposing the EU. Furthermore, the main competition from the mid 1990s came less from the mainstream, centre right, than from the emerging 'souverainiste' parties, mostly centre-right Eurosceptics such as Philippe de Villiers, carrying a similar message to that of the FN on the issue of France's role within the EU, but benefiting from more respectability. The emergence of those parties prompted a radicalization of the FN's tone in the 1994 and 1999 European elections, which presented a higher level of opposition as a means of introducing more difference between itself and the new parties (Interview: member of the FN's political executive and former MP, Paris, 09.05.2007). To the strong showing of the 'souverainiste' parties in 1999 must be added the challenge presented by a split in the party, resulting from internal dissent over calls for a more pragmatic approach in the party's discourse in order to turn the FN into a more acceptable coalition partner (Ivaldi 2005). By contrast, the change of platform (national rather than European) for the parliamentary election of 1997, and de Villiers' alliance with the centre right, led to a downplaying of the European issue and explains the return to a high level of positive references in the FN's manifesto. The limited moderation of the party's discourse after 2002 is an extension of the moderation sought by Marine Le Pen in advance of the parliamentary elections of 2007, highlighting the important role of leadership decisions. Her entrance into the political life of the FN in 2002, soon followed by her controversial nomination as vice-president of the party in April 2003, was marked by a decision to 'open up' the party in terms of policies as well as by seeking to expand the party's electoral base (Ivaldi 2005). Following Jean-Marie Le Pen's performance in the presidential election of 2002 (in which he beat the socialist candidate and acceded to the second round), this course of moderation sought to maximize the party's chances of gaining parliamentary seats for the first time since 1988.

Conclusions

Two conclusions emerge. First, parties of the extreme right are not uniformly Eurosceptic. This chapter finds that both parties broadly agree with the ideal of cooperation while rejecting current forms or practices such as the EU. Across time, parties have shifted from a positive to a negative attitude towards the EU, a change that has been found to apply not only to the FN and the FPÖ, but also to other parties such as the German Republikaner and the Dutch Centrumpartij (Mudde 2007). Change can, additionally, occur in a number of ways, from support to opposition, or from moderation to radicalization. More importantly, the development of the sectorial indicators shows that parties' position on the issue of European integration is primarily determined by reference to political and economic indicators. Culture plays only a limited role: parties' positions are underpinned by a discourse of acceptance of a 'European culture' based on a community of values and history, but this is not instrumentalized for electoral purposes. This is perhaps one of the more puzzling results of the in-depth analysis of these parties' discourses presented in this paper, indicating that, despite raging debates on the cultural definition of the European project and of its borders, issues of culture and identity are not at the foreground of the extreme right's support of or opposition to the EU.

Second, this chapter re-examines the claim that, unlike mainstream parties, extreme parties do not strategically adapt their discourse, and so are likely to remain more stable in their discourse. As the findings of this chapter illustrate, particularly with respect to the FPÖ, this is not the case: parties change over time, sometimes dramatically, in their overall attitude towards the EC/EU as a practical instance of cooperation, and this usually from positive to negative. Thus, as opposed to intellectual movements such as the Nouvelle Droite studied by Bar-On and Antón-Mellón in this volume, political parties do have to adapt to their competitive environment, leading to a blurring of ideological legacies. Furthermore, the internal composition of their discourse, and the respective emphasis on political, economic and cultural aspects, differs across countries as well as over time. This leads this chapter to conclude that strategic considerations play a role in extreme parties' positioning. Exploring a number of explanations for party positioning (ideology, responsiveness to public opinion and to shifts in the composition of the party's electorate, and party competition), responsiveness to the environment of party competition is found to explain the most change in the FPÖ and FN's position with respect to the EC/EU. These findings point to fruitful paths for further investigation of party positioning on the issue of European integration. In particular, the classification according to political, economic and cultural criteria can be used to refine analyses of party positions over time as well as in comparative perspective, across new and old member-states of the EU, and across party families beyond the extreme right.

Notes

1 Wüst, A. and Volkens, A. (2003) 'Euromanifesto coding instructions' (Mannheimer Zentrum für Europäische Sozialforschung, Working Paper 64). The full coding frame as well as the content analysis data can be obtained from the author.
2 10.5 per cent in 1990, 10.1 per cent in 1996, 18.2 per cent in 2002 and 38 per cent of references in 2004, as opposed to 0 per cent in 1986, 1994, 1995, 1999 and 2006.
3 Austria's first European election was held in October 1996, more than a year and a half after Austria's accession to the EU.

References

'Anfrage der Abgeordneten Dr Gugerbauer, Dr Haider an den Bundesminister für auswärtige Angelegenheiten betreffend Äußerungen des EG-Aussenkommissärs Willy de Clercq, zur "vollen Teilnahme am Europäischen Binnenmarkt" (25 February 1988)', *Beilage zu* den Stenographische Protokolle über die Sitzungen des Nationalrates der Republik Österreich XVIII, Nr. 1667-J.

Chari, R., Iltanen, S. and Kritzinger, S. (2004) 'Examining and explaining the Northern League's "U turn" from Europe', *Government and Opposition* 39(3), 423–50.

Downs, A. (1957) *An Economic Theory of Democracy* (New York, Harper & Row).

Freiheitliche Partei Österreichs (1986) 'Für eine Politik ohne Privilegien' (Parliamentary election manifesto).

Freiheitliche Partei Österreichs (1990) 'Für Österreichs Zukunft' (Parliamentary election manifesto).

Freiheitliche Partei Österreichs (1994) 'Österreich-Erklärung' (Parliamentary election manifesto).

Freiheitliche Partei Österreichs (1995) '20 Punkte für den Vertrag mit Österreich' (Parliamentary election manifesto).

Freiheitliche Partei Österreichs (1996) 'Österreichische Bundesregierung. Versprochen – Gebrochen' (European election manifesto).

Freiheitliche Partei Österreichs (1999) 'Heimvorteil für Österreich! Unsere Strategie für Österreich zur EU-Wahl!' (European election manifesto).

Freiheitliche Partei Österreichs (2002) 'Sozial & gerecht. Lebenswert & leistbar. Zukunftsorientiert & modern. Wir gestalten Österreich mit Sicherheit' (Parliamentary election manifesto).

Freiheitliche Partei Österreichs (2004) (European election manifesto, untitled).

Freiheitliche Partei Österreichs (2006) 'Programm' (Parliamentary election manifesto). Available at www.fpoe.at/index.php?id=459 (accessed 1 April 2008).

Freiheitliche Partei Österreichs (2008) 'Österreich im Wort' (Parliamentary election manifesto). Available at www.fpoe.at/fileadmin/Contentpool/Portal/wahl08/FP_-Wahlprogramm_NRW08.pdf (accessed 17 November 2008).

Front National (1985) *Pour la France. Programme du Front National* (Paris, Éditions Albatros) (Parliamentary election manifesto for 1986).

Front National (1989) 'Pour l'Europe des Patries. Le courage de dire, la volonté de faire' (European election manifesto).

Front National (1994) 'Contre l'Europe de Maastricht. Allez la France!' (European election manifesto).

Front National (1997) 'Un programme pour gouverner' (Parliamentary election manifesto).

Front National (1999) 'Pour une France libre, changeons d'Europe' (European election manifesto).

Front National (2000) 'Argumentaire: L'identité'. Available at www.frontnational.com/argumentaires/identite.php (accessed 30 March 2008).

Front National (2002) 'Programme du Front National pour les élections législatives de 2002' (Parliamentary election manifesto).

Front National (2004) (European election manifesto, untitled).

Front National (2007) '2007. Programme de gouvernement de Jean-Marie Le Pen' (Presidential election). Available at www.lepen2007.fr/pdf/Programmejmlp2007.pdf (accessed 30 March 2008).

Gabel, M. (1998) 'Public support for European integration: An empirical test of five theories', *Journal of Politics* 60(2), 333–54.

Grecu, R. (2006) 'Accession without integration? The impact of EU enlargement on the Romanian party system', in Lewis, P. and Mansfeldova, Z. (eds) *The European Union and Party Politics in Central and Eastern Europe*, pp. 210–30 (Houndsmill, Palgrave).

Hainsworth, P. (2004) 'The extreme right in France: The rise and rise of Jean-Marie Le Pen's Front National', *Representation* 40(2), 101–14.

Hurd, E. (2006) 'Negotiating Europe: The politics of religion and the prospects for Turkish accession', *Review of International Studies* 32, 401–18.

Ivaldi, G. (2005) 'Les formations d'extrême droite: Front National et Mouvement National Républicain', in Bréchon, P. (ed.) *Les partis politiques*, pp. 15–44 (Paris, La Documentation Française).

Johns, R.A. and Adamson, K. (2008) 'Europe in the ideology of Partidul Romania Mare and Vlaams Belang', in Neumayer, L., Roger, A. and Zalewski, F. (eds) *L'Europe contestée: 'Populisme' et 'Euroscepticisme' dans l'Union Européenne élargie*, pp. 233–52 (Paris, Éditions Michel Houdiard).

Kitschelt, H. (1995) *The Radical Right in Europe: A comparative analysis* (Ann Arbor, MI: University of Michigan Press).

Kopecký, P. and Mudde, C. (2002) 'The two sides of Euroscepticism: Party positions on European integration in East Central Europe', *European Union Politics* 3(3), 297–326.

Kramer, H. (1998) 'Austrian foreign policy from the state treaty to European Union membership (1955–1995)', in Luther, K. and Pulzer, P. (eds) *Austria 1945–1995: Fifty years of the second Republic*, pp. 161–80 (Aldershot, Ashgate).

Luther, K. (2007) 'Electoral strategies and performance of Austrian right-wing populism 1986–2006' (Keele, Keele European Parties Research Unit, Working Paper 24).

Mayer, N. (2002) *Ces français qui votent Le Pen* (Paris, Flammarion).

Merlingen, M., Mudde, C. and Sedelmeier, U. (2001) 'The right and the righteous? European norms, domestic politics and the sanctions against Austria', *Journal of Common Market Studies* 39(1), 59–77.

Mudde, C. (2007) *Populist Radical Right Parties in Europe* (Cambridge, Cambridge University Press).

Müller, W. and Strøm, K. eds (1999) *Policy, Office or Votes? How political parties in Western Europe make hard decisions* (Cambridge, Cambridge University Press).

Pelinka, A. (2005) 'Right-wing populism plus "X". The Austrian Freedom Party (FPÖ)', in Caramani, D. and Mény, Y. (eds) *Challenges to Consensus Politics: Democracy, identity and populist protest in the Alpine region*, pp. 131–45 (Brussells, P.I.E.–Peter Lang).

Plasser, F., Sommer, F. and Ulram, P. (1994) 'Entscheidung für Europa: Analyse der Volks-abstimmung über den EU-Beitritt Österreichs 1994', *Österreichisches Jahrbuch für Politik* (Vienna, Pölitische Akademie der ÖVP).

Sánchez-Cuenca, I. (2000) 'The political basis of support for European integration', *European Union Politics* 1(2), 147–71.

Taggart, P. (1998) 'A touchstone of dissent: Euroskepticism in contemporary Western European party systems', *European Journal of Political Research* 33(3), 363–88.

Vasilopoulou, S. (2009) 'Varieties of Euroscepticism: The case of the European extreme right', *Journal of Contemporary European Research* 5(1), 3–23.

Wessels, B. (2007) 'Discontent and European identity: Three types of Euroscepticism', *Acta Politica* 42(2/3), 287–306.

Wüst, A. and Volkens, A. (2003) 'Euromanifesto coding instructions' (Mannheimer Zentrum für Europäische Sozialforschung, Working Paper 64).

9

ISLAM AT ISSUE

Anti-Islamic mobilization of the extreme right in Austria

Sieglinde Rosenberger and Leila Hadj-Abdou

Introduction

Since the 1990s, taking issue with Muslim immigrants in a fear-laden way and constructing Islam as a threat to European and national communities has become one of the core mobilizing themes for right-extremist parties in Europe (Mudde 2007: 85–6; Zúquete 2008). Most prominently, after the terrorist attacks in New York 2001, a widespread tendency in the discursive anti-immigration strategies of extreme-right parties has emerged in addition to the trope of the undesired 'foreign other': the element of 'the alien Muslim'. Across Europe, extreme-right parties are denouncing Muslims as a minority lacking the willingness to integrate or, even worse, Muslims are being portrayed as a homogeneous group that cannot be integrated into a given national society owing to distinct ethnic, religious or traditional lifestyles. Thus, Muslims are constructed, either way, as a threat to liberal values, European heritage, social cohesion and the cultural integrity of a nation (Bunzl 2007; Mudde 2007; Van der Brug and Fennema 2003).

This paper aims to explore the formation of discursive mechanisms that enable the politicization of Islamic practices and Muslim immigration to Europe. The central question will be when, how and why anti-Islamic references have been brought into the public sphere by right-extremist political parties. In the following the term 'anti-Islamic mobilization' is employed as a conceptual mean to identify and assess the type of discourse employed by the far right that is directed against Muslim immigrants as an alien monolithic group, allowing for a devaluation of Islam as a backward and violent religion (Zúquete 2008: 324). Academic research has well demonstrated that extreme-right parties across Europe have a lot in common, often referring to each other when making use of anti-Islamism as a core issue of contestation and protest. However, systematically taking into account national particularities and institutional factors is decisive for a comprehensive analysis of the emergence of the anti-Islamic discourse. While extreme-right parties are being characterized as identity-oriented and exclusionary by nature, this paper supports the assumption that certain political opportunity structures significantly influence the scope and saliency of anti-Islamic mobilization.

In this chapter[1] we conduct a case study focusing on Austrian far-right parties, that is the Austrian Freedom Party (FPÖ) and the more recently founded Alliance for the Future of Austria (BZÖ).[2] First, the relationship between political opportunity structures and the evolution of anti-Islamic mobilization will be focused on. Second, the anti-Islamic discourse formation will be looked at through the lens of the critical concept of 'differentialist racism' (Stolcke 1999). In the past, Austria's extreme right has often been cited as an electorally successful right-wing party, pursuing an aggressive politicization of 'foreigners', establishing a discourse of exclusion and shaping the way for restrictive immigration policies (Betz 2001; Kitschelt 1995). As the following section will show, the Austrian extreme right, in terms of its current policy claims and anti-Islamic framing, for example, the culturalization of Islam and the use of an aggressive 'threat-of-Islam' communication frame, is in line with other European right-wing parties. However, the factual emergence of the discourse was delayed and its dynamics unfolded unevenly. The chapter argues that besides established ideological positioning towards nationalism and ethnic minorities, the intensity and timing of the rise of an anti-Islamic discourse is also the product of the complex interplay of institutional settings and party strategic purposes. Thus, it can be claimed to be the product of structural and discursive opportunities (see Williams in this volume).

The next section will identify and describe the national institutional framework and the dynamics of power relations that we believe have an impact on the emergence of anti-Islamic mobilization.

Uneven rise of anti-Islamic mobilization: structural opportunities

The formation of the anti-Islamic discourse type in Austria has to be critically assessed within the context of two relevant institutional factors: the formation of a coalition government between the Christian conservative ÖVP and the FPÖ in the year 2000 (lasting till 2006) and the inclusive mode of religious governance the state–church relationship in Austria is based upon.

Following France and the Netherlands, Austria – owing to labour migration and family unification – has the largest proportion of persons of Muslim faith in Western Europe (4.2 per cent in the 2001 census). However, in 1912, long before Muslims immigrated to Austrian territory, Islam had already been recognized as an official religion. The Islamic Religious Community in Austria (IRCA), officially established in 1979 and legally recognized by Austrian state authorities, serves as the official representational body of Muslims residing in the country (Kroissenbrunner 2003). Generally speaking, in Austria a religious pluralistic mode of inclusive governance is highly valued by political authorities and the population. With Islam recognized as one among fourteen faiths, religious believers enjoy a wide range of privileges (e.g. religious instruction in public schools, time off for prayer during working hours). Interestingly, Islam has been widely absent from political contestation for a long time. The rupture began in the late 1990s when the anti-immigration and anti-clerical FPÖ started to contest Islam by placing it at the intersection of immigration, religion and cultural/national identity (Dolezal *et al.* 2008; Luther 2005). However, against the background of an intensified anti-Islamic discourse employed by the extreme-right in Europe after 9/11, the FPÖ, well reputed for its tough stance on immigration, displayed a rather modest profile in this respect. What are the reasons for this exception?

Taking into account the institutional settings, power structures and aspects of party competition, three phases can be identified in the development of the FPÖ that led to the evolution and saliency of contestation of Islam: stage one covers the 1990s and lasts until 1999, when the FPÖ took up the role of an electorally successful opposition party mobilizing on grounds of anti-immigration ideas. Stage two stretches from 2000 to 2005, when the party was in government and pressured to change its political style from an opposition to a governmental party, more oriented towards compromises at the national and European level. Stage three starts after 2005, when tensions between ideological principles and pragmatic decision-making led to intense intra-party disputes and the party consequently split into two rivalling parties, the Strache-led FPÖ and the BZÖ, headed by Haider. Only then, anti-Islamic references and claims significantly characterized the political agenda of both parties.

In the following section, we briefly elaborate on these three stages, focusing on institutional aspects that played a role in shaping the politicization of Muslim immigrants and Islam.

Stage 1 (until 1999): anti-Islamic rhetoric on the fringes

Ever since 1986, when Jörg Haider took over the party leadership, the FPÖ has been mobilizing against 'foreigners'. Meanwhile, the party has launched several initiatives and policy proposals to stop and/or restrict immigration and deemed immigrant integration a superfluous political concern. Electoral campaigns have been underpinned by xenophobic resentment, anti-Semitic rhetoric and allegations designed to provoke envy and fear among non-immigrants (Reisigl and Wodak 2001). At that time the anti-immigration discourse was essentially based upon references that linked immigration with social and economic issues, such as the increase of unemployment that was argued to be caused by immigration and alleged misuse of welfare benefits. Moreover, the FPÖ introduced the concept of '*Überfremdung*', which was used for raising fears about immigration, posing a threat to Austrian values and national identity (Ter Wal 2002). By then religion was not an issue the party referred to, given its anti-clerical programmatic orientation. Only in the late 1990s, seeking to appeal to a wider electorate, the FPÖ slightly revised its former party line by identifying Christianity as the spiritual foundation of the

West. The 1997 party manifesto included an explicit reference to a '*wehrhaftes Christentum*', propagating a notion of Christianity willing and able to defend itself. It was precisely at this time that the party began to take political interest in Islam and announced that the existing legal right to build mosques needed to be discussed publicly (*Kurier*, 8 April 1997). However, in the election campaign in 1999 the topic of Islam and Muslims remained on the fringes of contestation (Geden 2006). It should also be considered that then the FPÖ was one of the electorally most successful far-right parties in Europe. In the general election in 1999 it took 26.9 per cent of the votes, ranking second behind the Social Democrats (SPÖ). Despite heavy protests by Austrian civil society groups and diplomatic measures initiated by EU-member states (Ahtisaari *et al.* 2000), the FPÖ became a partner in the new two-party coalition government led by the conservative Austrian People's Party (ÖVP).

Stage 2 (until 2004/05): relatively low level of anti-Islamic contestation

In government (from 2000 to 2005), the FPÖ developed a profile unlike other extreme-right parties in Europe. Most of all the party avoided taking an openly critical stance towards Islam, given the risks it would expose itself to, when playing the anti-Islamic card in a coalition government led by a partner favouring the inclusion of all recognized religions. As Oliver Geden (2006) concluded, the FPÖ as a government party felt obliged to tone down its anti-immigration posture in order to stay in office. Most surprisingly, even in the context of 9/11 in 2001, the FPÖ adopted a rather sympathetic perspective on Muslims in Austria. Senior party officials publicly declared their respect for the IRCA, advocated dialogue and tolerance, and maintained good relations with top officials in Arabic nations, Libya in particular (OTS 00515).

There are well-founded reasons to assume that the cautious behaviour towards Islam and Muslims was motivated by the diplomatic measures imposed by the EU-member states on the Austrian government in February 2000. As a response to international protests, the two governing parties ÖVP and FPÖ signed a declaration promising to prevent racism and xenophobia and to act in full accordance with European values (Government Declaration 2000). In the following years, the international community and the EU kept a vigilant eye on the FPÖ and the Austrian government. The government-leading ÖVP had a strong interest in presenting the governing coalition as a protector of minorities, especially minority religions, to the outside world. Consequently, the IRCA became a visible 'dialogue partner' of the Austrian government. It was during this period that various statements issued by the FPÖ underlined the universal right of religious freedom as well as the importance of dialogue with and among religious communities, including the IRCA. In 2004 the FPÖ did not utter one word of protest when the Minister of Education (ÖVP) issued a decree, in which the wearing of the headscarf by pupils was defined as a religious right that must not be infringed by any state institution (Gresch *et al.* 2008).

And yet, the reluctance to promote anti-Islamic feelings or promulgate restrictive policies on Islamic institutions and to stick to a pluralist approach towards Islam in Austria does not cover the entire story. While pleading the case for respect of religion and support of Muslims, declaring that religious provisions had to be followed and cooperation with Islamic religious communities was necessary, the FPÖ simultaneously expressed its demand to restrict and ban Islamic practices, such as halal slaughtering. Moreover, in 2004, the party started to debate over Turkey's future EU-membership and conflated the representation of Turkey as an Islamic country with warnings of the danger of radical Islam spreading across Europe (Geden 2006).

Stage 3 (after 2005): strong anti-Islamic mobilization

The transformation of the FPÖ from an opposition party with a distinct anti-establishment and anti-politics style into a governing party responsible for negotiations and policy decisions at the national and EU-level eventually resulted in major intra-party quarrels over core ideology and political pragmatism (Heinisch 2003).[3] In 2005, the party officially split into two parties, the Strache-FPÖ and the Haider-BZÖ. This was precisely the period when, under the influence of the Viennese FPÖ party leader, H.C. Strache, the anti-Islamic rhetoric gained in relevance. Consequently, conflicts over visible signs of Islam such as mosques, minarets and headscarves emerged and entered the political agenda. In other words: The anti-Islamic mobilization gained firm ground when two parties with very similar legacies, and personnel, were looking for support within the same electoral segment. It was H.C. Strache who seized the opportunity to play the anti-Islamic card, while the Haider-FPÖ had little scope to do so because of its participation in a government coalition with the much stronger Conservative Party.

When Islam became one of the major focal points of the Strache-FPÖ, it was used as a discursive tool in party activities. Key motions at party congresses and in parliamentary debates[4] portrayed Islam as a threat to the imagined Austrian nation and, by extension, to Europe. In line with that, the party launched an association named 'Verein-SOS-Abendland'[5] aiming to 'save Western cultures and customs' (*Neue Freie Zeitung*, 22 March 2007). In early 2008 the party released a policy position paper on Islam. The core message pointed out that occidental Christian culture is threatened and therefore needs to be defended by the FPÖ (*Wir und der Islam* 2008). However, the focal point of mobilization against Islam was local, regional and national election campaigns. The most prominent slogans constructing an irreconcilable dichotomy between the Christian 'us' and the alien 'them' were: '*Pummerin statt Muezzin*' ('Church bells instead of Muezzin', Viennese elections in 2005), '*Daham statt Islam*' ('Home instead of Islam', general elections in 2006), and '*Abendland in Christenhand*' ('Occident in the hands of Christians', European parliament elections in 2009).

While the Strache-FPÖ has taken the leading role in politicizing Islam in a pejorative and discriminatory way, the BZÖ came clearly second. In 2006, when the FPÖ ran an election campaign full of xenophobic statements and culturalized anti-Islamic references, the BZÖ brought itself into an awkward position. In a TV talk show the BZÖ leader read aloud a letter he claimed to be authored by a senior Muslim representative, who demanded the replacement of Christian crosses by Islamic crescents on Alpine mountain summits. Some time later, it turned out that the letter had been a fake written by a critical art group who wanted to show how eager certain people were to stir up fears about the alleged Islamization of the public sphere (Renner 2007). In 2007, the BZÖ took up the issue again, this time contesting the construction of mosques. In accordance with the controversy raised in Switzerland, the governor of Carinthia at this time, Jörg Haider, introduced a procedure in building regulations so as to generate a discretionary tool enabling him to restrict the construction of mosques (OTS 0104).

It is important to say that during that period, anti-Islamic discourse and policy proposals began to reach from the realm of the far right into the mainstream right. The Austrian People's Party (ÖVP) no longer intended to leave the Islam agenda to the Strache-FPÖ or the Haider-BZÖ and shifted its strategy from the non-discussion of religious issues to a politicization of Muslim immigrants' deficits in social integration. In 2005, the governmental consensus to keep religious issues out of party competition was breached by the ÖVP Minister of the Interior who labelled Muslim practices as alien to the ascribed Austrian value system and, therefore, as a hindrance to the social integration of Muslims into mainstream society (Hadj-Abdou 2008). Owing to heavy protest by parties on the political left, civil society and religious organizations, the statement was withdrawn within a day. However, the incident indicated that the 'Muslims-are-not-willing-to-integrate' discourse, which until then had been a ploy exclusively exploited by the extreme right, had begun to spill over into the political mainstream. Finally in 2007, when Jörg Haider laid emphasis on the mosque issue, several senior ÖVP politicians at regional levels expressed similar concerns and launched bills restricting the construction of Islamic buildings. Interestingly, ÖVP officials were careful to address Islamic practices outside the religious framework, defining the problem with reference to social cohesion and cultural incongruity (*Die Presse*, 28 August 2007).

The following section will take a closer look at European dimensions that can be identified as being decisive factors for the process of shaping anti-Islamic language and the emergence of policy proposals.

European discursive opportunities

Although, as we have attempted to demonstrate in the previous section, the emergence and rise of anti-Islamic mobilization within the Austrian extreme right evolved within the parameters set by national power structures and party competition, its scope and ideological substance goes well beyond national boundaries. Rather than limiting itself to national arenas and settings, along with the erosion of intra-European borders, anti-Islamic mobilization allows for new and old modes of representation of Europe as a space and a community, thus, to re-conceptualize Europeanism (cf. Bar-On in this volume). We argue that Islam evolves as a topic that facilitates the transgression of borders and political activity across national settings.

Interestingly, the extreme right has almost simultaneously been advocating anti-Islamic stances across Europe in nearly identical ways. Topics, frames and claims 'travel' from one national right-wing party to another, often regardless of actually existing conflicts and tensions or even the occurrence of Islamic practices (Akkerman and Hagelund 2007; Buruma 2006; Mudde 2007: 84 ff.). The observation that right extremist parties influence one another is perfectly valid for the Austrian far right. Issues raised and frames employed by Austria's extreme right are mostly not specifically referring to 'real' conflicts – they are embedded in the cross-national, anti-Islamic activism of the extreme right. For instance, when in 2007 the Swiss People's Party (SVP) launched a popular initiative aiming to statutorily forbid mosques and minarets in the Swiss constitution, the FPÖ brought in a similar motion to the Austrian Parliament within only a few days' interval (*Der Standard*, 30 June 2007). Another recent example illustrates these linkages: in the 2010 municipal elections in Styria, the FPÖ launched a free computer game, in which the users were asked to shoot as many mosques, muezzins and minarets as possible. The game was created by the same agency that also developed the material for the successful anti-minaret referendum of the SVP (*Salzburger Nachrichten*, 25 June 2010).

Moreover, cross-national associations fostering issue-based alliances ('Stop Islamization') have been set up, such as the City Alliance against Islamization[6] in 2008, where the FPÖ played a key role. This platform centres on the dangers of an alleged Islamization which for this purpose is being represented as not a local but a Europe-wide peril, threatening a very imprecise notion of European values and identities. Members of the City Alliance against Islamization speak out at different places across Europe, thus sharing their narratives and ideas.[7] Not only comparatively similar agendas, but even slogans and phrasings of striking resemblance can be observed. An example serves for better illustration: during the municipal election campaign in the city of Graz, the FPÖ candidate Susanne Winter, in a speech[8] given to party officials, referred to the prophet Mohammed as a child molester and argued for a banishment of Islam back to the place where it originally came from – strictly speaking 'beyond the Mediterranean Sea'. A very similar statement had previously been made by Filip Dewinter, the head of the Vlaams Belang: 'Organized, radical Islam has to be pushed back to the other side of the Mediterranean' (*Die Presse*, 23 November 2007).

Finally, it has to be said that aside from a great deal of congruency in the anti-Islamic narratives employed by extreme-right parties in several European countries, some policy issues brought into connection with anti-Islamic perceptions could only gain momentum through specific historic collective memories and pasts. Indeed, among the Austrian extreme right, the phrasing of a looming third Turkish siege, invoking the collective memory of the occupation of Vienna in 1529 and 1683 by the Ottoman Empire, gained some significance. In 2007, Strache coined this term at the national party congress in order to warn of an Islamization of Austria (*Die Presse*, 2 June 2007). This discursive strategy aggregated three different aspects: the discussion about Turkey's EU accession and its depiction as an Islamic country, the mobilization of fears against radical Islam, and recourse to the collective historical memory of the Turkish siege, which is now being transported to present times as a potential threat. This amalgamation furthermore allowed for an emphasis on the party's critical stance regarding Austria's membership to the EU. In 2006 the FPÖ launched the petition 'Austria stay free!' ('*Österreich bleib frei!*'), aiming to achieve a popular rejection of the treaty establishing a Constitution for Europe and to prevent Turkey's EU accession. In 2008, the above-mentioned petition was re-launched in the form of an Internet initiative with similar content on the party's Web page.[9] This development reached a climax in the 2010 municipal elections in Vienna. The FPÖ then published a booklet with the title *Sagas of Vienna* (*Sagen aus Wien*), which prominently featured a cartoon about the Turkish siege of Vienna, picturing at one side the Turkish conqueror with statements such as 'If I do not succeed this time, my successors will have to join the European Union' (FPÖ 2010: 9), and on the other side the city of Vienna with the statement 'The Sultan shall piss off. Turkey does not belong to Europe, not today and not in a hundred years' (ibid.: 10). The comic concludes with the remark 'Islam stay home! Our Vienna for our people' (ibid.: 15).

In the next section we take a closer look at the mechanisms of anti-Islamic politicization. We do so by analysing what is being represented as a 'problem' and what 'solutions' are being formulated accordingly. Finally, we will analyse the framing with respect to racialized and exclusionary elements.

'Islam is a threat': racialized and exclusionary politicization

Anti-Islamic mobilization implies a differentialist mode of racism. In this context, Islamic religion is framed as culturally alien and incommensurably different. 'The Muslim' is being socially constructed as the homogeneous 'other' in dichotomous relation with the self, aiming to exclude Muslim immigrants from access to institutions and benefits. The basic feature of differentialist racism (distinguished from biological racism) is that exclusion is based upon ascribed, essentialized cultural differences (cf. Silverstein 2005; Stolcke 1999; Weller 2006).

The anti-Islamic discourse employed after 2005 in Austria bore culturally racialized dimensions. Previously, Islam was not referred to as a monolithic bloc – the term was used to differentiate between ordinary Muslim people and Islamic fundamentalism and Islamic radicalism. During the campaign of the municipal election in Vienna in 2005 and the parliamentary election of 2006, the narratives shifted perceptibly: Islam was rejected as a whole and exclusionary measures proposed (bans on headscarves and the construction of mosques and minarets).

Following the methodology of frame analysis, we distinguish between two dimensions of the framing process in order to show in more detail how culturalized viewpoints and exclusionary dimensions entered the discourse. The first analytical dimension covers the problem definition (diagnosis frame); the second dimension is concerned with solutions that are being formulated to address the problem (solution frame) (Bacchi 2005).

Problem diagnosis: religious and cultural alien

Against the background of a pluralistic mode of religious governance in Austria and the legal obligation to treat all recognized denominations equally, the FPÖ frames Islam not as a minority religion but as a culture with distinct practices and values. Its counterpart, namely Christianity, is also being shifted from religion to culture, also expressed through the hierarchical concept of the *occident*. However it has to be noted that Islam is not only seen as a different culture but the culture itself is depicted as alien, backward, and therefore represented as an obstacle to the integration of immigrants into Austrian society. Even so, the meaning of these ascribed differences in culture or values often remains vague, that is, 'culture' and 'value' become strategic instruments, empty shells that can be filled with various (and sometimes contradictory) significations.

Especially from 2004 onwards, while the Strache-FPÖ was in the phase of establishment, references to Christian occidental culture gained relevance in political debates. In election campaign materials, illustrations of cathedrals and churches were used as symbols underpinning the party's proximity to occidental culture (Christianity), and contrasted with mosques, which were ascribed to the political opponent. In 2005, the FPÖ accused the political opponent of being a supporter of mosques; however, this was not a new phenomenon, the same argumentative strategy was applied in 1999.[10] The deployment of Christian symbols to underline the dissociation of Islam was done for the first time during the municipal election in Vienna 2005. St Steven's Cathedral was depicted together with the slogan, '*Damit der echte Wiener nicht untergeht*'[11] ('So the true Viennese shall not perish'), identifying the FPÖ Viennese party leader as the 'true' defender of the autochthonous culture. The electoral manifesto for the parliamentary election in 2006 called for the maintenance of (Catholic) religious instruction in public schools as a vehicle for national and European values (Election Programme 2006: 9). Finally, during the electoral campaign for the European Parliament in 2009, Strache attracted a considerable amount of media attention when he held up a Christian cross while giving a speech on the occasion of a demonstration against the construction of mosques (*Die Presse*, 27 May 2009).

Another popular tool for drawing a cultural demarcation line is the principle of gender equality, presented as a Western or even Austrian value. Along the same line as other European extreme-right parties (Akkerman and Hagelund 2007), the Austrian extreme right concentrates for that purpose on the illiberal gender-unequal practices of Muslims, while presenting itself as a proponent or defender of emancipated, autochthonous women: 'Austrian women must not subordinate to an Islamist world view' (OTS 00145). The argumentative strategy of portraying Islam as culturally backward is, thus, communicated through a culturalized version of the universal principle of gender equality. Again, taking into consideration the instrumentalization of gender equality for anti-Islamic mobilization, we can trace a process that began back then with critique directed against certain practices and went on to more generalizing racialized statements. In spring 2001, the Haider-FPÖ hosted an official event on Female Gender Mutilation (FGM). It was acknowledged that the social practice of FGM is being renounced by Muslim scholars and the Quran. Party representatives declared that female migrants must be supported by the state (OTS 0236). Meanwhile the differentiation between Islam and the practices of immigrants gradually eroded. It was replaced by a discursive formation creating a binary opposition between pre-modern Islam which oppresses women on the one side, and modern Austrian values characterized by gender equality on the other side. This pattern was significant for the framework of the debate on the accession of Turkey to the EU in 2004 and intensified after 2005 as a result of Strache-FPÖ activity. The party focused on the Muslim headscarf as a discriminatory practice against women. The headscarf was said to exclude women from public life, and force them into dependence on male family members.

Summarizing, it can be said that the most salient topics addressed were the erection of mosques and minarets, the wearing of headscarves, fundamental/radical Islamism, the purported unwillingness of Muslims to integrate and Turkish accession to the EU. Moreover, all these topics have been linked to each other in order to establish the predominant frame depicting Islam as a threat to the presumed national identity, to liberal European values, social cohesion and to gender equality as a marker of Western or even Christian civilization (see also Dolezal *et al.* 2008).

Problem solution: prohibition, denial of rights, and restrictions

Having analysed press releases, campaign materials and parliamentary documents of a period longer than ten years, three 'solutions' to the stated problems may be identified: the claim to prohibit, denial of rights and restrictive immigration policies.

Prohibitions, for instance of the headscarf, are presented as a measure designed to maintain the *Leitkultur* ideologically grounded in Christian values and modernity, freeing women from 'archaic tribe structures' (OTS 0205). In the national electoral campaign of 2006, an emotional slogan was 'Free women instead of compulsory veiling' ('*Freie Frauen statt Kopftuchzwang*'). Similarly, in the municipal elections in 2010 in Vienna one of the party slogans was 'We protect free women. The SPÖ compulsory veiling' ('*Wir schützen freie Frauen. Die SPÖ den Kopftuchzwang*'). The popular initiative launched by the FPÖ against the accession of Turkey to the EU in 2006 also employed the headscarf as a key motive for campaigning. A woman veiled with an EU flag symbolized the developments that the initiative aimed to oppose.

Individual and religious rights that Muslim immigrants are legally entitled to started to be called into question by the Strache-FPÖ. In contradiction to the official religious recognition of Islam, according to the party's rhetoric, Muslims should not be carriers of religious rights any more. By stating that 'Islam has nothing to do with religious freedom' (OTS 0138), religious freedom is thus interpreted in terms of promoting the cultural rights of the majority Christian community, rather than as a universal individual right to which any Austrian resident is entitled to. In 2008 the status of Islam as an officially recognized religion was questioned by the party. A senior party official, Andreas Mölzer, stated that an immigrant Muslim cannot be entitled to the same rights as were granted to autochthonous Muslim Bosnians during monarchy (OTS 0134). Prior to this, no political party had called this principle into question. By doing so, the party also challenged the cooperative, consensus-oriented mode of religious governance that had so far been considered to be a taboo for political parties (Suppanz 2003: 43).

Last but not least, by claiming that Muslim immigrants form parallel societies within Austrian cities, calls for restrictive immigration measures were a consequence derived from the ascribed unwillingness of Muslims to adapt and the threat of Islamic fundamentalism. Through the definition of integration as a one-way process, as the duty of immigrants to assimilate into the majority culture on the one hand, and the representation of Muslims as culturally alien on the other hand, the FPÖ constructs the inability of Muslims to integrate (OTS 0242).

The policy solutions derived from this unwillingness-to-integrate-construction and the fear-laden 'Islam is a threat' frame, are discriminatory and exclusionary on grounds of religious and ethnic diversity. The rhetoric is used to legitimize the denial of substantive rights to Muslim immigrants and their exclusion from core institutions of mainstream society. In the light of concrete policy proposals, both extreme-right parties are strongly in favour of a politics of control, prohibition, restriction and exclusion. Based on the view that Islam and Muslims are culturally alien, hence the nonconformity of Muslim minorities to Western norms and life-styles, the parties call for a variety of hard-line measures ranging from outlawing religious practices to the expulsion of Muslims 'beyond the Mediterranean Sea'. Both parties advocate a ban on Muslim headscarves, and call for a ban on the erection of mosques and minarets. Summarizing, the parties' demands call for a systematic exclusion of Muslims from structural, social and cultural modes of participation, institutions and benefits.

Conclusions

The aims and results of this paper are threefold. First, it has been argued that the occurrence and the uneven rise of anti-Islamic discourse among the two Austrian extreme-right parties FPÖ and BZÖ can be explained with strategic patterns of party competition,. dynamics in power structure and historically established modes of religious governance (most of all, the official recognition of Islam). Considering the time span from the late 1990s until today, European extreme-right parties began raising issues associated with Islam and Muslims, presenting them as a cultural threat to the values and integrity of nation-states and Europe. However, the Austrian extreme right acted differently from its fellow parties. Although anti-Islam references were moderately articulated against the background of international terroristic events, the Islam frame became dominant only during the election period of 2005 and 2006; after the split into two parties and their return to the status of opposition parties. Most notably, while in government, the Haider-FPÖ was reluctant to politicize Islam as a problem. Even 9/11 did not serve as a catalyst for enhanced politicization. The empirical data analysed for this paper strongly suggest that taking issue with Islam is not a governmental discourse type but, in the first place, employed by parties in opposition. While Haider held a leading role in the governing FPÖ, it was his internal rival Strache, leader of the FPÖ after 2005, who started to campaign with the issue of Islam.

Besides the findings indicating that the rise of anti-Islamic discourse follows party strategic goals and opportunity structures, the second aim of this paper was to identify the exclusionary framing mechanisms and policy proposals employed by the two parties. It has been shown that, bearing in mind the noteworthy time lag, the agenda of the extremist right in Austria highly resembles that of other European extreme-right parties (Zúqhete 2008). Islam has consistently been presented as a cultural marker of difference competing with a nationalistic narrative of social cohesion and a homogeneous identity. The solutions proposed to this alleged societal diagnosis advocate exclusionary policies. And yet, the anti-Islamic agenda of the extremist right mostly consists of electoral campaign rhetoric and polarizing slogans rather than specific policy formulations.

Third, in conflict with its ideological programme, the nationalistic-oriented extreme right has seemingly become both Christian and European in some aspects. It participates in European-wide initiatives, it takes up frames and slogans used by other extreme-right parties, it expresses commitment to Christian occidental values coupled with the rhetoric of a fixed European value community. In fact, the references to a European and Christian value-space are closely connected with claims of prohibition and serve as a means to justify even more restrictive measures to the detriment of immigrants. Against this background, the paper has highlighted that the discursive turn to Islamic practices and Muslim immigrants is another element of the long-established exclusionary politicization of immigration.

Notes

1 The chapter is based on election campaign material, press releases, media articles and party manifestos. The frame of analysis covers the period from January 1997 to October 2010.
2 In 2005 the FPÖ split into two factions, the FPÖ and the BZÖ. At the parliamentary elections of 2008 the FPÖ won 17.5 per cent of the votes, and the BZÖ 10.7 per cent.
3 In the early general election in 2002 the FPÖ suffered heavy losses, taking only 10 per cent of the votes (in comparison with 26.9 per cent in 1999) and the ÖVP won a landslide

victory (from 26.9 per cent of the votes in 1999 to 43 per cent in 2002). Despite this result, again ÖVP and FPÖ formed a coalition government, with a less influential role of FPÖ over public policies.

4   XXIII. Legislative Period: e.g. 248/A (E), 390/A (E), 1483/J.
5   See www.verein-sos-abendland.at/ (last retrieved 5 February 2009).
6   This cooperation originates from an alliance of the FPÖ with the Belgian Vlaams Belang and the movement pro-Köln. It was founded on the occasion of protests against the building of a mosque in the German city Cologne. See www.citiesagainstIslamization. com (last retrieved 10 August 2008).
7   It is moreover striking that Breivik, the far-right Norwegian terrorist, mentioned Austria several times in his writings, referring to debates that have been put on the agenda by the FPÖ (*Kurier*, 26 July 2011).
8   Shortly after having made those statements Winter became FPÖ candidate for the national parliamentary elections in 2008, and is since October 2008 national deputy. In 2009 Winter was condemned for her statements by the Austrian High Court because of incitement and vilification of religious doctrines.
9   See www.oesterreichbleibfrei.at/visionen.php (last retrieved 5 April 2008).
10 In the presidential elections 1999 the FPÖ put an emphasis on the fact that one candidate, Richard Lugner who is a builder, erected the first Austrian mosque (*Kurier*, 24 June 1999).
11 In the 2010 municipal electoral campaign in Vienna this slogan was even transformed into 'More courage for our Viennese blood' ('*Mehr Mut für unser Wiener Blut*'). The party gained with this slogan 25.8 per cent at the ballots, ranking second behind the Social Democratic Party of Vienna.

References

Ahtisaari, M., J. Frowein and M. Oreja 2000. 'Report commissioned by the President of the European Court of Human Rights', 8 September 2000: Paris: Report. Retrieved 9 January 2008 from www.austrosearch.at/pdf/reportwisemenaustria.pdf.

Akkerman, T. and A. Hagelund 2007. '"Women and children first": Anti-immigration parties and gender in Norway and the Netherlands', *Pattern of Prejudice*, 41(2): 197–214.

Bacchi, C. 2005. 'Discourse, discourse everywhere: Subject "agency" in feminist discourse methodology', *Nordic Journal of Women's Studies*, 13(3): 198–209.

Betz, H.-G. 2001. 'Exclusionary populism in Austria, Italy and Switzerland', *International Journal*, 57(3): 393–420.

Bunzl, M. 2007. 'Anti-Semitism and Islamophobia', in M. Bunzl (ed.), *Anti-Semitism and Islamophobia: Hatreds old and new in Europe*. Chicago: Prickly Paradigm Press, pp. 1–46.

Buruma, Ian 2006. *Murder in Amsterdam: The death of Theo van Gogh and the limits of tolerance.* New York: Penguin Press.

Dolezal, M., M. Helbling and S. Hutter 2008. 'Zwischen Gipfelkreuz und Halbmond. Die Auseinandersetzung um den Islam in Österreich und der Schweiz, 1998–2007', *Österreichische Zeitschrift für Politikwissenschaft*, 4: 401–18.

Geden, O. 2006. *Diskursstrategien im Rechtspopulismus. Freiheitliche Partei Österreichs und Schweizerische Volkspartei zwischen Opposition und Regierungsbeteiligung*. Wiesbaden: Deutscher Universitätsverlag.

Gresch, N., L. Hadj-Abdou, S. Rosenberger and B. Sauer 2008. 'Tu felix Austria? The headscarf and the politics of "non-issues"', *Social Politics*, 15(4): 411–32.

Hadj-Abdou, L. 2008. 'Das muslimische Kopftuch und die Geschlechtergleichheit. Eine Frage der Kultur oder der Religion?', *Femina Politica*, 17(1): 68–80.

Heinisch, R. 2003. 'Success in opposition – failure in government: Exploring the performance of the Austrian Freedom Party and other European right-wing populist parties in public office', *West European Politics*, 26(3): 91–130.

Kitschelt, H. 1995. *The Radical Right in Western Europe: A comparative analysis*. Ann Arbor, MI: University of Michigan Press.

Kroissenbrunner, S. 2003. 'Islam, Migration und Integration. Soziopolitische Netzwerke und "Muslim leadership"', in H. Fassmann and I. Stacher (eds), *Österreichischer Migrations- und Integrationsbericht*. Klagenfurt/Celovec: Drava, pp. 375–95.

Luther, K.R. 2005. 'Die Freiheitliche Partei Österreichs (FPÖ) und das Bündnis Zukunft Österreichs (BZÖ)', *Keele European Parties Research Unit. Working Paper 22*.

Mudde, C. 2007. *Populist Radical Right Parties in Europe*. Cambridge: Cambridge University Press.

Reisigl, M. and R. Wodak 2001. 'Austria first: A discourse-historical analysis of the Austrian "Anti-Foreigner-Petition" in 1992 and 1993', in M. Reisigl and R. Wodak (eds), *The Semiotics of Racism*. Vienna: Passagen Verlag.

Renner, F. 2007. 'Die Qual der Fernsehwahl', in T. Hofer and B. Tóth (eds), *Wahl 2006. Kanzler, Kampagnen, Kapriolen. Analysen zur Nationalratswahl*. Wien/Berlin: LIT Verlag, pp. 119–34.

Silverstein, P. 2005. 'Immigrant racialization and the new savage slot: Race, migration, and immigration and in the New Europe', *The Annual Review of Anthropology*, 34: 363–84.

Stolcke, V. 1999. 'New rhetorics of exclusion in Europe', *International Social Science Journal*, 51(15): 25–35.

Suppanz, W. 2003. 'Wir haben nun keine Tradition des säkularen Textes: Religion, Politik und ihre Kompetenzen in der politischen Kultur Österreichs', in M. Brocker, H. Behr and M. Hildebrandt (eds), *Religion–Staat–Politik. Zur Rolle der Religion in der nationalen und internationalen Politik*. Wiesbaden: Westdeutscher Verlag, pp. 33–46.

Ter Wal, J. 2002. 'Anti-foreigner campaigns in the Austrian Freedom Party and Italian Northern League', in R. Wodak and A. Pelinka (eds), *The Haider Phenomenon in Austria*. New Brunswick: Transaction, pp. 157–78.

Van der Brug, W. and M. Fennema 2003. 'Protest or mainstream? How the European anti-immigrant parties have developed into two separate groups by 1999', *European Journal of Political Research*, 42(1): 55–76.

Weller, P. 2006. 'Addressing religious discrimination and Islamophobia', *Journal of Islamic Studies*, 17(3): 295–325.

Zúquete, J.P. 2008. 'The European extreme-right and Islam: New directions?', *Journal of Political Ideologies*, 13(3): 321–44.

Reference materials

Press releases

OTS 0236: Hartinger: Jede fünfte Frau wird körperlich oder seelisch missbraucht. 8 May 2001.

OTS 00515: FP-Sichrovsky: Religionsfreiheit muss in Österreich garantiert werden. FPÖ gegen pauschale Verurteilung aller Mitglieder der Islamischen Glaubensgemeinschaft. 11 October 2001.

OTS 0156: Westenthaler: FPÖ bleibt Sicherheitspartei Nummer 1. Wer frei leben will braucht Schutz vor Terror und Kriminalität. 18 October 2001.

OTS 00885: FPÖ-Strache: Große Chance für den Tierschutz. Hoher islamischer Glaubensführer erlaubt Betäubung vor Schächtung. 24 January 2003.

OTS 0242: Mölzer: Nicht Europa, islamische Welt hat Grund zur Entschuldigung. 16 February 2006.

OTS 0205: Kickl: Kopftuchverbot wäre Befreiung für Frauen und Mädchen. 22 June 2006.
OTS 00145: Ausländerquote an Schulen: FPÖ: ÖVP-Modell zum Scheitern verurteilt. 10 July 2006.
OTS 0138: Mölzer: Festnahme von Islamisten – Zuwanderungs- und Einbürgerungsstop für Moslems. 13 September 2007.
OTS 0134: Mölzer: Grundsätzliche Diskussion über Islam erforderlich. 15 January 2008.
OTS 0104: LH Haider und LR Scheuch: Kärnten europaweiter Voreiter bei Bauverbot für Moscheen und Minarette. 11 February 2008.

Party manifestos, electoral programmes and position papers

Das Parteiprogramm der Freiheitlichen Partei Österreichs. Mit Berücksichtigung der beschlossenen Änderungen vom 27. Ordentlichen Bundesparteitag der FPÖ am 23. April 2005 in Salzburg (Party Manifesto 2005).
Österreich bleib frei! (Party Initiative Austria Stay Free!). Retrieved 5 April 2008 from www.oesterreichbleibfrei.at/visionen.php.
Sagen aus Wien. FPÖ Gemeinderatswahl 2010. Retrieved 2 September 2011 from http://issuu.com/hcstrache/docs/sagenbuch.
Wahlprogramm der Freiheitlichen Partei Österreichs. FPÖ Nationalratswahl 2006 (Election Programme 2006). Retrieved 1 September 2006 from www.fpoe.at.
Wir und der Islam. Freiheitliche Positionen zur Religionsfreiheit, zur islamischen Welt und zur Problematik des Zuwanderungs-Islam in Europa. Wien am 22. Jänner 2008 (Position Paper). Retrieved 1 February 2008 from www.fpoe.at.

Parliamentary documents

248/A (E)/NR/XXIII. GP: Entschließungsantrag der Abgeordneten Strache, Aspöck, Haimbucher und weiterer Abgeordneter betreffend Verbot des Bauens von Minaretten sowie die Verpflichtung für nicht abendländische Religionen zur Verwendung der deutschen Sprache bei der Abhaltung von Gottesdiensten und Predigten. 6 June 2007.
390/A (E)/NR/XXIII. GP: Dringlicher Antrag der Abgeordneten Heinz Christian Strache, Kolleginnen und Kollegen betreffend strikte Anwendung der Rechtsordnung zur Unterbindung der fortschreitenden Islamisierung und der damit verbundenen Terrorgefahr anstatt Errichtung eines Polizei und Überwachungsstaates. 27 September 2007.
1483/J XXIII. GP: Anfrage der Abgeordneten Rosenkranz, Kolleginnen und Kollegen betreffend Islamisierung Österreichs und radikal-fundamentaler Islamismus in Österreich. 27 September 2007.

Governmental document

Government Declaration 2000 'Verantwortung für Österreich – im Herzen Europas' signed by Jörg Haider and Wolfgang Schüssel. 3 February 2000.

PART III

Inside the box

Getting involved

10

THE BUILDING OF SOCIAL REPRESENTATIONS OF RIGHT-WING EXTREMISM

Birgitta Orfali

Generally, most disciplines in the social sciences, including social psychology, refer today to social representations. They often take this theory as a basis for their analysis of social phenomena. Going briefly back to the origins of social representations, this chapter shows first how deeply rooted they are in social knowledge and why they can be taken as an efficient theoretical tool to grasp the specificity of the contemporary extreme right. It will then analyse how extreme-right membership proceeds, taking examples in four countries (France, Italy, Hungary and Romania).[1] It is also worth mentioning that I had already set up (see Orfali 1990a) the premise of so-called internalist perspective (Goodwin 2006), which was then to be emphasized in Klandermans and Mayer's (2005) well-known analysis of European extreme-right activists.

This chapter deals with extreme-right membership by using the same methodological tools (i.e. interviews with right-wing extremists). This is certainly the best approach to understanding why people join these parties. I nonetheless combined the theory of social representations with the theory of active minorities to better grasp how extreme-right grass roots are indeed linked to communication on/about the extreme right. How people have discussed these parties and movements in recent decades has had an impact on the way activists consider themselves, and how society considers militants. There are true interactions between extreme-right minorities and society or the so-called majority, and these interactions play a role in the possible influence minorities may have on majorities, according to Moscovici (1979). Minorities and majorities act on one another and their interactions are simultaneous (the process of influence must take place within an action/reaction frame). Therefore, it is essential to understand how they build communication and use social representations in order to influence one another.

Social representations

In 1961, Moscovici published his work on psychoanalysis, its image and its public.[2] He referred to different authors, such as Durkheim, Piaget and Vygotski, and introduced us to an analysis of reality through the interdependence of the social and the psychological, giving social psychology the possibility of greater recognition within the social sciences. He underlined the importance of an epistemological reflexion on man and society and on common-sense rationality through the study of psychoanalysis and the process by which it penetrated into 1950s French society (Orfali 2000).

According to Moscovici, social representations refer to a modality of knowledge, which helps to elaborate behaviours and communication between individuals. Social representations therefore go back to the epistemological bases of common-sense knowledge and are specific because they are generated and transmitted through social exchanges, investing collective life and producing practices more or less different according to social groups. It is important to keep in mind the different levels of explanation in social psychology in order to understand how social representations operate. Interaction is of course an important presupposition in that respect but so also the intra-individual level, the inter-individual and situational level, the positional level and last but not least the level of beliefs, values, representations themselves, which can be summarized as a societal level, according to Doise (1982). All these different levels are combined within collective practices. They also appeal to other important dimensions, social, historical, cultural, symbolical and ideological. As true constructions, social representations induce implicit or explicit references, which can become certitudes in social thought. The fact that they are contextualized reinforces this aspect, especially since institutions and mass media are also solicited. This produces an obvious dynamic, generating or confirming social change. Through the example of the extreme right in some countries and from other contributions to this collection (to which it hopefully also offers a possible theoretical frame), this chapter analyses how social representations have helped social influence. Both theories (that of social representations and that of innovation), were suggested by Moscovici forty years ago: both deal with social change and allow the analysis of political change too.

Social representations are in fact the symbolic products of social thinking, communication and interaction among individuals and groups. They support and are simultaneously supported by their function in social life. These functions are moreover linked to the processes through which they evolve.

Two processes help the building of social representations

There are two main processes by which social representations are formed, namely, anchoring and objectification. The first process, anchoring, is making the meaningless meaningful. The second process, objectification, is aiming at the integration of the object (be it physical, social, imaginary or real) in the individual's and group's mind. It makes the abstract real. I would like to stress the importance of a reflexion on the extreme right through these two processes (already discussed in Orfali 2006).

Anchoring relies on collective memory and goes back to the social roots of a social representation. It refers to the representation in the social. When we wonder about extreme-right parties or movements, we are often dealing with the re-emergence of these and not with new groups emerging on the political scene in different countries. We are in fact using social representations. More specifically, we can observe the way the past can influence the present because we understand present parties and movements by reference to past parties and movements. The anchoring process helps us understand how a social representation is socially rooted, how a 'new' object that can appear meaningless (because it denies for example the lessons of history as extreme-right parties do) becomes meaningful, both before and after the construction of the representation.

Before the construction of a social representation, anchoring helps us understand the constitution of social relations: knowledge is given a functional dimension as it helps the interpretation of the environment. It has a function of mediation between the individual and the group, producing a common code, a common language and common references. Therefore we can link group communication to social influence. Within extreme-right parties, the internal communication is at first mainly articulated on the idea of sharing and exchanging feelings, opinions and ideas. There is a strong desire from members to find people who think and feel like them. In an earlier study I analysed the reasons for membership in the French Front National and showed how important the feeling of being in a sort of great 'family', sharing one and the same destiny, gives cohesion to the group and helps minority influence (Orfali 1990a; 1990b). Dechezelles shows something similar in her chapter on the cultural basis of youth involvement in certain rightist organizations, when she examines why young activists appropriate extreme-right values: 'it is worth examining the different ways in which party members experience their political involvement, their family socialization and their social origins'. The transformation into a social movement is then possible on the basis of this peculiar group certitude and relies on different styles of behaviour (consistency, investment, autonomy, rigidity and equality), which gives the minority both its specificity and social visibility and recognition.

After the building of the social representation, anchoring refers to a pre-existing knowledge that is used as a landmark for new forms of knowledge and that gives sense to the unfamiliar, the strange. Every new object is perceived according to the meaning the group gives it and is based on a hierarchy of values, a system of interpretation built in and by the group. The evaluation made by the group can favour the group's identity and it may also reinforce its cohesion. Sharing the same group mentality makes it possible to identify new objects and social phenomena in an identical spirit. Any new event is understood thanks to this specific mindset.

On the cognitive side, anchoring refers to a deeply rooted system of thought. The object is cognitively integrated in pre-existing notions and uses memory. Moscovici (1976) calls this opposition between the old and the new a 'cognitive polyphasia', explaining that the constituting thought has to build on a constituted thought. This in turn explains why it can exist in both a rigid and an innovative way. The fact that 'new' extreme-right movements have to be understood through a reference to 'old' ones shows how the cognitive process works: in any country, today's extreme right is necessarily related to some identical party or ideology from the past. In France, for example, the Front National will bring a reference to Pétain and the Nazi collaborationists (on this see also Wolfreys's chapter); in Italy, the fascists will be quoted when Alleanza Nazionale, Forza Nuova, Fiamma Tricolore or Azione Sociale are discussed.

The other process that is at work when we build social representations is objectification, which helps us understand how the object 'extreme right' is integrated in common-sense reality. It refers to the social in the representation. If we consider parties such as the Front National or Alleanza Nazionale, we observe that a specific object (here an extreme-right party) is structured and understood through the building of a specific image, often referring to both its positive and negative aspects, which tries to give sense to both words and things. The political debate about the extreme right has, for example, led to the renewal of a debate on democracy, its opponents and its defenders. Democracy is generally understood as a necessity but some people may dislike it and may quote Churchill, according to whom it is the worst political system but a better one has not yet been found. Social thought has this need to make things visual to be better understood, a need for more concrete elements to permit communication, while it still remains in the field of social and political life. Within social exchange, the ideas on the representational object have to be real. Objectification is what makes the abstract real.

Different phases assist this objectification process. First a selective construction aims at choosing between the information one has about the represented object. Everybody does not have the same opportunity and access to information, hence a difference in choice. The elements one has chosen have to coincide with the individual's existing value system. Through the classification of the information, an appropriation of 'true' information (i.e. those corresponding to known normative and cultural criteria) takes place.

Once chosen and privileged among other elements of information, the object has to be structured into a 'figurative kernel', reproducing in a visible way an important conceptual structure. The opposition – even the conflict – between different significant notions is helping the emergence of those that will best translate the meaning of the object. The concepts are not obvious though. Some of them are sometimes 'hidden', like the libido in Moscovici's work (1976) on psychoanalysis.

This figurative kernel is finally transformed: its elements become objective entities visible both in oneself and in others. Once they are integrated, the elements constituting the object of the representation are obvious and acquire a common-sense reality. A stable figurative kernel will be a tool to organize perceptions, judgements and behaviours both for groups and individuals within a socially constructed reality. This figurative kernel will be recognized both by in-group members and by out-group ones. The well-known '*Travail, Famille, Patrie*' in France, as well as '*Lavoro, Patria, Famiglia*' in Italy, can illustrate this point as members comment about it in a positive way while outsiders understand it in a negative way. But what is important is the fact that they both use it, either positively or negatively: there is then a true recognition of this concept as representative of the extreme right, at least in French or Italian society.

The objectification is easily rendered through discursive oppositions, as good/bad, ugly/nice etc. Language carries categories inducing a certain type of thinking. The word extreme right is, for example, not neutral. Quoting it means that we may refer to political or ideological oppositions, to cliché-thinking, and it needs a classificatory adjustment: *who speaks* (a member, a leftist or somebody who cares little or not at all for politics), *from where* (the point of view of a member, the point of view of somebody who is ideologically opposed to the party, the point of view of a voter), *about what* (a specific party, a political preference, politics in general), *how* (with the arguments of a proselytizer enjoying his party, with the arguments of one who may oppose the party, with voter arguments), *and with which effects* (convince family and friends that this is *the* party, accept or reject the implicit ideology, seduction/lassitude)?

Three levels are to be considered

Three levels are important to consider for understanding how social representations are meaningful for communication and communication is meaningful for social representations, in the context of the extreme right. The main question here is how do social representations emerge? We already mentioned the ambiguity, which takes place in the process of information. Different social groups have different access to information; they are involved in different ways and their members may answer differently to the group dynamics, especially where extreme positions or decisions are concerned, or even when social recognition is at stake.

The processes of anchoring and objectification also insert social representations within a more general and consensual frame, even if they explain communicative processes with the help of dialectics and favour social and political change.

Last but not least, the media system influences opinions, attitudes, stereotypes and social representations. There is a correlation between the aims of the media and the way representations are structured: diffusion will help the formation of opinions; propagation will assist the formation of attitudes, while propaganda will contribute to the formation of stereotypes. Communication on the extreme right will largely be dependent on these different modes of communication and types of influence. The extreme right can be perceived in terms of opinions or attitudes and can also have a stereotyped status. If we are to consider the social representation of the extreme right, we have to take into account this specific dimension through the degree of involvement of the members (see Orfali 1990a). But we also need to understand how social representations may help social influence because they refer to other communication tools, such as literature or music (Orfali 2005a). The perspective should not be divided into the externalist/internalist dichotomy. Trying to understand how people commit themselves in extreme-right parties or movements needs to combine both the reasons uttered by the activists themselves and communication at large. The micro- and macro levels have to be combined and not opposed in the attempt to understand why there still are people who join such parties across Europe. I have already demonstrated how one can combine both levels when I confronted 'active minorities and social representations', which share one and the same epistemology (Orfali 2002).

Effects of group membership

As Durkheim (1898) noted, *collective representations refer to the way the group is thinking of itself in its relations to the objects that affect it*. This idea of interdependence between the individual and the social in their relation to the object (symbol) is also relevant for social representations as it destroys the Cartesian dichotomy between the individual and the social, perhaps in favour of a more Hegelian understanding of reality.

How do people refer to the extreme right, an object obviously affecting them (both inside and outside the party)? First, there is the naming of the object. And this is not a neutral task. Are there differences according to the languages used and are these differences inducing different social representations (Moscovici 2000)? In fact, most languages use the word 'extreme' and what is perhaps stressed is the possible passivity and neutrality of the object itself? There is in fact a strong normative status in the process of naming itself. If we take Moscovici's (1984) suggestion about social psychology, we understand how interactions take place and favour a specific dynamic about the extreme right, where members do appreciate their parties in relation with other members' point of view but also in relation to other people, other members in other parties, outsiders from out-groups. The object is truly built through the tensions, which exist about the definition of the 'extreme right'.

Furthermore, the extreme right is not only an abstract entity but has a true meaning. This political tendency is convincing as far as it stresses the overwhelming power of an object (a specific ideology) in words referring to the movement itself. The social representation of the extreme right seems stronger than cultural differences. Oppositions have changed as well as social representations and we are now in a 'third wave' of right extremism (Goodwin 2006). This generates the necessity of both diachronic and synchronic analysis of the phenomenon – as has been done in some other contributions to this volume (see, for example, Turner-Graham, Williams, Camus, Virchow or Goodliffe).

Social representations evolve and transform according to practices evolving over time. These changes happen in parallel with social change and there is a dialectical relation between both social representations and social practices as there is between the two main processes working within social representations: anchoring and objectification. There still remains something of a dichotomy because of these permanent dialectics, but it is always articulated on a representation of the self, the other and the object. The position an extreme-right member has within his party induces a certain apprehension of reality and objects within this reality. Politics and political membership are at the same time real and imaginary, social and symbolic. They stand for the member's reality and even a definition of membership (as soon as one becomes a member of a group, be it social or political, one starts building expectations about one's status, one's roles in the group and has to define one's position within the group).[3] Different degrees of group participation lead to different identity definitions as I suggested when I theorized a typology of Front National members, opposing the men of order, the men of violence and the submitted men who organize the differences between '*militants*', '*adhérents*' and '*membres*' (Orfali 1990a). Either as true activists (*militants*), as less involved members (*adhérents*) or as simple members (*membres*), those who belong to extreme-right parties reconstruct their reality through the object of politics. In doing so, they adjust to their understanding of what social and political reality is. They constantly use a dichotomy between their everyday life and their membership because membership cannot remain neutral; it settles the individual in a process that he cannot avoid, in action for the party – even if this action is more or less important according to different individuals.

Investment in party activities is not the same for everybody but it may have the same function for everybody: it organizes the cognitive universe of the member and gives him/her tools to understand his/her own identity. This is what group membership usually gives to individuals. When the extreme right is considered, this is even more obvious. To become a member of an extreme-right party may bring cognitive dissonance (Festinger 1957), which the individual may try to reduce. Because the extreme right is stigmatized and rejected, members have to cope regularly with criticisms and negative opinions. The reduction of cognitive dissonance is then an important aspect when one analyses membership in these parties. As a woman I interviewed said: 'I don't care to meet people who don't share my ideas' (Orfali 1990a). Furthermore, a sort of 'paradoxical membership' reinforces this dimension: when Jews, women, workers or people from the West Indies become members, they want to get rid of their previous identity and the possible stigmatization linked to a specific religion, gender difference, status or ethnic characteristics (Orfali 2005a). The will to distance oneself from old identity criteria is strong enough to make legitimate the decision to enter a party, which stigmatizes one's original group. It is easier to cope with criticisms related to political membership than to criticisms made of one's religious, gender, status or ethnic belonging.

One has to notice that membership of extreme-right parties helps the individuals to deny previous membership and that this political membership prevails in the individuals' lives. Because they are willing to dissociate two worlds (the one before membership and the one after), members (specifically the paradoxical ones, but this is true for all members in fact, who constantly refer to a time before and a time after), do in fact reinforce a specific group dynamics. Activism in the party reinforces a true group mind and even 'party mind'.

The empirical data on the extreme right

A larger comparative study in four European countries – like the one I carried out in the 1980s – in France, Italy, Hungary and Romania can be very useful to check whether there is an identical process leading to membership in extreme-right parties.[4] The main questions were related to this process: why do people become members of extreme-right parties? How do people account for initial reasons for affiliating to the extreme right? We performed two kinds of thematic analysis: first, we compared participants' responses based on twenty-five interviews in each country; second, we analysed data across all four countries (100 interviews). We will here summarize the main results of this second analysis. We chose these four countries for the following reasons: two of them are situated in the West (France and Italy) and many different studies have already been done on their extreme-right parties and movements while the other two are situated in the East (Hungary and Romania) in the former communist bloc and few studies have been done on their respective extreme-right parties. Membership of the European Union is henceforth a common characteristic for all four countries, but for France and Italy it is an old membership while it is something quite new for Hungary and Romania. These four countries have differing experiences of the extreme-right phenomenon: re-emergence (France), historical heritage (Italy), post-communist nationalism (Hungary and Romania).

All the interviewees refer to a time before and a time after membership. Feeling much better after they became members, the interviewees all express the opposition between 'society as it is' and 'society as it should be'. In all four countries, extreme-right members live within the party, as they would like to live in society. The building of social representations is organizing their understanding of society. Joining the party means that one may have the possibility to change society. The fact that the reasons (explaining the decision to join an extreme-right party) always link personal experiences and political events, reinforce this aspect. All the interviewees go back to the time before membership and explain how odd, how different from other people they felt, while their life changed once they became members. A sort of renewal is felt that permits us to conclude that the intra-individual level is important in membership. There is at first a strong desire to organize cognitively one's world according to comfortable criteria. The uncomfortable feeling that existed before membership is forgotten once the decision to enter the party has been taken. Meeting people who have lived the same dissonance before membership helps reinforce the idea that one made the right choice by joining the party (Orfali 1989). This inter-individual level is then also important to explain the process of membership.

What is crucial is the fact that once a member, a person can relate with others who have gone through the same itinerary, who have lived the same doubts about the country, life in general, their own existence, values and norms. To find people who share the same experience is important as it reinforces group cohesion. The resentment felt before membership is forgotten and replaced by the will to become an activist in the party. Higher self-esteem is found and this may explain what Berman (1997) writes about militants who should not be seen as 'hapless victims of their economic or demographic environment, but as the active shapers of their own fate'. Though there are differences in membership (as I wrote when I opposed the men of order, the men of violence and the submitted men), a common feeling is shared by all members (Orfali 1990a). Otherwise there would be heavy turnover, but this is seldom the case when one enters an extreme-right party. The difficulty one meets when one wants to become a member (there is often opposition within one's family when it does not share the same political opinions or at work or with friends and relatives for the same reasons) is undeniable: once one becomes member of an extreme-right party, one does not quit it very easily. All the interviewees in all four countries express these difficulties in their relationship to others (family, work, relatives and friends). This reinforces the feeling of belonging to one and the same 'big family', that of the extreme right. It also organizes one's representations of the world, society and politics.

How do militants of the extreme right in France, Hungary, Italy and Romania express their certitudes on membership, their conviction that they have chosen the right way? We retained the main items, which rendered this choice 'obvious', and in this section we will consider the responses given by the interviewees, which show that there are common points in all four countries.

Proselytizing, a common feature in activism in general, is shared between militants in all four countries, but Hungary and Italy have more proselytizers in their extreme-right parties (64 per cent) than France and Romania (44 per cent). Conviction does not always express itself through proselytizing; it is often used by those less convinced than by those who are really convinced (Orfali 1990a). Indeed, proselytizing helps self-conviction.

Social polemic, which refers to the desire for debate and discussion rather than a desire to convince other people, is different in every country. All the Hungarian interviewees (100 per cent) are willing to discuss and want to consider different matters in an exhaustive way while the French and the Italian interviewees (64 per cent) consider this less important but more important than the Romanian interviewees (52 per cent).

Deep membership is truly important for the Italians (80 per cent), who appeared to be deeply committed by their political choice, while the French (68 per cent) show interest but a less intensive one. The Hungarians (60 per cent) and the Romanians (40 per cent) seem to be less convinced. One wonders here if the geopolitical situation of each country might explain these data: are Italy and France, as members of the Western countries, more orientated towards political commitment while Hungary and Romania, as part of recent dictatorship, would be less committed?

As for the use of *moral language*, which is recurrent among extreme-right activists, we notice that France and Hungary have the same percentage (76 per cent) which is quite high while Italy has only 56 per cent and Romania only 52 per cent. It would seem that the image of Italian or Romanian corruption, commonly adopted by other countries, is accepted as a categorization even by the Italians and the Romanians themselves and adopted into their own discourse.

Autonomy from the party's line is very important in Italy (84 per cent), Hungary and Romania (72 per cent) and less crucial in France (48 per cent). The Italian party system perhaps explains this, as there are numerous parties in the peninsula, which allows great freedom in political posturing, while Hungary and Romania used to live under communist pressure and are willing to profit from their new freedom since 1989.

The leader's charisma is important for 64 per cent of the French interviewees and for 52 per cent of the Romanian ones, while it is less important for the Italian (48 per cent) and Hungarian (36 per cent) ones. The levels of support for Jean-Marie Le Pen (and even more today with Marine Le Pen) for the Front National and of Corneliu Vadim Tudor for the Romania Mare Party explain these differences; Gianfranco Fini (the leader of Alleanza Nazionale) is also charismatic but, trying to appear as more moderate than before with phrases such as '*Basta con il fascismo*', he is considered a little less charismatic than the two others. Alleanza Nazionale has, moreover, been integrated into Silvio Berlusconi's People of Freedom and does not exist anymore as such. Jean-Marie Le Pen (his daughter too, but in a more moderate way) and Vadim Tudor are tremendous rhetoricians and use, even abuse, metaphors, expressions, the famous '*petites phrases*' that help to situate them in a true charismatic role. As for István Csurka, the leader of the MIÉP (the Hungarian Party of Justice and Life), he seems less charismatic, perhaps because of his constant use of drama and theatre expedient.

Regarding *racism*, the French seem to be much more racist than the other interviewees with 76 per cent expressing racist points of view, as against 44 per cent of Hungarians, 32 per cent of Romanians, and 'only' 16 per cent of Italians. Italians seem to be less racist because they showed empathy for immigrants, having members of their own family who migrated to the United States for example. The creation of so many 'little Italys' abroad has to do with the building of social representations on immigration and its consequences, and explains the interviewees' position on immigration. Of course, statistics are giving a general idea of the phenomenon and recent events in Italy have shown another aspect (Mammone 2009). The difference between speech and action is also underlined in these events, which oppose the interviewees' 'softer' answers. The desire to appear as 'gentle and moderate activists' introduces a bias, in any interview, while the acts can contradict the discourses.

As for *anti-Semitism*, the Hungarians reveal the strongest tendency with 72 per cent, as against 56 per cent of the French interviewees, 16 per cent of the Romanians and, in Italy, only 4 per cent (this last percentage is more or less the same as that found in the general population of the country: anti-Semitic attitudes were supposedly not the norm during fascism).[5] That the French express so anti-Semitic an attitude refers to the well-known theory of conspiracy (Taguieff 1988; 2005; 2006), the belief in the supremacy of the 'two-hundred families'. With this item of anti-Semitism, we discover how important social representations are: one cannot explain today's anti-Semitism without going back to ancient beliefs, the history of the country. Hungarians are therefore high scoring on this item because they have always rejected any minority in their country, especially the Jews, and the leader of the MIÉP recurrently uses this reference. Chapter 7 by Jean-Yves Camus explains the links between the extreme right, anti-Semitism and anti-Zionism and shows how an object is not defined alone but in relation to other objects in society.

Right-wing extremists generally favour *a traditional Church* though one has to retain the opposition between true churchgoers and non-believers. 'Although Catholic fundamentalists still retain strong positions within the apparatus of several extreme-right parties (Front National), the vote for the extreme right is generally weak among regular churchgoers and strong among non-believers', according to Camus (this volume), because 'the extreme right, like other political families, has had to adjust to an increasingly secular society'. Ninety-two per cent of the Romanian interviewees prefer such a Church (because religion was prohibited during the communist period. This is important, as well as the fact that the Orthodox Church is the main religion in the country, a religion that has lost a lot of its impact in the world in general; the Serbian war also induced this necessity for religious cohesion). Eighty per cent of the French interviewees (even if they do not themselves go to church) also favour this attitude while 72 per cent of the Hungarians and 56 per cent of the Italians agree. The Hungarians have the same concern as the Romanians about a traditional Church, which represents the possibility of saving the country's culture and past glory. The Italians score lower than the others (which can seem quite strange in the country of the Vatican but can be understood if we consider that religious pressure has been strong for a long time and that it has then induced a certain opposition to traditions, even though we will see hereafter that this is not really the case concerning sexual freedom). Once more, social representations are solicited to explain how attitudes are built (for or against) an object.

The interviewees score very high on the *abortion* item. They strongly oppose such a practice in all four countries (Hungary: 92 per cent; Italy: 84 per cent; Romania: 80 per cent and France: 76 per cent). This is perhaps the feature that is most significant when extreme-right ideology is discussed: there is a real rejection, which relies on the certitude that abortion is in fact killing. This certitude can be linked to the preference for a traditional Church but it is mainly articulated from a conservative point of view that can be found elsewhere in the world. Very often, this item is related to the conviction that murderers should be killed and there is a correlation, a dichotomy the theory of social representations permits to integrate: refusal of abortion/acceptance of death sentence (i.e. abortion refers to killing an individual – an innocent baby – while death sentence refers to killing somebody who betrayed society, who is guilty).

Sexual freedom is refused: by 88 per cent of the Hungarian interviewees, 76 per cent of the Romanians, 72 per cent of the French and 56 per cent of the Italians. The discourses always refer to the possibility of contracting diseases as a result of such freedom; the comparison with the decline of the country is always evoked (if society is so ill, it is because people are too free, especially sexually). The Italians are less opposed to this freedom in reaction to the weight Catholicism still has in the country.

The relations to the European Union are considered good by 76 per cent of the Italian and Romanian interviewees, while only 4 per cent of the French and 0 per cent of the Hungarians agree. As Williams explains in her chapter: parties of the extreme right are usually classified as Eurosceptics but she considers the change that is slowly occurring in this Euroscepticism. The French and the Hungarians in fact resist the European Union and express an important resentment (the Front National was opposed to the European Constitution and tried to influence society in that direction during the 2005 referendum; it succeeded and convinced people who were already convinced by the 'no' camp because French society and all the other parties were in fact very divided on the question). As for the Hungarians, the discourse of the leader of the MIÉP consistently opposes and demonizes Europe as being a symbol of the devil, and this can explain their total rejection. The Italians and Romanians recognize that they have had many benefits from Europe: the countries' economies have been much better since their entry into the Union.

Relations with the United States are favoured by 76 per cent of the Italians (once more, because of the numerous Italians who live there and because NATO was accepted after the Second World War). The Romanians are divided on this item (44 per cent) while the French do not really agree (28 per cent) and none of the Hungarians approve. Past relations with the US can explain these results: the French have always had an ambiguous relationship with the US, as have the Romanians, while the Hungarians reject the US as the symbol of the devil (thanks again to István Csurka's speeches). The negative image Hungarians have of the United States is also a result of the connection they make between the United States and Zionism, reminding us that there are 72 per cent anti-Semites among the interviewees in this country.

Reaction to a specific event had already appeared as an important reason for membership in France (Orfali 1990a): many activists related their decision to join the party in the 1984 interviews (published in 1990) to a specific event such as the TV broadcast '*l'Heure de vérité*', to which Jean-Marie Le Pen was invited, or the 1984 European elections where the Front National 'suddenly' emerged on the French political scene. Similarly, 100 per cent of the Hungarians claim that a specific event led them to join the MIÉP, the 2002 elections being very important in Hungary in that respect. In our recent data, 48 per cent of the French, 24 per cent of the Italians and 20 per cent of the Romanians put forward the role played by a specific event in their decision to become activists. The specific events are often related to politics (e.g. a referendum, or a change such as the *Tangentopoli* scandal in Italy) but they can also refer to an aggressive act that has occurred in someone's life. Whatever it refers to, it is always interpreted in an emotional and affective dimension. This is true of extraordinary events as we explained in Orfali (2005b) but it remains a valid feature in the social psychological process that induces membership (Orfali 2005a; 2010).

Do extreme-right members believe in the party's future? This was the last question aimed at understanding whether membership led to total submission to the party's ideology and group mentality or whether people could be true activists but not really believe in the party's success in local or national elections. The image of the leader played a role in this respect because many of the answers referred to Jean-Marie Le Pen and/or Marine Le Pen, Gianfranco Fini, Corneliu Vadim Tudor and István Csurka. Ninety-two per cent of the Romanian interviewees are confident in the future, as against 88 per cent of the Italians, 72 per cent of the French and less than half of the Hungarian interviewees (44 per cent). Overall, extreme-right party leaders have a key position as they induce a belief in the party's future.

In fact, culture is both desired and rejected by activists: it can be used as a pretext for membership (as discourses on the past cultural glory of the country always assume) and it can be used to communicate a specific ideology. Culture (for example music or literature and even sport) can serve as relay stations for extreme-right ideology because of its diffusion in society and the possibility of convincing in a softer way a larger part of the population ('equality' is a style of behaviour that specifically allows a greater influence on a larger part of the population, according to Moscovici 1979). In Orfali (2005a), I took the example of populist literature in Sweden,[6] which helped the building of a nationalistic sensibility, both on the local and on the national levels. Wasaloppet was also scrutinized in order to understand the true meaning of this national skiing competition for the Swedes and how it goes back to nationalistic values. Testa and Armstrong also analyse in this volume the meaning of football in Italy today. As for music, I analysed how a song such as 'La tribu de Dana'[7] (Dana's tribe in the album *Panique celtique*, by the French group Manau), adopted by teenagers in the 1990s, had roots in true nationalistic ideology. Teenagers used to repetitively sing this song and adopted, without knowing it, all the ideological references expressed in it. The process of influence can rely on modes of communication that are not explicitly political and can lead to acceptance of a hidden ideology, even by teenagers. As Moscovici (1976: 39) puts it:

> social representations are almost tangible entities. They circulate and crystallize all the time through a word, a gesture, a meeting, in our everyday life. Most of the social relations, most of the objects produced and consumed, most of the exchanged communications are impregnated with them.

Conclusion

Though nobody commands or prescribes extreme-right membership, some people do join and this chapter has tried to analyse their reasons. Taking the theory of social representations (Moscovici 1976) as a possible tool to explain the process of membership, I also went back to the theory of innovation, which was used in previous research on extreme-right motivations (Orfali 1990a; 2005a). This study thus attempted to understand whether there were links between parties in different countries, whether the process of affiliation relied on identical presuppositions. Specifically it is clear that both theories are relevant as one tries to get to the core of extreme-right membership. A social psychological perspective permits us to really understand the process of membership and the way ideology is articulated in relation to personal expectations within society. Billig (1978) showed this for the British National Front. But he insisted perhaps too much on the ideological reasons and, in our view, these need to be considered in relation to the personal expectations members have when they join such a party. These expectations can be realized through party activism and this is certainly the specificity of extreme-right parties: they suggest a minority action and consider all the other parties, indeed society in general, as the 'enemies' against which they have to fight.[8] Members then find what they are looking for, the possibility of overcoming a feeling of powerlessness that they felt before membership. This is even more striking when one considers that few members have been activists before, in other parties; they are often joining a party for the first time but 'strangely' they join an extreme-right party.

Notes

1 This comparative study was made thanks to the Groupe d'Étude pour l'Europe de la Culture et de la Solidarité (GEPECS) at Paris Descartes University, and thanks to the Laboratoire Européen de Psychologie Sociale (LEPS, research group on the extreme right that I led between 2002 and 2006). The researchers were: Ida Galli and Roberto Fasanelli (Italy); Ferenc Eros, Judit Ujlaky and Gergo Pulay (Hungary); Luciana Radut and Lavinia Betea (Romania); Birgitta Orfali and Erwan Lecoeur (France). The research was supported by the Fondation Maison des Sciences de l'Homme (FMSH) and by a Bonus Qualité Recherche (BQR) from Paris Descartes University.

2 In the present chapter, I refer to the 1976 edition.

3 There is a difference between 'membership' and 'the process of becoming member of a group' (cf. *L'adhésion – Militer, s'engager, rêver*, Orfali 2010).

4 This study has been published in a collective book (ed. B. Orfali) by the publisher L'Harmattan in 2012 under the title *L'adhésion à l'extrême droite: Étude comparative en France, Hongrie, Italie et Roumanie*.

5 They were seldom reported but for example in literature, as in the novel by Giorgio Bassani, *Il Giardino dei Finzi-Contini*.

6 Populist meaning here 'concerning people'.

7 'Dana's tribe' in the album *Panique celtique*, which means 'Celtic panic', by the French group Manau was in the ten top in 1998. It mixed rap music and Breton traditional songs.

8 The Oslo attacks on 22 July 2011 showed how the non-understanding of the evolution of society by a psychologically fragile person can lead to murder and terrorism as well as showing the fragility of democracy.

References

Berman, S. (1997) 'The life of the party', *Comparative Politics*, 30(1), 101–22.

Billig, M. (1978) *Fascists: A social psychological view of the National Front*, London, New York: Academic Press.

Doise, W. (1982) *L'explication en psychologie sociale*, Paris: PUF.

Durkheim, E. (1898) 'Représentations individuelles et représentations collectives', *Revue de Métaphysique et de Morale*, 6, in *Sociologie et philosophie*, E. Durkheim, Paris: PUF, 1951.

Festinger, L. (1957) *A Theory of Cognitive Dissonance*, Evanston: Row Peterson.

Goodwin, M.J. (2006) 'The rise and faults of the internalist perspective in extreme right studies', *Representation*, 42(4), 347–64.

Klandermans, B. and Mayer, N. eds (2005) *Extreme Right Activists in Europe: Through the magnifying glass*, London, New York: Routledge.

Mammone, A. (2009) 'The reality of racism in modern Italy: Berlusconi goes in mob-handed for injustice', *Tribune*, 20 March, pp. 14–15. Available at www.tribunemagazine.co.uk/2009/03/19/the-rise-of-the-extreme-right-in-italy/ (accessed March 2009).

Moscovici, S. (1976) *La psychanalyse, son image et son public*, 1st ed. 1961, Paris: PUF.

Moscovici, S. (1979) *Psychologie des minorités actives*, Paris: PUF.

Moscovici, S. (1984) 'Introduction to Moscovici' (ed.), *Psychologie sociale*, Paris: PUF.

Moscovici, S. (2000) 'What is in a name?' *Social Representations and Communicative Processes*, M. Chaïb and B. Orfali (eds), Jönköping: Jönköping University Press, pp. 12–28.

Orfali, B. (1989) 'Le droit chemin ou les mécanismes de l'adhésion politique', in *Le Front national à découvert*, N. Mayer and P. Perrineau (eds), Paris: Presses de la FNSP, pp. 119–34.

Orfali, B. (1990a) *L'adhésion au Front national – De la minorité active au mouvement social*, Paris: Kimé.

Orfali, B. (1990b) 'Le Front national ou le parti-famille', *Esprit*, 9, 15–25.

Orfali, B. (2000) 'Représentations sociales: un concept essentiel et une théorie fondamentale en sciences humaines et sociales', *L'Année Sociologique*, 50(1), 235–54.

Orfali, B. (2002) 'Active minorities and social representations: Two theories, one epistemology', *Journal for the Theory of Social Behaviour*, 32, 395–416.

Orfali, B. (2005a) *Sociologie de l'adhésion – rêver, militer, changer le monde*, Paris: Zagros.

Orfali, B. (2005b) *La société face aux événements extraordinaires – entre fascination et crainte*, Paris: Zagros.

Orfali, B. (2006) 'Extreme right movements: Why do they reemerge, why do they get banalised?', *Theory & Psychology*, 16, 715–36.

Orfali, B. (2010) *L'adhésion – Militer, s'engager, rêver*, Bruxelles: de Boeck.

Taguieff, P.-A. (1988) *La force du préjugé. Essai sur le racisme et ses doubles*, Paris: La Découverte.

Taguieff, P.-A. (2005) *La foire aux illuminés: Esotérisme, théorie du complot, extrémisme*, Paris: Mille et une nuit.

Taguieff, P.-A. (2006) *L'imaginaire d'un complot mondial – Aspects d'un mythe moderne*, Paris: Mille et une nuit.

11

NEO-FASCISTS AND PADANS

The cultural and sociological basis of youth involvement in Italian extreme-right organizations

Stéphanie Dechezelles

Taking into account the cultural dimensions of extreme-right parties, this chapter attempts to open the cultural 'black box' of these organizations through the comparison of two groups of young Italian activists inside Alleanza Nazionale and Lega Nord. It is shown that their collective cultural frames are not totally new and are composed of three main elements: an ideal model of society, a legendary narrative and a symbolic territory, which are inspired by old ideological references. But to understand why young activists appropriate such elements, it is worth examining the different ways in which party members experience their political involvement, their family socialization and their social origins. The mechanism that allows the individual appropriation of the above-mentioned elements is driven by certain shared biographical, familial and social experiences. Thus, in the case of the AN the transmission of intimated (family) memory is closely associated with political commemoration of past events, whereas in the case of the LN, the lack of family memory among young activists is compensated with topographical and historical inventions promoted by the party organization.

Extreme-right parties in contemporary Italy

Some significant changes occurred in the Italian party system during the early 1990s. These were owing to the slow but progressive disintegration of the electoral basis of key parties that were the backbone of the so-called 'First Republic' (1948–92), and the strong de-legitimization of the political elites involved in a corrupt political and economic system (*Tangentopoli*, i.e. 'Kickback City'). At that time, much of the political class was under investigation by the so-called *Mani Pulite* ('Clean Hands') judges in Milan who demanded a moralization of national politics. In line with public opinion, this 'quest for morality' was adopted by many political leaders and officials – even by those who would later be accused of corruption. In particular, opposition forces and their leaders saw it as a good way to obtain the political power and democratic legitimacy that they had never had. 'Change' and the need for a 'new elite' became the watchwords. One of the first outcomes of these turbulent times was the electoral victory of the first short-lived coalition between the right and the extreme right, led by the much discussed media tycoon Silvio Berlusconi in 1994. Berlusconi and his allies got back to power in 2001 and again in 2008. The initial Polo del Buon Governo e delle Libertà (1994) and then Casa delle Libertà (2001) were both pre-electoral alliances consisting of Berlusconi's own party, Forza Italia, some of the ex-Christian Democrats, Alleanza Nazionale (AN) led by Gianfranco Fini, and the powerful Lega Nord (LN) led by Umberto Bossi. Apart from Berlusconi's controversial role, and the rise of his party, the real 'shock' was the electoral successes of two parties that some key scholars of Italian political life labelled as 'extreme right' (Ignazi 2001): the heir of neo-fascism, AN, which had always been excluded from governments since the first democratic elections of 1948, and the regionalist, anti-Southern and xenophobic LN.

Officially created at the Fiuggi congress in January 1995,[1] AN represents the 'nationalist pole' of the domestic right-wing parties. After having controversially decided to abandon the positive reference to Benito Mussolini's fascism (against the wishes of most of the leaders and members), the AN leader Gianfranco Fini managed to increase the electoral score of the party throughout Italy – although, like the Movimento Sociale Italiano (MSI), the southern regions (*Mezzogiorno*) remain its electoral stronghold. From 1995 onward, the ideological turn of the party, together with Berlusconi's assistance, helped AN to emerge from the political wilderness. As a consequence, the party has increasingly been classified as a 'post-fascist' party by some social scientists. At the latest national elections in April 2008, AN even fused with Forza Italia in a new party named Popolo delle Libertà, whose precise organizational transformation is still unknown, but which seems more a conservative than a fascist party. Despite these changes, AN should still be considered as a 'far'-right party because of its ideological references, the political orientation of its members and voters, and its positions on immigration[2] or more recently on Italy's Roma population.[3] To sum up, its nature is controversial and contains not only conservative but also extreme-right features (Chiarini and Maraffi 2001).

The creation of the Lega Nord followed a different pathway. The LN was born in 1990–1 with a regionalist, anti-statist and anti-southerner stance. It appeared when several regional leagues that were created during the 1980s in the north of the country decided to merge in a federation under the leadership of Umberto Bossi (Diamanti 1993). After its growing electoral success in the northern provinces, the party of Bossi has progressively become a movement for the independence of Padania, the imaginary state located in Northern Italy, mostly in the Po valleys (Gold 2003), and, like other similar European extreme-right parties, has quickly adopted a radical rejection of immigration, Islam, the EU and homosexuals.

As Ignazi shows, the LN has now left its position as a regionalist protest party to adopt an extreme-right platform, particularly in its authoritarian and anti-immigrant rhetoric, whereas AN seems to have shifted towards the ideological centre and reinvented itself as a conservative party (Ignazi 2005). However, in spite of these contradictory ideological shifts, AN and LN belong to the broad family of European radical/extremist right-wing organizations because of their specific positions on moral values, law and order, and immigration (Eatwell and Mudde 2004; Dechezelles 2006b). Although they present themselves as a 'new' kind of party of the right, and some authors classify AN as a post-fascist party or LN as a populist one (Mény and Surel 2002), we consider that these two organizations share some of their references and values with past fascist and neo-fascist movements.

The cultural bases of political involvement

Despite the necessary compromises and the recent transformations of political competition (Katz and Mair 1994), the political parties and their members still retain several enduring cultural and ideological specificities. As both mediators and actors in democratic political life, parties are among the main suppliers of collective identities for both voters and, especially, activists. These identities are also revealed through the discourses developed by activists about their political organization and also through the various party literature and (internal and external) documents: this can be translated as the *activist culture*.

A sociological definition of the culture of a political organization is quite difficult. Both for social actors and social scientists, the notion of culture is controversial and must be used and defined as cautiously as possible.[4] In my analytical framework, it is the product of social constructions of collective frameworks of meaning that are generated by institutions and appropriated by individuals (Berger and Luckmann 1967; see Orfali in this volume). These are socially constructed and cannot be considered as an 'essence' but nor can one ignore the effects they can have on the social actors. The approach that is developed in this chapter is grounded in a comprehensive sociology and anthropology of culture (Geertz 1973). In such a perspective, the culture of an organization can be used as a tool to regulate exchanges, impose 'marks' and 'frameworks', indicate what is forbidden and what is possible, what is part of the group and what is alien to it, what is good and bad, ritual or subversive, ordered and disordered, relative and absolute, important or accessory for the whole group (Johnston and Klandermans 1995).

The culture of any political organization is made up of specific symbols, references, values, protest styles, rules and rhetorical lexis (Eliasoph and Lichterman 2003; Virchow in this volume). In other words, the affection for certain causes, the entry into activism and the way the activists behave is based not only on certain ideological principles and articulated doctrines, but also on the construction of common and collective references that activists are exhorted to assimilate and appropriate. Understanding the culture of a militant group consists of examining not only the process of production and appropriation of a collective framework, but also how it is used in internal and external relations in order to construct *similarity* – identity – and to assert *difference* – otherness (Barth 1969). Every collective identity is based on a double strategy of homogenization and differentiation: the creation of an inclusive and positive *Us* that can be opposed to the irremediably different and negative *Them*. However, it also involves paying attention to *evolutions*, *transformations* and *tensions* (Faucher-King 2005) because cultures are far from being considered as abstract essences or peaceful social constructions. Political cultures are never peacefully accepted, but generate struggles between rival groups and individuals who seek to impose themselves or to modify some elements of this culture. They also lead to further conflicts between different movements or groups to control references or symbols. This means that cultures are neither homogeneous nor stable. On the contrary, they are clearly affected by the struggles and tensions between the *émetteurs* (intellectuals, political leaders and streams) and the *récepteurs* (activists, elected representatives, sympathizers, voters).

Yet, youth organizations, and especially those of the extreme right, seem to defend their 'identities' – and the ways in which they are created and spread – much more than 'adult' organizations. Given this, detailed research on youth political organizations and their members should be central to understanding the parties to which they are linked and which might represent the future political elite. Indeed, cultural analysis of the parties allows one (1) to understand how they generate a group and shape the individuals according to their expectations, (2) to take into account the individual experiences of activism and the phenomena of generational heritage and, finally, (3) to partially comprehend the political and ideological reference points of future leaders.

This chapter essentially deals with young activists (i.e. those who are defined 'young' by the official party *statuto*: generally people between fourteen and thirty years old) of the youth organizations of extreme-right parties in Italy: Azione Giovani (AG) and the Movimento Giovani Padani (MGP).[5] The former is the youth section of Alleanza Nazionale while the latter refers to the Lega Nord. This study is also based on (1) data collected for a research project on the degrees of 'involvement' (*engagement*) within the right-wing youth organizations and extreme-right parties during the second Berlusconi government (2001–6), (2) internal documents and pamphlets, and (3) sixty interviews made in the northern regions of Veneto and Emilia-Romagna (Dechezelles 2006a). The main argument of this chapter is that the appropriation of a youth movement culture depends on two main mechanisms: (a) the *intériorization* of the three identification elements produced by the 'group' (an ideal society, a legendary narrative and a symbolical territory), and (b) common or shared family stories or individual experiences (which make the appropriation of collective cultural references easier).

The ideal society

The culture of all Italian extreme-right youth organizations includes a teleological project of the ideal society, which is made up of hierarchies, codes (behaviour, clothes and vocabulary) and specific forms of sociability. As for many other extreme-right movements, the ideal society for AN young activists is the family. In such a context, the links between individuals within Azione Giovani are modelled on domestic relations: they mutually consider themselves as faithful and obedient members of the same dynasty. The biological lexical field is often used to describe the links that all activists (the *members*, the *cells*, the *flesh*) have to maintain with the organization (the *nucleus*, the *stem*, the *body*). The young are then exhorted to follow a given 'discipline' and a strict hierarchical 'order'. Abnegation and self-sacrifice are therefore erected as fundamental values. As a consequence, all activities that arouse 'virile sentiments' are strongly promoted, especially fly-posting at night or leaflet distribution. Indeed, these can eventually help cultivate strong self-esteem and solidarity. Owing to the low frequency of violent confrontations between political groups in contemporary Italy, the epic tales of physical struggles during the 1960s– 80s gives status to the 'elders', which the 'youngsters' are encouraged to respect. They must also be educationally prepared both for street combat (i.e. physical education) and intellectual struggle (i.e. doctrinal education), even if they are asked by their leader to renounce violence (Dechezelles 2009). This also helps us to understand why the 'formation' of the AN youth includes studying the biography, methods, 'agonistic struggles', and epic 'actions' of fascist leaders (e.g. Léon Degrelle or Corneliu Zelea Codreanu) and movements (Italian *squadristi*, Romanian Archangel Michael company, Belgian Rexism), but also the actions of the MSI's young activists. Great importance is also attached to Julius Evola's radical philosophy. It is worth noting that Evola is considered as one of the main ideologues of the extreme right in Europe, and his books have now become a doctrinal reference for so-called 'new' or 'non-fascist' movements, including the MGP and the LN.

Another fundamental reference for the young AN activists is J.R.R. Tolkien's writings (especially the trilogy *The Lord of the Rings*). Their party has been ostracized by the mainstream political class and powerless for many decades. That is why the young AN activists identify themselves with the innocent *Hobbits*, who are also perceived, just like them, as the only people capable of saving the world from 'evil forces'. This omnipresent identification with Tolkien's mythology harks back to the 1970s when the young leaders of the Fronte della Gioventù (the MSI youth organization), such as Marco Tarchi, introduced the ideology of the French Nouvelle Droite in order to 'revitalize' Italian neo-fascism (Germinario 2002). Giorgio, an interviewee who joined the Fronte della Gioventù in the late 1980s, explains how Tolkien, inspired by the Scandinavian sagas where all opposing human feelings are represented (bravery, cowardice, cupidity, anger), is useful to provide an interpretative framework and a model for activists:

> Tolkien, with his adventure books like *The Lord of the Rings* or *The Hobbit*, has been considered by the Italian extreme right as an example to follow and as a world which we should reproduce in our private life as well as in our political activity.

In the case of the MGP, the group perceives itself through the symbolical representation of an *emotional community*. Just as in other recent European extreme-right parties, the young activists explain that their real conversion to and involvement in the party followed some 'conductive events' (Ihl 2002). This has often been an electoral meeting or a partisan social gathering they attended for the first time and where they were intrigued by the leader's speech (Zanoni 2001: 82–3). For the LN, these 'strong emotions' are valorized because they prove that the 'chosen' people/activists are not to be found among the hated 'professional politicians', but, on the contrary, among those who are pure and passionate. As they are strongly attracted to the 'emotional elements' of political involvement, the young LN activists abandon the study of ideological writings for a sort of 'affective evangelization' which is supposed to be more intuitive and faith-worthy. They also tend to prefer the use of poetry to express themselves, a point they have in common with other regionalist or irredentist movements (e.g. Occitan, Corsican or Irish): in documents published by the LN youth organization, there are indeed frequent quotations from poems written by 'famous' authors, Umberto Bossi or members of Arte Nord (the Padan poets association). They also participate in the actual organization of events on dialectal languages or local literature. Some of them contributed to the *Movimento Giovani Padani* novel, which aspires to be the glorifying saga of the brave knights of the Lega Nord (Capitanio 2003). Unlike the proud collective self-representation of the young AN militants, the LN young activists seem to share a common negative stigmata: they say they feel constrained to say nothing about their involvement for fear of ridicule or rejection. During the various interviews, they also explained that they feel relatively distressed when they express their ideas and reveal their political commitment outside their group's secure and reassuring environment. For this reason, they also attempt, through poetry or other means, to invert the negative labels attached to their party and to build an 'inspiring portrait'. Nevertheless, they share in common with the young AN activists some intellectual references, such as Alain de Benoist, the famous French founder of the New Right trend, who was invited several times by the MGP to summer school for the young elected members of the LN in the early 2000s.

The legendary narrative

The 'ideal society' of all right-wing extremist cultures is closely related to a legendary tale that defines the 'origins' and 'roots' of such a society (Coakley 2004). If young AN activists are not unique in evoking and celebrating the history of their own party, the importance of these activities in the socialization and the formation of activists is much greater than in other organizations. Nostalgia for fascism and for heroic times is central: even painful memories related to the most difficult moments of the party's history are perceived as propitious and part of shared, collective values (Tarchi 1995). In particular, the 'good activist' is the one who constantly pays tribute to the legendary *Great Men* of the party. Involvement in the group requires collective remembrance of remarkable events and past facts in order to guarantee their transmission and perpetuation. For example, Azione Giovani promotes the publication of books in which such events are ritualized:

when reading them, activists feel that they are now the heirs of a fascist golden past. AG also organizes collective excursions to the Duce's grave (in Predappio, his native village in Romagna), distributes posters that invite people not to forget, produces leaflets for several fascist and neo-fascist anniversaries. Owing to their frequent elective responsibilities in the secondary education system, young AN activists are used to denounce in their schools the so-called 'lies' or 'factious interpretations' in historical textbooks.

The customary lists of 'their' martyrs and 'their' deeds also incite activist groups to hate the *Enemy* (from the anti-Fascist Resister to the alter-globalization activist) and to demand some sort of 'compensation'. In particular, the internal literature regularly tells the story of young neo-fascist activists who were involved in the Movimento Sociale Italiano and who died in riots opposing them to young extreme-left activists.[6] There is also a continuing glorification of young nationalists who mobilized at Trieste in 1953, Budapest in 1956 and Prague in 1968 as well as the Dalmatian and Istrian Italians who were brutally killed in deep swallow-holes (*foibe*) in the Kras region by Yugoslav communist forces at the end of the Second World War. These victims are used to justify commemorative gatherings. This is the case of Treviso where many Azione Giovani activists go every year with other associations linked to Alleanza Nazionale or to local skinhead groups to commemorate the victims of the *foibe*. In the same way, young activists are vigorously involved in local campaigns aimed at renaming streets or public squares to honour 'their' heroes or the 'victims of communist barbarism'. Despite Gianfranco Fini's attempts to distance the party from its fascist and neo-fascists roots, it also seems that it is exactly this glorification of the 'heroic memory' of the MSI that influences and convinces young people to join it (Chiarini and Maraffi 2001; Ignazi 2005). Moreover, in such a context, it is not surprising that a fascist (and Nazi) symbol, the burning torch, is used as the AG logo (Cheles 1995). The torch represents a past that never dies but is reproduced by every generation.

Young LN activists express their fear of an 'occult' political world from which they feel excluded by seeking mythical origins in an invented past (Hobsbawm and Ranger 1993) and, specifically, by seeking supposed direct Celtic roots in opposition to the supposed Roman roots of the Southern people. The party leader, Umberto Bossi, is seen as a talented prophet who will make possible the liberation of the people of Padania. Hence, he can purify and regenerate the imagined Padania from violence and in the long term from the 'voracious' Roman and Italian state. In this historical revisionist context, Italy is in fact perceived as the dreadful product of two immutable, different entities: the kingdom of Piedmont–Sardinia and the kingdom of the Two Sicilies; Padania is instead portrayed as the only 'eternal nation'. In such a perspective, if Italy is *the* 'repulsive' land, Padania is the 'burning torch' for activists. Similarly, LN mythology considers the period when *Celti* and *Protoveneti* lived in northern Italy as the golden age which must be fundamentally 'restored'. The Po valley, with its hard-working populations oppressed by *Roma ladrona* (Rome, the thief), is therefore compared to a paradise which activists have to liberate from the oppressors. The invented 'barbaric heritage' is also useful to legitimate the lasting economic differences between the north and the south of the country: these are explained either by references to biological differences between peoples or a revisionist reading of history (Huysseume 2004). For this reason, the Movimento Giovani Padani activists seek to denounce as immoral all forms of domination and colonization undertaken by the Italian state – from the constitutional monarchy to the fascist dictatorship and the post-war democratic republic. As in the case of the Basque nationalists, this political discourse of 'oppression' seeks to convert their external image of being 'rich and selfish' into one of victims whose cultural and linguistic heritage is under threat.

The iconography of the MGP uses medieval symbols (knights, armour, battles) that are historically 'twisted' or equivocal in an attempt to mobilize memories of the Lombard League of the free northern towns that were opposed to Frederic of Hohenstaufen (twelfth century), as well as William Wallace, the Scottish leader who challenged the king of England, Edward the First (thirteenth century).[7] The federal leaders and the local sections of the party encourage young activists to join all 'Celtic' movements or events organized by the LN: cultural associations, seminars on Celtic history and civilization, bagpipe sessions, old sports (crossbow shooting), fancy-dress balls and Celtic concerts. These activities are also proposed during the two-party annual meetings (at Pontida in June and Venice in September) when young men can also prove their strength (tossing the caber, jumping over bonfires). These demonstrations also serve as a 'vehicle' for radical and racist theories through conferences and the sale of books, introducing into the LN youth organization some classical extreme-right authors (Ernst Jünger or Julius Evola) and references (medieval imaginary, Aryanism).

Far from being only a folkloric form of partisan mystification, these invented memorial frameworks lead youth activists to perceive themselves as the heirs of heroic ancestors and, moreover, to perpetuate the reproduction of a mythological memory. In such a context, the constant reminders of past struggles and martyrs have an essential pedagogical purpose: to infuse activists with a sense of loyalty and duty towards the ancestors of the party.

The symbolical territory

The 'territories of identification' of extreme-right youth organizations do not match the 'administrative' Italian provinces and regions. Young activists primarily refer to a 'national' territory (Italia for Azione Giovani, Padania for the Movimento Giovani Padani) which is a symbolical, imagined, hoped for, or artificially constructed space. This invented *topos* allows us to analyse the political culture through the lens of particular spatial references. Along with the cult of Imperial Rome, which is fully borrowed from the mythology of the fascist regime, it appears that young AN activists are also encouraged to refer to certain *closed spaces*. These are simultaneously considered as places for excluded, marginalized or outlawed people, and at the same time as fortresses or bastions in which neo-fascists can be protected. Indeed, since the collapse of fascism, the two neo-fascist youth organizations (the Fronte della Gioventù and Azione Giovani) have developed a rhetoric of 'confinement' and marginalization. The use of the word 'ghetto' is in fact recurrent in the propaganda of these youth organizations. This metaphoric image of the ghetto essentially evokes the situation of the Italian Social Republic (1943–5) where the Northern part of Italy was also controlled by the Nazis and where the Resistance was very efficient (Germinario 2005: 20; Mammone 2005), but also the exclusion of the MSI from every governmental coalition from 1948 till 1993. This lexical field refers to a space of forced reclusion, or to a secret place, but it is also the synonym of 'vermin'. Indeed, it is specifically a *rat* that these organizations have chosen as their symbol for many years.[8]

In a hostile external political environment, young AN activists seek refuge in party sections which are perceived as veritable *sanctuaries*. The local section represents a safe place, where everyone feels free to express his/her feelings. Here the young *camerati*[9] experience a sense of closed community. This also explains why meetings and social evenings inside the party building are just as fundamental as public demonstrations in the formation of the young activist. All interviewed young activists claimed to spend a lot of time inside the party buildings and to feel good in their warm collective atmosphere.

As previously suggested, the young LN activists defend and oppose their *Eldorado*, their bucolic space the Padania, to a discredited country – Italy – and an immoral supranational space: Europe. This became a key element within the identity strategy led by Padanist ideologues such as Gilberto Oneto and Giancarlo Pagliarini – a strategy pursued since the 1990s and particularly after the first Berlusconi government in 1994. The high point of this strategy was reached in September 1996, when Bossi invited the 'northern inhabitants' to come to the banks of the Po and support in Venice the proclamation of the 'independence of the free republic of Padania'. Being a rhetorical invention, Padania has no precise boundaries, no unitary language, and no ethnic homogeneity. It had never been mobilized by protest movements or regionalist parties before the LN. This explains the LN's efforts to create some supposed 'natural' frontiers for Padania (from the Alps to the Apennines, and from the Tyrrhenian sea to the Adriatic). Historically and geographically, these claims are completely inconsistent – but they have some effects on the partisan world as imagined by the LN, the internal literature and the activists themselves. The absence of precise historical and geographical references is echoed in the way the young activists present the story of their organization. Thus, in the already mentioned MGP novel, there are no precise details of time or space. On the contrary, they use expressions such as 'once upon a time', 'nowhere', 'everywhere' or 'here as elsewhere', and they invented a specific calendar that starts from 15 September 1996, the day Bossi declared the liberation of Padania in Venice (Capitanio 2003: 7–13).

The existence of an opponent is essential to build an identity and to provide some substance to a legendary narrative and an imagined territory. The historical 'enemy' is found in the rest of the Italian peninsula, and especially in the southern regions – the so-called despicable *Terronia*. The construction of an imagined country/space is thus essentially rooted in the racist 'rejection' of the population of the south. Southerners are portrayed as a distillation of all human deficiencies (e.g. laziness, fraud, ignorance) against which to set the virtues of Padans (e.g. courage, honesty). During the Venice LN meeting in September 2005, the MGP sold T-shirts on which was stamped a split peninsula: the north, the 'socially liberated' Padania, and the south, the 'united Terronia'. The latter is depicted as a sewer attracting rafts full of clandestine immigrants. For the last 10 years, the biggest enemy for Padan people has been the clandestine (and supposedly Muslim) immigrant.

Ideal society, legendary narrative and territory of identification are therefore the fundamental elements of the culture of extreme-right youth organizations in Italy. For both Azione Giovani and the Movimento Giovani Padani, the football stadium and terraces have also represented places to express part of their ideology (non-conformity, neo-fascism, nationalism or racism) (see Testa and Armstrong in this volume). Nevertheless, in order to understand how cultures are appropriated by individuals, it is also useful to analyse their social origins and shared experiences.

Shared common experience as a (pre-)condition for the appropriation of partisan culture

For a better understanding of the relationship between an organization and its members, it is necessary to examine connections between the party culture and individual biographical experiences. Within AN, the adulation of the glorious historical heritage is closely related to family stories and backgrounds. Indeed, the veneration of 'party ancestors' is rooted in the remembrance of heroic relatives. Family traditions are both perpetuated and transformed into political ones, as they are loaded with ideological meaning. Thus Benito, the Azione Giovani provincial secretary of Forlì, describes his fascist pedigree and the memory of his childhood which he associates with the involvement of his father in the MSI: 'I remember that when I was a child, I was six or seven years old, my father brought me to the MSI for the fascist Epiphanies. I remember the bags full of toys and the torch [logo] of the MSI.' In a similar vein, Enrico (a sympathizer whose father often voted for MSI or AN) points out that his grandfather participated in the actual construction of fascist sites in Africa (Ethiopia) and that his political orientation is 'something that is transmitted from father to son, from one generation to another'. The process of political identification is based on the indexation of the family story onto national history, and vice versa. Consequently, the veneration of fascism and the MSI coincides with and is equivalent to the homage paid to the members of one's own family – and, as suggested, this works both ways. Politics is in fact considered as a 'family issue' that the older activists must transmit to younger ones. This also gives activists the chance to identify themselves with and refer to close or familiar figures.

Fascist *Podestà* (ex-activists of the MSI or the Fronte della Gioventù) thus represent the family's heroes to be venerated and imitated. For some young activists, the first linkage between their families, fascist tradition and extreme-right political involvement is to be found in their own names: some of them are called Benito (Mussolini's first name), but also Alessandro (the first name of Mussolini's father), Giorgio (the old MSI leader, Giorgio Almirante) or even Galeazzo (as in Galeazzo Ciano, Mussolini's son-in-law). These indelible 'marks' confirm that the young AN activists are in the 'right place' within an extreme-right political organization and that they are fully involved in the perpetuation of a family engagement and a collective story.

The historical and family 'proximity' with certain past events/figures therefore allows the young activists to place themselves in a direct line of historical continuity with a private (family) and public (political) genealogy. Gianluca (local leader at Ravenna) explained that he decided to join the youth party organization when he came across a gathering of young Fronte della Gioventù activists in his home town. They invited him to watch a film about the victims of the *foibe*. His grandfather died in such circumstances and he explained that this is the reason behind his choice to start an activist career. Elena is the daughter of an ex-member of the MSI, her mother is a member of the AN, her sister is also a young activist in AG. She is also the granddaughter and grand-niece of fascist volunteers of the Spanish Civil War. During the interview, she speaks a lot about her family's past involvement and above all about her great-uncle Costantino. He was a volunteer in Spain, and then instructor of the first Ethiopian military school in the Italian army:

> I didn't talk about the [neo-fascist] party with him but we talked about uniform, duty, patriotism, fidelity and coherence. I can describe my uncle with these five words. And these five words became my political programme . . . To become part of the MSI for me was as natural as being part of my family.

In many different respects the 'small story' of the family matches the 'big history' of the fatherland and this can explain how the young AN activists easily appropriate a party culture emphasising the memory of past times. They are the living proof that the (political and biological) dynastic *thread* is not broken. The past engagement lives on through these young people.

In contrast, Movimento Giovani Padani give very few details about their 'family stories'. In addition to this 'volatile memory', we can also perceive a sort of modesty with respect to the intimate (family) memory. Unlike the young AN activists who give many details and seem proud to know them, it is hard to collect material to reconstruct the 'histories' of the young *leghisti*. When asked: 'Could you speak about your family story?', Valerio, as the secretary of the MGP in Piacenza, answered:

> I don't know if I have one . . . So, my grandparents . . . I have known only one of them. My grandmother . . . died more than ten years ago and the others died of illness when they were very young and . . . what else could I tell you?

The LN activists also differ from those of the AN because they consider both their ancestors and themselves as having endured governments and policies over which they could have no say. Even if they are members of a party in government, they still consider they are at the margins of political life in Italy. They consider there is nothing heroic in their partisan (and family) engagement. Their discourse often includes expressions denoting exclusion or marginalization. Rather than any previous family involvement in politics, what they usually share is a common rejection of 'politics'. During the interviews, this comes out more clearly than biographical details about their familial history. As Meri (provincial leader of Belluno in Veneto) notices:

> My grandmother often used to talk to me about the fascists. But she told me that the Partisans were not much better. She remembered some precise events when the [anti-fascist] partisans got into every house to steal things and that they were very hard with German soldiers . . . she told me that once they also killed a young local woman, one of them, because she had danced with some German soldiers.

Similarly, Mara (regional councillor of Vicenza in Veneto) recalls one of her uncles who disappeared during the Russian campaign: 'He never came back . . . He was my mother's brother, from whom we received only a very few censored letters . . . here it is, but let's talk about something else.'

The few memorial 'souvenirs' of the young LN activists often describe a world made up of 'little people', victims of abuses of power or fraud at the hands of southern Italians, gypsies and immigrants. In such a vein, they pay tribute to these ordinary people, 'their people' against 'the others' – their people 'without histories' against the 'official history'. Unlike the case of young AN activists, in the Movimento Giovani Padani there is thus no trace of 'pride': suffering, amnesia or death seem to be the watchwords. For example, Marco (ex-local leader in Rovigo) recalls two members of his family in the following terms:

> My grandfather . . . I never met him because he died when I was two months old. He was a servant . . . He participated in the Libyan war, in 1938, no in 1940, 1937–38 I think . . . It was first and foremost a war where nobody knew who they were fighting and without knowing why. These were little things my grandfather told my grandmother and she repeated them to my mother. For example, he said they fought in disgraceful conditions, without shoes, without ammunition . . . My great-uncle was in the Russian expedition in 1940–42 and he never came back. He sent postcards up until the end of 1942 but after that we don't know anything about him. Even when the USSR archives opened, we did research on him but nothing was found. I don't know what happened to him.

The ordinary sense of history of the MGP activists leads them to invent a legendary history to compensate for a lack of a family and national ideological narratives structuring their political involvement. In social terms, young LN activists are often strongly attached to their local 'land'. Most of them live in houses or farms inherited from their grandparents, their social origins are more than the national average linked with farming and agriculture and they often study for diplomas that are relevant to the territory (e.g. geometry or agriculture). They seem to have no option but to appeal to an indistinct history and geography which serves as a proxy for familial experience. It is then the projection of their family members' experiences.

Conclusions

It is not common to take into account the cultural dimension of extreme-right parties and the different ways in which party members experience their political involvement. The aim of this chapter was to open the 'black box' of these organizations through the comparison of the activist culture of two groups of young Italian activists (Alleanza Nazionale and Lega Nord). Each culture is a constructed artefact composed of three main elements: an ideal model of society, a legendary narrative and a fictional land. The mechanism that allows the individual appropriation of the above-mentioned elements lies in certain shared biographical and family experiences.

In the first case (AN), intimate (family) memories and political commemorations are inexorably associated and the transmission of such memories from one generation to the other works well. In the second case (LN), the thin 'family memory' has its corollary in the topographical inventions of the party organization. Finally, the process of appropriation of a common political culture is also rooted in shared social, professional and educational backgrounds or experiences.

This also leads to a better understanding of the differences, similarities, political transfers and conflicts between the two parties. This is specifically the case with recent political developments where the AN leadership seeks to manage the tension between the legitimate 'democratic' strategy, represented by its participation in the Popolo delle Libertà 'coalition' under Silvio Berlusconi, and an activist base that had been socialized with the myth of the 'purity of origins'. On the other hand, the LN constantly radicalizes its positions also in order to woo Berlusconi's electorate in northern Italy. Owing to the very good electoral results of the two parties in the 2008 election and their participation in the third Berlusconi mandate, these activist and ideological continuities could at times turn into problematic and dissonant features (Dechezelles 2007).

Notes

1 At the congress in this Lazio town, the post-war neo-fascist party, the Movimento Sociale-Destra Nazionale, disappeared. Led by Gianfranco Fini, the heir to the former national leader Giorgio Almirante, the majority of its components formed the Alleanza Nazionale and evolved towards a conservative and liberal party. Fini abandoned the reference to the fascist regime of Mussolini and recognized anti-fascism. This ideological evolution has seen it readmitted into the national political system and included in Silvio Berlusconi's

coalitions and governments. At the Fiuggi congress, another group led by Pino Rauti founded the radical post-fascist Movimento Sociale–Fiamma Tricolore.

2 Immigration, and the status of irregular immigrant workers already living in Italy, are regulated by the so-called Bossi-Fini Law (Law no. 189, 30 July 2002) and by a decree. Entrance into Italy is now limited exclusively to those in possession of an employment contract.

3 Particularly the mayor of Rome, Gianni Alemanno, who has decided to close every Roma camp in the Italian capital.

4 The expression 'political culture' is not used in the sense employed by proponents of the 'civic culture' or the 'political development' approaches. Further, it is not equivalent to the 'opinions' or 'attitudes' that survey researches usually seek to measure.

5 Both the AG and the MGP have specific student organizations: respectively Azione Studentesca and Azione Universitaria, and Movimento Studentesco Padano Federale and Movimento Universitario Padano. It is worth pointing out that this study is based on interviews with young members from all these groups.

6 For the use of Internet as a tool for neo-fascist groups, see Caiani and Parenti as well as Turner-Graham in this volume.

7 Several times Umberto Bossi declared *Braveheart* was his favourite film.

8 Marco Tarchi, ex-national leader of the Fronte della Gioventù, founded a radical and satirical magazine, *La voce della fogna* (*The voice of the sewer*) whose symbol was a black rat. The latter previously also appeared in the iconography of some small French extreme-right groups in the 1950s.

9 *Camerata*, also used by inter-war fascists, etymologically means 'room' (*camera*) and evokes intimacy and the sharing of a common, secret, space.

References

Barth, F. 1969. *Ethnic Groups and Boundaries: The social organization of culture difference*. Boston: Little Brown.

Berger, P. and Luckmann, T. 1967. *The Social Construction of Reality: A treatise in the sociology of knowledge*. New York: Anchor Books.

Capitanio, M. (ed.) 2003. *Tutto nacque all'improvviso, non certo per caso*. Milan: Lega Nord.

Cheles, L. 1995. '"Nostalgia dell'avvenire": The propaganda of the Italian far right between tradition and innovation', in Cheles, L., Ferguson, R. and Vaughan, M. (eds) *The Far Right in Western and Eastern Europe*. London and New York: Longman: 41–90.

Chiarini, R. and Maraffi, M. (eds) 2001. *La destra allo specchio*. Venice: Marsilio.

Coakley, J. 2004. 'Mobilizing the past: Nationalist images of history', *Nationalism and Ethnic Politics*, 10 (4): 531–60.

Crépon, S. 2006. *La nouvelle extrême droite: enquête sur les jeunes militants du FN*. Paris: L'Harmattan.

Dechezelles, S. 2006a. 'Comment peut-on être militant? Sociologie des cultures politiques et des (dés)engagements. Les jeunes militants d'Alleanza Nazionale, Lega Nord et Forza Italia face au pouvoir'. Ph.D. Political Science, Sciences Po Bordeaux.

Dechezelles, S. 2006b. 'Visages et usages de "l'extrême droite" en Italie. Pour une analyse relationnelle et non substantialiste de la catégorie "extrême droite"', *Revue internationale de politique comparée*, 12 (4): 451–67.

Dechezelles, S. 2007. 'Entre révolution et gestion. L'engagement des jeunes militant(e)s de la Ligue du Nord et d'Alliance Nationale face à l'expérience du pouvoir en Italie', in Delwit, P. and Poirier, P. (eds) *Extrême droite et pouvoir en Europe*. Bruxelles: Éditions de l'Université de Bruxelles: 225–46.

Dechezelles, S. 2009. 'Renouncing violence or substituting for it? The consequences of the institutionalization of Alleanza Nazionale on the culture of young neofascist activists in

Italy', in Leaman, J. and Wörsching, M. (eds, 2010) *Youth in Contemporary Europe: Converging cultures?* London: Routledge: 268–81.

Diamanti, I. 1993. *La Lega. Geografia, storia e sociologia di un nuovo soggetto politico*. Rome: Donzelli.

Eatwell, R. and Mudde, C. 2004. *Western Democracies and the New Extreme Right Challenge*. London and New York: Routledge.

Eliasoph, N. and Lichterman, P. 2003. 'Culture in interaction', *American Journal of Sociology*, 108 (4): 735–94.

Faucher-King, F. 2005. *Changing Parties: An anthropology of British political party conferences*. Basingstoke: Palgrave Macmillan.

Geertz, C. 1973. *The Interpretation of Cultures*. New York: Basic Books.

Germinario, F. 2002. *La destra degli dei. Alain de Benoist e la cultura politica della Nouvelle Droite*. Torino: Bollati Boringhieri.

Germinario, F. 2005. *Da Salò al governo. Immaginario e cultura politica della destra italiana*. Torino: Bollati Boringhieri.

Gold, T.W. 2003. *The Lega Nord and Contemporary Politics in Italy*. Basingstoke: Palgrave Macmillan.

Hobsbawm, E. and Ranger, T. (eds) 1993. *The Invention of Tradition*. Cambridge: Cambridge University Press.

Huysseume, M. 2004. *Modernità e secessione. Le scienze sociali e il discorso della Lega Nord*. Rome: Carocci.

Ignazi, P. 1994. *Postfascisti? Dal Movimento Sociale Italiano ad Alleanza Nazionale*. Bologna: Il Mulino.

Ignazi, P. 2001. 'Les partis d'extrême droite: les fruits inachevés de la société postindustrielle', in Perrineau, P. (ed.) *Les croisés de la société fermée. L'Europe des extrêmes droites*. La Tour d'Aigues: Édition de l'Aube: 369–84.

Ignazi, P. 2005. 'The extreme right: Legitimation and evolution on the Italian right: Social and ideological repositioning of Alleanza Nazionale and the Lega Nord', *South European Politics and Society*, 10 (2): 333–49.

Ihl, O. 2002. 'Socialisation et événements politiques', *Revue française de science politique*, 52 (2/3): 125–44.

Johnston, H. and Klandermans, B. 1995. 'The cultural analysis of social movements', in Johnston, H. and Klandermans, B. (eds) *Social Movements and Culture*. Minneapolis, MN: University of Minnesota Press: 3–24.

Katz, R. and Mair, P. (eds) 1994. *How Parties Organize: Change and adaptation in party organizations in Western democracies*. London: Sage.

Mammone, A. 2005. 'Gli orfani del Duce. I fascisti dal 1943 al 1946', *Italia contemporanea*, 239/240: 249–74.

Mény, Y. and Surel, Y. 2002. *Democracies and the Populist Challenge*. London: Palgrave Macmillan.

Tarchi, M. 1995. *Cinquant'anni di nostalgia. La destra italiana dopo il Fascismo*. Milan: Rizzoli.

Zanoni, P. 2001. *Bossi e la rivoluzione tradita*. Venice: Editoria Universitaria.

12

CREATING A EUROPEAN (NEO-NAZI) MOVEMENT BY JOINT POLITICAL ACTION?

Fabian Virchow

In the German neo-Nazi magazine *Hier & Jetzt*, an author associated with the group German Academy (Deutsche Akademie) dealt with the issue of internationalism. In view of increasing globalization he deemed a closer cooperation of nationalist forces an urgent necessity. 'Such cooperation,' he went on, 'has numerous synergetic advantages: exchange of experiences, coordination of joint activities, strategic and theoretical inspiration, financial and material support, as well as facilitating territorial evasion' (Schwarzenberger 2008: 26). While he remains sceptical of the idea of a 'Nationalist International' comparable to the Communist Internationale, he argues in favour of an informal alliance that should nonetheless have a name, a symbol and a body of representatives.

Although there is an extensive body of research on different aspects of the post-war extreme right in Europe, few investigations have so far focused on the issue of the transnational circulation of extreme-right ideas, cultures and praxeology (Zinell 2007). Also, the issue of political action and campaigning has been largely ignored by academics, despite the importance of political marches for the Storm-troopers in Germany and the Squadrismo in Italy.

This chapter addresses both the international and the transnational dimension of the European extreme right and the dimension of political action by investigating public demonstrations by extreme-right activists in several European countries. Here, the term 'international' is used to refer to cooperation between extreme-right protagonists from two or more different countries while the term 'transnational' is used to describe processes of cross-fertilization regarding ideology or patterns of action. Looking at three annual rallies in Budapest (Hungary), Wunsiedel (Germany) and Salem (Sweden) this contribution starts with a systematic reflection on the relevance of political action for the emergence, maintenance and dynamic of political movements. It then investigates these demonstrations and portrays them with regard to their respective causes, organizers, attendants, procedures and international dimensions. Finally, the question of whether, or to what extent, such transnational activities will contribute to the formation of a European (neo-Nazi) movement is discussed.

Performance and political action

Historical research has occasionally dealt with the importance of rallies and public demonstrations for the identity, formation and dynamic of fascist movements in the period before they come to power (Campbell 2003; Ehls 1997; Reichardt 2007). I strongly contend that demonstrations and public gatherings are an important factor for understanding the dynamic of contemporary political movements because the (lasting) involvement of individuals in political parties and movements is not the result of a rational decision alone nor does it depend solely on the agreement with the party programme. It also depends on how the organization/movement performs, how it connects with the individual follower through cultural and political symbols, myths and narratives. Also, the way the individual becomes integrated into the 'life' of a movement needs investigation. Finally, as Dechezelles suggests in this volume, the culture of a political organization is of major relevance.

Such a praxeological investigation reveals a broad set of effects, purposes and aims that the organizers of a rally may seek to achieve, or which may be experienced by the participants. Like all demonstrations/marches, those of the extreme right occupy public space in a physical and pointed way. In post-war Germany, public meetings and demonstrations/marches of the extreme right have never been viewed with equanimity. Protesters have always argued that political forces in the tradition of National Socialism are not entitled to basic rights such as freedom of speech and assembly. Over the last twelve years the extreme right has forcefully and successfully claimed these rights. Leading activists of the extreme right, especially from its neo-Nazi strand, admit that the specific thematic issue of the demonstration/march is not always important. What matters is that a march is held at all in order to demonstrate the existence of the extreme right and its determination not to be excluded from the public sphere.

In a middle-term perspective, the leaders of the extreme right feel confident that the rallies will help create an image of the extreme right as a political force capable of acting against all odds. Some factions of the extreme right attempt to use demonstrations/marches as a cover to air explicitly National Socialist terms, icons and political messages in public without being prosecuted. Also important is the neo-Nazi leaders' intention to exert pressure on the state authorities, civil society and left-wing protagonists by means of demonstrations. Building on the historical experience of the Stormtroopers, who organized marches through working-class areas in order to demonstrate their claim to power in the streets (and thus in the state as a whole), today's (German) neo-Nazi activists also intend to break the real or imagined 'predominance of the reds' by organizing public events at selected places. Another option would be to copy the Movimento Sociale Italiano's (MSI) attempt to present the forces of the extreme right as a bastion of public order, the theory of *Piazza di Destra* as it became known in Italy from the late 1960s (Mammone 2008: 222).

Violence is an important feature in marches of the Nationaldemokratische Partei Deutschland (NPD) and the neo-Nazi groups, but not in the sense that direct acts of violence against police forces, bystanders or counter-protesters dominate whole events. While in recent years there has been a growing number of outbreaks of violence perpetrated by so-called 'Autonomous Nationalists' closely related to public political manifestations (Schedler and Häusler 2011), the vast majority of the marches are still carried out in a highly disciplined manner. At the same time, there is a strong aura of violence designed to intimidate political opponents while producing a self-image of non-conformism. This aura of violence is derived from the habitus of the majority of the participants, from public knowledge of the accumulated potential violence of this political faction, and from the tone of the speeches and slogans that accompany the demonstration/march. When staging rallies, the extreme right deploys an extensive and comprehensive world of political symbols that are highly relevant for the cohesion of the organization and the spread of its appeal (Hennig 1989). Style and symbol are also relevant for the identity of a movement, and it is of no surprise that there is a long list of extreme-right movements whose names reflect the colour of their shirts.

Demonstrations fulfil several other useful functions for political movements. They provide an excellent opportunity to contact like-minded people from other cities, regions, or even countries. Contacts sometimes become friendships and visits are followed by return visits, thereby contributing to the emergence or consolidation of informal networks that cannot easily be dismantled by the state authorities. Rallies function as acts of initiation, where the neophyte openly declares his/her affiliation and is seen doing so by neighbours, teachers, workmates or relatives.

The repetition of this act of participation in demonstrations can contribute significantly to a progressive political socialization process whereby young people become strongly integrated into the movement milieu. These mechanisms of integration have not only an ideological but also a behavioural dimension. Rallies are a training ground for the inculcation of a particular code of behaviour, as expressed by slogans such as 'camaraderie', 'discipline', 'faith' and 'order'. Moreover, public demonstrations, especially the larger ones or those held near historical sites, are expected to invigorate those undertaking laborious day-to-day grass-roots activities. The feeling of belonging to a movement, bigger and potentially more influential than the small local group that most of the participants belong to is a *conditio sine qua non* for the emergence and the development of any movement.

To sum up, in its various facets the demonstration policy outlined above seeks to create a temporary emotional collectivity, which helps to recruit new followers, to stabilize the collective identity of the movement, to select cadres and to form ideological worldviews and attitudes. Contrary to Reichardt (2002), I do not believe that the adoption of an actor- and action-centred perspective in the study of the extreme right should replace ideology as a subject of investigation: far from it – it is the merging of both – ideology and praxeology – that counts. For example, an international extreme-right movement is likely to have much more success in getting its ideological message across to potential supporters if it offers them the opportunity to join like-minded people from other countries in action, rather than just reading about it in the movement's magazine. Only in action does it become clear who belongs. Collective identity, understood as a social process, needs permanent reproduction. Rallies and public demonstrations are a relevant factor in this respect, although not the only one.

International neo-Nazi rallies

There have been several post-war attempts to achieve closer international cooperation between extreme rightists or even to build a European-wide organization, from the European Social Movement, the New European Order (Nouvel Ordre Européen) and the Young European Legion in the early 1950s to the Nouvelle Droite in the late 1960s (Bar-On in this volume) and to neo-Nazi circles such as the European Movement in the mid 1980s. These attempts were often short-lived and/or involved no more than meetings between a few leading members. Despite a large degree of agreement on basic features of the worldview, the level of organizational institutionalization of an international extreme right in Europe remained low for a long time.

However, since the late 1980s a number of developments have significantly affected the evolution, performance and international cooperation of the extreme right in Europe. On a macro level, the dissolution of the Soviet Union and of other East European societies has been interpreted by the extreme right not only as a victory over 'communism' but, more importantly, as confirmation of the continuing potency of racial nationalism as the dominant factor in history, and also raising the possibility of a strengthened European entity capable of acting independently of the former superpowers. In addition, the manifold processes of globalization including a rise of international migration are translated by the extreme right into apocalyptic scenarios of decline, decadence and civil war. At the same time, the extreme right has exploited the trans-boundary links facilitated by technical innovations such as the Internet (see Turner-Graham or Caiani and Parenti in this volume) On a meso level, too, the emergence of a transnational 'White Power' music scene is widely celebrated by the extreme right as the most successful recruiting tool they have had for decades (see Langebach and Raabe in this volume). So, on the one hand, historical developments have been interpreted by the extreme right as proof of the urgent need for closer collaboration on the European level, and on the other hand the conditions for networking and mutual cooperation have significantly improved. International rallies are one expression of this development.

The significance of public demonstrations differs through time and place. While rallies are currently of minor importance for the extreme right in Italy and France they have become more relevant in Britain with the appearance of the English Defence League (EDL); they play a much bigger role in countries such as Sweden, the Netherlands, Germany and East European countries such as Hungary, or in Russia (Zuev 2010). The particular profile of the marches depends on the strategic and tactical perspectives of the organizers, country-specific political traditions, and legal and juridical restrictions. Thus, for example, while in Germany it is prohibited by law to display the swastika publicly or to wear uniforms marking one's political beliefs (Rösing 2004), other countries have no such restrictions: for example, in Russia, Sweden, Hungary and the Czech Republic extreme-right groups parade uniformed and in step.

In some cases extreme-right cross-border networking has resulted in an adaptation of tactics. This is the case, for example, with the Dutch People's Union (Nederlandse Volks Unie, NVU) that has developed a very close cooperation with neo-Nazis from North Rhine-Westphalia, a German state bordering the Netherlands. After several years of not indicating their rallies to the state authorities beforehand they learned from their German like-minded counterparts that it might enlarge their range of public acting to do so.

Extreme rightists also travel abroad to take part in rallies. One is the annual commemoration of Francisco Franco, the former dictator of Spain. It takes place around 20 November, which is the supposed anniversary of the death of Franco and of José Antonio Primo de Rivera, founder of the Falange. In 1997 roughly one hundred German neo-Nazis mainly from the NPD and the now defunct Free People's Bloc (Freiheitlicher Volksblock) travelled to Spain. The following years the number of participants from Germany fell to some twenty people. Since the late 1980s, only a very few marches organized by European extreme-right organizations have attracted significant international participation. Significance here is defined on three levels: (1) participating groups from outside the host country are clearly visible (e.g. banners, group logos); (2) participation is not an isolated event, but takes place regularly; (3) there are platform speakers representing groups not based in the host country.

While there are many public manifestations of the extreme right where speakers from other countries show up in order to create the impression of a movement with fulcrums across the globe, only a small number of marches have been conceptualized as international marches per se. Following the above criteria, there have been at least three important international public demonstrations over the last decade worthy of being investigated: the event in Budapest that is organized in mid February in order to honour the former Waffen SS, the rally in honour of Rudolf Hess in mid August in Germany, and the torchlight procession in the Swedish town of Salem in early December. The sections that follow seek to depict each of these demonstrations, their political and ideological context, the way they are organized and performed, and the international dimension of the gatherings.

Salem

Salem is a small Swedish town located some fifteen miles southwest of Stockholm. On 9 December 2000 seventeen-year-old neo-Nazi Daniel Wretström, drummer of the Swedish band White Legion (Vit legion), met his death in a dispute with a group of migrant youngsters. Ever since, Swedish neo-Nazi groups have staged annual rallies, attended by like-minded people from Scandinavian countries, Germany and the United States. Swedish neo-Nazis call Wretström 'Horst of our times' (Vår tids Horst) referring to Horst Wessel, a Stormtrooper whom the Nazi party (Nationalsozialistische Deutsche Arbeiterpartei, NSDAP) made a martyr after he was shot in Berlin in mid January 1930 (Siemens 2009).

The Salem march is organized by the Salem Foundation (Salemfonden) which runs a separate Web page[1] offering information in three languages: Swedish, English and German. The Web page also provides documentary material such as pictures and films used for the purpose of mobilization. There are also video clips with German and English subtitles[2] designed to interest non-Swedes in the Salem activities. Strict rules are drawn up by the organizers of the demonstration, which is organized as a silent march with rows of four. No smoking, alcohol or use of mobile phones is allowed. Torches are lit on the orders of the marshal.[3] Participants parade in a torchlight procession from the railway station to the place where Wretström died.[4] As the route is uphill, the sight of hundreds of torches and candles in the dark has a powerful emotional impact on those involved. On the site of Wretström's death a floodlit memorial engraved with runes has been built. The number of attendants reached 1,400 and 1,800 in the years 2002 and 2003 respectively. In 2004 the figure fell back to 1,600, and this decline continued with 1,400 in 2005 and 1,100 in 2006, reaching a low in 2007, 2008, 2009 and 2010 when around 1,000, 700, 600 and 700 neo-Nazis respectively joined the demonstration.

While the majority of participants come from Swedish neo-Nazi groups such as National Socialist Front (Nationalsocialistisk Front, NSF) or the Swedish Resistance Movement (Svenska Motståndsrörelsen, SMR) non-Swedish neo-Nazis took part in the Salem march from the start. In 2005, for example, neo-Nazis from Switzerland, the United Kingdom, Estonia, Norway, Germany and Denmark travelled to Salem. On this occasion, the Northern Relief Organization (Nordisches Hilfswerk, NHW), which is a neo-Nazi platform of German citizens and Scandinavians of German origin living in the Scandinavian countries, proclaimed that 'comrades travel as far as 2,000 kilometres to a suburb of Stockholm in order to honour him and his companions in misfortune', even though he was just an average Swedish youngster.[5] It is also noted that more than a hundred 'well-known comrades from Germany' plus delegations from several other countries participated in the commemorative march. On several occasions German neo-Nazis, beating their lansquenet drums, played a prominent role in the rally. They headed the procession together with those carrying the wreaths.

The international character of the Salem event is also demonstrated by the fact that several of the speakers are representatives of non-Swedish neo-Nazi and extreme-right groups. In 2002, spokesmen included Christian Worch from Germany and a representative from the UK-based magazine *Final Conflict*. The following year saw speakers such as Gareth Hurley who saw his appearance at the demonstration as a contribution to 'keeping alive the ancient ties between Scandinavia and the British Isles'. He further merged anti-Semitic statements with the myth of an autochthonous European population threatened by 'all manner of alien peoples and religions [that] are given their rights from one corner of Europe to the other'.[6] Roughly 200 neo-Nazis from Germany attended in 2003.

In 2004, it was up to Junge Nationaldemokraten (JN – youth wing of the NPD) leader Stefan Rochow, heading a group of a hundred German neo-Nazis, to give a speech. The following year German neo-Nazi Lutz Giesen spoke to the crowd and declared that 'we are here as Germans to jointly remember Daniel Wretström and the many dead of our movement'. His speech was translated by Thomas Ölund from the international Blood & Honour (B&H) network and co-founder of Salemfonden, and ended with an appeal not to give up the fight. This was received with great enthusiasm.[7] In 2007, White supremacist Preston Wiginton from Texas and NHW representative Stefan Günther were among the speakers. According to the Salemfonden Web page the latter 'spoke of gathering our strength by working together to build our own media for example' while the former stated that 'the Salem participants were sending out an echo across the world that would inspire like-minded people everywhere'.[8] Wiginton, who also addressed a racist rally in Moscow and is close to Nick Griffin, leader of the British National Party, declared that the Salem demonstration is inspiring for the American Movement.[9] Owing to Swedish police action that included the arrest and deportation of German neo-Nazis, the NHW published a call to resist police action and to increase the number of Germans joining the Salem action next time.[10] This appeal also stressed the European dimension of the Salem march by emphasizing that 'patriots from all over Europe' have lighted candles and torches for a young Swedish patriot and that, thanks to Daniel, 'many cross-national projects have emerged'.

The Salem march has an international and a domestic dimension. While it aims at the Swedish public and tries to bring the neo-Nazi movement in contact with a significant minority of the Swedish population that favours the exclusion and marginalization of immigrants, it is also regarded as a demonstration of unity by the groups supporting it. In 2007 and the following years the further decline in attendance was caused by disagreements between the relevant Swedish groups.

While the annual Daniel Wretström demonstration has been the biggest public neo-Nazi gathering in Sweden for some time, it is far from being the only one. There are, for example, regular rallies on the occasion of Sweden's National Day, 6 June. Comparing this People's March (Folkets Marsch) with the Salem demonstration, the Swedish neo-Nazis from *info14*,[11] an important Web page for Swedish extreme rightists (Säkerhetspolisen 2003: 41–2), argued that the latter is more important as it addresses concrete problems that have major relevance in contemporary Sweden.[12] Representatives of *info14* regularly travel abroad to attend the activities of like-minded groups.[13] One such stable connection exists with German neo-Nazis from the Rhine–Main–Neckar region where Swedish neo-Nazis took part in neo-Nazi 1 May marches and Remembrance Day activities.[14]

Furthermore, German neo-Nazi bard Frank Rennicke whose songs have been translated into Swedish appeared at the Nordic Festival in 2007 to entertain and ideologically arm neo-Nazis from the Scandinavian countries, the United States, Belgium and Germany. The same event saw speeches by Thomas Rackow, representative of the German JN, and French Emmanuel Brun d'Aubignosc, one of the founders of the international neo-Nazi media network Altermedia. On another occasion, German neo-Nazis from Mecklenburg–West Pomerania co-organized a one-day festival in the South Swedish district of Skåne.[15] Swedish neo-Nazis pay considerable attention to what their German counterparts do. For example, Robert Vesterlund, one of the main activists of the Salem Foundation, explained to his comrades why neo-Nazis in Germany use black flags as symbols while banners of this colour are not carried by the Swedes.[16] Some currents of the Swedish neo-Nazi movement imitate the concept of Autonomous Nationalists that has gained growing popularity among German neo-Nazi activists since the late 1990s.[17]

Finally, it should be mentioned that there are further joint activities of Swedish and foreign neo-Nazis on Swedish territory. One such example has been the rally on 7 July 2007 in front of the German embassy in Stockholm demanding the release of convicted Holocaust denier Ernst Zündel from a German prison. A delegation consisting of representatives from the Swedish NSF, the Danish National Socialist Movement (Danmarks Nationalsocialistiske Bevægelse, DNSB), the NHW and the Russian National Unity (Russkoye Natsionalnoye Edinstvo) were allowed to hand over a letter of protest.[18] This act of solidarity was welcomed by German neo-Nazis.[19]

In sum, there are plenty of opportunities for personal contacts between Swedish and non-Swedish neo-Nazis, allowing them to exchange ideas and knowledge and share in joint political action. Salem has been just one such occasion used by extreme rightists from several countries. However, its attractiveness for non-Swedish militants will depend to a considerable extent on the (temporal) unity of the different strands of Swedish neo-Nazism.

Wunsiedel

Wunsiedel is the small Bavarian town where Rudolf Hess's mortal remains were laid to rest after his suicide in mid August 1987 at the age of 93.[20] Hess had been taken prisoner by the British after his flight to England on 10 May 1941. He was sentenced to life imprisonment at the Nuremberg Trials, showing no signs of remorse, and from mid July 1947 until his death he was imprisoned in a British military gaol in Berlin-Spandau. Soon after his conviction the myth of Hess as an 'envoy of peace' was promoted by groups such as the Support Community Freedom for Rudolf Hess (Hilfsgemeinschaft Freiheit für Rudolf Hess) or the Rudolf-Hess-Society (Rudolf-Hess-Gesellschaft) that had close links to the German extreme right.

The day after Hess's demise, several small neo-Nazi gatherings in Germany (Hamburg, Berlin, Munich) and Austria (Vienna) took place. Neo-Nazis also besieged the cemetery in Wunsiedel for nearly two weeks so as not to miss the funeral. In 1988, the first Rudolf-Hess-Memorial march was organized by a group of neo-Nazis who successfully overturned a ban passed by the local municipality. In the end, some 120 Nazis attended the rally.

While the British authorities subsequently decided to demolish Spandau Prison to prevent it from becoming a shrine, the small town of Wunsiedel became the site for a prolonged attempt by German neo-Nazis to establish an international demonstration. Over the years, the Wunsiedel marches achieved growing importance and contributed to the unity of an otherwise quarrelsome extreme-right milieu. In 1989, the number of participants doubled with the participation of a group of Belgian neo-Nazis around the former VMO-activist Bert Erikson. The next year 1,100 neo-Nazis gathered in Wunsiedel, and this increase was celebrated as an important victory, encouraging the belief that next time even 'average citizens' would join the event. Instead, owing to political protests and counter-activities, the state authorities banned all marches in the area in 1991. The neo-Nazis switched to the city of Bayreuth where 1,500 showed up, among them a growing number of sympathizers from the United Kingdom, Italy, Spain, Austria and Belgium. Despite a further ban in 1992 that covered large parts of Germany, neo-Nazis staged a rally in the East German town Rudolstadt with 2,000 of their followers. The subsequent year the march took place in Fulda despite a comprehensive ban.

Since 1994, police forces have monitored the neo-Nazis very carefully and have blocked every attempt to organize a big rally. The neo-Nazis therefore switched their activities to Luxemburg (1994) where 180 of them were arrested in front of the German embassy, or to Roskilde in Denmark (1995). In 1996, the clandestine Wunsiedel-Committee for the first time called for a 'Month of Memory' instead of a single date for the march in order to have more flexibility. However, the attempt to stage a rally in Worms led to the arrest of 190 out of 250 participants. Despite this disaster, the neo-Nazis tried to organize another public demonstration on the occasion of the tenth anniversary of Hess's death in 1997. The police, using helicopters to transport its forces quickly, arrested more than 500 of them after an attempt to hold rallies in and near Braunschweig. The same day a small Hess memorial march took place in Køge (Denmark).

While there were some small Hess marches in subsequent years – Greve (Denmark 1998), Valkenburg (Netherlands) and Bern (Switzerland) in 1999, Echt (Netherlands) and Helsingør (Denmark) in 2000 – neo-Nazis were not able to organize a significant public commemorative event in Germany itself.

This led to some frustration and internal feuding. However, the neo-Nazis had more success with a campaign against an exhibition documenting the war crimes of the Wehrmacht on the Eastern Front. The protest rallies not only attracted support, but also helped unite the movement (Virchow 2006). The major breakthrough had been a rally in Munich on 1 March 1997, where some 5,000 extreme rightists joined the protest against the exhibition. A few months later, another 5,000 neo-Nazis took part in a similar rally in the city of Rostock, proving that demonstrations of this size were not an isolated case.

In 2001, German neo-Nazis again turned their attention to the issue of a legal Hess Memorial march in Wunsiedel. Encouraged by several decisions of the Federal Constitutional Court reversing judgements by lower courts, versed lawyer and neo-Nazi activist Jürgen Rieger made a rally in the Bavarian town possible by exploiting the liberal jurisdiction of the German constitutional court that gave freedom of speech and freedom of assembly priority over the eventuality of hate speech. Although the final decision was not announced until the previous evening, more than 900 neo-Nazis showed up in Wunsiedel on 18 August. The decision was greeted with enthusiasm by the German extreme right and triggered a dynamic development of the Hess memorial marches in Wunsiedel. The number of attending neo-Nazis rose to 2,600 (2002), 4,000 (2003) and 4,500 in 2004. There also was an intensified distribution of posters and leaflets in many parts of Germany celebrating Rudolf Hess.

During this period, the Hess memorial march was strictly controlled by Jürgen Rieger: he opens the event, and this is followed by music from an extreme-right singer-songwriter. During the march itself participants remain silent while Wagnerian music is played. Slogans on banners refer solely to the person, the actions and the fate of Rudolf Hess. Flags are carried in the lowered position. The march moves slowly. Overall the procession is reminiscent of ritualized mourning (Dörfler and Klärner 2004).

In 2005, the Federal Constitutional Court confirmed a ban decreed by a lower court on the basis that the law on incitement had been tightened shortly before. Caught by surprise, the neo-Nazis were not able to organize a replacement event but split up into several smaller gatherings. Foreign sympathizers organized protest meetings elsewhere in Europe, as in Stockholm where sixty to seventy neo-Nazis from NSF, MNR and *info14* showed up.[21] The following years the demonstration remained banned. Rieger's attempt to have the tightening of the law on incitement declared to be incommensurate with basic democratic rights finally failed in November 2009.

From the very beginning the Hess memorial march had a strong international component. In 1993, for example, neo-Nazis from Belgium, France and the United Kingdom joined the Fulda march, with John Peacock (BNP) and Claude Cornilleau (Parti nationaliste français et européen) acting as speakers. In the early 2000s extreme-right activists from countries such as Sweden, Denmark, Italy, France, Finland, the United Kingdom, Belgium, Austria, Switzerland, the Netherlands, Russia, the Czech Republic and Spain travelled to Wunsiedel, and in 2004 20 per cent of the participants were non-German.

The Wunsiedel rally was part of a 'demonstration calendar' of the extreme right in Germany. According to this calendar, there are each year three public demonstrations that call for nationwide, or even international participation. Attendance is a must for the movement's followers. These events include a march held in Dresden in mid February to commemorate the Allied bombing of the city in early 1945 (Biddle 2008; Kirwin 1985), described by the extreme right as a 'bombing Holocaust'. This rally grew to 7,500 participants in 2008 but was successfully challenged by anti-fascists in subsequent years. Regularly on 1 May, in the capital or in several cities simultaneously, the extreme right holds an event celebrating Nazi social policy, declaring that it eliminated unemployment and that a strong nation-state acting on a policy of national preference is a precondition to serve the 'national interest' in times of globalization that is said to be favouring US interests. Finally, there has been the march in Wunsiedel in praise of Rudolf Hess.

In addition, there is an average of two to three neo-Nazi marches every weekend, each attracting up to 400 participants (Virchow 2006; 2011). On several occasions non-German neo-Nazis join such events. When the NPD organized a 1 May demonstration in Berlin in 2004 some of the 2,300 demonstrators came from Romania, Spain, Austria and the United States. Part of a crowd of 3,300 on 8 May 2005 were neo-Nazis from Finland and South Africa, while delegates of extreme-right organizations from Greece, Norway, Sweden, Belgium, Spain, Austria and Romania brought messages of support.

Budapest

The Hungarian capital is the location of a 'Day of Honour' (Becsület Napja) annually organized around 10 February. The Red Army finally liberated Budapest on 13 February 1945, but the 'Day of Honour' refers to the attempt by Hungarian troops and German Waffen-SS units on 10 February the same year to escape the city that was encircled by Soviet and Romanian troops.

The public demonstration has taken place at least since 1998, and is used to reaffirm the commitment of Hungarian neo-Nazis to their historical examples such as the Arrow Cross Party (Nyilaskeresztes Párt, NP) and its leader Ferenc Szálasi. The NP was a pro-German anti-Semitic national socialist party that ruled Hungary from 15 October 1944 to January 1945. During this period, some 550,000 Hungarian Jews were murdered (Varga 1991). After the war, Szálasi and other Arrow Cross leaders were tried as war criminals by Hungarian courts.

The 'Day of Honour' was organized by the Hungarian Section of Blood & Honour (Ver es Becsület) until the group was banned in 2004 owing to its National Socialist character. After that, the rally was sponsored by 'private' individuals such as János Endre Domonkos, former leader of the Hungarian B&H branch or groups such as Pax Hungarica (Pax Hungarica Mozgalom) or the Movement for the Unity of the Homeland (Hazáért Egység Mozgalom), also closely tied to the B&H network. The annual event is supported by groups such as Bloody Sword (Véres Kard) or Hungaria Skins.

The 'Day of Honour' is held largely on Budapest's Heroes' Square (Hősök tere).[22] In the centre of the square is the Millennium Memorial, one of Budapest's major landmarks with statues of important figures from Hungarian history. Located in the very centre of the monument is a 36-metre column with a statue of the archangel Gabriel on the top. The ceremony of the 'Day of Honour' is carefully structured. It starts with rhythmic drum rolls. Participants pass the drummers while entering the fenced-off square through a narrow corridor. Two men in military uniforms wearing historical steel helmets lead the procession, which lines up in strict formation according to the instructions of the event organizers. Then, speakers address the audience and wreaths are laid, while the two 'soldiers' stand guard over a wooden cross erected near the lectern. The cross bears the inscription 'Blood & Honour' and a German steel helmet on its top.[23] Several dozen red and white striped Árpád flags, like those last used by the NP in 1945, provide the backdrop for the ceremony.

While the various Hungarian neo-Nazi groups provide the majority of participants, there is a significant contingent from other European countries. On 14 February 1998, 500 to 600 neo-Nazis obeyed the call of Blood & Honour Hungary and the Hungarist Hungarian National Front (Magyar Nemzeti Arcvonal, MNA) to join the 'Day of Honour'. Among them were about 150 German-speaking neo-Nazis. Two years later, again some 140 German and Austrian neo-Nazis were among the crowd of 450. A report in a neo-Nazi magazine highlighted this international dimension: 'Many non-Hungarians had accepted the invitation. One could see Slovak nationalists as well as Serbians. Even some Russian comrades were present to show they don't agree with the cruelties once exacted by the communists against Hungarians.'[24]

Some 600 neo-Nazis gathered at Budapest's Heroes' Square in 2005 where German NPD activist Eckart Bräuniger addressed the crowd as he had already done in 1999 and 2004.[25] Two years later his Goebbels-like tirade[26] was translated to a thousand-strong audience of Hungarians, Belgians, Bulgarians, English, Croatians, Austrians, Swiss, Slovenians, Czechs and Germans, this last group numbering 100 neo-Nazis. Other speakers had been the Hungarians Zsolt Illés and Tudós-Takács János, British B&H-organizer Stephen Swinfen, the representative of the Spanish group National Democracy (Democracia Nacional) Luis Munoz, NPD leader Udo Voigt, and Bavarian NPD official Matthias Fischer, an activist in the far-right German–Hungarian Friendship Association. In the evening, a neo-Nazi rock concert took place where two German bands performed.

In 2008, 1,100 to 1,500 neo-Nazis came together beneath a huge banner with a trilingual slogan reading 'Heroes of Europe' (a tribute to the Waffen SS) in English, German and Hungarian. A speaker from Germany declared: 'We, the youth of Germany and Hungary proclaim to the world that our grandfathers and great-grandfathers were not criminals ... Profess yourself in nation and history and dare to speak out loud: Glory and Honour for the Waffen SS.'[27] In 2009, some 2,000 extreme rightists attended the demonstration. Among the speakers had been German neo-Nazi Ralph Tegethoff.

The rhetoric and semantics of the speeches reveal many parallels with pre-1945 fascism and their general line is staunchly anti-communist. They also disseminate the idea of a Jewish conspiracy and call for a struggle for the survival of the European peoples, invoking the Waffen-SS as an example to emulate.

Although Blood & Honour is banned in Hungary, its insignia, slogans and ideology are very much in evidence at every 'Day of Honour'. To organize a public event around anti-Semitic invective and cultic admiration of the Waffen SS would be unthinkable in many European countries, and this indeed constitutes the added value of the 'Day of Honour' for the attending neo-Nazis. Among those coming from abroad, Germans have a privileged position as their country is the birthplace of the Waffen SS. They not only provide a significant proportion of the speakers, but, in 2008, the German national anthem was played alongside the Hungarian one. The same year Czech neo-Nazis carried a banner with the German language slogan 'National Resistance – Bohemia and Moravia'. Hungarian Web pages run by neo-Nazis welcome the involvement of Germans.[28] For their part, German neo-Nazis are impressed by the 'Day of Honour':

> The demonstration professionally organized by our Hungarian comrades commanded our complete respect . . . The national anthems of Hungary and Germany were played and sung. This 'Day of Honour' on Budapest's Heroes' Square is a powerful confession of a Europe of Nations and Free Peoples, against a Europe of Big Business and Globalizers!'[29]

In Hungary, the freedom that followed the collapse of communism and that was part of the transformation into a market economy also unveiled dark strains of nationalism, chauvinism and anti-Semitism. Anti-immigrant sentiment, prejudice against homosexuals and the glorification of Hungary's fascist past is the centre of attention of several extreme-right groups in contemporary Hungary (Bernáth et al. 2005), among them the Party of Hungarian Justice and Life (Magyar Igazság és Élet Pártja, MIÉP) and the Movement for a Better Hungary (Jobboldali Ifjúsági Közösség, Jobbik). When the population's discontent grew in the wake of the governmental crisis in 2006, many extreme-right groups sought to exploit it and direct it towards violence. Members of Jobbik participated in the riots, as well as followers of groups such as the MNA, which has a paramilitary unit[30] and also takes part in the 'Day of Honour'.[31]

Jobbik has several representatives in local government and runs a professional Web page in English.[32] The group gained a lot of attention after it founded the Hungarian Guard (Magyar Gárda, MG) in 2007 and started to march in columns through small towns such as Tatarszentgyörgy (9 December 2007) in order to intimidate the gypsy population.[33] The MG was subdivided into battalions and companies and in late summer 2008 counted 1,500 members, who train in martial arts and learn to shoot. Jobbik and the MG maintain several contacts with extreme-right organizations throughout Europe such as the BNP, the NPD and the Czech National Party.

Transnational political action

This contribution addressed the issue of demonstrations/marches as an important dimension in the development and the dynamics of an international extreme-right movement. The rallies in Salem, Wunsiedel and Budapest play an outstanding role in the particular national context and are well known in the international context of the neo-Nazi extreme right. The proportion of non-nationals participating in these rallies is up to 25 per cent and the organizers of these marches regularly invite non-nationals as speakers in order to demonstrate the international character of the movement. Those who attend these demonstrations from abroad are official representatives as well as ordinary members of extreme-right parties and movements. The international dimension of these rallies is accentuated by participants wearing banners and sweatshirts with slogans such as 'German–Hungarian Friendship' (Német–Magyar Barátság) or 'Brothers in Arms Germany Hungary'.

The local organizers provide an obligatory frame of procedure in which the order of events is highly ritualized and integrates religious dimensions and procedures. Also, each of these marches connects the cause of the event to a message participants should take up and act on (e.g. 'Fight Multiculturalism'). The three international demonstrations are embedded in the movement's broader culture, as exemplified by the use of the Internet for education/propaganda and by its efforts to entertain through the products of an extensive White Power–Rock Against Communism music business. This also produces effects of intertextuality and follow-up communication. Taken together international demonstrations of the extreme right may play an important role in the process of growing transnationalism and internationalism of the European extreme right.

As far as demonstrations are concerned as a field of cross-border transfer it has proved quite difficult to show *exactly* how a particular concept of demonstration policy used in one country has been discussed and transferred to another context. Certainly there is fascination among German neo-Nazis that the Swastika can be shown in public in the Scandinavian countries and that the MG in Hungary behaves in many respects like the pre-1933 Stormtroopers. However, there are also examples where the transfer of knowledge and experience is obvious. One is the change of tactics of neo-Nazis in the Netherlands. Traditionally they had relied on 'spontaneous' rallies without any prior contact with the police or the local administration, and they might have continued to do so had they not learned the value of a more legalistic tactic under the influence of German neo-Nazis and their own experience when taking part in rallies in Germany. The other example is the emergence of the concept of 'Free Nationalists' in Sweden. This approach was first adopted in Germany in the early 1990s when several neo-Nazi organisations were banned by state authorities, and it was an attempt to become less vulnerable to state repression. Swedish neo-Nazis followed suit, albeit, as with the NSF, dismissing some excesses seen in a far-reaching copy of style and appearance of the autonomous left.[34] This latter example also shows that transnationalism or cross-border transfer of a political concept or a propaganda idea does not automatically result in the strengthening of the movement. In the Swedish case, the difference of opinion on the concept of 'Free Nationalism' contributed to the drop in participants at the Salem march.

In addition, while there is talk about 'steadfast brotherhood in arms' many extreme rightists have visions of a Greater Germany, a Greater Hungary, or a Greater Romania. Nationalism, as the very foundation of the extreme-right worldview, will always be an obstacle to any idea of an extreme-right Internationale. This, too, can be seen at work in the international marches: in 2004, Austrian neo-Nazis were challenged for carrying the Austrian national flag. For their German 'comrades', Austria is still the Ostmark. On another occasion German neo-Nazis aggressively asked their comrades from Czechoslovakia to strongly condemn post-war resettlement of ethnic Germans as a precondition for being allowed to join the march.

Notes

1   www.salemfonden.info/.
2   http://de.youtube.com/watch?v=zs91gIL_Ltk; http://de.youtube.com/watch?v=KQNhDBr-Hq8&feature=related.
3   www.widerstand.info/meldungen/816.html#more-816.
4   http://de.youtube.com/watch?v=wEPdJwtmWnU&.
5   http://de.altermedia.info/general/salem-2005-wurdiges-gedenken-fur-daniel-wretstrom-ein-aktionsbericht-des-nordischen-hilfswerks-141205_4226.html#more-4226.
6   http://de.youtube.com/watch?v=DuoLCbcGIwI.
7   http://de.youtube.com/watch?v=39vX8jeem7c.
8   www.salemfonden.info/index_eng.php.
9   www.nordischeshilfswerk.org/bewegung_txt.php?artikelid=62; www.info14.com/2007–12–17-framgangsrikt_salem_trots_massivt_motstand.html.
10   http://nordischeshilfswerk.org/bewegung_txt.php?artikelid=54.
11   The number refers to the so-called '14 Words' coined by US neo-Nazi David Eden Lane: 'We must secure the existence of our people and a future for White children.'
12   www.info14.com/2007–12–08-salem__svenskt_deltagarantal_okade.html.
13   www.info14.com/2007–01–07-info-14_deltog_pa_aktivitetsvecka.html.
14   www.info14.com/2007–05–07-forsta_maj_i_tyskland__info-14_pa_plats.html; www.info14.com/2007–11–15-heldengedenken__en_hyllning_av_fallna_hjaltar.html.
15   www.info14.com/2006–07–08-nationalistisk_festival_i_skane.html.
16   www.info14.com/2007–01–27-foredrag_i_vasteras.html.
17   www.nordischeshilfswerk.org/bewegung_txt.php?artikelid=55. The so-called 'Autonomous Nationalists' have emerged in Germany in 2003 as a neo-Nazi youth culture. While its worldview does not differ much from other neo-Nazi groups they copycat elements of visual performance and style of action of the radical left-wing autonomous movement.
18   www.nordischeshilfswerk.org/bewegung_txt.php?artikelid=58.
19   *HNG-Nachrichten* 9/2007, pp. 10–11.
20   In July 2011 the local administration liquidated the tomb after consultation with the remaining family.
21   www.info14.com/2005–08–21-protest_mot_demonstrationsforbud.html.
22   In 2011, the event took place in a forest near to Budapest with only 100 attendees after it had been banned by the police (http://becsuletnapja.com/english). Yet, several other commemorative events, partly organized by Jobbik and the Youth Movement of the sixty-four castle districts (Hatvannégy Vármegye Ifjúsági Mozgalom; HVIM), were organized in the towns of Debrecen, Karcag, Mosonmagyaróvár, Hatvan and Pér.
23   http://de.youtube.com/watch?v=krqOHLQtSTU, 01:07.
24   *Der Angriff* No. 1, pp. 22–3.
25   http://de.youtube.com/watch?v=6gdBzrULUuQ&NR=1.
26   http://de.youtube.com/watch?v=KLRd9Tim3fY.
27   http://de.youtube.com/watch?v=I-4RC84seYE&feature=related.
28   www.l88.hu/about1745.html.

29 www.widerstand.info/meldungen/2096.html#more-2096.
30 http://de.youtube.com/watch?v=97i1QgNY6_E.
31 *Front* No. 4, 22 February 2005, p. 8.
32 www.jobbik.com/.
33 http://de.youtube.com/watch?v=9ac4dApwFMg.
34 Leading neo-Nazi activists in Germany reacted to he ban of several of their organizations in the first half of the 1990s by creating a network of loosely connected local/regional groups (*freie Kameradschaften*) (Virchow 2004). This model, which avoids the formal structures of a political party, has been further sharpened by some by copying performative rituals of the radical left autonomous movement. The latter step that has included staging a 'black bloc' on neo-Nazi rallies has been criticized by the Swedish groups.

References

Bernáth, G., G. Miklósi and C. Mudde. 2005. 'Hungary', in C. Mudde (ed.), *Racist Extremism in Central and Eastern Europe*. London: Routledge, pp. 80–100.

Biddle, T.D. 2008. 'Dresden 1945: Reality, history, and memory', *The Journal of Military History* 72(2): 413–49.

Campbell, M.W. 2003. 'Keepers of order? Strategic legality in the 1935 Czechoslovak general election', *Nationalities Papers* 31(3): 295–308.

Dörfler, T. and A. Klärner. 2004. 'Der "Rudolf-Hess-Gedenkmarsch" in Wunsiedel', *Mittelweg 36* 13(4): 74–91.

Ehls, M.-L. 1997. *Protest und Propaganda. Demonstrationen in Berlin zur Zeit der Weimarer Republik*. Berlin/New York: de Gruyter.

Hennig, E. 1989. 'Die Bedeutung von Symbol und Stil für den Neonazismus und die Rechtsextremismusforschung in der Bundesrepublik', in R. Voigt (ed.), *Politik der Symbole – Symbole der Politik*. Opladen: Westdeutscher Verlag, pp. 179–96.

Kirwin, G. 1985. 'Allied bombing and Nazi domestic propaganda', *European History Quarterly* 15(3): 341–62.

Mammone, A. 2008. 'The transnational reaction to 1968: Neo-fascist fronts and political cultures in France and Italy', *Contemporary European History* 17(2): 213–36.

Reichardt, S. 2002. *Faschistische Kampfbünde: Gewalt und Gemeinschaft im italienischen Squadrismus und in der deutschen SA*. Cologne: Böhlau.

Reichardt, S. 2007. 'Fascist marches in Italy and Germany: *Squadre* and SA before the seizure of power', in M. Reiss (ed.), *The Street as Stage: Protest marches and public rallies since the nineteenth century*. London: Oxford University Press, pp. 169–89.

Rösing, J. 2004. *Kleidung als Gefahr? Das Uniformverbot im Versammlungsrecht*. Baden-Baden: Nomos.

Säkerhetspolisen. 2003. *Verksamhetsåret*. Stockholm: SÄPO.

Schedler, J. and A. Häusler. 2011. *Autonome Nationalisten. Neonazismus in Bewegung*. Wiesbaden: VS Verlag für Sozialwissenschaften.

Schwarzenberger, D. 2008. 'Inter-Nationalismus', *Hier & Jetzt* 11: 26–9.

Siemens, D. 2009. *Horst Wessel. Tod und Verklärung eines Nationalsozialisten*. München: Siedler.

Varga, L. 1991. 'Ungarn', in W. Benz (ed.), *Dimensionen des Völkermords. Die Zahl der jüdischen Opfer des Nationalsozialismus*. München: Oldenbourg, pp. 331–51.

Virchow, F. 2004. 'The groupuscularization of neo-Nazism in Germany: The case of the Aktionsbüro Norddeutschland', *Patterns of Prejudice* 38(1): 56–70.

Virchow, F. 2006. 'Dimensionen der "Demonstrationspolitik" der extremen Rechten in Deutschland', in A. Klärner and M. Kohlstruck (eds), *Moderner Rechtsextremismus in Deutschland*. Hamburg: Hamburger Edition, pp. 68–101.

Virchow, F. 2011. 'Die "Demonstrationspolitik" der extremen Rechten – Eine Zwischen-bilanz', in H. Klare and M. Sturm (eds), *Dagegen!' Und dann . . .?! Rechtsextreme Straßen-politik und zivilgesellschaftliche Gegenstrategien in NRW*. Münster: ten Hompel, pp. 17–23.

Zinell, A. 2007. *Europa-Konzeptionen der Neuen Rechten*. Frankfurt/Berlin: Peter Lang.

Zuev, D. 2010. 'A visual dimension of protest: An analysis of interactions during the Russian march', *Visual Anthropology* 23(3): 221–53.

PART IV

Widening interests

Music, Internet, sport

13

THE ITALIAN EXTREME RIGHT AND ITS USE OF THE INTERNET

A 'bi-front' actor?[1]

Manuela Caiani and Linda Parenti

Introduction

Throughout the world, the usage of the Internet by extremist groups is on the rise. Analyses reveal that today, almost without exception, all major (and many minor) extremist and insurgent groups have websites (Zanini and Edwards 2001: 43). According to Weimann (2006a) there are some 4,800 terrorist or terrorist-related websites that currently exist. Arab and Islamic groups are regarded as having the largest presence on the Internet, but others, such as right-wing extremists, are also active participants on the Web (Whine 2000).

As highlighted in Turner-Graham's chapter in this volume, several sources stress that in Europe as well as in the USA right-wing extremists (such as White supremacists) have begun exploiting the Internet for several political purposes such as spreading their propaganda, rallying their supporters, preaching to the unconverted and also intimidating political adversaries (ADL 2001,[2] Tateo 2005, see also FRA 2010: 123 and Te-Sat 2010: 14). Indeed,

> the Web, boundless, difficult to control, in a state of continuous change, is the ideal place for those at the boundaries between legal politics and illegal activities, for those who want to recruit, diffusing violent, racist or just subversive ideas, for those who want to 'increase in number to assault the World', as various comrades of the Web claim.
>
> (Fasanella and Grippo 2009: 156)

Italy is not an exception (Roversi 2006; Padovani 2008). In fact, the interest in the phenomenon has increased in recent years (e.g. Criscione 2003; de Koster and Houtman 2008; Fasanella and Grippo 2009) and watchdog civil society organizations and political activists (e.g. the Osservatorio Democratico; Indymedia Italia;

AntiFascismo Militante; etc.) monitor, archive materials, and investigate the Italian extreme right (Padovani 2008). Some studies focus on the way these extremists' websites portray immigration issues or the historical fascist period (see Criscione 2003; Padovani 2008: 755); others concentrate on the links of the Italian extreme-right websites and their attempt to create national and international Web communities (e.g. for the use of 'Webring' see Qin *et al.* 2007; Caiani and Wagemann 2009). According to some estimates, about 150 websites are run in Italy by extreme-right groups and political parties. Likewize, a 2002 study conducted by UISP (Unione Italiana Sport) on 'racism, soccer and the Internet', found that among the websites maintained by soccer fan clubs, the Italians ones were among the most racist (Wetzel 2009: 365). Some of these websites are easily reachable, and apparently 'neutral'. Others are more complex to access and more violent and radical, at the borderline between legality and illegality according to Mancino Law (Fasanella and Grippo 2009: 158). Furthermore, extreme-right organizations do not only use the Internet as a simple showcase. In addition, communication technologies 'afford opportunities to debate, mobilize, reflect, imagine, critique, archive, and inform' (Downing and Brooten 2007: 538, as quoted in Padovani 2008). In Italy in the 1990s, the first sites of the so-called 'multimedia antagonism', linked to companies that produce and commercialize right-wing music, appeared on the Web (on music and the extreme right, see Langebach and Raabe in this volume). Ever since, these sites, advertising concerts and 'cultural' initiatives, have played a central role in the ideal re-composition of the Italian extreme-right family, offering new 'spaces for the confrontation and debate among the various souls' of the extreme right, such as AN, Fiamma Tricolore, and Forza Nuova (Caldiron 2001: 336). The Internet thus represents not only a new forum of communication for these political forces in which an 'electronic community' of like-minded people can be created, but also a stimulus and a means to renovate themselves, adopt new topics and action strategies, modernizing their identity by embracing technological and cultural changes. For example, in 1997, Alleanza Nazionale organized a multimedia conference on 'populism and new media' (Caldiron 2001: 336).

Studies stress that the Internet is exploited by extreme right-wing groups for various political goals. Political scientists have shed light on how they use the Internet to spread their *propaganda*, including books, magazines, leaflets and other kinds of materials inciting violence (Stern 1999; Whine 2000). Concentrating on the American extreme right, Glaser *et al.* (2002) suggest that racists often express their views more freely on the Internet. Other scholars and watchdog organizations show that right-wing groups use the Internet to recruit new members (Qin *et al.* 2007). Zhou *et al.* (2005) stress how the Internet can facilitate the formation of 'international' communities among racists and extremists, which through the Web can reach a global audience and build contacts with other right-wing groups. In parallel, a recent qualitative study conducted by a team of Dutch researchers (de Koster and Houtman 2008) has shown that the Internet is very often used by right-wing extremist activists to create and reinforce a 'sense of community'. Furthermore, besides the capacity of the Internet to generate collective identities (Myers 2000;

Arquilla and Ronfeldt 2001) and solidarity (Chase-Dunn and Boswell 2002), scholars also underline the role of this new medium in helping the processes of mobilization. In particular, many social movement studies have shown the crucial function of the Internet in the development of transnational social movements and in the organization of collective action (Bennett 2003; Petit 2004).

Despite the increased academic attention in (extremist) politics on the Web (Whine 2000), this literature focuses mostly on left-wing social movements. The empirical research on the extreme right is scarce (Burris *et al.* 2000; Zhou *et al.* 2005), mainly qualitative and generally limited to the US case. Against this background, this chapter, based on a formal content analysis of different types of right-wing websites, focuses on the Italian extreme right and aims to explore *the degree and the forms of the political use of the Internet by Italian extremist right-wing organizations.* We do not limit our analysis to extreme-right political parties, but also include non-party organizations and violent groups. Following a brief presentation of the methodology used, we will describe the different types of organizations and sites that comprise the (online) universe of the Italian extreme right. We will then present the results of our content analysis, expose the main characteristics of right-wing organizations' websites and explain how they are used to fulfil different political purposes. Differences and similarities in the use of the Internet between several types of extreme-right organizations will also be illustrated with empirical evidence. In the conclusion, the chapter will try to link the empirical results with the more general research question on the role of the Internet for extreme-right organizations, reflecting on the contrast between the 'novelty' of the medium used by these organizations and the traditional old fascist message transmitted.

Data and methodology

To build our 'dark Web collection' (Qin *et al.* 2007: 75) and then codify the Italian extreme-right organizations' websites thus identified, we have used a 'snowball' technique. First, in order to map all Italian extreme-right organizations that are active online, we started with the most important Italian extreme-right groups (and respective URLs), reached on the basis of secondary sources (e.g. watchdog organizations, academic and scientific literature, etc.). Then, through their weblinks to other extreme-right organizations, we discovered the websites of minor and less well-known Italian groups, eventually identifying one hundred organizational websites. We then classified them into broader extreme-right categories (they are: extreme-right political parties and movements; nostalgic and revisionist associations; commercial associations; subcultural youth and skinhead groups; neo-Nazi organizations; cultural, traditional, radical Catholics; and New Age and neo-mystical groups, see section 3).[3]

Second, we conducted a quantitative Web content analysis of the identified extreme-right websites (in a proportion of 50 per cent of websites analysed for each category, see section 3). A formalized codebook, constructed by relying on similar studies on extremist websites (e.g. Gerstenfeld *et al.* 2003; Zhou *et al.* 2005;

Qin *et al.* 2007), was used to capture systematically their content (for similar Web content analysis of terrorist websites, see Weimann 2004). Using several indicators, the codebook aimed at analysing how and how much extreme-right groups exploit the Internet for several political purposes such as enhancing the group's communication and identity (e.g. providing Web-interactivity with members and sympathizers; hosting martyrs stories and leaders' speeches; presenting narrative about operations of the group, etc.; for this dimension of the political use of the Internet and the empirical indicators used to investigate it, see Zhou *et al.* 2005); sharing ideology (e.g. 'pin-pointing' enemies through the website);[4] presenting the mission and the doctrine of the group, etc. (ibid.); offering information and propaganda (e.g. news reporting, showing of slogans, banners and seals, etc., Qin *et al.* 2007); and recruitment and training (or, expressed in other words, 'command and control', Zhou *et al.* 2005; advertising for groups' events and initiatives, activation of the members in online and offline actions, offering multimedia materials etc., see della Porta and Mosca 2006). The quantitative Web content analysis has been integrated with a qualitative investigation of the websites and organizational documents available on the websites (e.g. leaflets, magazines, etc.). Although we are aware that we cannot assume what these organizations do on the virtual arena of the Internet to reflect their actual political activities and mobilization from the Web, we are nevertheless convinced that the Internet is a good channel for expressing their views, especially for those who wish to escape the censorship of the public gaze, and thus a good instrument for researchers to study these groups, which are otherwise difficult to investigate (Burris *et al.* 2000; see also Caiani and Parenti 2009).

Types of Italian extreme-right websites

According to Mudde (2007), what characterizes the extreme right in Europe is its lack of political and ideological homogeneity. Likewise, far for being a united family, the panorama of the Italian extreme-right groups appears as extremely diversified, insomuch as scholars have described it as a 'plural' (Caldiron 2001) and 'fragmented' right (Caiani and Wagemann 2009). This is also what emerged from our 'dark websites collection', which reveals the existence of many different types of online extreme-right groups, ranging from established extremist right-wing parties to several extra-parliamentary groups, from the revisionist, neo-Nazi to the fundamentalist Catholic right. Some of them are characterized by neo-fascist or even neo-Nazi positions, such as MSI-Fiamma Tricolore, Forza Nuova and Fronte Sociale Nazionale.

In the category 'political party and movements' (twenty-four organizational websites found), we have included the groups that define themselves as political parties and movements and are openly involved in political activities such as elections, political debates and policy issues (Tateo 2005: 13). As for what concerns the parliamentary and extra-parliamentary extreme right, we can mention the party Movimento Sociale Italiano–Fiamma Tricolore (founded in 1995 by some ex-MSI members led by Pino Rauti who refused to follow AN's path of moderation and the way that it has distanced itself from the fascist past); Fronte Sociale Nazionale (founded in 1997, following a split within the MSI–FT); Forza Nuova (originating from the MSI diaspora in the transition to AN); Libertà di Azione (also known as Azione Sociale, led by Benito Mussolini's granddaughter, Alessandra) and some very recent groups such as Rinascita Nazionale (founded in 2000). Another conspicuous sector of the Italian extreme right on the Web is represented by non-party 'nostalgic, revisionist and negationist' organizations (thirty organizational websites identified).[5] These are groups that refer to the twenty years of fascist rule in Italy and the Salò Republic and that are apologists for Benito Mussolini (see for example the websites of the organizations Il Ras, Cuore Nero, Federazione Nazionale Combattenti della RSI).[6] Furthermore, we found some more specifically 'cultural organizations' that can be divided between traditional associations and New Age and 'neo-mystic' groups (seven websites identified).[7] Above all the latter are characterized by their frequent reference to Celtic mythology (Tateo 2005: 15). Yet another (smaller than the previous ones) category of the galaxy of the Italian extreme right that we detected contains 'neo-Nazi' groups and sites (four identified)[8] that refer to German National Socialist (NSDAP) ideology, the Third Reich and Hitler. Furthermore, it is possible to identify a broad range of youth sites that includes skinhead groups, hooligans and music groups (twenty-two organizational websites identified).[9] These groups focus on music (which they define as 'antagonistic', Tateo 2005) and sport as their main interests, and their sites are often characterized by fascist or Nazi symbols. Contacts between skinheads and some soccer hooligan groups are also very frequent in Italy (Gnosis 2006). Music labels and fan magazines are associated with many of these music groups. Moreover, after the summer of 2002, a rather atypical phenomenon emerged, especially in Rome, namely, the occupation of buildings by young people belonging to the extreme right. The first occupations by such 'right-wing anarchists' led to the emergence of various 'squatted centres' (*centri sociali*) (di Tullio 2006). This is a peculiarity of the Italian case. The most important issues for these groups are the right to free housing and the fight against usury, but also include cultural issues and social justice. Furthermore, there are various 'commercial extreme-right organizations' that collect and sell military souvenirs (e.g. uniforms), purportedly as 'memorabilia' (eight websites identified).[10] Within commercial organizations we also included the 'publishers' (see for instance Settimo Sigillo, Libreria Europa) that produce and sell only right-wing books (Nazi and fascist texts).[11]

The Internet as a medium for propaganda and 'activation'

Studies on right-wing extremism from political scientists (Whine 2000) as well as from non-governmental organizations fighting anti-Semitism and racism (e.g. Stern 1999) concur in pointing out that today the Internet is largely used by these groups for spreading their ideology and their message. Moreover, studies on terrorism and political violence stress that lone individual Web consumers may overcome their feeling of isolation and find on right-wing websites a common cause that resonates with their own ideas. Responding to the extremist ideology of a virtual community, some may make a decisive step from sharing thoughts to engaging in tangible actions (Post 2005). This is confirmed also by right-wing activists and leaders themselves: for example, Don Black, a former Alabama Ku Klux Klan leader, underlines that White Separatists are seeing more Internet activity turn into 'real-world activism . . . The criticism we have always heard is that people do not do anything but sit behind their computer and post on message boards. We are actually turning people out to meetings and getting people involved in activism.'[12]

This raises two important questions: to what extent and in what ways do right-wing extremist organizations use the Internet as a tool for diffusing propaganda? How do right-wing radical groups use the Internet to set their agenda and encourage mobilization?

Our data show that Italian right-wing websites use the medium of the Internet forcefully for different political persuasion tasks and that they do so by skilfully using a wide variety of styles and forms of discourse (on this point see also Tateo 2008: 291), such as reproduction of documents, historical photos, newspaper articles, poetry and song texts, and various material explicitly recalling fascist iconography and rhetoric (e.g. classical texts from the Nazi/fascist past or Nazi symbols and bibliographical references). To offer some specific examples from our database: more than 60 per cent of the Italian extreme-right groups we investigated offer on their websites 'articles, paper and dossiers' and more than half (52 per cent) have a 'news section' covering (often a very biased selection of) media news. Also, in order to diffuse their views among visitors and sympathizers, almost half of the organizations offer bibliographical references (43.6 per cent) that are very rich in content and refer to an extremely wide range of issues. They vary from documents concerning historical issues and very traditional *topoi* of the extreme-right discourse (such as revisionist and negationist documents, documents that 'testify' to the crimes of communism, documents recalling traditional 'conspiracy theories' (Mudde 2007), but also biographies of current and past fascist intellectuals, soldiers and leaders (on the importance of the 'legendary narrative' for the construction of group's identity see also Dechezelles in this volume);[13] war tales of the Nazi/fascist and the RSI period). It is also possible to find articles on current political and social issues such as the corruption of the Italian political system and parties (e.g. very frequent are documents that trace the development, interpreted as 'betrayal' of Alleanza Nazionale under Fini since the Fiuggi congress in 1995)[14] or cultural issues.[15] Finally, also very frequent are documents that express the organization's view on several ethical issues, such as abortion, gender, homosexuality (e.g. see www.destra2000.interfree.it). In terms of differences between various types of extreme-right organizations, 'bibliographical references' are above all present on the sites of political parties and movements (63.7 per cent), which are also the main sites that offer 'articles, paper, and dossiers' (100 per cent).

Nevertheless, the message of the extreme-right organizations is not only propagated through traditional 'written' means of communication, but also with more innovative tools such as visual/audio tools. For instance, the majority of right-wing organizations' websites (51 per cent) use 'hate' symbols that 'advocate violence against, separation from, defamation of, deception about, or hostility towards others based upon race, religion, ethnicity, gender or sexual orientation' (Franklin 2006, as quoted in Tateo 2008: 290). Moreover, some extreme-right groups, such as right-wing commercial organizations (100 per cent) and nostalgic and revisionist groups (93 per cent) rely more than others on such 'hate' icons. As has been noted, aggressive banners and seals are particularly diffuse in right-wing youth-oriented websites (Padovani 2008).

The most common hate symbols are the swastika/*Hakenkreuzen* or burning crosses, eagles, *fascii littori*, symbols and photos of fascism, Mussolini and Hitler. Furthermore, showing a good degree of technical sophistication, extreme-right groups use them as animated and flashy banners (47.8 per cent), portraying symbols or representative figures, instead of as statistics or figures.

The significant presence of hate symbols and messages on the Italian extreme-right websites can be interpreted in the light of the lack of control and/or censorship that the Internet allows, and which in Italy (as well as in Spain) is particularly unregulated (Wetzel 2009: 365), despite the fact that the country has laws against the promotion of the Nazi ideology and the denying of the Holocaust. For example, on the website of the political party Fronte Sociale Nazionale (www.frontenazionale.it) we find a wide range of anti-Semitic stereotypes and images, such as the Star of David bleeding, 'the global plutocratic Mafia' and the 'Talmudic Judaism' (on anti-Zionist and anti-American propaganda on the Internet see also Wetzel 2009: 350). On the top page of the site Il Ras (www.ilras.tk) the visitor is welcomed by a skull close with the communist symbol 'hammer and sickle' in front of it, an Italian flame waving, a 'No entrance' road sign for Che Guevara and a 'wanted only dead' banner for Che Guevara. Similarly on the site *Il Duce*, we find a child who urinates on communist symbols and on the American flag.

However, beyond serving as a medium for propaganda, the Internet is also used by the Italian extreme-right groups as a means of 'agitation' (Wetzel 2009: 350), that is to organize mobilization events outside the Web, as well as to promote online actions directly. Official sources for instance stress that right-wing extremists also attack their political opponents through the Internet (e.g. for example publishing lists of personal data of political opponents, such as the names of family members or the addresses, Te–SAT Report 2007: 37–8).

Our data show that Italian extreme-right organizations quite often use the Internet for this 'activation of members' function, although less often than for communicating their propaganda as stressed above. However, from our analysis we could appreciate that when they try to mobilize members through the Web, this is done according to several strategies. The most common feature is to use the organizations' websites to disseminate among activists and even simple sympathizers their own 'event calendar/agenda', information on meetings, demonstrations and concerts (about one-fifth of the organizations, 21.7 per cent). A significant number of groups (17.4 per cent) also display on their website the event calendar of other right-wing organizations. This seems to suggest that the Web can serve to foster a sense of solidarity and collective identity between extremist organizations, and to build relations of cooperation that eventually can also be used in offline reality (Cinalli 2004). Most importantly, about 19 per cent of groups use the Internet to publicize their own 'on-going political campaigns'. This is the case of the numerous campaigns against immigrants and foreigners (e.g. against the Roma)[16] publicized on the website of the party Forza Nuova.

Another example is the campaign for the '*Mutuo Sociale*' ('Social Mortgage'), which was launched on the Internet in 2006 by a network of Italian right-wing organizations with the goal of providing home ownership for Italians – but not for non-Italians – who cannot afford to buy a property at market rates.[17]

Nevertheless, beside the traditional topic of immigration (on the topic see also the political campaign '*Italia libera dagli extracomunitari*', 'Free of foreigners'),[18] right-wing groups promote Internet campaigns on a wide variety of issues, sometimes also mirroring the radical left-wing counterpart social movements (Caiani and Parenti 2009). It is very common to find leaflets on abortion and related issues (see for example the site of *Forza Nuova*),[19] and usually they can be downloaded. Likewise, political parties and movements' websites often provide a summary of international geopolitical issues with ready-made arguments: campaigns for the boycott of Israeli and Chinese goods, against the USA and its 'imperialist wars'[20] and against the European Union are commonly found. Sometimes the same organizational websites even refer to YouTube videos posted by the group to explain their campaign further (for example the campaign of Forza Nuova against the Lisbon Treaty).

Thus, whereas right-wing organizations to a large extent use the Web to help their offline political initiatives, the organization of proper online 'protest' actions (such as for example 'net-strikes', Mosca 2006)[21] are very uncommon. When it happens, these types of actions are usually 'online petitions'. The group Repubblica Sociale Italiana, for example, publishes on its website a petition to ask that Foggia (a southern city in Italy) be declared as a Second World War 'martyr symbol' and that a day of collective remembrance for all Italians killed during the Anglo-American 'invasion'[22] be instituted. Protests staged directly on the Web are much more frequently used by left-wing movements (della Porta and Mosca 2006: 543). However, there is an interesting 'interplay' between the offline and online reality for Italian extreme-right organizations, particularly among 'Ultras' extreme-right soccer hooligan groups: they often utilize the Internet to organize and coordinate through the Web actions that are going to be staged in the 'real' world[23] or, more often, as a sort of showcase to illustrate actions already staged offline.[24] These websites are considered as sort of 'electronic business cards' that contain relevant information on the identity and the history of the group (ibid.: 538). On the (limited) use of the Internet by extremist groups to organize or publicize their actions online it should be noted that organizations are aware that the Internet is at the same time an opportunity and a danger: the Web is an opportunity for mobilizing and increasing their potential audience, but at the same time, it is also a useful instrument for police investigation and political adversaries to obtain information on illegal and violent actions.[25]

Extreme-right virtual communities: a new technological tool for old messages?

Do Italian extreme-right organizations use the Internet to form online communities and foster the collective identity of their group? This is of crucial importance since, as Virchow in this volume suggests, the continued involvement of individuals in political movements is not a result of a rational decision alone, but depends on the manner by which the organization/movement gets connected to the individual follower through cultural and political symbols, myths and narratives. Internet arenas of discussion, such as those represented by online forums, chat and mailing lists, can play an important role in terms of the construction of the collective identity of the group. Within such 'agora', enemies and allies are identified (Atton 2006) and the 'causes' of social and political problems are framed (Snow and Benford 1988), thus reinforcing the group identity and fostering solidarity between its members (on this point, see also Weimann 2006b and Dechezelles in this volume).

As underlined, the presence of an online sense of community and the associated actions can be inferred from the content of the websites (de Koster and Houtman 2008: 157). Analysing the features of online neo-Nazi rhetoric, Thiesmeyer (1999) has shown that extreme-right websites try to create a sense of community.

The content analysis of Italian right-wing websites reveals that, similarly to what has been noticed in the case of the British National Party, identity is often constructed through a process of (self) victimization of right-wing extremist groups: they tend to present themselves as the victims of the mainstream political actors (e.g. the ruling political class, established political parties, the judiciary, etc.) or, as is more often the case, as oppressed by the same actors who are usually the target of their actions (Atton 2006: 581). For example, instead of defining themselves as 'racist' (a racist party), they tend to define themselves as victims of 'racist acts' by various other political actors (e.g. victims of the aggression of communists, victims of immigrants who steal Italian jobs, etc.). In documents posted on their websites (either leaflets, press releases, etc.) it is frequent to find complaints that extreme-right groups receive unfavourable treatment from the state and the judicial system when compared with the extreme left. On this point, scholars have stressed that the societal and political consensus against right-wing extremism is frequently exploited by the activists for their propaganda (Wagemann 2005: 25). Rather diffused among extreme-right organizations is the argument that presents Italians (as well as the extreme-right organizations themselves) as victims of immigration, communism and Muslims, and that, building on this, demands the right to regain their 'lost hegemony' over the territory. The nationalistic dimension is strong in the public discourse of Italian extreme-right groups, especially – as Testa and Armstrong stress in this volume – in youth subcultures. On the website of the organization Veneto Fronte Skinhead, for example, newspapers are often accused of reporting exclusively on aggression against immigrants (by Italians), but not the opposite.[26] The left, as well as immigrants, are thus seen as the harshest enemies. On the website of the Fronte della Nuova Gioventù, leaflets dedicated to communists' acts of aggressions incite supporters to react and regain their 'territory'.[27] 'Italy for the Italians' and opposition to multiculturalism are, thus, some of the most important themes used by right-wing extremist groups to reflect their identity online.

It is indeed fairly usual (30 per cent of the groups analysed) to find the names of the group's leaders or members who are 'persecuted' (e.g. imprisoned) because of their fascist faith. In this sense they are considered as 'martyrs'. The Veneto Fronte Skinhead's website for example, displays among the news of the week, the Courts' orders to imprison 'comrade XXX', and members and sympathizers are invited by the group to support him symbolically and materially.[28]

The fostering of such collective identities also works through 'virtual' spaces open to discussion and interactivity on the Web (see Qin *et al.* 2007). Our data show that advanced Internet-based communications tools, such as online forums and chat rooms, are used by the Italian extreme-right groups: 30.4 per cent of the organizations offer a newsletter which, if subscribed to, provides information about the group; 28.3 per cent have on their websites 'forums of discussion' and/or mailing lists; 17.4 per cent of the right-wing sites contain 'questionnaires' and 'online surveys' where the groups ask the activist or sympathizer to express his/her own opinion on a variety of matters, from political to technical issues concerning the usability of the website. For example, on the website of the historical-revisionist group Il Ras, we find these three items: 'Do you agree to politics in the stadiums? Do you agree with our comrades who actively support the liberation of Palestine? Do you think we can improve some sections of this site?' (www.ilras.tk). Chat lines, where communication between activists and members is more instantaneous, are present in 17.4 per cent of the websites. Nostalgic and revisionist organizations are those among the most likely to contain a 'forum of discussion' (56.3 per cent) as well as 'chatlines' (31.3 per cent), whereas the presence of a published 'newsletter' is equally well distributed among all types of extreme-right groups. A recent study on the use of the Internet by radical left-wing organizations showed that 36 per cent of these groups have forums for discussion and/or mailing lists, 51 per cent offer newsletters, while chatlines and online surveys are present only in 10 per cent (della Porta and Mosca 2006).

One type of information that is often posted on the extreme-right websites (in 64.3 per cent of cases) is the 'policies or rules' document that strongly regulates, and sometimes limits, participation to forums or mailing lists. For instance, in some right-wing websites participation is allowed only to those 'who share the group ideology',[29] or 'who are true nationalists', or 'who are fascists'. In these cases, the desire to distinguish between 'in-group' and 'out-group' is evident. Such restrictions serve to reinforce the identity of the group by operating a clear discrimination between insiders and outsiders (Wageman 2005). However, on many occasions, many extremist websites are rather willing to showcase fairly mainstream views and use the Internet for the purpose of 'image control' (Gerstenfeld *et al.* 2003: 40) and/or 'content management' (Preece 2000). Indeed their pages frequently contain assertions that the group or the website is non-violent and not hate-oriented. For example, the site Il popolo d'Italia (www.popoloditalia.it) declares on the main entrance page of its discussion forum:

> Besides a respect for all users, language should be maintained that does not border on vulgar and does not disturb the moral dignity of the other users. Therefore it is severely forbidden to swear, post vulgarities or violent affirmations. Such discussions will be cancelled by moderators and the user may be punished.

Similar claims that underline the rules of 'net-etiquette' are easily found on many other sites.[30] Furthermore, as underlined by Langebach and Raabe in this volume, non-conventional tools of political consensus making – for example, 'White Power music' for right-wing youth subcultures – may play an important role in identity formation, as well as mobilizing members and sympathizers. Our results seem to suggest that the Italian right-wing groups are willing to exploit all the potentialities of the Internet for this purpose and indeed their websites have a strong emphasis on multimedia usage. Multimedia materials are very common (52.2 per cent), in particular, political audio downloads (such as, for instance, audios reproducing the national Italian anthem or anthems of political parties, etc.) as well as audios such as sermons and speeches (e.g. by leaders of the fascist or Nazi regimes).[31] Italian extreme-right organizations also make a frequent use of music and videos, hosting fascist and Nazi songs,[32] or posting songs and videos of extreme right-wing bands (see the site Lorien),[33] including the recording of musical events, gigs and concerts organized by the group (see for example the sites of Casa Pound[34] and Blocco Studentesc).[35] Common also are historical videos of Mussolini (see the site Il Ras). As has been underlined, all this material plays an important role in emphasizing the existence of a numerically significant group behind the site and is crucial in transmitting the group's 'ideology' (Tateo 2005). Right-wing subcultural youth groups, and revisionist and nostalgic organizations are the most likely to use multimedia materials on their sites (respectively around 70 per cent of the former, and 60 per cent of the latter). In the latter case, the use of multimedia materials serves the revisionist agenda of these organizations, and their willingness to rewrite history and to document the crimes of communism (Tateo 2005).

Conclusions

Against the background of an increasing academic interest in (extremist) politics online (de Koster and Houtman 2008) and a paucity of systematic empirical studies concerning extreme right-wing movements, this chapter, focusing on the Italian extreme right and conducting a formalized content analysis of different types of right-wing websites, aimed at contributing to fill this gap, by exploring the degree and the forms of the political use of the Internet by Italian extremist right-wing organizations.

First, our analysis demonstrates that these extremist groups exhibit a good level of Web knowledge and a considerable degree of Internet usage, through which they appear to pursue several different political goals. Our study has in fact indicated that, for the Italian case, extreme-right organizations use the Web largely as an instrument for propagating their ideology and expressing their views on a wide range of social, economic and political issues, showing their ability and willingness to explore the new potentialities offered by the Internet for communicating with potential 'recruits'. A clear feature emerging from this part of the analysis has been the richness of the content of the extreme-right Web propaganda, with the use of a variety of typical right-wing extremist rhetoric.

Second, Italian extreme right-wing organizations also emerged as quite effective in supporting communication and interactions with potential members and sympathizers, skilfully using Web technologies such as multimedia materials and various spaces for virtual discussions. In this sense, when promoting debates on the Web (such as online forums and chat rooms), they create electronic communities of like-minded people on their websites, and encourage the fostering of a collective identity (for this aspect of the websites' usage by right-wing organizations see also Padovani 2008).

Finally, if online actions are rare for extreme-right organizations (namely political actions performed directly online), nevertheless, such groups use the Internet to activate their members and promote mobilization outside of the Web (namely in the real world). They increasingly rely on the Internet in order to advertise the organizations' political campaigns and initiatives.

However, despite the novelty of the medium used (and the ability to adapt themselves to the new virtual tools), the Italian right-wing extremist groups reproduce an old message on their websites: a traditional fascist/Nazi rhetoric and view of the world. The symbols, icons, as well as the sophisticated Internet techniques (e.g. multimedia materials) used on their websites promote a precise and well-defined identity based on a clear separation between 'insider groups' and 'outsider groups', a stigmatization of political adversaries or ethnic and social minorities (e.g. homosexuals), often accompanied by an exaltation of fascism and Nazism. Considering this, our research confirms the importance of understanding how right-wing minorities build communications and use 'social representations' to influence society (Orfali, in this volume). Acting between tradition and innovation, activists of many extreme-right groups multiply their online presence, transforming themselves – as a representative of the Italian political party Alleanza Nazionale explains – into *legionari* (literally, legionnaires) of the [Web] space' (Caldiron 2001: 338).

Our research has demonstrated that through the Internet, these various groups are able to build a coherent and unifying ideology (see also Roversi 2006: 106ff.), which – in spite of the 'novelty' of the medium used – resonates with the old fascist rhetoric/paradigm. As the sociologist Roversi stresses, the 'dark pages' of the Web are characterized by nostalgia for the fascist era, racism, videos of clashes with the police, threats of revenge posted on the Web, and they create propaganda and proselytize against several social adversaries. More than a 'global village', the Internet appears 'as a space where differences are reproduced and emphasized, where distinct non-negotiable identities prevail' (Roversi 2006).[36] Considering this, the Italian extreme right may be described as constituting a 'two-front' actor, extremely innovative in its strategies of action and means of political consensus building, as well as 'traditional' in its message, although spread through these new modes of communication.

Notes

1 Although the authors share responsibility for the whole chapter, Manuela Caiani contributed the final text of sections 1, 4 and 6; and Linda Parenti of sections 2, 3 and 5.
2 www.adl.org/poisoning_web/introduction.asp.
3 Extreme-right websites have been classified into the broader extreme-right organizational categories on the basis of the self-definition of the group and the predominant tenets of the sites' content (for details on this method and the categories used, see also Tateo 2005).
4 Namely, classify others as either enemy or friend.
5 See for example, Il Ras (www.ilras.tk/).
6 Il Ras (www.ilras.tk/), Cuore Nero (www.ilcuorenero.it), FNCRSI (http://fncrsi.altervista.org).
7 E.g. Sodalizio del cerchio antico (http://utenti.lycos.it/sodalizio/indice.htm).
8 E.g. Parole dal Terzo Reich (www.paroledalterzoreich.com).
9 E.g. Casa Pound (www.casapound.org/); Blocco Studentesco (www.bloccostudentes co.org).
10 E.g. Il Presidio (www.ilpresidio.org/index.html).
11 The list of the extreme-right websites identified is available from the authors on request.
12 'Right-Wing Extremist Groups Becoming More Active After Post-9/11 Lull', *Newhouse News Service*, 14 July 2004.
13 E.g., see the revisionist organization Decima Mas (www.decima-mas.net/).
14 E.g., see the revisionist organization Controstoria (www.controstoria.it/).
15 E.g., see the cultural association Raido (www.raido.org), on neo-celtic and neo-mystic religion; see the association Centro Studi la Runa (www.eleuteros.org/tof).
16 The online campaign named 'Italy to Italians' for example is set to protest against the 'barbaric immigrations':

> Desperate Italians would often have accepted miserly payments usually given to immigrants, but they haven't been accepted for work just because they're Italians and they could not be blackmailed. Let's break this double grip: denounce those who employ immigrants illegally, exclude delinquents and begin a human repatriation of new slaves!

(See, www.forzanuova.org/pdf/IMMIGRAZIONESELVAGGIA2%5B1%5D.pdf.)

17 The '*Mutuo sociale*' project had a double goal: on the one hand reclaiming the right to property for Italians and on the other hand making the same right to property more difficult for immigrants and foreigners.
18 See the site Italia Libera (http://xoomer.alice.it/ilfasciolibero/base.htm).
19 See the Forza Nuova site (www.forzanuova.org/).
20 See the site Fascismo in Rete (www.Fascismoinrete.cjb.net/).

21 As for what concerns *online actions*, our data show that only very few right-wing groups organize them (only four groups out of forty-six).
22 See the site RSI, www.italia-rsi.org/. The purpose of the online petition was to remember that the Italians were not only victims of the Nazi front, but also of the Anglo-Americans.
23 For example, in February 2007, when a police officer (*Raciti*) was killed outside the stadium after a derby, different groups of Ultras utilized the Web to organize offline actions to protest against police and to show videos of such protests on their websites.
24 For example, videos posted on the Web showing violent clashes between the police and the right-wing Ultras groups (see also 'L'odio unisce le curve', *La Repubblica*, 4 February 2007).
25 The police have sometimes used online videos to identify and arrest violent Ultras (see '*I filmati su YouTube incastrano i tifosi teppisti*', *La Repubblica*, 22 November 2007).
26 See the press releases on the website of Veneto Fronte Skinhead (www.veneto fronteskinheads.org/comunicati.html).
27 See the press releases on the website of Fronte Nova Gioventù (www.fdng.org/ documenti/materiale/volantini/manifestazione_aggressioni_comuniste.jpg).
28 www.venetofronteskinheads.org/.
29 For example see the site Fascismo e Libertà (www.fascismoeliberta.it/).
30 E.g., see also www.popoloditalia.it, the site Il Foro Mussolini, (http://foroitalico. altervista.org/secondapagina.htm), the site Brigata Nera (http://it.geocities.com/ brigatanera88/), the site Spedizione Punitiva (www.spedizionepunitiva.tk/) and Il Ras (www.ilras.tk).
31 For example, see the links present on the site Benito Mussolini (http://spazioinwind. libero.it/mussolini/index2.htm).
32 For example, see the links found on the site of the cultural association Gente d'Europa (www.geocities.com/gente_europa/).
33 www.lorien.it/.
34 www.casapound.org.
35 www.bloccostudentesco.org/home.html.
36 Interview with A. Roversi, Sociologist of Communication, 'Politica e calcio, la violenza in rete', *La Repubblica*, 17 January 2006 (translated by the authors).

References

ADL. 2001. Available at: www.adl.org/poisoning_web/introduction.asp.
Arquilla, J. and Ronfeldt, D. 2001. 'The advent of netwar (revisited)', in J. Arquilla and D. Ronfeldt (eds), *Networks and Netwars: The future of terror, crime, and militancy*, Rand, Santa Monica: 1–25.
Atton, C. 2006. 'Far-right media on the Internet: Culture, discourse and power', *New Media and Society*, 8(4): 573–87.
Bennett, W.L. 2003. 'Communicating global activism: Strengths and vulnerabilities of networked politics', *Information, Communication and Society*, 6(2): 143–68.
Burris, V., Smith, E. and Strahm, A. 2000. 'White supremacist networks on the Internet', *Sociological Focus*, 33(2): 215–35.
Caiani, M. and Parenti, L. 2009. 'The dark side of the Web: Italian right-wing extremist groups and the Internet', *South European Society & Politics*, 14(3): 273–94.
Caiani, M. and Wagemann, C. 2009. 'Organizational networks of the Italian and German extreme right: An explorative study with social network analysis', *Information, Communication & Society*, 12(1): 66–109.
Caldiron, G. 2001. *La destra plurale*, Manifestolibri, Rome.

Chase-Dunn, C. and Boswell, T. 2002. 'Transnational social movements and democratic socialist parties in the semiperiphery', paper presented at the Annual Conference of the California Sociological Association. Available at: http://irows.ucr.edu/papers/csa02/csa02.htm, retrieved 9 March 2010.

Cinalli, M. 2004. 'Horizontal networks vs. vertical networks within multi-organizational alliances: A comparative study of the unemployment and asylum issue-fields in Britain', *European Political Communication Working Paper Series*, Issue 8/04, University of Leeds.

Criscione, A. 2003. 'Fascismo virtuale. La storia della Rsi nei siti Webdella destra radicale', *Zapruder*, 2: 122–30.

de Koster, W. and Houtman, D. 2008. 'Stormfront is like a second home to me: On virtual community formation by right-wing extremists', *Information, Communication & Society*, 11(8): 1155–76.

della Porta, D. and Mosca, L. 2006. 'Democrazia in rete: stili di comunicazione e movimenti sociali in Europa', *Rassegna Italiana di Sociologia*, 4(Oct–Dec): 529–56.

di Tullio, D. 2006. *Centri Sociali di destra*, Castelvecchi, Rome.

Fasanella, G. and Grippo, A. 2009. *L'orda Nera*, Rizzoli, Milano.

FRA. 2010. *Fundamental Rights: Challenges and achievements in 2010*, European Union Agency for Fundamental Rights, Vienna.

Gerstenfeld, P.B., Grant, D.R. and Chiang, C. 2003. 'Hate online: A content analysis of extremist Internet sites', *Analysis of Social Issues and Public Policy*, 3(1): 29–44.

Glaser, J., Dixit, J. and Green, D.P. 2002. 'Studying hate crime with the Internet: What makes racists advocate racial violence?', *Journal of Social Issues*, 58(1): 177–93.

Gnosis. 2006. 'Relazione sulla politica informativa e della sicurezza', *Rivista Italiana di intelligence*, May–August 2001. Available at: www/sisde.it/gnosis/RivistaRelSam.nsf/ServNavig/1, retrieved August 2009.

Mosca, L. 2006. *Searching the Net*, Report on Work Package 2 for Demos Project: 86–110.

Mudde, C. 2007. *Populist Radical Right Parties in Europe*, Manchester University Press, Manchester/New York.

Myers, D.J. 2000. 'Media, communication technology, and protest wave', paper presented at the Social Movement Analysis: The Network Perspective, Loch Lomond, Scotland.

Padovani, C. 2008. 'The extreme right and its media in Italy', *International Journal of Communication*, 2: 753–70.

Petit, C. 2004. 'Social movement networks in Internet discourse', paper presented at the annual meetings of the American Sociological Association, San Francisco, 17 August 2004. IROWS Working Paper #25. Available at: http://irows.ucr.edu/papers/irows25/irows25.htm, retrieved 9 March 2010.

Post, J.M. (ed.) 2005. 'Psychology', in *Addressing the Causes of Terrorism*, report of the working group at the International Summit on Democracy, Terrorism and Security, 8–11 March, Madrid, The Club de Madrid Series on Democracy and Terrorism, 1: 7–12.

Preece, J. 2000. *Online Communities: Designing usability, supporting sociability*, John Wiley & Sons, Chichester, UK.

Qin, J., Zhou, Y., Reid, E., Lai, G. and Chen, H. 2007. 'Analyzing terror campaigns on the Internet: Technical sophistication, content richness and Web interactivity', *International Journal of Human–Computer Studies*, 65: 71–84.

Roversi, A. 2006. *L'odio in rete. Siti ultras, Nazismo ondine, jihad elettronica*, Il Mulino, Bologna.

Snow, D.A. and Benford, R.D. 1988. 'Ideology, frame resonance, and participant mobilization', in B. Klandermans, H. Kriesi and S. Tarrow (eds), *From Structure to Action*, JAI Press, Greenwich, CT: 197–218.

Stern, K.S. 1999. *Hate and the Internet*, American Jewish Committee, New York.

Tateo, L. 2005. 'The Italian extreme right on-line network: An exploratory study using an integrated social network analysis and content analysis approach', *Journal of Computer-Mediated Communication*, 10(2): art. 10.

Tateo, L. 2008. 'The fascist discourse in computer mediated communication: The dual strategy model of the Italian extreme right', *Psicologia & Societade*, 20(2): 287–96.

Te-Sat. 2007. *Report on EU Terrorism Situation and Trend*, Europol.

Te-Sat. 2010. *EU Terrorism Situation and Trend Report*, Europol.

Thiesmeyer, L. 1999. 'Racism on the web: Its rhetoric and marketing', *Ethics and Information Technology*, 1(2): 117–25.

Wagemann, C. 2005. *The VETO Database on Frames–Germany*, Work Package Report for START Project Patterns of Radicalization in Political Activism.

Weimann, G. 2004. *www.terror.net: How Modern Terrorism Uses the Internet*, Special Report, US Institute of Peace.

Weimann, G. 2006a. *Terror on the Internet: The new agenda, the new challenges*, United States Institute of Peace, Washington, DC.

Weimann, G. 2006b. 'Virtual disputes: The use of the Internet for terrorist debates', *Studies in Conflict and Terrorism*, 29(7): 623–39.

Wetzel, J. 2009. 'Country Report Italy', *Strategies for Combating Right-Wing Extremism in Europe*, Bertlesmann Stiftung (ed.), Gütersloh, Bertelsmann Stiftung: 327–74.

Whine, M. 2000. 'The use of the Internet by far right extremists', in T. Douglas (ed.), *Cybercrime: Law, security and privacy in the information age*, Routledge, London: 234–50.

Zanini, M. and Edwards, S.J.A. 2001. 'The networking of terror in the information age', in John Arquilla and David Ronfeldt (eds), *Networks and Netwars: The future of terror, crime and militancy*, Santa Monica, CA, RAND, MR-1382-OSD.

Zhou, Y., Reid, E., Qin, J., Chen, H. and Lai, G. 2005. 'U.S. domestic extremist groups on the Web: Link and content analysis', *IEEE Intelligent Systems*, 20(5): 44–51.

14

'AN INTACT ENVIRONMENT IS OUR FOUNDATION OF LIFE'

The Junge Nationaldemokraten, the Ring Freiheitlicher Jugend and the cyber-construction of nationalist landscapes

Emily Turner-Graham

On 17 July 2011, five days before unleashing the attacks on Norway that he claimed were 'atrocious but necessary', Anders Behring Breivik opened accounts on the social networking websites Facebook and Twitter. On Facebook, he painted a brief but later telling portrait of himself, identifying as a Christian and a conservative and his interests as Freemasonry and bodybuilding (BBC 2011). On Twitter he offered only a quote from John Stuart Mill – 'One person with a belief is equal to the force of 100,000 who have only interests.' Six hours before the attacks, he posted a video on the video sharing website YouTube visually detailing his manifesto '2083 – A European Declaration of Independence', depicting the threats to Europe he perceived from 'Cultural Marxism' and 'Islamic Colonization' (*The Telegraph* 2011). As a final deed before putting his violent plans into action, on the day of the attacks he sent out a mass email containing his 1,500-page manifesto. Before physically attempting to bring to life his extremist vision of how the world should be by first detonating a bomb at government buildings in central Oslo and then committing the mass shooting of sixty-nine people at an Arbeiderpartiet (Labour Party) youth camp on the Norwegian island of Utøya, Breivik carefully assembled his ideal world in the virtual realm online. Building a cyber environment more to his liking was an important first step towards creating such a world in actual reality. Although the horrific acts of Breivik are of course an extreme example, the Internet is increasingly providing a wide range of extreme-right groups with a forum to develop and test their vision of an ideal world online before committing to their plans in reality.

Since the Second World War, the extreme right has remained a persistent and significant force throughout the world but most especially in Europe, at its geographical source. Its influence is at the very least constant, if not in fact on the rise, owing in part to its ability to consistently claim as its own, issues pertinent to considerable percentages of the population (*Spiegel Online* 2008). Environmentalism has long since been one such issue and now, as this issue takes on a renewed significance and becomes more pressing to the world community than ever before, the extreme right, with its ever-mobile Janus face has similarly stepped up its focus upon it. While maintaining long-held rightist views that national identity and national landscapes are closely interconnected, many extreme-right parties have now also contemporized their mobilizing passions by creating a virtual nationalist world online, using the 'intact environment' of the Internet as a testing ground to electronically mould the 'intact [racial] environment' they seek to apply to the world at large (RFJ 2003).

The extreme right has become increasingly adept at manipulating these new media in order to transmit its message. The youth wings of a number of extreme-right parties provide particular examples of this, targeting Europe's young people on issues of special concern to them – such as the environment – and using means to communicate with young people 'in a way [in which] they're used to being communicated to' (Wells 2008, p. 5). As such, the cyber-efforts of the Junge Nationaldemokraten (JN), youth wing of Germany's 'neo-Nazi' Nationaldemokratische Partei Deutschlands (NPD), and Ring Freiheitlicher Jugend (RFJ), youth wing of Austria's increasingly extreme-right *Freiheitliche Partei Österreichs* (FPÖ) will provide the focus of this chapter. Focusing on these groups seems particularly interesting: based in two countries that entertained a complex relationship with a Nazi past, these two extreme-right youth groups show a degree of convergence in the way they use new electronic media: as such they point to the development of a transnational extreme-right youth community. The success of the FPÖ's increasingly determined campaign for the youth vote was made clear in Austria's last general elections in 2008, in which 44 per cent of first-time voters cast their votes for the FPÖ (*Neue Freie Zeitung* 2008).

Given the relative newness of the medium itself, academic research on the wide and varied transmission of right-wing ideology on the Internet remains relatively limited. Yet, prominent American white supremacists, such as David Duke, have predicted that the Internet will be 'the tool of the White revolution' (Kaplan *et al.* 2003: 139–40). Less academic attention still has been given to the many youth groups who adhere to extreme right-wing ideas and the way they use the Internet, despite the fact that young people use the Net as an everyday means of communication. In the same way as Caiani and Parenti's chapter in this volume on the Italian extreme right's use of the Internet, this chapter will make considerable use of the medium itself as a key primary source.

Blood and soil on the information superhighway

The JN and the RFJ both have an extensive Internet presence. Visitors can easily move from the main website for each group (www.jn-buvo.de/ and www.rfj.at), to individual websites for their region (for example, the JN Bremen group:

www.npd-jugend.de/ or the RFJ in Oberösterreich: http://ooe.rfj.at/). As well as these clearly party-related sites, NPD and RFJ produce clips posted on YouTube. The JN also offers its Volksfront (People's Front) broadcasts online which – among other online material – produce a bulletin every week of 'critical news' believed to be relevant to NPD supporters and given a particularly youthful focus by the style of its JN newsreader. The NPD also targets the Internet generation with the much discussed downloadable 'Hate-rock' songs of their *Projekt Schulhof* (Project Schoolyard) campaign (the British National Party conducts a similar campaign), while young people in Austria can similarly download FPÖ leader H.C. Strache's hard-hitting 'H.C. Rap', 'Viva H.C.' and the new track, 'Wiener Blut' (Viennese Blood), from the Net and onto their iPods and mobile phones. Over a couple of weeks in 2006, 158,000 listeners downloaded Strache's first rap song within an overall Austrian population of 8,316,487 (Rauschal 2006). Similarly, one can 'friend' or 'like' the NPD, FPÖ, H.C. Strache or a number of other extreme-right politicians on Facebook (Strache currently has 104,586 Facebook friends). H.C. Strache is especially skilled in the use of Facebook, slipping in the traditional extreme-right complaints about the European Union, for example, alongside wishing his 'friends' a sunny weekend (Strache 2011). A bridge between the actual and the virtual world has clearly been built by the extreme right's youth groups.

In 1993, in the early stages of the Internet's development, Roland Bubik, a member of the New Right (discussed in detail by Bar-On and Mellón in this volume) recognized that 'new possibilities for influencing people are arising in the area of communications networks'(Hooper 2002). A concentrated Internet presence allows for a number of opportunities that were not possible in the pre-Net era. First, the Net brings a worldwide and highly visual (and thus accessible) awareness to the cause it represents. Second – and this is of key importance in attracting an often socially vulnerable youth audience – such Internet sites create an immediate identification and a sense of 'groupness'(Wallace 1999: 55). It is 'a place of congregation', providing an instant sense of community in an increasingly disjointed, disconnected world (Reymers 2002). Indeed, in the case of the extreme right, it allows for the development of 'virtual groupuscules'(Kaplan *et al.* 2003: 149) as well as for the 'exchange of communicative gestures and symbols' (Reymers 2002) which allow for self-validation through 'the recognition and negotiation of meaning' (Reymers 2002). The Internet allows young people especially to make in-roads into that significant part of their lives, 'the search for identity' (Reymers 2002). The making of a public statement (of sorts) in cyberspace allows for the confirmation of an individual's nationalist identity, stating viscerally 'this is who I am' but also allowing for the aspirational recognition and exploration of 'this is who I ought to be' (Wallace 1999: 79).

But, significantly, it does this within a void of sorts, a virtual reality. An online community immediately makes the visitor feel accepted and validates their views – irrespective of how bizarre or politically incorrect they may be – simply by its presence (Wells 2008). As a result – combined with the Internet's comforting 'anonymous factor' (Wallace 1999: 79) – the establishment of more radical positions than may otherwise have been taken in 'real time' is possible. As such – particularly in a setting that is both political and adolescent – moderate voices can often be drowned out (Wallace 1999: 76–8). Add to this the polarization that can take place as a group's radicalism grows, as well as the pressing demands of online group conformity (Wallace 1999: 59–64), and the Internet is clearly a potent medium even before – or if – its users meet at party meetings and excursions. This is made clear in the case of Patrol 36, a neo-Nazi group in Israel, who filmed their various physical attacks on their Jewish compatriots and then posted them online in order to impress their ideological brothers abroad (*Foreign Correspondent* 2008).

Equally, the Internet allows for the easy spreading of profoundly radical material which, given the significant restraints placed upon the display of Nazi-related paraphernalia throughout much of Europe, is a major point in favour of its intensive use by the extreme right. The natural attraction of many teenagers to some form of rebellion is dramatically catered to by the offensive extreme-right material available on the Net. As a representative of the British National Party's (BNP) music label, Great White Records, phrases it: 'Young people love anything that's seen as rebellious . . . in our opinion if they're going to rebel we'd like them to do it our way and listen to our music . . .' (MacIntyre 2006).

This 'rebellious' stance has recently been confirmed by BNP leader, Nick Griffin, who is touting the party as 'the Sex Pistols of British politics' (*Dateline* 2009). Further, the Internet allows for the repetition of a message and the embedding of a vision which other mediums do not. As Nick Griffin states: 'People will listen to a song over and over again and . . . take all the words in in a way you'd be very lucky to get one in one hundred [people] to come and listen to a speech' (MacIntyre 2006).

Since environmental issues rely heavily on the visual, the Internet has proved to be an ideal medium for the coupling of nationalism and environmental issues in the extreme-right's campaign for Europe's youth, as well as an ideal medium for refreshing this long-held cause in its connection to extreme-right ideology. The coming 'white revolution' has been virtually created online, for fellow travellers and potential adherents alike to already bear witness to. A community and a corresponding environment is created that does not yet exist in reality. The Internet is thus also a means of projecting desires and creating a landscape of ideas: 'Any field in which . . . [an] . . . idea can germinate and be shared is a field of potential meaning to the individual, and therefore a locus of the elements of identity'(Reymers 2002). Further, the landscape of the Internet is a 'large scale immersive 360 degree panorama venue [that] seamlessly blends image with thematic content' (Reymers 2002).

Within an environmentalist stance, the extreme right chiefly has the opportunity to launch an appeal to 'old ideals' of 'traditional[ism] . . . and a stable order' (Olsen 1999: 2). Yet in doing so it can also present itself from a fresh perspective – especially by way of the Web – as the polar opposite of the left, and most particularly now 'the postmaterialist New Left and its political agenda' (Olsen 1999: 2), which can then easily segue into a broad-spectrum attack on the EU, globalization, immigration, the Muslim community and the threat of terror. The malleable discourse surrounding environmentalism can be seen to have moved increasingly to the centre of most extreme-right platforms throughout Europe.

As Jonathan Olsen states, it would be easy to 'dismiss the Radical Right's engagement with ecological questions as a Trojan horse, a crude and superficial attempt to smuggle in an extremist politics via a populist green posturing' (Olsen 1999: 2). Yet as Olsen acknowledges and as this chapter also concurs, this stance is part of a long-standing rightist position and understanding of the world which, post-September 11, has now been renewed in vigour, especially through the cyber-focused eyes of youth.

This is particularly so in the cases of Germany and Austria. The 'defense of small-scale communities against an homogenizing one-world culture and, above all, the protection of the local environment against the forces of global capitalism' are modern representations of elements of the Romantic and later *völksich* traditions that have long coloured right-wing German and Austrian understandings of the interconnection between national identity and the natural environment (Olsen 1999: 2). The Internet, with its capacity to not only spread a message around the world but also, conversely, to allow for the development of localized 'tiny geographical units' (Reymers 2002) is the perfect medium for *völkisch* thought in the twenty-first century.

It is important to understand what is meant by these traditions, by contemporary representations of nature which draw on them and so, in short, what is meant by the term 'the environment' for the extreme right. '[E]nvironmentalism . . . has as much to do with protecting a piece of ourselves, a sense of our identity, as it does with protecting forests, rivers, and lakes'(Olsen 1999: 5) – or, as both the NPD and the FPÖ have more simply put it '*Umweltschutz ist Heimatschutz!*' ('Environmental protection is Homeland protection!') (NPD Greiz 2008; RFJ Leizen 2008). It is interesting to note that in the aftermath of the earthquake, tsunami and resultant nuclear reactor catastrophe in Japan in 2011, both the FPÖ and NPD have variously declared themselves online to be anti-nuclear within the same context (Strache 2011; JN 2011).

There has always been – and continues to be – a rejection by the extreme right of 'Enlightenment universalism', that is, 'a world view in which a system of places is a human, not a natural construction . . .' (Olsen 1999: 5–6). For the extreme right, all ethnic or cultural groups have a geographical area with which they are naturally and inherently connected. This area both forms and consistently informs their ethnic and cultural characteristics. Under a *völkisch* understanding of national identity, particular races were tied to particular areas and judgements were made upon those races depending on the environment with which they were connected. Jews, for example, originally emanated from the desert and were therefore viewed as shallow, arid, 'dry' people, devoid of profundity and totally lacking creativity. As a result they were in fact spiritually barren (Mosse 1964: *passim*). 'True' Germans, by contrast, having always lived in dark, mist-shrouded forests, were deep, mysterious and profound and imbued with the all-important and oft-mentioned 'life force'. Further, as they were constantly surrounded by darkness, they were imbued with a dynamic, creative urge as they strove towards the sun. Clearly, the opposite action was anticipated from a desert people, already in the sun.

'All humans have the right to a homeland': the online environmental policies of the NPD, the JN, the FPÖ and the RFJ

While efforts have been made to move away from overt statements on race following the Second World War and the very obvious connections that could be damagingly made with the Nazis' policy of *Blut und Boden* (Blood and Soil), there are still very clear intimations – particularly in the virtual world depicted on the Internet – that ethnic groups are bound to certain areas and that to wrest people away from their naturally determined locale is damaging not only to national identity but also to national health and the environment. Not only are people naturally connected to one area but this connection is an organic product of nature itself (Olsen 1999: 6).

The NPD and the FPÖ, though currently located at different points on the extreme-right spectrum, both espouse environmental policies essentially in keeping with this overall rightist belief system. Put briefly, the NPD seeks to deport immigrants and asylum-seekers from Germany and to restore the 'eastern lands' (such as Silesia in Poland) (Olsen 1999: 17). They are also profoundly opposed to the European Union (EU) as it currently stands and argue instead for a union based upon a 'Europe of the Peoples' (Olsen 1999: 17). This deliberately vague term almost certainly correlates to the oft-used term 'Europe of Fatherlands' currently espoused by Heinz-Christian Strache, leader of the FPÖ, and also Die Republikaner, another German extreme-right party (*Die Republikaner* 2007). This notion is a common thread in extreme-rightist discourse and suggests that the EU at present is a 'Diktat' and does not respect the rights of individual countries and as such, their individual identities. The NPD believe strongly in a connection between national identity, the population and the environment, and they argue for this triumvirate in quite traditional terms, highlighting the superiority of the German people and the subsequent incapability of other national groups to live within Germany's borders. Bar-On and Williams discuss this theme using different national examples in other chapters of this volume.

Recent online policy statements by the NPD resonate with the long-held idea of the environment representing far more than just a backdrop to human affairs. The destruction of nature, they argue, 'can be traced to the destruction of traditional homogeneous ethnic communities, and this in turn [has led to] the alienation brought about by unbridled economic growth' (NPD Bayern 2009). Indeed, for the NPD, environmental policy is intimately interconnected with all other stances of the party: '[t]he protection of nature should not depend on one-sided economic considerations. The preservation of the natural conditions of life is more important than the profitability of factories' (NPD Bayern 2009). The correlation between human beings and their environment is such that sustainable development is regarded as a 'people's economy' in which 'people and ecology are harmonized: the economy cannot be allowed to destroy Germany's environment and alienate its people' (NPD Bayern 2009).

On the JN's website, this stance – in which German national identity, Germany's future and the German environment are firmly tied together – is elaborated upon in a piece entitled 'On German distress', as well as emphasizing the key role to be played by youth.

> You [distress] are apparent all over our country! What has happened to this country over the last decades? What is happening to our German people, our German culture, which can be seen in our country's forests, lakes and rivers? We can see it day after day with our own eyes: corruption, destruction and foreign domination is becoming clear to everyone in our everyday lives, at school, at university or in factories! And do we want young Germans to become accustomed to it? Do we want to accept this unchallenged? . . . [T]he refusal to be politically active make German youth become a petty bourgeois mass: some try their luck in a professional career, [looking for satisfaction] in consumption and prosperity, others in a brainless tavern [or] disco at the weekends, indulging in drug taking, into the left camp. The idolization of all foreigners, the national self-oblivion – the national self hate – [makes for] the indeterminable dissolution . . . of the German people! . . . The consumer and waste-oriented society with its McDonalds and Coca Cola imperialism, idiotic Hollywood productions, degenerate music, deviant pornos and cities of cold concrete silos without meaningful leisure alternatives for our youth – this is life today in the standard international civilization. We became alienated and so today we are mentally incapacitated from the character of our national identity: drinking, stuffing ourselves with food, watching rubbish on the idiot box, reading *Bravo* and *Bild*, visiting the disco at the weekend, driving a fast car and [smoking] a joint occasionally – should that be the sum of our much-sworn-to liberty, the essence of our lives? If you recognize this too, the wrongful way in which our lives are determined, if you believe that these problems demand our time [to find] a solution, [a solution] that places the people at the centre of political activity, even if you feel the golden cage in which our people have been imprisoned and robbed of our national identity, then it's time that you also made a contribution to the removal [of] this wrong thinking.
>
> (JN 2009)

Therefore, immigration is seen by the NPD and the JN as a threat not only to German national identity but also to the German environment.

> All humans have the right to a homeland and to protection from expulsion. The right to a homeland is a human right. It exists independent of

intergovernmental agreements, and neither can it be abolished by them. The right to a homeland is that most important of collective human rights and the basis for the preservation of the peace. The word 'homeland' is understood worldwide in spatial, ethnic and cultural terms. Thus the homeland, which for its *Volksgruppen* develops a history over centuries, as well as cultural traditions, achievements and protected objects [*Schutzobjekten*]. Nationality and culture are substantial bases for becoming human . . .

We demand:

A liveable environment, which is our homeland, and its protection is decided by us.

The preservation of the German right to self-determination – no voting rights for foreigners!

The preservation of the German identity – no dual-nationality!

Immediate completion of mass immigration and gradual repatriation of strangers living here to their homeland.

Promotion of German culture and ending of the deliberate re-education and *Überfremdung* by politics and the media.

(NPD 2005)

The website of the JN's parent party, the NPD, advertises the right-wing magazine *Umwelt und Aktiv* which encapsulates these sorts of ideas in its promise to address *Heimatschutz* (homeland protection), *Tierschutz* (animal protection) and *Umweltschutz* (environmental protection) (*Umwelt & Aktiv* 2011).

In Austria, under the leadership of Heinz-Christian Strache, it has been widely acknowledged that the FPÖ are pursuing an ever more radical path (Turner-Graham 2008). Certainly there are suggestions that the RFJ are making increased connections with Austria's neo-Nazi scene (Öllinger 2007, http://rfjwatch.wordpress.com/ 2011). With regard to the environment especially, for example, the FPÖ can be seen to be moving ever more towards a similar position to that of the NPD. Importantly, also like the NPD, the FPÖ posts all of its policies and their visual accompaniments online.

While preserving much of past leader Jörg Haider's pre-existing agenda, Strache has also changed aspects of the FPÖ programme. This can be seen in Strache's reference to Austria's need to become a '*Volksgemeinschaft*' (Strache and Mölzer 2006: 73) – a problematic and nazified word previously avoided for its racialist overtones and instead replaced with the more 'pastoral . . . notions' suggested in the word '*Heimat*' when defining Austria's national identity (Carter 2005: 39). Strache has made his own ethnic identification clear: 'first Austrian, then German, then European' (Strache and Mölzer 2006: 74). But his views on European identity more broadly are complex. Europe, he repeatedly states, is a 'Christian–Western community of values' (Strache and Mölzer 2006: 75, *passim*). Strache is a pan-German and to a degree a pan-European but his Europe is a very specifically delineated one.

There should be no European superstate, he declares, but there should be a solitary core idea of Europe (*Kerneuropa*).

The direction in which Strache is taking the FPÖ is particularly clear in the party's stance on the environment. In fact, an ethnic–cultural–environmental triptych which both references the past and yet speaks of a postmodern present seems to be evolving under Strache. The notion that cultural diversity poses a threat to national identity is primarily proffered as the FPÖ's current position and material on the Internet and cartoons in online party newspapers such as the *Neue Freie Zeitung* support this with a distinct objectification of other groups within Austrian society. The RFJ's use in their mission statement of the slogan 'an intact environment is the foundation of life' (RFJ 2003) immediately following 'environmental protection is homeland protection' (RFJ 2003) and the overall context of FPÖ and RFJ policy makes clear again the close correlation here of a triumviratic ethnic, cultural and environmental identification.

The online 2003 Mission Statement of the RFJ elaborates further on these means of identification, clarifying first their ethnic understanding of self: 'The RFJ commits itself without reservation to the Austrian state and its history. Austria has been embedded since its inception with the German people and culture' (RFJ 2003). Then clearly outlines who has no role in the Austrian state:

> [F]oreign infiltration threatens our people. [With] over 800,000 foreigners legally living here . . . roughly at least 300,000 illegals and also, in the last 20 years, over 350,000 naturalized foreigners, Austria has far exceeded its capacities. The RFJ demands, therefore, a strict management of the asylum laws and an immediate lowering of the immigration quota to zero. Beyond that, incentives must be created for inducing foreigners already living here to return to their homeland.
>
> (RFJ 2003)

Having made these sorts of distinctions, the ideal type of Austrian is then put forward, as the RFJ manifesto states that 'the Farming Community [is] the Cornerstone of our Culture' (RFJ 2003). This makes a clear connection between Austrian national identity and the Austrian rural landscape, which then segues into support for a 'Europe of the Peoples': 'The wealth of Europe lies in the variety of its traditional peoples and cultures, whom it should seek to protect as the highest basic value of a European constitution' (RFJ 2003).

The FPÖ 2011 Party Programme picks up on similar themes, making clear the on-going perceived correlation between the Austrian natural environment and Austrian national identity. Under the heading of 'Homeland, Identity and Environment', it is stated:

> We are committed to protecting our Austrian homeland, our national identity and our distinctive natural environment . . . We are aware of the

connection with our ancestors and the responsibility for our children and we want to preserve a home for future generations, which enables independent living in an intact environment . . . The . . . majority of Austrians are part of the German people, their language and their cultural community.

(FPÖ 2011)

'Dedicated to the homeland': visions from a virtual nationalist world

The RFJ – obviously, as a youth organization – have made considerable use of the Internet to impart their message on the construction and maintenance of Austrian space. The RFJ in Oberösterreich, for example, has headed its page with the message *Der Heimat verpflichtet* (Dedicated to the Homeland) (RFJ Oberösterreich 2009). Accompanying this caption are various appealing views of the region – the town squares at Branau and Freistadt; the lake at Vöcklabruck, a traditional church at Gmunden replete with Eastern-style dome and mountains in the background; the Altstadt streetscapes of Schärding and Linz; the clear blue skylines of Perg and Wels dotted with traditional buildings, a smattering of more modern constructions and the mountain range looming large behind them. Although also taking these local images to the furthest corners of the world, the Internet is primarily idealizing and defining familiar surrounds for RFJ members in appealing high definition while the caption compels their connection to this landscape. In a reminiscently *völkisch* style, it is creating a community between members – as Austrian citizens – and their environment, and so giving them a sense of belonging defined by what is around them.

The RFJ in Innsbruck has similarly made use of powerful imagery in its video clips available online, accessible either through their website or the popular youth website, YouTube. 'RFJ Tirol – Fight for your Homeland!' is a recent offering. It begins on an historical note, stating: 'Andreas Hofer [the Tyrolean who led forces against Napoleon] gave his life for his homeland and with him, thousands of our forefathers. His fight for freedom, for tradition and for sovereignty lives again in us' (RFJ Tirol 2008).

Old paintings of Hofer's struggle for the embodiment of Austrian nationalism – the Tyrolean landscape then merges seamlessly with modern photographs of the region, suggesting both the eternal nature of the landscape and the persistent need to defend it. To underline how this defence might translate in modern life, the clip then segues into recent footage of RFJ Tirol members walking through the hallowed Austrian forest carrying Austrian flags and then cleaning a Second World War memorial that had been covered in graffiti by the local *Antifa* (anti-fascists). These FPÖ youth are at one both with the Austrian environment and with their historical and current national obligations. 'If honourless people visually pollute our holy memorials,' the caption reads, suggesting both the built and the natural memorials shown, 'We must come to the fore' (RFJ Tirol 2008). The seamless visual flow of the clip allows for both a serious and an encouraging message to be easily imparted. It concludes with an obvious if partly peculiar appeal to its youthful audience:

> Because we love our homeland . . .
> Because it's fun to fight for the homeland
> Because we are true patriots
> Will you also fight for your homeland
> Because Tirol needs us!
>
> (RFJ Tirol 2008)

The message of Austrian land being invaded by alien forces is made even more visually palpable in another video posted on YouTube by the Tyrolean RFJ. Entitled 'Watch out!', it begins with standard scenes of 'our beautiful Tyrol', wildflowers, green fields, snow-capped mountains, cows. Then the screen becomes black and the text reads, 'Stop! We [will] keep to the truth'. The idyllic scenes of the Austrian countryside are then interspersed with shots of Muslim women and their children, black people in tribal dress dancing wildly on the streets of Innsbruck, Muslim men at prayer and a mosque being built with an Austrian mountain in the background. Strikingly, the clip then moves into material on the lengthy animosity between Austria and Italy over South Tyrol, which still remains an autonomous Italian territory. A grab-bag of 'invaders' of Austria are thus easily spliced together. 'Watch out!' the video reiterates as it concludes.

Owing to both the ease with which a plethora of images can be selected for viewing on the Internet and the fact that YouTube groups clips together under a common theme, a clip by 18TYROL88[1] entitled 'Stop [the] Islamization [of] Europe' can then be simply accessed from the sidebar by young viewers of the RFJ's message (18TYROL88 2008). The comparative subliminal subtleties of the FPÖ's youth videos is made clear by 18TYROL88's visual diatribe. With a text banner running almost continually along the bottom of the screen, the clip joins together a vast number of images that infer both that Islam is a danger to Europe and that Europe is in increasing agreement on this fact. 'The minaret and Muslims [are not about] religious practice', the text proclaims, 'They are symbols of power and conquest' and '[a] minaret stands not for religious freedom but for a political goal' (18TYROL88 2008). The sentiment that Islam is most obviously an affront to Austria's landscape and overall environment is made clear in a further declaration, 'Oriental dwellings should not happen in our Alpine land. Just as oriental clothing, music and culture [should not happen]' (18TYROL88 2008). An equally forceful heavy metal song is superimposed over this hard-hitting montage to round out the clip's overall impression. Part of the song runs:

> They rule the land
> They're in command
> They hold all strings in hand

They are invisible
Out of sight
They've designed
A secret place
To play their games . . .
Now connect
Don't even ask
Until we're out of it
Everything's at highest stake
Come take a look . . .
You've reached
The promised land
You've crossed the line
You've reached the end.
            (Blind Guardian 2006)

The NPD, and its youth wing the JN, similarly exalt a *völkisch* vision of the German homeland. The NPD webpage has been emblazoned for some time with the confident motto '*Hier ist Deutschland*'. The scene the slogan captions is invariably a rural one or otherwise a photograph from a stereotypically German small town, an old castle amidst forest, an aged stone wall covered in snow, ornate Fachwerk-style buildings (NPD Greiz 2008). The strident tone of the slogan leaves little possibility in the viewer's mind that Germany could be visually depicted in any other way. In 2011, the NPD continued to enforce this message with the line 'We want to live' superimposed upon a natural scene. German national identity and indeed German national survival are inextricably linked with the landscape (JN 2011).

The NPD clearly states in its party programme its belief in the relationship between German identity and the German environment under the heading, 'Nature is the basis of life' (NPD Greiz 2008). As with the *völkisch* thinkers of the nineteenth century and the National Socialists of the inter-war era, the NPD puts forward, 'German landscapes are cultural landscapes . . . [h]umans are a part of nature. Therefore nature is not simply only the "environment" of humans' (NPD Greiz 2008). But, like the RFJ, they give this connection of national self and environment a contemporary – and thus apparently – relevant perspective by also noting:

> Environmental protection cannot be seen as separate from cultural develop-ment . . . The materialism of the last decades has advanced the destruction of the natural basis of life in an irresponsible way. Unrestrained economic growth, radical landscape change, ambitious industrial projects, industrial-ization of agriculture, urbanization of villages as well as the destruction of urban structures are irresponsibly advanced by established parties, organiza-tions and interest groups.

(NPD Greiz 2008)

Similarly, the NPD argues that 'All genetically modified goods must be subject to compulsory labelling in Germany' (NPD 2008). Having couched their environmental policy in modern and essentially appealing terms, the NPD then return to a more recognizably *völkisch*/National Socialist position of yearning for a traditional, rural lifestyle within which a 'true' German identity will be found: 'The one-sided bias of material values and economic obligations has led inevitably to the destruction of traditional links and cultures. Humans are alienated and without roots, they are losing their identity' (NPD Greiz 2008).

Further, they then focus particularly upon the treatment of animals, putting forward, in a manner that recalls the Nazis' Animal Protection Law of 1933, that

> [There must be] [t]he protection of animals and the biodiversity of species in the animal and plant world. The avoidance of unnecessary cruelty to animals is a self-evident matter for people. Offences are to be punished criminally [under the NPD].
>
> (NPD Greiz 2008)

The Volksfront–Medien site – easily accessible from both NPD and JN links – provides, like the RFJ sites, a myriad of video clips supporting their rightist message. The creation of a germanized landscape is a key theme to many of them. The '*Kritische Nachrichten der Woche*' (Critical News of the Week) for 5 April 2008 examined the story of ethnic Germans expelled from Eastern Europe following the Second World War; 1 May being celebrated in Nazified terms as the 'day of work' (*Tag der Arbeit*); Germany's apparent social problems with its Turkish population; the seemingly excessive number of foreigners now living in Germany; a new exhibition in Berlin surveying Hitler's post-war architectural ambitions to build 'Germania'; the killing of an NPD youth apparently by 'foreigners'; the permission for Muslim students to pray at school and the FPÖ's successes in provincial Austrian elections. In an environmental viewpoint governed by the connecting of identity, population and landscape, this news report brought in past attempts to germanize Europe, the apparent aberration Europe had become under the influence of multiculturalism and the moves of right-wing activists elsewhere to redress the balance (JN 2008). In a clip recalling the more aggressive of the RFJ-related Web-videos, an advertisement for an anti-mosque demonstration that took place in Frankfurt-am-Main last year is also available, depicting a mosque and the sound of a call to prayer, and a scene of Muslim men kneeling in prayer is overlaid with the line: 'Our future? The Germany of tomorrow?' An aggressive, hard rock soundtrack then breaks in, accompanied by stark black and white footage of JN demonstrators marching and the confrontational slogan 'Not with us!' (JN 2008).

The Volksfront–Medien site, in its Net-borne attempts to bring an extreme-right message to Germany's youth, also offers 'political cabaret' in which Santa will only distribute gifts to Germany's children if they concede 'guilt' over 'Holocaust memories' and a call to attend the NPD's May 1 rallies attempts to illustrate what Germany's presently bleak industrial landscape could become under extreme-right leadership. Other videos arrogantly proclaim 'I am a nationalist!' and others still focus on the music of nationalist folk singer Frank Rennicke (JN 2008 and 2011).

It cannot be plausibly argued that the extreme right can gain any sort of substantial power through the influence of the Internet alone. What can be easily seen, however, is the vast array of new opportunities for spreading their message and so attracting new members the Web provides, particularly to Net-savvy youth. The fascist movements of the inter-war period placed strong emphasis on the performance of highly visible events in public places. Pageants, paramilitary parades, secularized religious ceremonies and rituals accompanied by symbolic or sometimes real punch-ups with their enemies were the stock-in-trade of these events, the purpose of which was to provide a means other than the ballot box for demonstrating popular legitimacy (Kaplan *et al.* 2003: 139–40).

> Within neo-fascism, a second style of political expression has developed – the 'Groupuscule' or a 'small vanguard group' – who wait, prepared for action, on the societal fringes but generally shun the mainstream political system and impart their message instead through a combination of violence and virulent propaganda.
>
> (Kaplan *et al.* 2003: 140)

The Internet has captured both of these styles of extreme-right display. Cyberspace now provides any group with a transnational, indeed worldwide, stage upon which they can enact their 'ceremonies and rituals' – either 'symbolic' or 'real' – for any audience and through which they can gain impetus and ideological unity from one another. Equally, it provides an anonymous infinity of virtual alleyways and dark corners for any groupuscule, however extreme their standpoint, to develop and accrue followers. It is the perfect forum for an extreme-right *Kampf um die Köpfe*.

When figures were last released in 2011, 42 per cent of the FPÖ's support came from people aged under thirty, with 24–29 per cent of the vote – on a par with the main parties, the SPÖ (Sozialdemokratische Partei Österreichs) and the ÖVP (Österreichische Volkspartei) (*Die Presse* 2011). The NPD, while not making as strong a showing, is nonetheless represented in two of Germany's sixteen parliaments. Given these positions, with regard to environmentalism, the Internet allows extreme-right groups to construct a cyber-landscape – either visually on YouTube clips or with words and downloadable music on their websites. While waiting for their vision of a neo-*völkisch* 'Europe of the Fatherlands' – that is, today's extreme-right version of identity as it relates to landscape which has been updated to a renewed relevance and reconstructed upon the bones of old nationalist understandings – to transpire in actual reality, the JN and the RFJ can craft it in virtual reality and, at the same time, find electronic common ground. In doing so, they also expose in real-time the cutting edge of extreme-right ideology to a

postmodern generation at once enlightened and anaesthesized by today's technological bombardment.

Note

1   The YouTube pseudonym '18TYROL88' has clear neo-Nazi overtones; based on their
    position in the alphabet, the numbers '18' and '88' can be decoded thus: 18 – AA – Adolf
    Hitler; 88 – HH – Heil Hitler. Though the references given here focus on their YouTube
    JN material content from 2008, the material has not changed much up to 2012.

References

18TYROL88. 2008. http://de.youtube.com/watch?v=OGCd8pkpGD4 (accessed January 2009).

BBC News. 25 July 2011. 'Profile Anders Behring Breivik'. Available at: www.bbc.co.uk/
news/world-europe-14259989 (accessed December 2011).

Blind Guardian. 2006. 'Otherland'. Available at: www.lyricsmania.com/.../a_twist_in_the_
myth_lyrics_31873/otherland_lyrics_345207.html (accessed September 2011).

Carter, Elizabeth L. 2005. *The Extreme Right in Western Europe: Success or failure?*. Manchester
University Press: Manchester.

Dateline. 30 August 2009. Interview with Nick Griffin. Special Broadcasting Station, Australia.

Foreign Correspondent. 2008. The Australian Broadcasting Commission.

Freiheitliche Partei Österreichs. 2011. Available at: www.fpoe.at/ (accessed December 2011).

Freiheitliche Partei Österreichs. 18 June 2011. *Parteiprogramm der Freiheitlichen Partei Österreichs*.
Available at: www.fpoe.at/ (accessed December 2011).

Hooper, John. 16 November 2002. 'Flirting with Hitler', *The Guardian*. Available at: http://
guardian,co.uk/weekend/story/0,3605,839755,00.html (accessed September 2011).

Junge Nationaldemokraten. Facebook Page. Available at: www.facebook.com/pages/JN-
Junge-Nationaldemokraten/206417776064788 (accessed December 2011).

Junge Nationaldemokraten. 2008. Available at: www.volksfront-medien.de (accessed January
2009).

Junge Nationaldemokraten. 2009. 'Wer wir sind – Vom deutschen Elend'. Available at:
www.jn-buvo.de/index.php?option=com_content&task=view&id=12&Itemid=26
(accessed January 2010).

Junge Nationaldemokraten. 2011. Available at: www.jn-buvo.de/ (accessed January 2012).

Kaplan, Jeffrey, Leonard Weinberg and Ted Oleson. 2003. 'Dreams and realities in
cyberspace: White Aryan resistance and the world church of the creator'. *Patterns of
Prejudice*, 37 (2): 139–55, 139–40.

MacIntyre, Donal. 2006. 'Nazi Hate Rock', Channel 5, Britain.

Mosse, George L. 1964. *The Crisis of German Identity: Intellectual origins of the Third Reich*.
Grosset & Dunlap: New York.

Neue Freie Zeitung. 9 October 2008. 'Die Jugend hat das Vertrauen in die 'alten Gro_parteien'
verloren!', p. 8. Available at: www.fpoe.at/fileadmin/Contentpool/Portal/PDFs/NFZ/
2008/nfz4108.pdf (accessed December 2008).

NPD. 23 May 2005. 'Die Vielfalt der Kulturen erhalten! Überfremdung und Einwanderung
stoppen!'. Available at: www.npd-bodensee-konstanz.de/inhalte/vielfalt-erhalten.html
(accessed September 2008).

NPD. 2011. Available at: www.npd.de/ (accessed January 2012).

NPD Bayern. 2009. 'Eine intakte Natur ist Grundlage unserer Zukunft!'. Available at:
www.npd-bayern.de/index.php/menue/56/thema/258/such_0/umwelt/Eine_intakte_
Natur_ist_Grundlage_unserer_Zukunft.html (accessed January 2010).

NPD Greiz 2008. Available at: www.npd-greiz.de/material/umwelt.pdf (accessed January 2009).

Öllinger, Karl. 2007. 'Ist der RFJ rechtsextrem? Neue Fakten'. Available at: www.gruene.at/uploads/media/RFJ_Neue_Fakten.pdf (accessed September 2008).

Olsen, Jonathan. 1999. *Nature and Nationalism: Right-wing ecology and the politics of identity in contemporary Germany*. St Martin's Press: New York.

Die Presse. 21 January 2011. 'Umfrage: FPÖ schafft Anschluss an "Großparteien"'. Available at: http://diepresse.com/home/politik/innenpolitik/627076/Umfrage_FPOe-schafft-Anschluss-an-Grossparteien (accessed March 2011).

Die Presse. 22 January 2011. 'FPÖ-Neujahrstreffen: "Drittes Kapitel" Kanzlerschaft'. Available at: http://diepresse.com/home/politik/innenpolitik/627565/FPOeNeujahrstreffen_Drittes-Kapitel-Kanzlerschaft?_vl_backlink=/home/index.do (accessed March 2011).

Rauschal, Andreas. 20 September 2006. 'Tanz den HC Strache!'. *Wiener Zeitung*. Available at: www.wienerzeitung.at/DesktopDefault.aspz?TabID=4701&Alias=Wahlen&cob=248879&currentpage=14 (accessed September 2008).

Die Republikaner. 6 October 2007. 'Kongreß der Republikaner'. Available at: www.rep.de/content.aspx?ArticleID=7fc08d65-7502-42d9-94c4-4ce5f90a25b8 (accessed September 2008).

Reymers, Kurt. 2002. 'Identity and the Internet: A symbolic interactionist perspective on computer-mediated social networks'. Available at: http://sociology.morrisville.edu/info space/identity.html (accessed September 2008).

RFJ. 2003. 'Umweltschutz ist Heimatschutz'. Available at: www.rfj.at/standpunkte/index.php (accessed September 2008).

RFJ. 2008. 'Strache ist lebendiges Vorbild für die Jugend'. Available at: www.rfj-sbg.at/main.php?_sessionid=ff0a88c7c6ae21e01925f2a8&_pid=19&_spid=0 (accessed January 2009).

RFJ. 2011. Available at: www.rfj.at/ (accessed January 2012).

RFJ Liezen. 2008. Available at: www.rfj-liezen.at/site/ (accessed January 2009).

RFJ Oberösterreich. 2009, 2011. Available at: http://ooe.rfj.at/standpunkte/ (accessed January 2012).

RFJ Tirol. 2008. Available at: www.rfj-tirol.at/rfjvideo08 (accessed January 2009).

RFJ Watch. 2011. http://rfjwatch.wordpress.com/ (accessed January 2012).

Spiegel Online. 10 March 2008. 'Far right attacks reached new record in Germany in 2007'. Available at: www.spiegel.de/international/germany/0,1518,druck-540550,00.html (accessed December 2008).

Strache, Heinz-Christian. 2011. Facebook Page. Available at: http://de-de.facebook.com/HCStrache (accessed December 2011).

Strache, Heinz-Christian and Andreas Mölzer. 2006. *Neue Männer braucht das Land*. ZZ-Edition: Wien.

Telegraph. 'Norway: Andres Behring Breivik YouTube video posted hours before killings'. 24 July 2011. Available at: www.telegraph.co.uk/news/worldnews/europe/norway/8657669/Norway-shootings-Anders-Behring-Breiviks-YouTube-video-posted-hours-before-killings.html (accessed December 2011).

Turner-Graham, Emily. 2008. 'Austria First: H.C. Strache, Austrian Identity and the current politics of Austria's Freedom Party', *Studies in Language and Capitalism*, pp. 181–98. Available at: www.languageandcapitalism.info/wp-content/uploads/2008/11/slc3–4_turner-graham.pdf (accessed January 2009).

Umwelt & Aktiv. 2011. Available at: www.umweltundaktiv.de/ (accessed January 2012).

Wallace, Patricia. 1999. *The Psychology of the Internet*. Cambridge University Press: Cambridge.

Wells, Rachel. 20 April 2008. 'Dear iGod, your inbox is overflowing', *The Age*, p. 5. Available at: www.theage.com.au/news/national/dear-igod-your-inbox-is-overflowing/2008/04/19/1208025558711.html (accessed September 2008).

15

INSIDE THE EXTREME RIGHT

The 'White Power' music scene

Martin Langebach and Jan Raabe

Introduction

'White Power' music is an international phenomenon. Nowadays, in countries such
as Germany, it is the most important medium used to attract young people to the
extreme-right movement. Through the lyrics the musicians spread 'old' Nazi
messages and racist ideology. First of all, this chapter defines the terms used for this
kind of music in Germany and gives a brief summary of the development of the
music scene. We focus in particular on the situation in Germany. With the largest
'White Power' music scene and market worldwide, it is an impressive example of
the importance of music to the extreme right. Subsequently, the chapter addresses
the relevance of this kind of music to the socialization of teenagers and its potential
for the mobilization of the extreme-right movement and its political parties.

Importance of extreme-right music and its origins

'White Power' music, neo-Nazi music or White Noise – there are different terms
for the music of the extreme right in the international context. In Germany scholars
and journalists have begun to use the term *RechtsRock* (Dornbusch and Raabe 2002).
This neologism consists of the term *rechts* (right) to characterize it as a phenomenon
of the political (far) right and '*Rock*' for rock music. *RechtsRock* does not signify a
particular kind of music. It simply refers to the lyrics, which are based on nationalism, racism, anti-Semitism or on the glorification of National Socialism/fascism.
The term therefore embraces so-called 'Rock against Communism' (RAC),
'National Socialist Hardcore' (NSHC) and 'National Socialist Black Metal'
(NSBM). In the international context we use the English term 'White Power' music
instead of *RechtsRock*.

The development of 'White Power' music is intimately linked to parties and organizations of the extreme right, but it is not their invention. It started thirty years ago, when Ian Stuart Donaldson became a member of the National Front in Great Britain.

A key figure: Ian Stuart Donaldson

The roots of 'White Power' music lie in a campaign by the National Front (NF) in Britain in the late 1970s. With racist slogans they tried to win the support of, among others, British skinheads, whose subculture displayed attitudes similar to those of the NF (Clarke 1976; Pearson 1976). In April 1979 Ian Stuart Donaldson became a member of the party. He was the leader of Skrewdriver, a punk group founded in 1977, but he soon switched to the skinhead subculture. His decision to become a skinhead was driven by the belief that 'punk music at the time was becoming too left-wing' (Pearce 1987), as Joe Pearce, editor of the Young National Front (YNF) newspaper *Bulldog* and friend of Donaldson, wrote in a personal reminiscence. Nevertheless, the group was very popular among skinheads and also punks at that time. Skrewdriver became the figurehead of the Rock Against Communism campaign, which was initiated by the YNF in 1979 as an 'answer' to the Rock Against Racism movement. Joe Pearce and Ian Stuart Donaldson also started the White Noise Club and White Noise Records. Their first record was the Skrewdriver EP 'White Power' in 1983. Meanwhile, Skrewdriver also became famous among skinheads in other Western European countries and, after a delay of one or two years, also in Eastern Europe. The band signed a contract with the German record label Rock-O-Rama, which released and distributed Skrewdriver's records until Donaldson died in a car accident in 1993 (see also Cotter 1999: 117–21).

Donaldson and Skrewdriver were never just an NF music group. According to their own self definition they were a nationalistic and, above all, a neo-Nazi rock group. Because of their success outside Great Britain their political perspective widened. While, in their 1983 song 'White Power', they still focused on the nation as the political frame of reference, one year later Skrewdriver discovered a European dimension. As Donaldson sang in the song 'Europe Awake' (1984):

> Europe what have they got to do to make you come alive?
> What has happened to the heritage that once was yours and mine?
> A capitalistic economy, the communists roam the streets.
> The old people aren't safe outside, what solution do we seek.
> [Refrain] Europe awake, for the white man's sake.
> Europe awake, before it's too late.
> Europe awake, Europe awake now.
> We've got to get together soon, and take our nations back.

'White Pride' worldwide

The international dimension of 'White Power' music originates in the nature of the music and the scene itself.[1] It emerged from the punk and skinhead subcultures and spread worldwide like other youth cultures. Nowadays, 'White Power' music is a globalized phenomenon and the fans are aware of this international dimension. The interlinkage exists in the knowledge about bands and fans from other countries and in two main common themes in the music: all of them consider themselves to be members of the 'white race' and they are all anti-Semitic. In every other respect the lyrics tend to vary from country to country, and on occasions inter-national unity can be superseded by national interests, which still have priority over the extreme right. For instance, the German and the Polish 'White Power' scenes are hostile towards each other for historical reasons. Also, some protagonists from Western Europe and the USA still have problems with participants in 'White Power' music from Eastern Europe, because the latter supposedly do not belong to the 'white race'.

This music scene varies from country to country. While Russia, Hungary, Italy and above all Germany have huge scenes with lots of bands and fans, there are very few supporters in Great Britain, Norway or Canada. Also, the connections between the 'White Power' music scene and the parties of the extreme right are rather variegated. Given this, a comparison of all of these would be too complex for this chapter, hence we will characterize the importance and the function of the music by focusing on its development and appearance in Germany.

From England to Germany

The extreme-right music scene in Western Germany was small in the 1980s, as in other countries. It consisted of a few skinhead bands and several hundred sympathizers. There were also supporters in the German Democratic Republic, but no local bands. They mainly looked to groups from Great Britain and West Germany (Niederländer 1989; Waibel 1996), but immediately after German reunification, they merged with the West German scene and grew. 'We sell more records in Germany than anywhere else', said Ian Stuart Donaldson in an interview in 1993: 'Also Germany has probably got the biggest skinhead scene in Europe' (Stuart 2004: 18). In 1993, the scene supposedly consisted of around 5,400 skin-heads (Innenministerium des Landes Nordrhein-Westfalen 1995). There was an increase, not only in the number of records sold, but also in the number of records released and in the number of record labels. In 1989, one label released six records (albums). Five years later nineteen labels released forty-six CDs. In 2010, 108 records were produced by twenty-nine German record labels – today Germany still has the largest 'White Power' music scene worldwide. During the last twenty-five years, over 1,800 records have been published by around 950 groups. Nowadays, at least around 220 bands and twenty-five balladeers are active and they play around 180 concerts and small concerts (also called 'ballad evenings') in Germany in one year.

Some of the producers of 'White Power' music, like PC Records, release more than twenty records a year. The number of copies sold is undisclosed. We assume for new bands about 1,000 copies and for well-known groups such as Die Lunikoff Verschwörung, the successors to the notorious group Landser, the number of copies exceeds 10,000. At the moment, many bands and musicians are starting to create their own MySpace and Facebook profiles and many songs are presented to the public on YouTube. Furthermore, the scene has special Internet platforms with thousands of users. The German scene is extensively linked to bands, producers and supporters from other countries. The number of supporters of the 'White Power' music scene should not be underestimated: the German Federal Office for the Protection of the Constitution lists an estimated 9,500 subculture-orientated and other right-wing extremists with a propensity to violence for 2008 (Bundes-ministerium des Innern 2009). We suspect that this number is only the tip of the iceberg, but unfortunately alternative studies do not exist.

Organizations from within the scene

Protagonists of the 'White Power' music scene have founded at least two inter-national organizations: the Hammerskins Nation, and Blood & Honour. The former was created by Wollin Lange und Scan Tarrant, two skinheads from Dallas, Texas, in 1986:

> The Hammerskin Nation is a leaderless group of men and women who have adopted the White Power Skinhead lifestyle . . . The HSN brotherhood is a way of achieving goals which we have all set for ourselves. These goals are many but can be summed up with one phrase consisting of 14 words. 'We must secure the existence of our people and a future for white children'.
>
> (www.hammerskins.net)

Their German 'chapter' was founded in 1994. Today they have chapters in thirteen different countries. The number of members is unknown, as is that of Blood & Honour. The latter was established by Ian Stuart Donaldson, after he fell out with the NF in 1985 and spent some time in prison. It defined itself as an organization from the skinhead scene for the skinhead scene. Politically, it was dedicated to National Socialism: 'We will follow the example of the one incorruptible ideal: National Socialism, and its great martyr Adolf Hitler' (*Editor* 1987: 2). Today Blood & Honour has 'divisions' in seventeen countries. The German 'division' was established in 1994. Their members produced a magazine, established a record label and organized concerts. From 1998 onwards they became active in the Nationaler Widerstand (National Resistance) and took part in rallies with their own banners and speakers. On 14 September 2000, Blood & Honour was banned in Germany because of their agenda, which was related to the manifesto of the NSDAP (German National Socialist Party). It can be assumed that they continue as an underground movement. Blood & Honour is also an important organization of the extreme-right movement in other countries. Apart from concerts, Blood & Honour Vlaanderen, for example, also organized memorials for the Waffen SS, and Blood & Honour Hungary organize the 'Day of Honour' every year.

International cross-links

The German 'White Power' music scene has manifold connections to musicians and fans from other countries. These links have developed thanks to a variety of activities: supporting foreign bands and attending their concerts, accessing the same Internet sites, visiting or performing at concerts in other countries, celebrating with foreign fans at concerts, having interviews with foreign bands in fanzines, producing CDs with foreign bands, becoming involved in international organizations outside of the music scene/subculture.

Since 1985, 'White Power' bands from different countries have appeared together on compilations such as 'No Surrender' and have been on stage together, in Germany at least since 1989. In 1991, for the first time several musicians from different countries played together as a band using one name: German–British Friendship. In the corresponding song on the mini-CD they sing in English: 'We are the same race, we have the same faith! We have the same roots, we are all wearing boots! No more brother's war! We have suffered enough! We fight the red peril, we are strong enough!' Since that time, various bands have shown their international linkage with similar Friendship Projects, e.g. in 1996 Steelcapped Strength and Volkszorn with their CD entitled 'Swedish–German Friendship', in 2002 Final War and Stoneheads with 'American–Austrian Friendship', in 2003 Odal Sieg from Chile and the Vinland Warriors from Canada with 'Southland–Vinland Friendship', in 2004 No Surrender plus Bannerwar from Greece and Sokyra Peruna and Whites Load from Ukraine with their 'Hellenic–Ukrainian Friendship' or in 2009 KG23 from Canada and Blue Max and Strong Survive with the 'Vinlandic–German–Croatian Strike Force'.

Today, German 'White Power' bands play concerts in different countries and foreign bands perform in Germany. In addition to these 'normal' events, concerts are organized in several countries to mark the anniversary of Ian Stuart Donaldson's death on 24 September 1993. In 2011 for example, there were concerts in Ukraine, Hungary, Great Britain, France, Italy, Belgium, Sweden and Australia. Besides these concerts there are at least three large festivals with an international dimension: the 'Veneto Summer Fest' of the cultural Association Veneto Fronte Skinheads in the North of Italy, the 'Sons of Europe' Festival in Budapest, Hungary and, the most international of all, the 'Fest der Völker' ('Festival of the Nations') near Jena, Germany, named after a film by Leni Riefenstahl about the Olympic Games in Berlin in 1936. The first event took place in 2005 and was visited by around 500 people. In 2006, it was banned because of the football World Cup in Germany. The following year 1,700 visitors came and around 1,200 in 2008. Most participants were from Germany. The person responsible for the festival is a member of the NPD, but the neo-Nazis who organize it are from the so-called *freie Kameradschaften* ('free fellowships'). The 'Fest der Völker' has an explicitly trans-national concept, for example the appeal was translated into different languages. In the English appeal of 2006 and also that of 2007, the organizers complained that 'Because of the globally led politics, the will and interests of the people of Europe are pushed into the background.' They also criticized the 'continuous stream of foreign people towards Europe', and the cultural collapse caused by mass immigration, loss of roots and Americanization, which are 'connected with globalistic development'. They closed the appeal with the statement:

> We are against it! Together with the nations we will put a spoke in the globalist's wheel! Together with continuing the uprooting of the Nations, there will always be an increase in a healthy nationalism. Our main focus is on sovereign national states with their own national economy. A Europe of native countries, living together peacefully and having equal rights partnerships to secure one's own autarky. The ideal of the future is speaking the language of the nations and not that of a 'United World'! Europe will live or go down with us![2]

At each of the three festivals to date, activists from six (2005), nine (2007), nine (2008) and seven (2009) countries spoke. In general they spoke in their first language and were translated into German. The line-up of the 'White Power' bands was also international. They came from seven (2005), three (2007), five (2008) and four (2009) countries. The mass of the people, the songs, different flags and speeches created an atmosphere of a transnational comradeship of 'White People' in Europe.

Extreme-right music as a factor of socialization and mobilization

Today music is the most important medium for the extreme right to spread its ideology. However, the bands do not seek to promote a specific party or organization, although the NPD in particular uses it for activating and mobilizing people. The musicians play this type of music for their own sake. The musicians want to communicate their views to an interested audience. For the audience, the music has a variety of different impacts:

The lyrics affirm the self-assurance of the neo-Nazi and cultivate a collective identity (Corte and Edwards 2008)

In general, the lyrics of 'White Power' music are written in the native language of the country to which the musicians belong – exceptions can only be found in the NSHC and NSBM groups. The musicians have a strong interest in the recipient understanding the message they want to spread and focus on at least three target groups:

a) Skinheads: the songs have the task of communicating the in-group feeling of this subculture by appealing to them directly: 'We're German Skinheads, short hair, radical! We're German Skinheads, patriotic, national!', sings the group Spreegeschwader in the song 'Deutsche Skins' (German Skins). However, the number of songs focusing on skinheads has decreased with the diversification of the music over the last ten years.

b) Today the lyrics address many more people who are active in the so-called 'Nationaler Widerstand'. A song by the group Stahlgewitter, named after a novel about the First World War by Ernst Jünger, is even entitled 'Nationaler Widerstand'. The chorus of the song employs a slogan used at many demonstrations: 'Here comes the national resistance'. They combine it with a vow of commitment to their country and dedicate this declaration to their role models, the German soldiers of the Second World War: 'Here comes the national resistance, without compromise we stand by our country – betrayed by the suits, the lefties and commies . . . Old combatants, we shake your hands! Soldiers of the Wehrmacht – we commemorate your heroic deeds!'

c) Anybody who is patriotic and dissatisfied with the situation of his or her 'fatherland': the lyrics try to combine these feelings with the political aims of the extreme right. The German group Sleipnir, which is named after the eight-legged horse of Odin, the supreme god of Norse mythology, thus sing in their song 'Rebellion' about patriotic young people who are willing to change the situation:

> They don't wear bomber jackets, yet they are nationalist. (They) go to football matches or parties, yet their heads aren't shaven. It's difficult to determine who they are and what they want, but if it has to do with Germany, than you hear them rumbling from far away. A young people's revolt! On the streets, in the alleyways – they come from everywhere! The youth of today revolts! In the cities, in the villages – our numbers are rising!

The main subject of the lyrics of 'White Power' music is their own country, as well as a few songs (around 5 per cent) that are about drinking alcohol, going to football matches, having parties and falling in love with/having sex with a girl (from their own 'folk'). Thus Germany is the main frame of reference for lyrics written by German musicians. Some of these lyrics make it clear that the Germany they talk about is not the present German state. They refer to a Germany within the borders of 1937, which also includes parts of what is now Poland, Russia or the Czech Republic. Within such a framework, it is possible to identify two main discourses: the glorification and the violation of the country.

The glorification of Germany emphasizes the beauty of the landscape and nature and focuses mainly on the country's past. Some musicians postulate explicitly some form of continuity, as the group Kraftschlag does in their song about an old man who lives in the same street as the vocalist and who is still a National Socialist:

'We've saddled our legacy on our shoulders. We will carry the swastika full of pride.' The vocalists sing about the community of the people, the glory of the army and its soldiers, 'German' values such as fidelity, honour and courage and the beauty of the people. Thus, the music forms a 'collective memory' (Eyerman and Jamison 1998: 21–5). The past is also a blueprint for their criticism of today's Germany. They claim the country has been threatened in several ways since the end of the Second World War:

a)   through the American re-education programme, Germans were implanted with a guilt complex. Now they are ashamed of their own history and are no longer proud of their heritage;

b)   through capitalist materialism, which numbs the minds of the people and destroys every altruistic feeling;

c)   through liberalism, which promotes individualism instead of collectivism and destroys the unity of the people. Individualism is responsible for the dissolution of common ethical and gender values, and for evils such as feminism, homosexuality and paedophilia;

d)   through foreign (that is to say, non-white) immigration which threatens ethnic homogeneity.

According to this ideology, Germany's enemies can be separated into two different groups, internal and external. The internal enemies include not only left-wingers, especially anti-fascists, and all democratic politicians who are supposedly contributing to the decline of a once glorious nation, but also people whose lifestyles are not acceptable to the extreme right: punks, hip-hop fans, homeless people or homosexuals. The external enemies are the USA and Israel, in particular Jewish people. Even if the latter have German citizenship they are declared to be non-Germans according to the anti-Semitic Nuremberg Laws of 1935. Although German neo-Nazis have good relations with their comrades in the USA, the country and its ideals in general constitute an enemy. In the anti-Semitic message of the lyrics, American Jews and supporters of Israel are one of the main problems. On the basis of an anti-Semitic conspiracy theory they are responsible for anti-German politics, especially for the re-education and the so-called *Schuldkult*, the 'cult of guilt'. Regular terms such as East Coast (this is perceived as the home of a supposed Jewish pressure group in the financial and cultural heart of the USA) and ZOG (Zionist Occupation Government) are used to describe the supposed conspirators (Lööw 1998: 127–31).

Clearly the lyrics are inspired by traditional extreme-right themes, but they are less sophisticated than the documents of political parties usually are. The lyrics are much simpler, with a low level of abstraction. The song writers are not usually classical ideologists.

'White Power' music contributes to the socialization of the listeners

'Rock music, in comparison with books, demonstrations and leaflets, has the advantage that you can check it out day by day without getting bored', the well-known German 'White Power' group Landser (1999: 31) pointed out. Music in general is omnipresent in the everyday life of teenagers and young adults in Germany (Langness *et al.* 2006: 78). When young people start to listen to 'White Power' music, it is generally only as one style of music among others. Thus we found some 14-year-old boys who listened to Landser as well as German hip-hop and techno music, the latter two styles having no political content. Two reasons can be ascertained: some teenagers are interested in this music because they see it as something really extreme. They use it to distinguish themselves from their parents, teachers and other teenagers. However, if they do not agree with the message of the lyrics, even at a most basic level, they are going to give it up very soon. For others, music has become an important factor of their self-socialization. The recipients listen to the lyrics and their messages deliberately. In the course of this he/she forms his/her own opinion about society, its past, present and future. Along with the music, the recipients get in touch with the lifestyle of the musicians, which implies, in addition to their conviction, specific aesthetics based on the use of signs and symbols. The bands are the outposts of their subculture, which becomes interesting for those who are fans of the music. The recipients who become followers of this subculture acquire its lifestyle as well. Furthermore, Pfaff found that the acquisition of such a lifestyle could lead to participation and political protest, but that this did not necessarily reflect genuine political conviction (Pfaff 2006).

The biographies of some of today's well-known German neo-Nazi activists under the age of forty show the relevance of 'White Power' music and its subculture to their own political career:

> I first got in touch through tapes of 'Onkelz', 'Störkraft', 'Endstufe' and so on, when I was twelve or thirteen years old. At that time my hair was much longer than today and I was committed to Metal . . . At the age of sixteen I had my head shaved and I totally indulged in skinhead music. You met in a small gang – none of them are around anymore – and infested the region. You met other like-minded people and went to the first concerts and parties. It was a great time. I joined the FAP, which was banned shortly after, and later on the HNG, and all the rest of it.
>
> (Marx 2006)[3]

Enrico Marx was born in 1976 in Eastern Germany and grew up in the south of Saxony–Anhalt, where he still lives. He has been one of the most significant activists in that region for ten years.

'White Power' music is used by parties and organizations of the extreme right to mobilize their supporters

For young people music is the gateway to the extreme right and they are mobilized by it to participate in the actions of the extreme-right movement and its parties. This can be seen at any demonstration of the extreme right: a lot of the mostly young participants wear T-shirts or badges bearing the names of 'White Power' music groups. Overall, we have identified five different levels of mobilization:

a)   agreeing with the content of the lyrics;
b)   becoming part of the 'White Power' scene. This includes the acceptance of and adaptation to its lifestyle, which has changed among the supporters of far-right music in Germany. Bit by bit, the skinhead style has been displaced by various forms of expression. Today, young supporters of the neo-Nazi movement may have totally different appearances, such as skinhead or punk, copying a member of the Hitler Youth, or they look like young radical left-wing activists, many of them have a completely 'normal' style. However, the formation of the collective identity is still clearly visible because of the typical clothes and an enormous number of different signs and symbols. Also, according to their self-image, these young people perceive themselves on this level to be part of a scene ('White Power' music) rather than part of the extreme-right movement. Going to concerts is one of the important points at this level;
c)   being mobilized for protests, especially demonstrations and rallies;
d)   becoming a member of a party or another organization of the extreme-right movement;
e)   using violence and terror to fulfil political aims. The lyrics define who the enemy is. The music itself could be a stimulus for or background to grievous bodily harm and murder.

Excursus: concert mobilization in Germany

Ian Stuart Donaldson argued in an interview for the documentary *Lieder der Verführung*:

> Going to a concert and listening to a group that you agree with is a lot more enjoyable than a political meeting. And we can get over to a lot more people that way. And, may be, if they listen to the lyrics, they believe in what they say.

Concerts are one of most obvious and regular events and a significant step towards mobilization on the 'White Power' music scene, because they create a common feeling of comradeship and strength. The vocalists perform their lyrics in front of the audience. The audience in return accepts the message and listens without disagreeing and sometimes even participates by singing along with the band. The concerts are also a good indicator of the importance of the 'White Power' music scene to the extreme right. In Germany in 2010, around 200 'White Power' rock and ballad concerts took place. The top events had more than 1,600 visitors, and the average concert had about 100 to 200. Most of these concerts are not organized by political parties or organizations, but by the network of fans, producers and musicians. It is more like a grass-roots movement. One reason for this is the circumstances of the concerts: most of them are illegal, so they have to be organized clandestinely. No publicity about the concerts is available; information is passed by word of mouth by people who know each other. Being able to gather more than 1,000 people for a rock show without the police getting to know about it shows the sophisticated structure of the network of fans of German 'White Power'.

Excursus: mobilization by parties and the extreme-right movement in Germany

Since at least the early 1990s there has been a connection between the 'White Power' music scene and the extreme-right parties in Germany. Especially in the east of the country, young neo-Nazi skinheads became members of newly founded parties. Some of these parties returned the favour by organizing concerts. The Deutsche Alternative (DA), for example, organized a concert with Störkraft and Skrewdriver as early as 1991 in Cottbus.

After the rise of racial violence between 1991 and 1993, the German government banned several parties including the DA, because of their aim of abolishing the democratic system, which they pursued in an actively militant and aggressive manner. As a reaction to this, militant neo-Nazis started following the concept of leaderless resistance and were reorganized into the aforementioned *freie Kameradschaften* (FK). The first of these were founded in the mid 1990s. Today, there are around 200 FK in Germany. Some of them are small and have less than ten members, others are bigger. The larger ones such as the now banned Mecklenburgische Aktionsfront or Nationaler Jugendblock Zittau have around sixty members. The henchmen of the FK are usually between eighteen and twenty-five years old and evidently come from the subcultural neo-Nazi scene (based on 'White Power' music). The 'co-operation between them is guaranteed by regular meetings and by longstanding contacts between their leaders' (Virchow 2004).

Other activists of the extreme right started joining the Nationaldemokratische Partei Deutschlands (NPD). This oldest party of the far right in Germany was founded in 1964. Until 1969, it prospered and won several seats in some of the state parliaments in Western Germany. But with its collapse in the election of the Bundestag in 1969, the NPD declined into an irrelevant splinter party. In 1996, the party started its comeback with Udo Voigt as the new chairman. He rebuilt the NPD not only though their classical party structure, but also by seeking to integrate elements of social movements. In 2004, the party and some of the most important leaders of the FK arranged a joint venture under the title 'Eine Bewegung werden' ('becoming one movement') – the NPD was named the spearhead of the movement. In the election for the state parliament in Saxony in the same year, the NPD won seats with 9.2 per cent of the votes. Primarily, people between eighteen and thirty-five years of age had voted for the NPD (Statistisches Landesamt des Freistaates Sachsen 2004: 16). It was re-elected in Saxony in 2009 with 5.6 per cent. In the state parliament in Mecklenburg–West Pomerania in 2007, the party won 7.3 per cent of the votes. The NPD achieved this increase by directing its political appeal at young people. Its first success was a rally against the exhibition 'Crimes of the German Wehrmacht: Dimensions of a War of Annihilation 1941–1944' in Munich on 1 March 1997, which was organized by the NPD. The majority of the 5,000 extreme-right participants were aged between eighteen and thirty. One year later the NPD organized their first 'Tag des nationalen Widerstandes' ('Day of national resistance') in Passau with a Bavarian brass band and also the popular balladeer Frank Rennicke. Four thousand people responded to the invitation.

With this event the NPD began its successful strategy of winning over extreme right-wing youth culture. In 2000, Voigt was asked in an interview by the neo-Nazi magazine *Hamburger Sturm* whether one or more German bands played a similar role in the NPD to that of Skrewdriver in the National Front. He replied: 'If German groups manage in the future to express themselves in a positive manner about the NPD, compose music for the NPD or commit themselves to the NPD, I can imagine one day they might take over this role' (Voigt 1999: 55). The following year, the monthly journal of the NPD, called *Deutsche Stimme*, arranged their first media festival with a mixture of political speeches and gigs by 'White Power' rock bands. In the first year, 1,500 predominantly young people attended. In 2002, there were 1,800 visitors, 3,800 in 2003, 5,000 in 2004, and 7,000 in 2006. That was when the organizational role of the NPD ended, and the party changed its strategy. Nowadays, it arranges summer festivals with the same mixture of political speeches and even political music, but on a regional basis. In 2010 the NPD organized around thirty-eight such events. The most successful was the 'Rock for Germany' in 2009 in Gera, Thuringia, which was also the start-up for their election campaign for the state parliament of Thuringia. More than 5,000 people came to see Die Lunikoff Verschwörung and also the speaker of the NPD. In 2010 the party started again with their *Deutsche Stimme* media festival. Two thousand joined it in 2010 and more than 1,600 in 2011.

In 2004, more than fifty FK and producers of 'White Power' music produced a multimedia CD, which was called *Anpassung ist Feigheit. Lieder aus dem Untergrund* ('Adjustment is cowardice. Songs from the Underground') and also a website with the address www.schulhof.net ('*Schulhof*' means school yard). Both contain 'White Power' songs in different styles and convey different information about the 'Nationale Widerstand' and its agenda. The aim was to distribute around 200,000 free copies of the CD to young people in order to win them over to extreme right-wing ideas. Before this could be accomplished, however, the CD was banned because it violated the Youth Protection Law. Only a few months later, the NPD produced a CD of their own as publicity material during their election campaign for the state parliament of Saxony. Its title was *Schnauze voll? Wahltag ist Zahltag* ('Fed up? Election day is payday!'). Around 30,000 copies of it were given to young people in the last few weeks before the election. In subsequent years, the NPD produced several editions of this so-called school yard CD. Some of them are available as downloads from their media server (for the importance of the World Wide Web to the extreme-right movement, see Turner-Graham's chapter in this volume).

Meanwhile, Christian Worch, one of the leading neo-Nazis of the FK, set out to make rallies more attractive to participants. In an internal letter of 27 September 2001, he told the other leaders of the party that he was willing to let a band called Oidoxie play live on stage at the end of a rally in Leipzig: 'On the one hand we'd like to offer something specially for the younger protesters who are also interested in music. And on the other hand we'd like to pave the way for the legalization of other music events.' This second point addressed one of the main problems of the 'White Power' music scene: many of their concerts were curtailed by the police, mainly because they were against the law. In the following years, bands played short gigs at a few demonstrations, but this did not usually have any particular effect on mobilization.[4] Nor did it help to legalize the concerts.

Shortly after the NPD's success in the elections in Saxony in 2004, however, the party started to support the music scene by staging concerts. NPD members of parliament are invited to make a speech at the beginning. In terms of legality, the concerts thus became political events and the police were unable to disrupt them. Although this had no effect on the basic legalization of this kind of concert, it gave the 'White Power' music scene the impression that their problems were being addressed. Today, the NPD is the party for which 'White Power' music listeners vote.

Profits

It is worth mentioning at this point that the profits from the sale of 'White Power' music CDs and merchandize are important for ensuring financial resources. One condition for the success of the mobilization is the level of resources the movement can mobilize, not least money. In this respect, the cultural sector, and thus the 'White Power' music scene, differs from all the other sectors of political movements. Generally, you need resources to generate your message, whereas in the cultural sector it is possible to generate resources. This creates a special dynamic in this field. People can earn money while producing propaganda CDs. If you compare the number of people working professionally in different sectors of the extreme-right movement you can see how important this aspect is: the NPD had around 200 professionals working for them in 2005. Across all the shops and Internet distributors we estimate that at least 150 persons earn their living from 'White Power' music. The fact that you can make profit with right-wing propaganda CDs means that even people who do not agree with the lyrics are willing to produce and sell such products. For example, Herbert Egold, the founder and owner of Rock-O-Rama Records, one of the most important labels in the history of 'White Power' music, particularly for its propagation throughout Europe and across the world, was not a right-winger, he was simply a businessman. The second important point is the dimension of the business: as of today, seventy shops and 100 Internet shops in Germany sell almost exclusively 'White Power' music and paraphernalia. Many of the owners of the labels and shops take the money for their private use, but a few of them contribute some of their profits to the movement. For example, the earnings from the special 'Solidarity' compilation are used for printing leaflets, building infrastructure or for campaigns. The profits from a concert of the Blood & Honour Vlaandern were spent on buying a new public address system for a neo-Nazi group in Dortmund. Corte and Edwards have confirmed this transfer of the money to right-wing organizations (Corte and Edwards 2008: 13). In Germany, the NPD's Internet shop, DS-Versand, offers more than 800 different CDs and a range of related merchandize. Many important NPD activists are involved in this business too, such as Thorsten Heise, member of the federal administration of the NPD. He owns a record label and has produced forty-five CDs in the past seven years. He is also involved in the international business of producing 'White Power' music. Thus, these protagonists can reach a considerable audience. They earn money from their political involvement and are 'employees of the scene', which means that they can act more openly than in a 'normal' job. The fact that it is possible to make money from White Power music is one of the main reasons for the rapid and vigorous development of the White Power music scene.

Conclusion

The modernization of the extreme-right movement in Germany, as in many other countries, would not have been possible without 'White Power' music. It gave a fresh image to 'old' political aims. In addition, through the medium of music, listeners receive the political content of the songs in a totally different way from when they are reading a leaflet or a book – media that are no longer popular with young people today. The lyrics of the songs give them a collective identity as nationalists. Because of the internationality of the music scene, it also promotes a transnational collective identity under the slogan 'White Power' (a dimension that not all structured political parties are promoting or can always promote). The transnational identity of the music scene comes alive when bands play concerts abroad, when fans travel for a concert or festival to another country or when bands from different countries produce a CD together. These contacts sustain the international network of the 'White Power' music scene. Last but not least, music is an important factor for mobilizing support for the extreme-right movement, for their ideas, their rallies, their finances and their election campaigns.

Notes

1 The international dimension is a consequence of the music and the youth culture themselves, because they cannot be 'localized' in a single country. Like every youth culture, the 'White Power' music and youth scene is international in the way all youth cultures are.

2 web.archive.org/web/20071012070122/www.f-d-v.de/england/index.php. Please note that this text – like the sentence 'connected with globalistic development' – is taken from the English section of their homepage.

3 The FAP (Freiheitliche Deutsche Arbeiterpartei) was a neo-Nazi party that was banned in 1995. The HNG (Hilfsorganisation für nationale politische Gefangene und deren Angehörige e.V.) is an organization that supports neo-Nazis in prison ('POWs').

4 In a few cases, an evening concert was organized to take place after a demonstration to mobilize more people to participate in the demonstration (e.g. see Virchow's contribution to this volume). It did not have any noticeable effect.

References

Bundesministerium des Innern. 2009. *Verfassungsschutzbericht 2008*. Berlin: Vorabfassung.

Clarke, J. 1976. 'The skinheads and the magical recovery of community', in Hall, S. and Jefferson, T. (eds), *Resistance Through Rituals: Youth subcultures in post-war Britain*. London: HarperCollins Academic, pp. 80–3.

Corte, U. and Edwards, B. 2008. 'White Power music and the mobilization of racist social movements', *Music and Arts in Action*, 1(1), 4–20.

Cotter, J.M. 1999. 'Sounds of hate: White Power rock and roll and the neo-Nazi skinhead subculture', *Terrorism and Political Violence*, 11(2), 111–40.

Dornbusch, C. and Raabe, J. (eds) 2002. *RechtsRock. Bestandsaufnahme und Gegenstrategien*. Hamburg, Münster: Unrast Verlag.

Editor. 1987. 'Editorial', *Blood & Honour*, 2, 2.

Eyerman, Ron and Jamison, Andrew. 1998. *Music and Social Movements: Mobilizing traditions in the twentieth century*. Cambridge: Cambridge University Press.

Innenministerium des Landes Nordrhein-Westfalen. 1995. *Verfassungsschutzbericht 1994*. Düsseldorf.

Landser. 1999. 'Das Interview', *Blood & Honour Division Deutschland*, 8, 30–1.

Langess, A., Leven, I. and Hurrelmann, K. 2006. 'Jugendliche Lebenswelten: Familie, Schule, Freizeit', in Shell Deutschland Holding (ed.), *Jugend 2006. Eine pragmatische Generation unter Druck*. Frankfurt am Main: Fischer Taschenbuch Verlag, pp. 49–102.

Lööw, Helene. 1998. 'White Power rock 'n' roll: A growing industry', in Kaplan, J. and Bjorgo, T. (eds), *Nation and Race: The developing Euro-American racist subculture*. Boston: Northeastern University Press, pp. 126–47.

Marx, E. 2006. *Barbarossa Records*. Available at: www.nd-b.com/ww/nazilaeden/antwort_babarossarec.htm, accessed 31 August 2007.

Niederländer, L. 1989. *Forschungsbericht: 'Das politische Wesen der Skinheadgruppierungen und ihre Sicherheitsrelevanz'*. Berlin: Humbodt-Universität.

Pearce, J. 1987. *Skrewdriver: The first ten years – The way it's got to be!* London: Skrewdriver Services. Available at: www.unitedskins.com/home.htm, accessed 15 April 1999.

Pearson, G. 1976. '"Paki-bashing" in a north east Lancashire cotton town: A case study and its history', in Mungham, G. and Pearson, G. (eds), *Working Class Youth Culture*. London: Routledge & Kegan Paul, pp. 48–81.

Pfaff, N. 2006. *Jugendkultur und Politisierung: Eine multimethodische Studie zur Entwicklung politischer Orientierungen im Jugendalter*. Wiesbaden: Verlag für Sozialwissenschaften.

Statistisches Landesamt des Freistaates Sachsen. 2004. *Wahlen im Freistaat Sachsen 2004. Sächsischer Landtag. Ergebnisse der Repräsentativen Wahlstatistik*. Dresden.

Stuart, I. 2004. 'The voice of the resistance!' (Interviews), *Blood & Honour*, 30, 17–20.

Virchow, F. 2004. 'The groupuscularization of neo-Nazism in Germany: The case of the Aktionsbüro Norddeutschland', *Patterns of Prejudice*, 38(1), 59–73.

Voigt, U. 1999. 'Parteivorsitzender der NPD im Gespräch mit dem Hamburger Sturm', *Hamburger Sturm*, 21, 55–7.

Waibel, H. 1996. *Rechtsextremismus in der DDR bis 1989*. Cologne: PapyRossa Verlag.

16

THE ULTRAS

The extreme right in contemporary Italian football

Alberto Testa and Gary Armstrong[1]

Since the inception of the Italian nation, politics in all its guises has proved integral to all realms of society. As one of the most significant of Italian cultural practices, football (*il calcio*) has been no exception to political contestation and has constantly mirrored political circumstances. This chapter illustrates this most notably by detailing how football might be used as a tool to spread neo-fascist as well as racist and ultra-nationalist thought in Italy and Europe. Thus, it is a form of mobilization. Because of these correlations, the game has long been regarded as a legitimate arena for struggles by actors across the political spectrum. As early as the 1930s, Mussolini's Partito Nazionale Fascista (Fascist National Party) recognized its value (Martin 2004; Foot 2006). Since then, the Italian political spectrum, ranging from liberals to a multitude of right and left organizations and even those promoting pro-Catholic political sentiment, have valued the game, and the arena in which it is enacted, as both a tool and a locale for their proselytizing (Porro 1992; Ginsborg 2001).

Two diverse hard-core football followings in Italy are the Ultras and *ultrá*. The term Ultras is our neologism and it is used to describe neo-fascist (Italian) football supporters' gatherings. The Ultras grew out of but are different from the *ultrá*. The latter are best described as hard-core fans (invariably male and aged between sixteen and forty) who since the early 1970s have manifested behaviours that at times exceed what is considered the 'norm' in linguistic and bodily comportment and were – and still are – prepared to indulge in violent practices against rival fans.[2] The very existence of the *ultrá* is embedded in Italian football's traditional parochial rivalries and wider political–ideological configurations. The football club and its tradition is the most important focus of their existence. Their support utilizes popular songs promoting both the city and footballing traditions. By contrast, the Ultras put the group above the football club – they have an ever-present ideological *motif*, namely neo-fascism, and exist both inside and outside of the football stadium. In contrast to the *ultrá*, the Ultras are more instrumental – but 'real' football fans all the same who also celebrate their own style, which is best signified by the sale of their own merchandizing. They will fight in the name of football but their confrontations are inextricably linked to political antagonisms.

The *curve* and the Ultras

In some Italian instances, the very structure that hosts the game carries political resonance. This is particularly the case with the main football arena in Rome – the Olympic Stadium – which, similar to others throughout Italy, has become the place to articulate both a metaphorical and literal bridge to a footballing – and often a political – past. Begun in 1927 and finished in 1937, whereupon it became known as Foro Mussolini (Mussolini's Forum) as part of il Duce's fascist project, the Olympic Stadium has hosted sports events and fascist parades and in 1938 hosted a rally in honour of the invited Adolf Hitler. As a consequence, the main street to the stadium is dominated by an obelisk bearing the dedication to '*Mussolini Dux Dux*' adorned by symbols and mottos celebrating the fascist regime (Caporilli and Simeoni 1990). This football–political connection remains today. On match day for the two Roman teams that call it home, the stadium stands sell not only football-related merchandize but busts of Mussolini and other fascist regalia.[3]

Renamed Foro Italico (Italian Forum) after Mussolini's demise in 1943, restructuring for the XVII Olympics in 1960 saw the arena renamed the Olympic Stadium. It is when entering this locale that both sets of Roman Ultras – who follow AS Roma and SS Lazio – become most visible and audible. Ostensibly a non-locale and a culture-free zone, the Olympic Stadium on match day hosts tens of thousands sharing their assumed right to comment and narrate. It is a stage for a variety of narratives and performances: some quintessentially masculine and football-specific; others overtly political; others subtly non-conformist; still others that are gratuitously transgressive.

On match day the Olympic Stadium *curve* (terraces behind the two goalposts) manifest a subtle social order that is controlled by the Ultras. Some of this is based on individual notoriety; all of it is based on manifestations of power. Although seat numbers are allocated and tickets printed, the 'ordinary' fan will not necessarily occupy the paid-for seat. Hierarchy and seniority, gained within the Ultras' micro-social system, count more than the outside logics based on the power of money or the demands of bureaucracy. A person who has sat for years in a seat will understandably be unhappy to give up his/her place when commanded to by the Ultras. Complaints about such behaviour, however, would be seen as a challenge to the informal and unwritten rules in force; the unfortunate spectator needs either to find another seat, or stand.

Numbering some 200 members in the instance of the Boys, who are a sub-group among a greater collective of thousands, and 6–7,000 for the Irriducibili of Lazio, such stadium gatherings are not marginalized or ostracized by the tens of thousands of others in attendance. At times therefore, the chants and banners the Ultras' display bear critical and accusatory messages that articulate the rage of tens of thousands of fellow fans when directed at 'their' players and club officials. Comments articulated or displayed are usually succinct; narratives are short, thus 'fitting' the tempo of the game that the *curve* collectively watches. At other times, the banners pronounce upon and denounce wider political issues, often manifesting an aversion towards a chronically inefficient and decadent political system. Marco, one of the leading charismatic[4] figures of the Boys, explained the association of place and practice:

> The football stadium allows us to bring our battles – via the media – to 40 million Italians. Before in the stadium you would rarely find socio-political issues raised by the Ultras. It is the only place that we can speak freely about our ideas without being charged with subversive association. In other places we would be repressed. We are people that do not want to be made stupid by consumerist repression, we want to discuss and to confront. The stadium ends are ours, here we can express who we are and impose our rules. We go to the stadium and articulate our ideas because the state does not allow the individual to freely speak out because of rampant political correctness. We fight this lack of freedom mostly with negative campaigns but when the state allows us to express our values, we also send constructive and positive messages.

What the Ultras do is not entirely new; such messages have been sent via the football stadium for decades.

Us and them: football and politics

Political violence was evident in Italian football stadiums in the 1970s but the overt politicization of the football *curve* in the 1980s corresponded with a society-wide disillusionment with formal politics. This change was coterminous with the political scandal remembered by the Italian nation as *Tangentopoli* (Barbaceto *et al.* 2002). The revelations around the criminal workings of the political class saw the electorate lose faith in any integrity the Italian political system had left. The Ultras that emerged out of this combined awareness of this public outrage and the consequential demands for socio-political change with the age-old youthful celebrations of collective identity and enjoyment of transgression. For the Ultras, thus, the worlds of football and political processes are inseparable.

The Ultras identify themselves with *non omologazione* (non-conformity) and express their loathing for political and social 'conformism' both within and outside the football stadium. Theirs is and has always been an oppositional and non-conformist stance. Their action-oriented ideology sees them identify with the ancient neo-fascist figure of the Warrior who, regardless of the consequences, will fight 'the system'. The Ultras are also ardent football fans and watch a game that is forever changing – mostly for the worse in their opinion – as it allows itself to be violated by corporate takeovers and transnational TV broadcasters. Concomitantly, the world around them changes as strange accents are spoken in the streets they call home. In the globalized society of contemporary Italy, the streets of the capital are seen by many of its citizens as an ecology of fear; they believe the eternal city is being overtaken by thieves and murderers from foreign lands. In this society of strangers trust is hard to establish, a scenario exacerbated by the absence of a political will that seeks accommodation with the newly arrived or seeks a revision of concepts pertinent to citizenship. In these lacunae the appeal to the myth of an eternal yesterday of Roman greatness is seductive to many. In this milieu the Ultras seek allies, both local and international.

Within football, for instance, the Ultras respect *i camerati* (an Italian fascist term for comrades) regardless of nationality. As a consequence, their oppositional nature is at times very accommodating. A shared transnational enthusiasm for football and neo-fascist ideology has given rise to Ultras *gemellaggi* (twinning-friendships) based on a sense of mutual *rispetto* (respect). The Boys Roma had such twinnings with equivalents in both football support and neo-fascist ideology at Benfica Lisbon and Hammarby of Sweden. The Irriducibili had twinnings with Espanyol and Real Madrid of Spain, Werder Bremen, Lokomotiv Leipzig and Lipsia of Germany, Panathinaikos of Greece and Paris St Germain of France. Both Boys and Irriducibili had a strong twinning with the Ultra Sur of Real Madrid, a neo-fascist group, ever-nostalgic for the regime of General Franco, in 2007. Such twinnings arise from contact made via the *direttivo* (management board) of the Ultras that is then communicated to the more peripheral supporters in the gatherings. The origin of such relationships is often attributable to personal contacts – representatives of the Ultra Sur attend games as guests of the Boys' *Direttivo* (management board) who display the team scarves of the twinning clubs in their Head Office. The twinning is first and foremost a declaration of friendship based on a shared enthusiasm for neo-fascism; where this common belief system originates needs further investigation.

Modernity and its discontents

Using the anti-rationalistic and anti-humanistic ideas of thinkers such as the Italian Julius Evola (1934, 1953, 1961), the Italian neo-fascists see their battles as against the 'modern' world, which deliberately neglects their coveted sense of tradition. The doctrine also stresses the subordination of the individual ego to the collective and seeks a revaluation of the idea of nation, considering it as an organic community of people that exists in opposition to a liberal, hyper-individualistic society. How this is played out and rationalized is a crucial aspect of this inquiry. We thus spoke to core Ultras to ascertain meaning.

When asked what it meant to be *di destra* (extreme right), one such individual, Todde (Boys)[5] answered that he did not recognize himself in the concept generally and associated himself more with being 'old right' (characterized by the bureaucratized dimension of fascism) and even with the Marxist–Leninist left. Arguing that such political concepts were probably obsolete, Todde spoke of the necessity for political renewal to overcome the conservative middle-class culture and to build a socialist front that celebrates a sense of nation. He recited a poem written by one of the Boys (author unknown), which highlighted the duality of nation and brotherhood. The poem has been regularly published in the Boys' monthly fanzine titled *The Honour of Rome*:[6]

> I walk along the streets bold and proud. I am the son of an ancient
>> EMPIRE
> I serve my fatherland, I am Italian
> I am proud to make the Roman SALUTE
> Attached to affections and to the religion [Catholic]
> Never will I bend my will in front of the 'master' [Italian authorities]
> The motto that I follow is
> Will, Power and Freedom
> I do not love the weak and promiscuous
> I am not violent
> I do not wish to repress
> But I wish that everyone remains in their nations
> People respect me
> Because they know I am a perfect citizen
> I wait for the Celtic Sun to rise
> In the hope that everything will improve.

The oft-recited poem stresses the masculine sense of public possession. Those reciting the poem were invariably quick to perform the fascist salute as they said the words, fully aware of this gesture's ancient origins. A triumvirate of affirmative abstractions, hence, portrays those reciting the poem as proclaiming neither their pursuit of violent conflict nor any wish to impose their will upon others. At the same time, the poem is dismissive of those weak in body and in the face of temptation. Meanwhile, it anticipates the arrival of a better world – in the morning. For the Boys, and Ultras like them, their ethnic bond is based on a generalized sense of shared kinship and is expressed in their proclamation of a fatherland united by a common religion – namely, Christianity. Such pride expressed by the two groups also brings prejudice – the selection of those constructed as the cultural 'other' is at times perplexing. Such a vision inevitably provokes academic and media analysis.

Interpreting the Ultras

The manifestations of neo-fascist ideology expressed by the Ultras should not be understood primarily as a means to reinforce social and personal identities and traits of masculinity (Roversi 1992). Neither should they be explained using Goffman's concept of 'frame' and the metaphor of the war supposition (Dal Lago and de Biasi 2002). In seeking to explain their origin and *raison d'être*, this inquiry uses the conceptual sociological frameworks of Max Weber (Ferrarotti 1965; Freund 1968; Rossi 1982) and the new consensus theory on fascism best explained by Griffin (1998, 2000). The theoretical boundaries of this inquiry consider contemporary Italian neo-fascism's role as an agenda of social change and locate it within the proclamations around the concept of 'Third Way' nationalism as first propounded by Mussolini's fascist ideology in the 1920s. Fascism was born in Italy after the First World War and was also characterized by a 'socialistic' or trade unionist and radical component represented by the revolutionary syndicalists (RS). Mussolini's socialistic component was inspired by the writings of George Sorel (1847–1922), particularly his proposition of the social myth (von Hendy 2002). Sorel influenced both right and left. His anti-intellectualism and his passion for revolutionary activities (in place of rational discourses) made him one of the most influential intellectuals in Mussolini's ideology. Sorel's arguments manifest a combination of spiritual themes and Marxism. True socialism, according to Sorel, could only appear after a period of violent revolution perpetrated by a disciplined proletariat (Jennings 1999). However, this required provocation.

In Sorel's reasoning, the nature of man is based on acting spontaneously via the concept of free will. In order to act, a whole range of images (which he termed 'myths') have to be present in the human conscience, which might influence the instinct, producing action. Sorel divided these images into 'spontaneous' and 'instinctive'. The idea of myth is very important in framing the logic of the Ultras. For the Ultras, football and football support are based on a celebration of faith, loyalty and courage, crucial to which are narratives of heroism and warrior-like behaviour. This produces a potent and unmediated mix that constitutes a belief system. Myth is a projection, but essentially different from utopian visions, which are intellectual representations that can be rationally examined and discussed, having a value more theoretical than practical.[7] Myths do not describe things. Their function is to determine action via mass inspiration. Myth is a project different from seeking a utopian vision. Myth is best considered a representation that lends itself to rational examination. Myth is the immediate expression through images of the will that wait to be transformed into accomplishment. It is not important if the myth is not realizable; its purpose is to be the engine of human action in its appeal to those seeking radical change.

For those who embrace fascism and its modern manifestations, the myth of the golden age and a glorious past on which to build an 'ideal' Italian society (see Dechezelles in this volume) is ever-contrasted to an uncertain and worrying present. In the neo-fascist Ultras, the past is forever interpreted and reinvented to give new meaning in the present. These beliefs include but also exist beyond football. The game and its paraphernalia are to the Ultras in many ways representative of the contemporary state of decay, which requires some form of (neo-fascist-led) renewal. The myth expressed by fascism and adapted by the Ultras to their everyday experience in and outside the football stadium is transformed into a sense of accomplishment. The Ultras have issues both political and personal to accomplish.

The romance of the local

Amid this feeling of political decay, another political reference was provided by worries over the post-1990s immigration to Italy, especially from Eastern Europe and the inability of the Italian state to manage the newly arrived. This issue presented a theoretical challenge to neo-fascism. The ideologies of nationalism and racism are sometimes related, sharing historical origins and characteristics (Miles 1993). These overlapping concepts are certainly present in the Ultras' articulations, as Giovanni, the ideologist of the Irriducibili,[8] demonstrates in his statement:

> The Italian extreme right still represents the fundamental values of Italian society – the family and the concept of fatherland. When the family is substituted by single parents or 'natural unions' or when people are no longer proud to be part of the Italian nation, and when those who arrive from abroad have more rights than Italians; then our society will dissolve.

These words stress two important foundations of the desired neo-fascist society: *Patria* (fatherland) and family. These beliefs have a long neo-fascist pedigree. The *Decalogo del Balilla* ('The Commandments of the Balilla'), written in 1929, argued: 'Ama la Patria come i genitori; ama i genitori come la Patria [Love your fatherland as you love your parents, love your parents as you love your fatherland]' (cited in Galeotti 2000). Such love, however, came at a price – some had to be excluded. Exclusion was based on a sense of shared identity. Giovanni explained those who were not wanted in the Fatherland:

> It is useless to speak about 'multi-ethnic' models of coexistence or even 'European' models. To have social peace every nation has its own identity which needs to be respected. We can see the English situation where social peace is forever disturbed by the multi-ethnic society imposed by the UK government and championed by Tony Blair. We are not 'rough racists'; we support the concept of tolerance, but this exists only when there is reciprocity, otherwise it is all bollocks. For example when a Muslim wants to build ten mosques here in Italy he has to allow us Christians to build ten churches in his country. It would be more equal if they allow us to put a crucifix in Muslim schools just for the principle of reciprocity.

In Giovanni's discourse, fascism and its nationalistic and 'racist' elements play an important role. But the exaltation of *Patria* does not necessarily translate to the exaltation of one 'race' over and above all the others. The exaltation of the fatherland is underlined by differences founded more in cultural and religious identity than in biological differences – even if the latter are at times stressed. This may be explained by considering the roots of the Ultras' ideology: Italian fascism was less obsessed with biological racism than Nazism, although this does not mean that there were no 'biological racist' currents within Italian fascism (these strands were present well before the Racial Laws of the late 1930s, Cassata 2008). Such complexities are often found in ideological discourse, particularly when one considers the many forms of non-racist nationalisms (cf. Smith 1995).

To make sense of the Ultras' ideas pertaining to nationalism, it is important to clarify the nationalistic dimension of Mussolini's fascism. Italian fascism in the 1930s was a combination of state and romantic nationalism. State nationalism projected the idea of nation as a community composed of individuals contributing to the state's maintenance and strength. The general feature of such nationalism was to be the assertion of the primacy of national identity over claims of class and religion. In romantic nationalism – a particular strain of nationalism originated as resistance to the universalism and rationalism of the Enlightenment – linguistic, cultural and historical factors are considered the most important 'glue' to national identity and specific territory (McLean 1995). It is, however, the romantic nationalistic dimension of fascism that appears most to influence the Italian youth neo-fascist movement (hence also the Ultras, a fully fledged part of it). We identify this nationalism as 'revolutionary', a 'Third Way' between a celebration of the processes of globalization – which the neo-fascists believe homogenize and erase national identities – and a 'false patriotism'. According to neo-fascists, *l'Italia* is an entity based on commercialization and capitalism, which neglects the expression of glorious local traditions. Italian politicians deny the country a significant political and moral role at the international level, accepting subservience to the Anglo-Saxon ways of life based on consumerism and individualism.

Revolutionary nationalism coheres around the idea of a nation sharing a sense of common participation within collective destinies. Such people seek a Europe constructed on the bases of ethnic and cultural identities and traditions; a Europe based on autonomies and regions. This type of nationalism sees Europe as an empire of *patrie* (fatherlands) following a social and fascist tradition and is the classical approach of much of the post-war extreme right who saw a united Europe as a better option than a narrow fascistic nationalism (see Tamir Bar-On in this book). Significantly, it sees Europe as neither white nor Christian but as an alliance of national-revolutionary forces, which encapsulate the traditionalist and integralist qualities of both the former Soviet empire and Islam. This Third Way, though, is expressed by people who feel threatened by globalization – such protagonists are anti-English and anti-American because both have manifested historical opposition to Italy. They also seek ideological comfort from those who think like them even if speaking a different language. But while willing to make football-related, cross-boundary links with similar neo-fascists, such people are also super-patriots around their national team and thus willing to denigrate other – European – peoples. Such thinking needs gurus.

The local and the global

Among a variety of long-standing Italian thinkers, the neo-fascists follow the more recent ideas of Jean Thiriart and the French Nouvelle Droite (New Right) intellectual Alain de Benoist (on the latter see the chapters by Bar-On and Antón-

Mellón). A dominant theme within both these philosophies is anti-Americanism and the fight against globalization, which is considered a domain of international finance controlled by Jews and Freemasons. For the Ultras and other Italian neo-fascist groups (as for de Benoist), the enemy of the state is the value-oriented, materialistic and commercially obsessed society of the USA.

This convergence is exemplified by two Italian neo-fascist groups – including football supporters – which in the twenty-first century are the inheritors of the ideological populist ideas of Mussolini's fascism (de Felice 1965; 1978), crucial to which was the concept of the *Terza Posizione* ('Third Position') – a political philosophy which sought to mediate between rampant capitalism and state-sponsored socialism. Crucial to the Third Positionist Movement was a strategy that engaged *il popolo* (people) in revolutionary action. This required both violence against political opponents and cultural programmes to educate youthful enthusiasts (Streccioni 2000). The movement was best represented in Rome by the social welfare campaign pursued by the Casa Pound Italia (CPI)[9] social movement and Forza Nuova (New Force – FN) political party. Both entities claim to follow the philosophy of Julius Evola and the ideas of Nicola Bombacci; both 'gurus' are also quite popular among the whole Italian extreme-right movement which, as Caiani and Parenti in this volume illustrate, is quite variegated. Bombacci was a friend of Mussolini and a former communist who became the advisor of Mussolini during the period of the Italian Social Republic in 1943 (Salotti 2008). Evola, who died in 1974, remains a guru of the Italian extreme right. Stated simply, Evola's philosophy condemned modernity and democracy and propounded totalitarian and racist arguments.

The notion of tradition was crucial to Evola's thinking; his ideal society had a hierarchy based on superiority of birth. Only individuals born into the higher caste were capable of attaining the most elevated levels of spirituality. Such qualities were inherited and not based on economic or material criteria. At the top of this system stood the warrior caste. Such men personified obedience to authority and a love of discipline and order while manifesting a willingness to sacrifice themselves and others in the never-ending pursuit of honour. The first battle for such warriors was against oneself; the warrior forever wrestled with his own weaknesses. According to Evola, modern man has less capacity than the warrior to win over his ego because he is too easily charmed by temptations that pervert the spirit. In following Evola's teachings, the Ultras were aware that they too had to resist their inner demons and be aware of external manipulations. The path to purity was difficult – but piety was theirs for the taking.

The wretched of the earth?

In the Ultras' discourses, as mentioned earlier, globalization is to blame for the crises brought about by mass immigration. The forces of globalization push populations of the Third World to the First, particularly Western Europe. However, for the neo-fascist, the real enemies of Italy were not the journeying immigrants but who and what pushes such people to migrate. While such movement generated dangers for migrants via their perilous journeys, their arrival created danger for 'us' (indigenous Europeans) because the arrival of the poor caused the erosion of indigenous Western cultures. The defence of Western cultures was not all they stood for. At times, many proclaimed their support for those subject to Judeo-Christian imposition.

Unsurprisingly for neo-fascists, the Ultras had no time for Jews and the state of Israel. The anti-Israel stance was visually evident; in many instances, the Irriducibili in their *curva nord* location in the Olympic Stadium displayed the Palestinian flag, which accompanied their chants in praise of the repressed: 'Palestina never give up'. In the course of the research, the Boys Roma expressed several times their hostility to 'Zionism', publishing in 2006 an article in their fanzine *The Honour of Rome* titled 'Libertà per La Palestina' ('Freedom for Palestine'). However, sympathy for the Muslim dispossessed might be considered pragmatic.

This attitude should be considered along with the hostility expressed towards the most public of Christian nations, which is also the nation that has no fewer than 113 military bases in Italy, the USA. The anti-American stance of revolutionary nationalism is evident in the following statement released by the Irriducibili in the summer of 2006 pronouncing upon the former Iraqi President Saddam Hussein:

> As *Irriducibili* we well understand unfortunately on our skin the inefficiencies and injustices of our judicial system. And many times because of this we were convinced that perhaps in no other country in the world there existed a judicial system worse than the Italian one. Actually, we have found one in Iraq; we laugh at a tribunal that by its nature should be impartial. Is a tribunal impartial composed of judges appointed by a 'joke' government in a 'joke' state that does not have any national sovereignty? Can it be considered impartial when the judges are appointed by those who have arrested him? What will be the likely outcome of the process? Which sacrosanct defence rights have been granted to Saddam Hussein?
>
> We hope that the same justice that will kill Saddam Hussein one day (hopefully soon) will punish those who committed crimes such as the slaughters of Sabra and Sahila, the massacres in Iraq by the Anglo-American troops using white phosphorus; the civilians killed during the invasion of the country, the Palestinian population who no longer have houses destroyed by bulldozers, the torture in the concentration camps of Abu Graib and Guantanamo Bay. For the past crimes (Vietnam, Dresden, Roma, Berlin, Hiroshima, Nagasaki, Baghdad, Kabul, Belgrade) and so on . . . We are full of hope, but we also know that it will be difficult because the tribunals that will judge these '*signori*' are designated by those themselves!

To those who consider hard-core football supporters as the representatives of the inarticulate, such articulations might lead them to believe that the Ultras were clearly manipulated by organized political forces. This is a widely held belief – but it is not true.

Manipulated or innovative?

Media coverage of the Ultras has depicted them as puppets of wider Italian neo-fascist political formations. While some held membership of such entities in their life beyond the Ultras, both Boys and Irriducibili stressed their total independence from all other neo-fascist entities. Those seeking to recruit in the *curve* for such entities faced hostility and even assault in their proselytizing. This may surprise the reader, but has to be considered as an act of piety – the Ultras wanted total control of their football locale – against assumed interlocutors. It also gave them a further sense of virtue in their contempt against those they considered 'compromised' by the 'system' – be it political institutions or football organizations.

If association with a group outside the stadium was sought, it was with an entity that espoused social activism over abstract ideology. This was, for instance for the Boys, CPI, an association popular among the Roman (and indeed national) neo-fascist youth. Its most famous slogan was its proclamation to promote 'Fascism of the Third Millennium', which signified an attachment to tradition but at the same time a revision of fascism to address current issues. The peculiarity of this youth group was the presence of many women militants who held the same status, dignity and opportunities as men. The CPI campaigned on social issues such as disability rights, and collected medicines for the impoverished in countries such as Iraq.

This populist streak of the organization is found via the contemporary Third Positionist Gabriele Adinolfi. An ideologist rather than a politician who eschewed political parties for political movements, Adinolfi's political commitment was prolific: the organizer of several editorial ventures, most notably *Orion* and *Rinascita* (Rebirth), Adinolfi also ran a website blog of counter-information called *Noreporter* and offered a variety of cultural activities as well as political debates around Evola and Bombacci. One of the most popular projects of Adinolfi and CPI was the 'Social Mortgage'. The aim of the project is to create a regional organization with public money to build a public infrastructure to improve the quality of life. The project was supported by the Boys and Irriducibili who advertised such ideas via banners in the Olympic Stadium. Casa Pound has strong ties with Padroni Di Roma, an Ultras group located in the *curva sud* of the Olympic Stadium, but also – via the twinning with the youth centre Cuore Nero (Black Heart) of Milan – has connections with the northern Italy *curve*, such as those of Inter-Milan, Monza and AC Milan.

The CPI was the most respected political entity in the Ultras' existence. Its penchant for direct action and its bottom-up approach to politics was admired. While at times the CPI was dismissive of what many perceived as the futility of football-related disorder, the two entities could share space in the city, an accommodation arising out of a sense of mutual admiration. The need for a cultural programme saw the CPI organize rock concerts throughout Italy attended by tens of thousands willing to listen to rock lyrics that condemned banking, the European Union and a variety of other issues pertinent to neo-fascist politics. The latest estimate indicates that CPI could count over 300 militants and 200,000 sympathizers throughout Italy (*L'Espresso* 22 May 2009).

Attacking from the right

The Ultras exist in a framework wherein narratives – both football related and politically inspired – of idealized scenarios of masculinity are ever-present. They seek to combine notions of the Warrior with abstractions drawn from a variety of Western thinkers. They represent, therefore, an 'irrational' combination of theory and action and are most visible when in the football stadium. Claiming the stadium as their agora, they are, in our analysis, implicitly admitting that they prefer the Assembly over representative democracy. They accuse, tease and cajole in the stadium but in doing so represent a primitive form of monitoring democracy; a more sophisticated range of possibilities be it via auditing and regional assemblies or the technologies of civil society are evidenced today, which permit the citizen to resist or oppose (Keane 2009). The Ultras prefer noise, slogans and when necessary direct action/confrontation. They believe they represent the will of the people – even those too supine to realize their conformity.

In reality, however, the Ultras have little to offer by way of visions of a new social order. Their *leitmotif* instead is based around articulating a variety of fears and a sense of political disillusionment. The Ultras and the neo-fascists share an ideology that will never take power by democratic means but they do constitute an emerging and pan-European social movement (see Virchow in this volume; music might be another route to consider in this pursuit; on this point see Langebach and Raabe's chapter). They contest – with violence – their political opponents and at times the police are sent to repress them. They refuse to be defeated.[10]

The state – via both its agents and the electoral process – is tasked to control those disillusioned with democracy and willing to turn to violence to resist or provoke change. For the Warriors seeking moral and political regeneration, a full-frontal attack upon the state is not possible. They must instead, in the words of Evola, enter the state of *Apolitia* (a spiritual distance from materialistic society) and, to borrow from a Chinese proverb, 'Ride the Tiger' (Evola 1961). In doing so, the passenger frustrates the beast's potential to attack and harm them. Ride long enough and the possibility arises of their defeating what seeks to destroy them.

The fascist dimension of the Ultras needs to be addressed from two perspectives: theoretical and empirical and both inside and outside of the football stadium. As this chapter has shown, these dualities are inter-connected but their belief system drives the participants to action – most notably in and around football stadia. It is this that particularly disturbs the state. The neo-fascists outside of the stadium gaze upon the assumed decadence of Italian society. In the stadium such passivity ends when individuals gather with the ideologically inspired like-minded. In such a milieu, individuals can make the transition from theory to action without the need for consistency in thought or action. Opposed to globalization and the commercial logic of contemporary football, the Ultras enjoy the skills of the foreign-born footballer who wears a team shirt that promotes global finance. Dismissive of the game's materialism and its never-ending pursuit of efficiency and profit, the Ultras appreciate the abstract qualities of faith and courage that the game provides for both players and fans. Resisting the socio-political *sistema* (status quo) and celebrating their non-conformity, their songs and myths celebrate the very nation that now criminalizes them. They follow a long-standing (and quintessentially Italian) political ideal and celebrate it in that most traditional and Italian of contexts – *il calcio*.

The football stadium has always been an exceptional zone in Italian society. Today this locale is subject to an ever-expanding state-regulated exceptionalist logic – those who enter are filtered and those considered enemies of the state barred.

Notes

1 The authors are indebted to Dr Andrea Mammone for his helpful feedback on an earlier draft of this chapter. Our thanks are also due to Professor Nicola Porro (Cassino University, Italy) for his advices and to Gianpaolo, Yuri, Katia, Paolo, Fabrizio T., Fabrizio P. and most importantly Paolo Zappavigna who introduced us to the Ultras and *curva*'s world.

2 The word *ultrá* finds its etymology in French political discourse. During the Restoration period (1815–30) the word *ultrá-royaliste* indicated partisan loyalty to the Absolute Monarchy. The *ultrá-royaliste* championed the interests of property-owners, the nobility and clericalists. They were the supporters of authority and royal tradition in contraposition to the philosophies of human rights and individual freedoms espoused by followers of the Enlightenment (Regoli 2006).

3 The authorities turn a blind eye to such enterprise. Consequently, the merchandize is sold in defiance of the Mancino Law passed in 1993 that prohibited the use of political symbols linked to fascism. Such artefacts are to be found on sale on stalls in Predappio (the burial place of Mussolini). In Rome, the same artefacts are on sale in the popular Via Sannio Market and in Via Conca d'Oro. Badges in praise of Mussolini are also sold by entrepreneurs outside the Coliseum.

4 The concept of 'charisma' emerges as a constant attribute admired and desired in both the Boys Roma and Irriducibili group. It is a theme common in many extreme-right groups throughout Europe and it is well explored in Orfali's chapter.

5 Todde was twenty-four years old (at the time of this interview) and belonged to an 'ordinary' Italian middle-class family with a university background in law.

6 This publication is sold by Ultras via their Head Office and also on the match-day *curve*.

7 In evaluating Sorel, it is important to realize that the end of the nineteenth century was a period when the philosophical doctrine of *vitalismo* (vitalism) prevailed over rationalism. In *vitalismo*, life has peculiar traits that are not present in inanimate substance and cannot be explained entirely using the laws of physics. The key concepts in *vitalismo* were: humanity, history, experience, corporeal nature, instincts, irrationality, subjectivity, perspective, value of the individual thing, change, disease, death. One of the most prestigious exponents of the conception of life was Friedrich Wilhelm Nietzsche (1844–1900).

8 Giovanni is forty years old, from a middle-class family and has an educational background in the humanities.

9 The CPI, before becoming a national association, was a small gathering named after a
   Roman building squatted in 2003 by youth of the Occupazioni Non Conformi (Non-
   Conformist Occupations – ONC). The name 'Pound' was chosen in honour of the
   American poet Ezra Pound who lamented the negative influence of money and usury
   promoted by the banking system (Accame 1995). On the other hand, FN is one of the
   major neo-fascist parties in Italy.
10 While the Ultras might see their role as bringing some sense of Athenian 'people power'
   to the football stadium, we might consider that democracy has been over-concerned with
   the notion of *demos* (people) at the expense of the role of *kratos* (rule), which has frequently
   utilized force – strength and domination is integral to order and stability (Runciman
   2009). When the Assembly was superseded by representative democracy and with it
   elections, political parties and charismatic leaders, the result was a democratic process
   that saw Europe become the global killing fields in the first half of the twentieth century.
   Democracy suffers from founding myths; it is frequently chaotic and forever needs a sense
   of purpose.

References

Accame, G. 1995. *Ezra Pound economista. Contro l' usura*. Roma: Settimo Sigillo.
Barbaceto, G., P. Gomez and M. Travaglio. 2002. *Mani Pulite la veria storia*. Roma: Editori
    Riuniti.
Caporilli, M. and F. Simeoni. 1990. *Il Foro Italico e lo Stadio Olimpico. Immagini dalla storia*.
    Roma: Tomo Edizioni.
Cassata, F. 2008. *'La difesa della razza'. Politica, ideologia e immagine del razzismo fascista*. Torino:
    Einaudi.
Dal Lago, A. and R. de Biasi. 2002. *Introduzione all'etnografia sociale*. Bari: Editori Laterza.
de Felice, R. 1965. *Mussolini il Rivoluzionario: 1883–1920*. Torino: Einandi.
de Felice. R. 1978. *D'Annunzio Politico: 1918–1939*. Bari: Laterza.
Evola, J. 1934. *Rivolta contro il mondo moderno*. Milano: Hoepli.
Evola, J. 1953. *Gli uomini e le rovine*. Roma: Edizioni dell'Ascia.
Evola, J. 1961. *Cavalcare la tigre*. Milano: Vanni Scheiwiller.
Ferrarotti, F. 1965. *Max Weber e il Destino della Ragione*. Bari: Laterza.
Foot, J. 2006. *Calcio: A history of Italian football*. London: Harper Perennial.
Freund, J. 1968. *Sociologia di Max Weber*. Milano: Il Saggiatore.
Galeotti, C. 2000. *Mussolini ha sempre ragione*. Milano: Garzanti.
Ginsborg, P. 2001. *Italy and Its Discontents 1908–2001*. London: Penguin Books.
Griffin, R. 1998. *International Fascism: Theories, causes and the new consensus*. London: Arnold.
Griffin, R. 2000. *Revolution from the Right: Fascism*. Retrieved 6 August 2004, from Oxford
    Brookes University: http://ah.brookes.ac.uk/history/staff/griffin/fasrevolution.pdt.
Jennings, J. 1999. *Sorel: Reflections on violence*. Cambridge: Cambridge University Press.
Keane, J. 2009. *The Life and Death of Democracy*. London: Simon & Schuster.
L'Espresso. 2009, May 22. 'Benvenuti a Casa'. Retrieved 6 June 2009, from http://espresso.
    repubblica.it/multimedia/6043835.
McLean, I. 1995. *Concise Dictionary of Politics*. Oxford: Oxford University Press.
Martin, S. 2004. *Football and Fascism: The national game under Mussolini*. Oxford: Berg.
Miles, R. 1993. *Racism after 'Race' Relations*. London: Routledge.
Porro, N. 1992. 'Sport, political system and sociology in Italy'. *International Review for the
    Sociology of Sport* 27(4): 329–40.
Regoli, R. 2006. *Ercole Consalvi. Le Scelte per la Chiesa*. Roma: Editrice Pontificia Università
    Gregoriana.
Rossi, P. 1982. *Max Weber. Razionalitá e Razionalizzazione*. Milano: Il Saggiatore.

Roversi, A. 1992. 'Football violence in Italy'. *International Review for the Sociology of Sport* 26(4): 311–31.

Runciman, D. 2009. 'What a way to run a country', review of *The Life and Death of Democracy*. *The Observer* (books). 7 June.

Salotti, G. 2008. *Nicola Bombacci: Un comunista a Salo*. Milano: Ugo Mursia Editore.

Smith, A.D. 1995. *Nations and Nationalism in a Global Era*. Cambridge: Polity.

Streccioni, A. 2000. *A destra della destra*. Roma: Edizioni Settimo Sigillo.

Von Hendy, A. 2002. *The Modern Construction of Myth*. Bloomington: Indiana University Press.

INDEX